D0833068

The Pinocchio Intermediate Vocabulary Builder

Books by Mark Phillips

Metallica Riff by Riff
Guitar for Dummies
Honeymooners Trivia
Sight-Sing Any Melody Instantly
Sight-Read Any Rhythm Instantly
The Wizard of Oz Vocabulary Builder
Tarzan and Jane's Guide to Grammar

The Pinocchio Intermediate Vocabulary Builder

Mark Phillips

Based on
The Adventures of Pinocchio
by Carlo Collodi

A. J. Cornell Publications
New York

The Pinocchio Intermediate Vocabulary Builder

All Rights Reserved © 2004 by Mark Phillips

No part of this book may be reproduced or transmitted in any form
or by any means, graphic, electronic, or mechanical, including
photocopying, recording, taping, or by any information storage
retrieval system, without the permission in writing from the
publisher.

For information address:
A. J. Cornell Publications
18-74 Corporal Kennedy St.
Bayside, NY 11360

Cover illustration by Debbie Phillips
Cover design by Jonathan Gullery

Library of Congress Control Number: 2004090148

ISBN: 0-9727439-2-8

Printed in the Unites States of America

Introduction

Why I Wrote This Book

When I was a student, I had a terrible vocabulary. That's because I didn't like to read — and, as parents and teachers have always told us, reading is the only effective way to build a vocabulary. Once I tried to improve my vocabulary by memorizing the definitions of 1000 words (that appeared on little flash cards that came in a pretty box). I was able to memorize the meanings of *abase, abash,* and *abate,* but by the time I got to *abdicate,* my mind became fuzzy — and I still had 996 words to go! The unpleasant alternative was to do a lot of reading. But how many books would I have had to read to learn all the words I needed to know? And what guarantee was there that the books I chose would even contain the words I needed — assuming I even knew what those words were?

When I was in the seventh grade, I did feel duty bound to read one particular book because it was written by a relative of mine. I learned something about the study of vocabulary by reading that book: If you learn a word in context you'll remember what it means. For example, in one scene it said that an eleven-year-old boy "brandished" a toy sword. Well, at that time, I had never heard of the word *brandish* (but I looked it up and found that it meant "to wave in a threatening manner"). What a vivid mental picture I had! Of course that's what it meant. What else would an 11-year-old boy do with a toy sword?

Because I didn't want to have to read a lot of books, I wished there existed one good book of fiction that was fairly short and just happened to contain all the words I'd ever need to know (for my SATs or just for intelligent-sounding conversation). That way, I could learn the necessary words in context and remember what they meant. But no such book existed.

As an adult, after having finally built a vocabulary through reading — hey, you have to do something to get through those boring hours of commuting to work on public transportation! — I decided to create the book I wished for as a teenager. Because the story of *The Wizard of Oz* is known and loved by everyone, and because it's rich in characters and situations, I chose it as a vehicle for the book I had in mind. I made a list of the best high school/college/adult-level vocabulary words — 1,850 of them — and, reworking and rewriting L. Frank Baum's classic story from beginning to end (but maintaining the overall plot), I sprinkled the words — in contexts as meaningful as I could make them — throughout. After writing *The Wizard of Oz Vocabulary Builder,* I realized that a book with about 1,000 easier vocabulary words would be useful to students in junior high school or middle school. Thus was born *The Pinocchio Intermediate Vocabulary Builder.*

How to Use This Book

In the story, all the vocabulary words appear in **bold type**. Read with a pencil in hand. As you go, underline any word you already know. If you think you know a word but aren't 100 percent sure about it, check the definition. For any word that's new to you, read the definition carefully. By the time you get to the end of the story, you will have learned many of the words (because you learned them in context). Your next step is to go back to Chapter 1 and read the entire story a second time, again with pencil in hand. This time through, you'll be able to underline many more words than you did the first time. As you go, re-check the definitions of any words you've forgotten. Every time you re-read the story you not only learn new words, but you reinforce the meanings of the words you've already learned. You'll probably need to re-read the story several times, each time underlining more and more words until they all have been accounted for.

By the way, if you see any words in *plain* type whose meanings you don't know, look those up in any standard dictionary. But generally, for all the boldface words, use the definitions included here rather than those in a dictionary. Why? A dictionary might show five different meanings for the same word, yet four of those might rarely be used by anyone. And there's no little sign pointing to the fifth one that says: *This* is the one you really want. And dictionaries aren't always user-friendly. You might read a definition in a dictionary and *still* not understand what a word means because the definition might contain other difficult words or because the dictionary doesn't show you *how* the word is used—it doesn't use it in context.

Once you're familiar with the special words presented in this book, you'll probably start noticing them everywhere—in newspapers, in other books, on TV shows, or in movies. You might even become possessive of them—every time you come across one, you'll proudly think to yourself: *Hey! That's one of my words!*

Contents

Chapter 1: Geppetto Makes a Puppet   1
Chapter 2: The Cricket   5
Chapter 3: The Pears   9
Chapter 4: New Feet and a New Schoolbook   16
Chapter 5: The Puppet Theater   20
Chapter 6: Fire-Eater   27
Chapter 7: Fire-Eater Sneezes   31
Chapter 8: The Fox and Cat   36
Chapter 9: The Red Lobster Inn   49
Chapter 10: Killers   65
Chapter 11: The Blue-Haired Fairy   71
Chapter 12: The Doctors   75
Chapter 13: Medicine   82
Chapter 14: The Field of Wonders   94
Chapter 15: Pinocchio Goes to Jail   108
Chapter 16: The Snake   133
Chapter 17: The Watchdog   139
Chapter 18: The Weasels   143
Chapter 19: The Pigeon   149
Chapter 20: The Land of the Busy Bees   161
Chapter 21: Pinocchio's Mother   171
Chapter 22: Pinocchio Goes to School   178
Chapter 23: The Fight   187
Chapter 24: The Fisherman   205
Chapter 25: The Snail   212
Chapter 26: Lampwick   221
Chapter 27: Playland   231
Chapter 28: Donkeys   245
Chapter 29: The Circus   258
Chapter 30: The Shark   278
Chapter 31: The Reunion   288
Chapter 32: A Real Live Boy   294

Chapter 1 "Geppetto Makes a Puppet"

Once upon a time a block of firewood found its way into the room of a kind but poor old wood carver named Geppetto. It was a small but comfortable room on the ground floor, with a tiny window under the stairway. The furniture couldn't have been much simpler: an old chair, a rickety bed, and a broken-down table. In a back corner stood a **decrepit**[1], old stove.

As soon as he saw that piece of wood, Geppetto was filled with joy. Rubbing his hands together happily, he said to himself: "This has come in the nick of time. Now I can make myself a beautiful wooden puppet that can dance and turn somersaults. With it I can travel the world and earn my supper."

Geppetto took out his tools to begin cutting the wood into the proper shape, but first stopped to ask himself: "What should I call him? I think I'll call him Pinocchio. I once knew a whole family by that name, and they were all lucky."

After choosing the name for his puppet, Geppetto set to work. He made the hair, the forehead, and the eyes. All of a sudden the newly made eyes moved back and forth, then stopped and stared at him! Seeing this, Geppetto asked, "Why are you staring at me?"

But there was no answer.

After the eyes, Geppetto made the nose, which began to grow as soon as it was finished. It grew and grew until it became so long that it seemed endless. Poor Geppetto kept cut-

---

[1] **decrepit** A person described as *decrepit* is weak or frail from old age or illness; he's worn out, wasted away. A thing described as *decrepit* is in a state of disrepair or decay (from hard use or time); it's broken-down, beat up, shabby, etc. *In 1835 American showman P. T. Barnum shamelessly exhibited a decrepit, hymn-singing woman as the 161-year-old nurse of George Washington.*

1

ting it and cutting it, but the more he cut, the longer the nose grew. In **despair**[1], he finally left it alone.

Next he made the mouth. No sooner was it finished than it stuck out its tongue at him!

Eager to finish what he'd started, Geppetto ignored the insult and went on with his work. After the mouth, he made the ears, the chin, the neck, the shoulders, the stomach, the arms, and the hands.

As he was about to put the finishing touches on the fingertips, Geppetto suddenly felt his face being poked. "Pinocchio, you bad boy!" he yelled. "You're not even finished yet, and you're already rude to your poor old father. That's very bad, my son. Very bad!"

The legs and feet still had to be made. As soon as they were done, Geppetto felt a sharp kick! Though thoroughly **exasperated**[2] by the puppet's antics, Geppetto didn't yell. Instead, he said to himself: "Well, I guess I deserve it. I should have realized this might happen before I started to make him. But now it's too late."

He took hold of the puppet and put him on the floor so that he might walk. Pinocchio found that his wooden legs were too stiff to move, so he lay on the floor and just wiggled them

---

[1] **despair** As a noun, *despair* is a state of being without hope (and the feeling of sadness or powerlessness that accompanies that state). As a verb, to *despair* is to lose all hope. *Franklin D. Roosevelt became President (1933) during the Great Depression, when the economy was in collapse and the nation was in despair.*

[2] **exasperate (exasperated)** To *exasperate* someone is to annoy or irritate him; to make him angry, disturbed, etc. The noun is *exasperation*. *In films featuring the (early 20th century) comedy team Laurel and Hardy, the thin, dimwitted Stan Laurel continually exasperated his fat, bullying partner, Oliver Hardy.*

about **haphazardly**[1], as a baby does in a crib. Now, with his legs **limbered**[2] up a bit, he got back up and took a few **faltering**[3] steps. When he nearly tumbled over, Geppetto took his hand and patiently taught him how to put out one foot in front of the other.

With a little practice, Pinocchio was able to walk all by himself. Very soon after that he was able to run all around the room! He came to the open door, and with one leap he was out into the street. Off he ran!

Poor Geppetto ran after him but wasn't able to catch up. "Stop him! Stop him!" Geppetto shouted. But the people in the street, seeing a wooden puppet running by, were too amazed to move.

By sheer luck, a policeman stood directly in Pinocchio's path. Hearing the commotion, he looked up. As the wooden boy ran by, the officer grabbed him by his long nose and returned him to his father.

Geppetto grabbed Pinocchio by the back of the neck and started to drag him home. As he was doing so, he shook him two or three times and said to him angrily, "We're going home now. I'll deal with you when we get there!"

---

[1] **haphazard (haphazardly)** If something happens (or occurs) *haphazardly*, it happens with no specific pattern; that is, it happens or seems to happen randomly, by chance, unpredictably, etc. *Looking at a map of Pittsburgh, we noticed that the streets appeared to wind haphazardly, like strands of spilt spaghetti.*

[2] **limber (limbered)** Something (a person, tree branch, etc.) described as *limber* bends easily; it's flexible. As a verb, to *limber up* is to make oneself limber (as by stretching or flexing). *People limber up before exercising to prevent tears in their muscles and tendons.*

[3] **falter (faltering)** When speaking of physical motion, to *falter* is to move unsteadily or stumble. When speaking of action or purpose, to *falter* is to hesitate or be indecisive. *In a 1947 speech before Congress, President Harry Truman said, "The free peoples of the world look to us for support in maintaining their freedoms; if we falter in our leadership, we may endanger the peace of the world — and we shall surely endanger the welfare of our nation."*

Pinocchio, on hearing this, threw himself to the ground and refused to take another step. One person after another gathered around the **mutinous**[1] child until a small crowd had formed.

"Poor puppet," said one man. "I'm not surprised he doesn't want to go home. Geppetto's certainly not an **abusive**[2] father, but there's no doubt that he'll give the boy a good spanking."

"Geppetto's a good man," added another, "but if we leave that poor puppet in his hands, who knows what he might do!"

Hearing these comments, the policeman suddenly ended matters by setting Pinocchio free and placing Geppetto under arrest! Then, hoping to **disperse**[3] the crowd, he yelled, "Okay, break it up. Show's over."

While poor old Geppetto was being led off to the police station, Pinocchio ran wildly through the town, taking one short cut after another toward home.

---

[1] **mutinous** A *mutiny* is a revolt against authority, especially a rebellion of sailors against their superior officers (as on a ship). To describe a person as *mutinous* is to say that he's rebellious, unruly, uncontrollable, etc. *After English explorer Henry Hudson reached Hudson Bay (1610), his mutinous crew set him adrift in a small boat; he was never seen again.*

[2] **abusive** To be *abusive* is to mistreat someone either verbally (by using harsh, insulting language) or physically (through maltreatment, battering, etc.). *The 1981 biographical film* Mommie Dearest *portrays Academy Award–winning actress Joan Crawford (1908–1977) as an abusive mother.*

[3] **disperse** This word can mean "to drive off into various directions; scatter" (as in *after the concert, the crowd dispersed*), or "to vanish; disappear; break up and scatter out of sight" (as in *by noon the fog had dispersed*), or "to spread over a wide area" (as in *disperse knowledge* or *disperse leaflets and pamphlets*). *The Knights of the Round Table dispersed after the death of King Arthur.*

Chapter 2 "The Cricket"

On reaching home, Pinocchio found the front door **ajar**[1]. He slipped into the house, locked the door behind him, and threw himself on the floor with a sigh of relief. But his happiness lasted only a short time, for just then he heard **intermittent**[2] chirping sounds.

"Who's that?" asked Pinocchio.

"I'm a cricket who's been living in this room for many years!" answered the voice.

Pinocchio turned and saw a cricket crawling slowly up the wall.

"But now this room is mine," said the puppet with a **proprietary**[3] attitude, "so please get out. And don't come back."

"I won't leave this spot," answered the cricket, "until I've told you something very **consequential**[4]."

"Tell me, then, and hurry."

---

[1] **ajar** If something (a door, for example) is *ajar*, it's partially open. *When the vacationing police officer returned to his hotel room and found the door ajar and a strange woman inside, he said, "Either you're the chambermaid or you're under arrest!"*

[2] **intermittent** Something (a sound, for example) described as *intermittent* stops and starts; it goes on and off (usually at irregular intervals). *Fireflies emit intermittent flashes of light to attract mates.*

[3] **proprietary** A *proprietor* is the legal owner of something (a property or business, for example). *Proprietary* means "relating to or befitting a proprietor." For example, to have a *proprietary* attitude toward something is to act as if you own it. And to describe a product (a medicine, for example) as *proprietary* is to say that it may be made and sold only by one who has the legal right to do so. *An auctioneer generally acts as an agent for the seller and has no proprietary interest in the merchandise being offered.*

[4] **consequential** This word describes matters that have important or significant consequences (results, effects, etc.) or people who are important or influential. *The consequential Supreme Court case Brown versus Board of Education (1954) ended racial segregation in public schools.*

5

"Boys who refuse to obey their parents and run away from home will never be happy. When they're older they'll be very sorry."

"All I know is that tomorrow morning I'll leave this place forever. If I stay here the same thing will happen to me that happens to all boys and girls. I'll be sent to school, where I'll be forced to study. And I hate to study! It's much more fun, I think, to chase butterflies and climb trees!"

"You fool! Don't you know that if you do that, you'll grow into a donkey and you'll be laughed at by everyone? Why don't you at least learn a trade, so that you can earn an honest living?"

"Can I tell you something?" asked Pinocchio, who was beginning to lose patience. "Of all the trades in the world, there's only one that really suits me."

"What's that?"

"Eating, drinking, sleeping, and playing all day."

"I'm telling you for your own good, Pinocchio," said the cricket in a calm voice, "that there are **dire**[1] **repercussions**[2] for people who live that way. They generally end up in the hospital or in prison."

"Be quiet! If you make me angry, you'll be sorry!"

"But Pinocchio, I'm already sorry — for you."

---

[1] **dire** This word can mean "causing or warning of great suffering, misfortune, trouble, disaster, etc.," as in *dire consequences,* or it can simply mean "desperate, urgent, very bad, etc.," as in *dire poverty. According to a July 1962 Atlantic magazine article entitled "A Marriage on the Rocks," for married people, divorce "is always a threat, admittedly or not, and such a dire threat that it is almost a dirty word."*

[2] **repercussion (repercussions)** An (often important) effect or result of some event or action is known as a *repercussion* (the word is generally used in the plural: *repercussions*). People sometimes use this word to suggest that the effect or result in question is indirect or unfavorable. *In its description of the website The Bankruptcy LawFinder, the Internet Directory points out that "the prospect of filing for bankruptcy can have devastating repercussions on an individual's life."*

"Why?"

"Because you're a silly, wooden-headed puppet."

These words **infuriated**[1] Pinocchio beyond all reason. He jumped up in a rage, took a hammer from the bench, and threw it with all his might at the cricket. The poor insect was crushed against the wall.

If the cricket's death bothered Pinocchio at all, it was only for a few minutes. As the day wore on, a queer, empty feeling at the pit of his stomach reminded him that he had had nothing to eat.

A boy's appetite grows very fast, and in a few moments the queer, empty feeling had become hunger, and the hunger grew bigger and bigger, until soon he was as hungry as a wolf.

Poor Pinocchio ran around the room, **rummaged**[2] through all the boxes and drawers, and even looked under the bed in search of a piece of bread or a cracker. But he found nothing.

And meanwhile his hunger grew and grew. Finally he wept and thought to himself: "The cricket was right. It was wrong of me to disobey my father and to run away from home. If he were here now, I wouldn't be so hungry! Oh, how horrible it is to be hungry!"

And as his stomach kept grumbling more than ever and he had nothing to quiet it with, he thought of going out for a

---

[1] **infuriate (infuriated)** To *infuriate* someone is to make him furious; that is, to make him extremely angry, to enrage him, etc. *In Greek mythology Paris (a prince of Troy) was asked to choose the most beautiful of the goddesses; he selected Aphrodite (goddess of love) and, in doing so, infuriated the other two contestants, Hera (wife of Zeus) and Athena (goddess of wisdom).*

[2] **rummage (rummaged)** To *rummage* through or in something (a box, drawer, attic, basement, etc.) is to search through it carefully (as by looking under things, turning things over, pushing things aside, etc.). *In their search for food, raccoons often rummage through garbage cans.* Note: As a noun, *rummage* means "miscellaneous articles; odd and ends."

walk to the nearby village in the hope of finding some kind person who might give him some food.

Chapter 3 "The Pears"

Pinocchio hated the dark streets, but he was so hungry that, in spite of it, he ran out of the house. The night was pitch black. It thundered, and bright flashes of lightning now and then shot across the sky, **illuminating**[1] the entire town. A cold, angry wind blew, raising clouds of dust and making the trees shake and moan.

Pinocchio was terrified of thunder and lightning, but his **rabid**[2] hunger made him forget his fear. He ran as fast as he could toward the village. He arrived tired out and panting, with his tongue hanging out like a dog's.

The whole village was dark and deserted. The stores were closed, and all the doors and windows were shut. It seemed like a ghost town.

Pinocchio, in desperation, ran up to a doorway, threw himself upon the bell, and pulled it wildly, saying to himself: "Someone will surely answer that!"

He was right. An old man in a nightcap peered through an **aperture**[3] in the upstairs window curtain. He called down angrily, "What do you want at this hour of the night?"

---

[1] **illuminate (illuminating)** To *illuminate* an object is to throw light on it; to light it up; to brighten it with light. To *illuminate* a subject or topic is to make it more clear or understandable. The noun is *illumination. Astronomers tell us that the degree of fullness of the moon depends on the amount of overlap between the half of the moon's surface that faces us and the half that's illuminated by the sun.*

[2] **rabid** Technically, this word means "affected with (the disease) rabies," as in *rabid dog.* But when people describe something (hunger or thirst, for example) as *rabid,* they mean that it's uncontrollable, raging, etc. And when they describe a person as *rabid,* they mean that he's fanatically enthusiastic or devoted (to some thing or cause), as in *rabid hockey fan. Adolf Hitler's rabid anti-Semitism was expressed in his autobiography,* Mein Kampf.

[3] **aperture** An *aperture* is a small opening in something; a slit, crack, break, gap, etc. *You can whistle by forcing air either through your teeth or through an aperture formed by puckering your lips.*

9

"Will you be good enough to give me a bit of bread? I'm dying of hunger."

"Wait a minute and I'll be right back," answered the old fellow, thinking he had to deal with one of those naughty boys who love to roam around at night ringing people's bells while they're peacefully asleep.

After a minute or two, the same voice cried, "I have something I think you'll find **invigorating**[1]. Get under the window and hold out your hat!"

Pinocchio had no hat, but he managed to get under the window just in time to feel a shower of ice-cold water pour down on his head, his shoulders, and his whole body.

He returned home as wet as a rag, freezing, and tired out from weariness and hunger. As he was too weak to stand, he sat down on a little stool and put his feet on the stove to dry them.

There he fell asleep. While he slept his wooden feet began to burn. Slowly, very slowly, they blackened and turned to ash.

Pinocchio slept so soundly that he was unaware of his feet. At dawn he opened his eyes just as a loud knocking sounded at the door. "Who is it?" he called, yawning and rubbing his eyes.

"It is I," answered a voice. It was the voice of Geppetto, who had finally been released from the police station.

The poor puppet, who was still half asleep, had not yet discovered that his feet were burned and gone. As soon as he heard his father's voice, he jumped up from his seat to open

---

[1] **invigorate (invigorating)** To *invigorate* someone or something is to give it or fill it with strength, energy, or liveliness (as in *the Beatles invigorated popular music*). As an adjective, if something is *invigorating*, either it's strength-giving, enlivening, etc. (as in *an invigorating cup of tea*) or it's refreshing, stimulating, etc. (as in *an invigorating sea breeze*). *In his third inaugural address (January 1941), President Franklin D. Roosevelt said, "A nation, like a person, has a body — a body that must be fed and clothed and housed, invigorated and rested, in a manner that measures up to the [goals] of our time."*

the door. But as he did so, he staggered and fell flat on the floor.

"Open the door for me!" Geppetto shouted from the street.

"Father, I can't," cried the puppet, rolling on the floor.

"Why not?"

"Because someone has eaten my feet."

"Who?"

"The cat," answered Pinocchio, seeing that the cat was busily playing with some wood shavings in the corner of the room.

Not knowing what else to do, Geppetto gave his son an **ultimatum**[1]: "Open this door right now or I'll give you a spanking when I get in!"

"Father, believe me, I can't stand up," moaned Pinocchio. "Oh, dear! Oh, dear! I'll have to walk on my knees for the rest of my life!"

Geppetto, thinking that all these tears and cries were only more of the puppet's tricks, angrily **clambered**[2] up the side of the house and went in through the window.

At first he found nothing **amiss**[1]. But upon discovering Pinocchio stretched out on the floor and really without feet, he

---

[1] **ultimatum** An *ultimatum* is a statement or demand (generally presented at the end of a negotiation or dispute) that expresses the threat of some penalty if the demand is not met. *After Germany's World War II surrender (May 1945), the U.S., the USSR, and Great Britain issued an ultimatum to Japan either to surrender or risk total destruction.*

[2] **clamber (clambered)** To *clamber* (up or over something) is to climb (up or over it) awkwardly or with difficulty, using both hands and feet. *According to the* Cambridge Biographical Encyclopedia, *when Australian aviation pioneer Sir Patrick Gordon Taylor flew over the Tasman Sea in 1935, "one engine cut out, and oil pressure was lost on another; [and so he] spent the rest of the flight clambering across the wings every half-hour, transferring oil from the dead engine into the ailing one."*

felt very sad and his anger disappeared. Picking him up, he caressed him and said to him with tears running down his cheeks: "My little Pinocchio, my dear little Pinocchio! How did you burn your feet?"

"I don't know, Father, but believe me, the night has been a terrible one and I'll remember it as long as I live. The thunder was so noisy and the lightning so bright. And I was hungry. And then the cricket said I was a fool and I threw the hammer at him and killed him. And I couldn't find anything to eat and I went out. And the old man with a nightcap looked out the window and **doused**[2] me with **frigid**[3] water. And I came home and put my feet on the stove to dry them, and I fell asleep. And now my feet are gone, but my hunger isn't! Oh! Oh! Oh!" And poor Pinocchio began to scream and cry so loudly that he could be heard for blocks around.

---

[1] **amiss** This adjective means "not the way it should be; wrong, improper, incorrect, etc." *According to NASA, once the Mars Pathfinder's airbags were installed (September 1996), "a detailed 'walk through' of the whole lander was performed by some of the best spacecraft mechanical engineers around; they looked for anything that might appear to be amiss."* Note: The word is also used as an adverb, meaning "in a wrong way; improperly, incorrectly, etc.," as in *speak amiss.*

[2] **douse** To *douse* something is to throw water (or some other liquid) over it; to drench it. *When, in September 1997, forest fires threatened the fabled stone fortress Machu Picchu in the Peruvian Andes, helicopters doused the mountainsides with water.* Note: When speaking of light or fire, the word is often used informally to mean "put out; extinguish," as in *he doused his flashlight.*

[3] **frigid** This word is used to describe something (air temperature, for example) that is extremely cold. It's also used figuratively to describe people who are cold in feeling or manner. *A scientific study of steel samples from the Titanic show that the ship sank (after hitting an iceberg during its 1912 maiden voyage) not because of a gash in its hull, but because the hull was made of a type of steel that became brittle and fractured easily in (the North Atlantic's) frigid water.*

Geppetto, who had understood nothing of all that jumbled, **incoherent**[1] talk—except that Pinocchio was hungry—felt sorry for him. He pulled three ripe pears out of his pocket and offered them to him, saying, "These pears were for my breakfast, but I give them to you gladly. Eat them and stop weeping."

"If you want me to eat them, please peel them for me."

"Peel them?" asked Geppetto, **aghast**.[2] "I would never have thought that you were so **finicky**[3] about your food. Bad, very bad! In this world, even as children, we must get used to eating everything, and liking it, for we never know what tomorrow may bring!"

"You may be right," answered Pinocchio, "but I won't eat the pears if they're not peeled. I don't like them."

And kind, patient Geppetto took out a knife and began to peel the pears. Though he worked quickly around their **spherical**[4] bases, the **tapered**[1] tops proved troublesome, and

---

[1] **incoherent** To describe language or thought as *incoherent* is to say that it shows no logical connection of ideas; it's confused, fragmented, disordered, etc. An *incoherent* person is one who is characterized by such language or thought. *People who suffer from (the mental illness) schizophrenia often exhibit incoherent speech and inappropriate behavior.*

[2] **aghast** To be *aghast* is to be struck by or filled with amazement, shock, surprise, terror, etc. *According to the* Cambridge Encyclopedia, *after (English scientist) Sir Isaac Newton (1642–1727) determined that all celestial bodies (stars, planets, moons, etc.) have a gravitational attraction to one another, he "was aghast at the implications for the unfortunate investigator; with so many bodies, each pulling all the others, how could anyone hope to cope with the mathematics involved?"*

[3] **finicky** People who are *finicky* are excessively or overly fussy or particular about something (food, for example); they're difficult to please; they're picky. *The 9-Lives cat food TV commercial claimed that "the cat who doesn't act finicky soon loses control of his owner."*

[4] **spherical** A *sphere* is a round, three-dimensional object; a ball. To describe something as *spherical* is to say that it has the shape or approximate shape of a sphere. *The challenge for mapmakers is to avoid distortion when they transfer the features of a spherical body (the earth, for example) to a flat piece of paper.*

he worked more slowly. Finally finished, he placed the three peeled pears before his son and put the peels in a row at the side of the table. Pinocchio ate one pear in an instant and started to throw the core away — but Geppetto held his arm.

"Oh, no, don't throw it away! Everything in this world may be of some use!"

"Do you think I would ever eat that core?" cried Pinocchio angrily.

"Who knows?" replied Geppetto calmly.

And later the three cores were placed on the table next to the peels.

Pinocchio had eaten the three pears, or rather devoured them. Then he yawned deeply, and cried, "I'm still hungry!"

"But I have nothing more to give you."

"Really? Nothing?"

"I have only these cores and these peels."

"The fruit was sweet and **succulent**[2]," said Pinocchio, "but these cores and peels are dry and bitter." Then, feeling a sharp pang of hunger, he said, "Oh, very well. If there's nothing else, I'll eat them."

At first he made a face, but, one after another, the peels and the cores disappeared. "Ah! Now I feel fine!" he said after eating the last one.

---

[1] **taper (tapered)** Things that are *tapered* (pant legs, church spires, pool cues, etc.) become gradually narrower or thinner at one end. *The Washington Monument is a tapered, 555-foot shaft whose exterior is faced with white marble and whose interior is lined with memorial stones from all 50 states.*

[2] **succulent** This word is used to describe food that is juicy and tasty. By extension, it can describe anything interesting or enjoyable (gossip, for example). *American author F. Scott Fitzgerald (1896–1940) once joked that "the kiss originated when the first male reptile licked the first female reptile, implying in a subtle, complimentary way that she was as succulent as the small reptile he had for dinner the night before."*

"You see," observed Geppetto, "that I was right when I told you that one must not be too fussy about food. We never know what life may have in store for us!"

Chapter 4 *"New Feet and a New Schoolbook"*

As soon as his hunger was satisfied, Pinocchio started to grumble and cry that he wanted a new pair of feet. But Geppetto, in order to punish him for his mischief, let him alone the whole morning. In the afternoon, too, Geppetto ignored his son's **relentless¹ badgering²**. Then, after dinner, he said to him, "Why should I make your feet over again? To see you run away from home again?"

"I promise you," answered the puppet, sobbing, "that from now on I'll be good."

"Boys always promise that when they want something," said Geppetto.

"I promise to go to school every day and to study hard."

"Those sound like **noble³ aspirations⁴**, but boys always say that when they want their own way."

---

¹ **relentless** To be *relentless* is to be steady and persistent; to be never stopping, as in *the relentless beating of the drums. When heavyweight boxer Mike Tyson turned professional in 1985, he was known for his relentless punches, which knocked out opponents early in fights.*

² **badger (badgering)** To *badger* (someone) is to nag, pester, bother, or annoy (him). *After her three-year-old whined for a lollipop for an hour, the young mother — who'd once promised herself that she'd never yell at her children — lost her temper and screamed, "Stop badgering me!"*

³ **noble** People, deeds, or thoughts described as *noble* show high moral character (generosity, courageousness, righteousness, goodness, etc.). *In 1957 journalist Leonard Warren observed, "[In opera] tenors are noble, pure, and heroic...but baritones are born villains."*

⁴ **aspiration (aspirations)** An *aspiration* is a strong desire for high achievement (as in life, career, etc.); a goal, aim, ambition, etc. The word is often used in the plural. *In 1984 journalist Hugh Newell Jacobsen said, "When you look at a city, it's like reading the hopes, aspirations, and pride of everyone who built it."*

"But I'm not like other boys! I'm better than all of them, and I always tell the truth. I promise you, Father, that I'll learn a trade, and I'll take care of you in your old age."

Geppetto, though trying to look **stern**[1], felt his eyes fill with tears and his heart soften. He said no more, but, taking his tools and two pieces of wood, he set to work.

In less than an hour the feet were finished—two slender, **nimble**[2] little feet, strong and quick, modeled as if by an artist's hands.

"Now close your eyes and sleep!" Geppetto said.

Pinocchio didn't feel the least bit sleepy, but he closed his eyes and pretended to sleep while Geppetto attached the two feet with a bit of glue, doing his work so well that the seams between the legs and the **appended**[3] **extremities**[4] could hardly be seen.

As soon as Pinocchio felt his new feet, he gave one leap from the table and started to skip and jump around, mad with joy. Finally he stopped and said, "To show you how grateful I

---

[1] **stern** This word is used to describe people, manners, or facial expressions that are strict or severe. *Stern* people are inflexible and uncompromising, and they often appear grimly serious, hard, or withdrawn. *In a famous U.S. Army recruitment poster, a stern-faced Uncle Sam says, "I want you."*

[2] **nimble** To be *nimble* is to be quick and light in movement; to move with ease and agility. *According to the* **Cambridge Encyclopedia,** *whereas most birds fly away when disturbed, New World quail "prefer to run away, trotting on nimble feet like little clockwork toys."*

[3] **append (appended)** To *append* something (to something else) is to add it on or attach it. *A postscript (P.S.) is a message appended at the end of a letter, after the writer's signature.*

[4] **extremity (extremities)** This word refers to the outermost or farthest point or portion of something. When used in the plural *(extremities)* it often refers to the hands or feet (the end parts of bodily limbs). *Frostbite is caused by prolonged exposure to freezing temperatures and most often affects the ears, nose, or extremities.*

am to you, Father, I'll go to school now. But to go to school I'll need a suit of clothes."

Geppetto did not have a penny in his pocket, so he made his son a little suit out of paper with pictures of flowers on it, a pair of shoes from the bark of a tree, and a tiny hat from a piece of bread.

Pinocchio ran to look at his reflection in a bowl of water, and he felt so happy that he said proudly, "Now I look like a gentleman."

"Indeed," answered Geppetto. "But remember that fine clothes do not make a gentleman unless they are neat and clean."

"Very true," answered Pinocchio, "But in order to go to school, I still need something very important."

"What?"

"A schoolbook."

"To be sure! But how will we get it?"

"That's easy. We'll go to the bookstore and buy it," explained the puppet.

"And the money?"

"I don't have any."

"Neither have I," said the old man sadly.

Pinocchio became **downcast**[1] at these words, for when poverty shows itself, it destroys all joy — even in children.

"Wait here!" cried Geppetto all at once, as he jumped up from his chair. Putting on his old coat, full of holes and patches, he ran out of the house without another word.

After a while he returned. In his hands he had a brand-new schoolbook for his son, but the old coat was gone. The poor fellow was in his shirtsleeves, and it was snowing outside.

---

[1] **downcast** If you're downcast, you're low in spirits; you're sad, depressed, discouraged, etc. *In May 1944 teenaged Jewish refugee Anne Frank wrote in her diary: "I have often been downcast, but never in despair; I regard our hiding as a dangerous adventure, romantic and interesting at the same time."* Note: The word can also mean "directed downward," as in *downcast eyes.*

"Where's your coat, Father?"

"I sold it."

"Why did you do that?"

"Because it made me too warm."

Pinocchio understood the **import**[1] of the white lie instantly, and, unable to restrain his tears, he jumped on his father's neck and kissed him over and over.

---

[1] **import** The *import* of something (spoken words, gestures, actions, etc.) is that which is implied or signified by it. For example, if spoken words don't clearly spell something out, the *import* is the true meaning or idea of those words. *Speaking of an acquaintance, Hellen Keller once remarked, "She grasps the import of whole sentences, catching the meaning of words she doesn't know."*

Chapter 5 "The Puppet Theater"

When it stopped snowing, Pinocchio hurried off to school with his new book under his arm. As he walked along, he busily planned his **agenda**[1]. He thought: "In school, today I'll learn to read, tomorrow to write, and the day after to do arithmetic. Then, clever as I am, I can earn a lot of money. With the very first pennies I make, I'll buy Father a brand-new cloth coat. Cloth, did I say? No, it'll be of gold and silver with diamond buttons. That poor man certainly deserves it. After all, isn't he in his shirtsleeves because he was kind enough to buy a book for me? On this cold day, too! Fathers are indeed good to their children!"

While dwelling on these **visionary**[2] desires, he thought he heard beautiful music coming from somewhere in the distance—but because it was faint, the direction it came from was difficult to **discern**[3]. He stopped to listen more carefully, tilting his head this way and that. Finally, he determined that

---

[1] **agenda** An *agenda* can be a (written or mental) list of things to do, or it can be a course of action to be followed regularly. *According to* The Reader's Companion to American History, *"Although the future of the U.S. space program is promising, NASA must tackle several issues before its agenda of both unmanned and manned missions can be [carried out]."*

[2] **visionary** People who are *visionary* tend to be dreamy, unrealistic, fanciful, etc. To describe ideas, plans, schemes, etc., as *visionary* is to say that they're unpractical or unachievable. As a noun, a *visionary* is a dreamer, a romantic, an idealist. *The title character of (Spanish novelist) Miguel de Cervantes'* Don Quixote *(1605) is a visionary who imagines himself a knight destined to right wrongs.*

[3] **discern** To *discern* something is to perceive it and recognize the difference or distinction between it and something else through either one of the senses (sight, hearing, etc.) or the intellect, as in *through the fog, we were unable to discern the outlines of the building. Looking at the night sky, it's impossible to discern any matter lying between stars (but scientists tell us that such matter indeed exists).*

it was coming from a little street that led to a small village along the shore.

"What can that music be?" he wondered. **Enraptured**[1] by its charm, he stood listening, forgetting about everything else. Then, suddenly coming to his senses, he thought: "What a pity that I have to go to school today! Otherwise—"

There he stopped, very much puzzled. He felt he had to make up his mind for either one thing or another. Should he go to school, or should he follow the music?

"Today I'll follow the music, and tomorrow I'll go to school," he decided **arbitrarily**[2]. "There's always plenty of time to go to school."

He started running down the street. Soon he was close enough to hear the **subtle**[3] **nuances**[1] of the various instru-

---

[1] **enraptured** To be *enraptured* by something (a work of art, for example) is to be carried away by it (as from overwhelmingly strong, pleasurable emotions); to be transported, captivated, delighted, enchanted, thrilled, spellbound, etc. *In its description of a website concerning Greek mythology, the* Internet Directory *says, "Take a trip back in time as you page through Greek myths and stories, revisiting the ancient creatures that have enraptured students of literature for thousands of years."*

[2] **arbitrary (arbitrarily)** An *arbitrary* decision is one based on individual will, momentary personal preference, or whim (rather than on reason or principle). *In algebra class, when we were told that we can choose any letter — not just* x *— to represent an unknown quantity, I arbitrarily chose k.*

[3] **subtle** This word is used to describe things (odors, colors, humor, meanings, differences, etc.) that are so slight, faint, or delicate that they are difficult to detect; they're not immediately obvious; they're understated. *[British political leader] Winston Churchill (1874–1965) once gave the following advice about public speaking: "If you have an important point to make, don't try to be subtle or clever; use a pile driver; hit the point once; then come back and hit it again; then hit it a third time — a tremendous whack."*

ments, and the music sounded even more beautiful than before. He ran as fast as his little wooden legs would carry him.

Suddenly he found himself in a large square, full of people standing in front of a wooden building painted in **vibrant**[2] colors. He stared at the building for a few moments while he caught his breath, then asked a little boy near him, "What's that?"

"Read the sign and you'll know," answered the boy.

"I'd like to read it, but somehow I can't today."

"Why not?"

"Um...I can't **decipher**[3] the handwriting."

"Oh, really? Then I'll read it to you. It says 'Great Puppet Theater. Marionette Show Today.'"

"When did the show start?"

"It's starting right now."

"And how much does it cost to get in?"

---

[1] **nuance (nuances)** A *nuance* is a slight degree of difference between two nearly identical things (as two colors, tones, feelings, meanings, etc.). The word also signifies any expression or appreciation of such slight degrees of difference. In 1966 *American author and poet Paul Goodman said, "To translate [literature from one language to another] one must have a style of his own, for otherwise the translation will have no rhythm or nuance."*

[2] **vibrant** In one sense, if something (a color or a sculpture, for example) is *vibrant*, it's stimulating, lively, spirited, exciting, etc. Country Life *magazine once spoke of a place "under the sea where the light plays on vibrant corals [and] tropical pinks."* In another sense, if something (a city or a novel, for example) is *vibrant*, it throbs or pulses with energy or activity. *According to* Grolier's Encyclopedia, *"The houses [of New Orleans' French Quarter] are flush with the sidewalks, and balconies overlook the streets, giving [the area] an intimate, vibrant atmosphere.* Note: If you say that a sound or musical instrument is *vibrant*, you mean that it has a strong, deep tone (as in *the vibrant tone of a cello*).

[3] **decipher** To *decipher* something that's unclear is to make out the meaning of it; read it; interpret it. To *decipher* something written in code is to convert it into ordinary language. *In 1973 Austrian zoologist Karl von Frisch received a Nobel Prize for deciphering honeybees' "dance language" (through which they communicate the direction and distance from their hive to nectar sources).*

"Five cents."

Pinocchio, who was wild with curiosity to know what was going on inside, lost all his pride and said to the boy shamelessly, "Will you lend me five cents until tomorrow?"

"I'd like to lend it to you," answered the other, poking fun at him, "but somehow I can't today."

"Then will you buy my coat of flowered paper for five cents?"

"For kids our age a floral pattern is **passé**[1]; it's been **superseded**[2] by solid colors or stripes. Besides, if it rains, what could I do with a coat of paper? It would be ruined."

"Do you want to buy my shoes?"

"Shoes of bark? They're only good for lighting a fire."

"What about my hat?"

"Some bargain! A cap made out of bread! Is that supposed to be **aesthetically**[3] pleasing?"

"Well—" said Pinocchio, who was too **naïve**[1] to understand that the boy was **intimating**[2] that the cap looked ugly.

---

[1] **passé** Anything *passé* is out of fashion (or style); outmoded; out of date; etc. *American novelist Raymond Chandler (1888–1959), speaking of slang, once said, "I've found that there are only two kinds that are any good: slang that has established itself in the language and slang that you make up yourself; everything else is apt to be passé before it gets into print."*

[2] **supersede (superseded)** If something *supersedes* something else, it comes after it (in time) and replaces it; it takes the place of it. *In the 1980s, record players were superseded by CD players.*

[3] **aesthetic (aesthetically)** The branch of philosophy concerned with the nature of beauty or art is known as *aesthetics*. The adjective *aesthetic* means "having or showing an appreciation of beauty or good taste (as distinguished from the practical or scientific)." *Whereas tattoos were once applied for practical reasons (to signify one's rank, for example), today they are generally applied for purely aesthetic purposes.*

"Look," the boy interrupted, "I don't know you, but let me give you some advice about clothes. At the least you should try to **conform**[3] to the way your **peers**[4] dress—because if you **deviate**[5] from the **norm**[6], you'll be laughed at. But better still, look to see what the best-dressed boys wear—then try to

---

[1] **naïve** People who are *naïve* (pronounced *nigh-EVE*) lack worldly experience and tend to believe whatever they're told; they're simple, trusting, unsophisticated, unsuspicious, childlike, etc. The noun is *naïveté* (pronounced with the accent on the last syllable, which rhymes with *bay*). *In 1989 American author Florence King said, "We want a President who is as much like an American tourist as possible—someone with the same goofy grin, the same innocent intentions, the same naïve trust."*

[2] **intimate (intimating)** To *intimate* something (an idea, for example) is to express it in an indirect manner; to hint at it, imply it, suggest it. *At one time angels were popular features on graves; their presence intimated that, just as they had protected the departed during his lifetime, they did so now in death.*

[3] **conform** To *conform* is to act or be in agreement with accepted standards or expectations (as in conduct, dress, law, business, etc.). The noun is *conformity*. *In his book* The Naked Civil Servant *(1968), British author Quentin Crisp said, "The young always have the same problem—how to rebel and conform at the same time; they have now solved this by defying their parents and copying one another."*

[4] **peer (peers)** Your *peers* are the people who have equal standing with you (in age, rank, class, etc.). *Actor Tom Cruise's childhood was complicated by his family's frequent moves, but he used sports as a way to fit in with his peers.*

[5] **deviate** To *deviate* is to turn aside from a particular course, or to depart from what is considered normal. *Canadian Prime Minister John Diefenbaker (1895–1979) once said, "There was no member of my family who was a lawyer, but I never deviated from that course from the time I was eight or nine years of age."*

[6] **norm** A standard regarded as typical or normal is known as a *norm*. *Although cars with rear wheel drive were the norm for many years, most cars today have front wheel drive.*

emulate[1] them. Anyway, I don't want to buy anything from you."

Pinocchio, still without the five cents he needed, was almost in tears. He was just about to make one last offer, but didn't have the nerve. He hesitated for a long time, unable to make up his mind. At last he said, "Will you give me five cents for my brand-new schoolbook?"

"I'm a boy, so I don't buy things from other boys," said the little fellow **cryptically**[2].

"Sorry to **intrude**[3]," said a **canny**[4] used book salesman who happened to be standing nearby and **eavesdropping**[5], "but I might give you five cents for your book. But first I have to make sure that the price you're asking isn't too high. You see,

---

[1] **emulate** To *emulate* something is to try to equal it (to become as good as it) by imitating or copying it. *With their 1966 album* Pet Sounds, *the Beach Boys tried to emulate the Beatles' imaginative use of recording techniques.*

[2] **cryptic (cryptically)** If something (a remark or gesture, for example) is *cryptic*, it's mysterious, ambiguous, or puzzling. *Although (16th-century French physician and astrologer) Nostradamus's predictions of the future have fascinated people for centuries, experts point out that his forecasts were written in cryptic language.* Note: The word is also used to refer to messages written in (a secret) code.

[3] **intrude** When you *intrude*, you force yourself upon another (or others) without his invitation or permission; you butt in, horn in, stick your nose in, etc. *Penguins show little fear of humans; in fact, they sometimes use their wings to beat the shins of people who intrude on their nesting grounds.*

[4] **canny** People who are *canny* are shrewd and cautious (as in business or in dealing with others); they're sharp-witted, slick, thrifty, etc. *Scottish-born U.S. industrialist Andrew Carnegie's canny investments made him wealthy by age 30.*

[5] **eavesdrop (eavesdropping)** To eavesdrop is to secretly listen in on someone's private conversation. *In 1961, in a unanimous opinion that the Constitution bars the police from electronic eavesdropping, U.S. Supreme Court justice Potter Stewart said, "At the very core [of the 4th Amendment] stands the right of a man to retreat into his own home and there be free from unreasonable governmental intrusion."*

there's a **glut**[1] of schoolbooks in the marketplace right now, so even though it has some educational value, it has very little **monetary**[2] value. Here, let me see it."

Pinocchio handed over the book and the salesman made a show of **appraising**[3] it. Then, acting as if he were doing Pinocchio a tremendous favor, he agreed to the price. Taking a nickel from his pocket he handed it to Pinocchio, then disappeared into the crowd.

And to think that poor old Geppetto sat at home shivering in his shirtsleeves because he had to sell his coat to buy that schoolbook for his son!

---

[1] **glut** A *glut* is an excessive amount of something (goods on the market, for example); an oversupply. *In 1947 a glut of fresh oranges (in the U.S.) lowered prices from $4.00 to $.50 per box.*

[2] **monetary** This word means "pertaining to money." *In 1971 French president Georges Pompidou referred to the U.S. dollar as a "basic monetary yardstick that constantly loses value as a result of purely internal politics," then added that "the rest of the world cannot be expected to regulate its life by a clock which is always slow."*

[3] **appraise (appraising)** To *appraise* something is to judge or evaluate it so as to estimate its value, worth, quality, etc. *Jewelers not only make jewelry — they also repair and appraise it.*

Chapter 6 "Fire-Eater"

Quick as a flash, Pinocchio disappeared into the puppet theater. It was full of people, who were enjoying the show and laughing till they nearly cried at the zany[1] physical antics of the marionettes and the savage topical[2] references in their jokes and songs.

Pinocchio sat mesmerized[3] in the last row. Then suddenly, without any warning, the leading puppet stopped acting, pointed to the rear of the theater, and yelled wildly, "Look, look! Am I dreaming? Or do I really see Pinocchio there?"

"It is Pinocchio! It is Pinocchio!" yelled all the marionettes. "Pinocchio, come up to us! Come to the arms of your wooden brothers!"

At such a loving invitation, Pinocchio stood up, and with one leap found himself in one of the middle rows. With another leap, he was on the orchestra leader's podium[4]. With a third, he landed on the stage.

---

[1] **zany** If something is *zany*, it's comical in a clownish, crazy, or outlandish way; it's wacky, silly, goofy, etc. *Jim Carrey's zany performance in the film* Ace Ventura: Pet Detective *catapulted him to fame in 1994.*

[2] **topical** This word describes things (humor, references, etc.) that pertain to the here and now; that is, things of current or local interest (to listeners, viewers, etc.). *The topical folk songs Bob Dylan wrote in the early 1960s ("Blowin' in the Wind," for example) expressed the hopes and angers of his generation.*

[3] **mesmerize (mesmerized)** If you're *mesmerized* by something, you're captivated by it; you're spellbound, fascinated, hypnotized, etc. *Mass murderer Charles Manson mesmerized his (mostly female) followers with drugs and religion.*

[4] **podium** A *podium* is a platform or stand used by an orchestra conductor or public speaker (for holding notes, etc.). *For theatrical effect, Philadelphia Orchestra conductor Leopold Stowkowski (1882–1977) insisted that spotlights be focused on the podium.*

It's impossible to describe the shrieks of joy, the warm embraces, and the **exuberant**[1] greetings with which that strange company of wooden actors and actresses received Pinocchio.

It was a touching sight, but the audience, seeing that the play had stopped, became angry and began to **clamor**[2] for the play to continue.

The yelling was of no use, for the marionettes, instead of going on with their act, made twice as much noise as before, and, lifting Pinocchio on their shoulders, carried him around the stage in triumph.

Concurrent[3] with this **jubilant**[4] celebration was the sudden arrival onstage of the theater's owner. His name was Fire-Eater, and he was **infamous**[5] for his frightful appearance and

---

[1] **exuberant** To be *exuberant* about something is to be extremely or uninhibitedly happy or enthusiastic about it. *According to* Webster's World Encyclopedia, *"the celebration of the Buddhist New Year is an occasion of great joy; in their exuberance, [people] squirt water on whomever they meet in the streets, regardless of whether it is a friend or a stranger."*

[2] **clamor** As a verb, to *clamor* is to make a loud or noisy outcry (about something). As a noun, a *clamor* is such an outcry. *At the end of the 1997 film* Titanic, *wealthy passengers in lifeboats await rescue amid the clamor of poor passengers drowning in the cold Atlantic water.*

[3] **concurrent** When two things (events, occurrences, etc.) happen at the same time, they are said to be *concurrent*. The adverb *concurrently* means "at the same time." *The early Egyptians had two completely separate calendars running concurrently, one for religious purposes and one for agricultural use.*

[4] **jubilant** People or celebrations described as *jubilant* are filled with great joy, happiness, delight, merriment, etc. The noun is *jubilation*. *In the United States, the Fourth of July is an occasion for parades, patriotic speeches, and noisy jubilation.*

[5] **infamous** If you refer to a person or thing as *infamous* (pronounced *IN-fuh-miss*), you mean that it's well known for a bad or evil reputation. *Salem, Massachusetts, was the site of the infamous 1692 witchcraft trials.* The noun is *infamy* (pronounced *IN-fuh-me*). *President Franklin D. Roosevelt referred to December 7, 1941 (on which Japanese planes attacked the U.S. naval base at Pearl Harbor, Hawaii) as a "date which will live in infamy."*

ruthless[1] cruelty. He was large and **burly**[2], with teeth like yellow fangs and eyes like glowing red coals. But his most **prominent**[3] feature was his tangled black beard that hung all the way down to his feet! In his huge, hairy hands he held a long whip made of green snakes and black cats' tails twisted together, which he constantly swished through the air in a threatening manner.

At his unexpected appearance, the **furor**[4] in the theater abruptly ended. The audience was speechless; no one dared even to breathe. The poor marionettes, one and all, **cowered**[5] in fear.

---

[1] **ruthless** People who are *ruthless* show no pity or mercy; they're cruel, harsh, hard-hearted, etc. *Heinrich Himmler (1900–1945), who (during World War II) headed the Gestapo and was responsible for the death of millions of Jews in concentration camps, is considered by many the most ruthless of all Nazi leaders.*

[2] **burly** People who are *burly* have large, wide bodies; they're heavy, strong, beefy, muscular, etc. *Characters featured in "Popeye" cartoons include the spindly Olive Oyl and the burly Bluto.*

[3] **prominent** If an object is *prominent*, it stands out so that it can be easily seen; its immediately noticeable. *The most prominent feature on the planet Jupiter is the Great Red Spot (an oval larger than the planet Earth).* If a person (or group, organization, etc.) is *prominent*, he stands out above others; he's widely known, important, distinguished, etc. *During the 1950s and '60s, Martin Luther King, Jr., was the most prominent member of the American civil rights movement.*

[4] **furor** A *furor* is a public uproar; a commotion, frenzy, etc. *In 1966 John Lennon provoked a public furor when he claimed that the Beatles had become more popular than Jesus.*

[5] **cower (cowered)** To *cower* is to shrink back (crouch, cringe, draw back, etc.) in fear or shame. *In 1951 U.S. author Henry Miller said, "Every genuine boy is a rebel; if he were allowed to develop according to his own instincts, society would undergo such [an extreme change] as to make the adult revolutionary cower and cringe."*

"Why have you brought such **pandemonium**[1] to my theater?" the huge fellow screamed at Pinocchio.

The puppet didn't wish to **attribute**[2] blame to himself or to anyone else in particular. With shaking knees he answered **evasively**[3], "Believe me, sir, it's not my fault."

"Enough! Be quiet! I'll deal with you later."

As soon as the play was over, Fire-Eater went to the kitchen, where a big lamb chop was slowly turning over the fire. More wood was needed to finish cooking it. He called in a couple of the wooden actors and said to them, "Bring Pinocchio to me! He looks as if he's made of well-seasoned wood. He'll make a fine fire for cooking."

At first the marionettes hesitated. Then, frightened by a **sinister**[4] stare from their master, they hurriedly left the kitchen to obey him. A few minutes later they returned, carrying poor Pinocchio, who was squirming like a fish out of water and crying pitifully, "Father, save me! I don't want to die! I don't want to die!"

---

[1] **pandemonium** This word signifies a state of noisy disorder or commotion. *In November 1986 the* New York Times *said that "pandemonium paid a visit backstage" at the opening of Radio City Music Hall's Christmas spectacular when "a camel stepped on the foot of a Rockette [and] human Christmas trees bumped into eight maids a-milking."*

[2] **attribute** If you say that something is *attributed* to you, you mean that it's thought of (by people) as resulting from, caused by, or produced by you. *The saying "Any man who goes to a psychiatrist ought to have his head examined" has been attributed to film producer Samuel Goldwyn (1882–1974).*

[3] **evasive (evasively)** People (or things) described as *evasive* tend to escape (from things) or avoid (things), usually by cleverness or trickery; they're hard to pin down; they're dodgy, shifty, slippery, etc. *If someone asks you for certain information that you don't want to reveal, an evasive but usually inoffensive answer you might give is "A little birdie told me."*

[4] **sinister** Anything *sinister* suggests or threatens evil or danger. *Actor Boris Karloff (1887–1969) specialized in portraying monsters and other sinister characters in such films as* Frankenstein *(1931) and* The Mummy *(1932).*

Chapter 7 "Fire-Eater Sneezes"

Though Fire-Eater looked ugly and heartless, his **disposition**[1] was not nearly as nasty as most people imagined. Proof of this is that, when he saw poor Pinocchio being brought to him, struggling with fear and crying, he felt sorry for him and began to weaken. Finally, he could control himself no longer and gave a loud sneeze.

At that sneeze, one of the wooden actors, who until then had looked miserably sad, smiled happily and, leaning toward Pinocchio, whispered to him, "Good news, my brother! Fire-Eater has sneezed, and that's a sign that he feels sorry for you. You're saved!"

Strangely, whereas most people cry when they feel sorry for someone, Fire-Eater had the strange **quirk**[2] of sneezing each time he was moved to pity.

But after sneezing, Fire-Eater, mean as ever, shouted at Pinocchio, "Stop crying! It gives me a funny feeling down here in my stomach and...Achoo! Achoo!" Two loud sneezes finished his speech.

"Are your father and mother still living?" asked Fire-Eater.

"My father, yes. My mother I have never known."

"You never knew your mother? Then who raised and **nurtured**[1] you?"

---

[1] **disposition** Your *disposition* is your usual or natural attitude, mood, or state of mind (as in *he had a cheerful disposition*). *In 1987, actor Roddy McDowall, speaking of his roles as a child star, said, "I really liked Lassie, but that horse, Flicka, was a nasty animal with a terrible disposition."*

[2] **quirk** A *quirk* is a peculiarity or oddity of behavior or personality (a strange or odd mannerism, for example). (Uncle Tom's Cabin *author) Harriet Beecher Stowe (1811–1896) once said, "Every man has his own quirks and twists."*

"My kind, loving father. He's like a father *and* mother to me."

"Your father must be a very good man. I think he would suffer terribly if I were to use you as firewood. Poor old man! I feel sorry for him! Achoo! Achoo! Achoo!" Three more sneezes sounded, louder than ever. "However, I should be sorry for myself, too, right now. My fine dinner is spoiled. I have no more wood for the fire, and the lamb chop is only half cooked. Never mind. In your place I'll burn some other puppet. Guards!"

At the call, two security guards **affiliated**[2] with the theater appeared. They were tall and wore helmets on their heads. In their hands they carried very large swords—the type favored by **medieval**[3] knights.

---

[1] **nurture (nurtured)** To *nurture* someone (a baby or child, for example) is to promote his growth and development (feed him, educate him, encourage him, etc.). *In 1985, comparing office workers to family members, personnel consultant Gerald Slaton said, "There are the daddies, who want to be in charge, the mommies, who do the nurturing, and the various children [competing] for their attention."*

[2] **affiliation (affiliated)** An *affiliation* is a close connection or association between two or more people, groups, or organizations. Sometimes the associated elements are independent and equal, but more often one is dependent on, subordinate to, or part of the other. *Radcilffe College for women is affiliated with Harvard University (in fact, Radcliffe students are instructed by the Harvard faculty).*

[3] **medieval** This word describes anything that pertains to, is characteristic of, or is in the style of the Middle Ages (the period of European history roughly from the fifth century to the fifteenth century). *According to medieval astronomical theory, the area of space immediately beyond the stars was the dwelling place of angels.*

Fire-Eater said to them, "Some of our bit part players are not true **thespians**[1]. For them acting is merely an **avocation**[2]. Take one of them and bring him here to throw on the fire. I want my lamb chop well done!" With unthinking **subservience**[3], the guards carried out the order. As they approached the fire, the new victim was so frightened that his legs doubled up under him and he fell to the floor. Pinocchio, at that heartbreaking sight, threw himself at the feet of Fire-Eater and, weeping bitterly, asked in a pitiful voice that could scarcely be heard, "Have pity on my wooden brother, I beg of you, sir!"

"There are no sirs here!"

"Have pity, Your Excellency!"

On hearing himself addressed as Your Excellency, Fire-Eater sat up very straight in his chair, stroked his long beard, and, becoming suddenly calm, smiled and said to Pinocchio, "What would you like me to do?"

"I beg for mercy for my poor brother, who has never done the least harm in his life."

---

[1] **thespian (thespians)** A *thespian* is an actor or actress. (Ancient Greek poet and playwright Thespis is considered the founder of drama, and the word derives from his name). *In her 1971 book* Julie Harris Talks to Young Actors, *the Tony-winning actress reflects on her career and gives advice to aspiring thespians.*

[2] **avocation** A *vocation* is one's regular work or profession. An *avocation* is an activity engaged in for enjoyment outside of one's regular occupation (a hobby, for example). (Alice in Wonderland *author*) Lewis Carroll's vocation *was writing, but his avocation was photography (he excelled especially at photographing children).*

[3] **subservient (subservience)** If you're *subservient* you are (or act as if you are) under the control or authority of another; you're obedient, servile, submissive, etc. *In 1992 Oscar-winning actor Michael Caine said, "The basic rule of human nature is that powerful people speak slowly and subservient people quickly — because if they don't speak fast nobody will listen to them."*

"There's no mercy here, Pinocchio. Even though you've **wreaked**[1] **havoc**[2] in my theater, I've spared you. But I can go only so far. I'm hungry and my dinner must be cooked, so this puppet must burn in your place."

"In that case," declared Pinocchio, **heedless**[3] of the consequences, "my duty is clear. Guards, tie me up and throw me on those flames. It's not fair for someone else to die in my place!"

These brave words, said in a piercing voice, made all the other marionettes cry. Even the guards cried like babies.

Fire-Eater at first remained hard and cold. He said, "So what if it's not fair? Life is filled with **inequities**[4]. In war some soldiers die while others are merely wounded. Why? Because life isn't fair!" But then, little by little, he softened and began to sneeze. After about a dozen sneezes, he opened his arms wide and said to Pinocchio, "You're a brave boy! Come to my arms and kiss me!"

---

[1] **wreak (wreaked)** To *wreak* (pronounced *reek*) something damaging or unwelcome is to give expression to it (as in *wreak anger*), bring it about or cause it (as in *wreak havoc*), or inflict it (as in *wreak punishment*). *The 1976 film* Carrie *concerns a high school girl who uses her power to move objects by telekinesis in order to wreak revenge on classmates who'd tormented or humiliated her.*

[2] **havoc** The action of bringing about destruction or disorder, or the result of being destroyed or thrown into disorder is known as *havoc*. *When Washington State's Mount St. Helens erupted in May 1980, it killed over 60 people, triggered fires, and wreaked havoc on farmlands.*

[3] **heedless** To *heed* something is to pay careful attention to it. If you're *heedless*, you don't pay careful attention; you're unthinking, unmindful, incautious, reckless, inattentive, careless, etc. *English playwright Sir Richard Steele (1672–1729) once wrote, "[Staggering] downstairs with heedless [speed], I [stepped into] a pail of water."*

[4] **inequity (inequities)** An *inequity* (pronounced with the accent on the second syllable) is an instance of unfairness or injustice. *In the 1980s (in the U.S.), such measures as school busing and affirmative action were instituted to correct past inequities in education and employment.*

Pinocchio ran to him and, scurrying like a squirrel up the long black beard, gave Fire-Eater a loving kiss on the tip of his nose.

"You're all pardoned!" announced Fire-Eater. Then, sighing and sadly shaking his head, he added, "Tonight I'll have to eat my lamb chop only half cooked. But watch out next time, marionettes."

At the news that pardon had been granted, all the puppets ran to the stage and, turning on the lights, they danced and sang till dawn.

Chapter 8 "The Fox and Cat"

The next day Fire-Eater called Pinocchio aside and asked him, "What's your father's name?"

"Geppetto."

"That's a nice name. You know, my name, "Fire-Eater," is really a **misnomer**[1]. I don't actually eat fire; I only looked as if I might, or so I'm told. Now tell me, what does your father do for a living?"

"He's a wood carver."

"Does he earn much?"

"A mere **pittance**[2]; in fact, his earnings are so **meager**[3] that in order to buy me a schoolbook, he had to sell the only coat he owned — a coat full of patches."

"Poor fellow! I feel sorry for him. Here, take these five gold pieces. Give them to him with my kindest regards."

Pinocchio thanked him over and over. He kissed each marionette in turn, then even kissed the guards, and, beside himself with joy, set out on his homeward journey.

He had gone barely half a mile when he met a crippled fox and a blind cat walking together like two good friends. The

---

[1] **misnomer** A name that's wrongly or unsuitably applied to someone or something is known as a *misnomer* (pronounced with the accent on the second syllable). *The term* Indian *is a misnomer for* Native American *(the error originated with Christopher Columbus, who, believing he had sailed around the world and reached India, mistook Native Americans for inhabitants of India).*

[2] **pittance** A *pittance* is a very small amount of something, especially a very small monetary wage, payment, or allowance. *The original creators of Superman sold their rights to the character early in its existence for a pittance and never shared in the fortune made by the copyright owners.*

[3] **meager** If something is *meager*, it's lacking or deficient in quantity or size; it's scanty, insufficient, inadequate, limited, etc. *In his second inaugural address (January 1937), President Franklin D. Roosevelt, referring to the Great Depression, said, "I see millions of families trying to live on incomes so meager that the [shadow] of family disaster hangs over them day by day."*

fox leaned on the able-bodied cat for support, and the cat let the sharp-eyed fox lead him along.

"Good morning, Pinocchio," said the fox, greeting him courteously.

"How do you know my name?" asked the puppet.

"I know your father well."

"Where have you seen him?"

"I saw him yesterday standing at the door of his house."

"What was he doing?"

"He was in his shirtsleeves trembling with cold."

"Poor Father! But after today he'll never suffer again."

"Why?"

"Because I've become rich."

"You, rich?" said the fox, and he began to laugh out loud. The cat was laughing also, but tried to hide his **mirth**[1] by stroking his long whiskers.

"There's nothing to laugh at," cried Pinocchio angrily. "These, as you know, are five new gold pieces." And he pulled out the gold pieces that Fire-Eater had given him.

At the cheerful tinkle of the coins, the fox unconsciously held out his paw that was supposed to be crippled, and the cat widely opened his eyes—but closed them again so quickly that Pinocchio didn't notice.

"And may I ask," inquired the fox, "what you're going to do with all that money?"

"First of all," answered the puppet, "I want to buy a fine new coat for my father, a coat of gold and silver with diamond buttons. After that, I'll buy a new schoolbook for myself so that I can go to school and study hard."

"Look at me," said the fox. "For the silly reason of wanting to study, I've lost a paw."

---

[1] **mirth** A state of gladness, merriment, gaiety, glee, etc., especially when expressed by laughter, is known as *mirth*. *The dental anesthesia nitrous oxide is often called "laughing gas" because it produces mirth when inhaled.*

"Look at me," said the cat. "For the same foolish reason, I've lost the sight of both eyes."

At that moment, a blackbird, perched on the fence along the road, called out sharp and clear, "Pinocchio, don't listen to bad advice. If you do, you'll be sorry!"

Poor little blackbird! If he had only kept his words to himself! In a flash the cat leaped on him and ate him, feathers and all. Then the cat cleaned his whiskers, closed his eyes, and became blind once more.

"Poor blackbird!" said Pinocchio to the cat. "Why did you kill him?"

"I killed him to teach him a lesson. He's too **meddlesome**[1]. Next time he'll keep his mouth shut."

Suddenly the fox turned to the puppet and said, "Do you want to double your gold pieces?"

"What do you mean?"

"Do you want a hundred, a thousand, two thousand gold pieces for your measly five?"

"Yes, but how?"

"It's very easy. Instead of returning home, come with us."

"Where?"

"To Dupeland."

Pinocchio thought awhile and then said firmly, "No, I don't want to go. Home is near, and I'm going where my father's waiting for me. How worried he must be that I haven't returned yet! I've been a bad son, and the cricket was right when he said that a disobedient boy can't be happy. I've learned this the hard way."

"Well, then," said the fox, "if you really want to go home, go ahead, but you'll be sorry."

"You'll be sorry," repeated the cat.

---

[1] **meddlesome** People who are *meddlesome* butt into the affairs or business of others; they're nosy, interfering, etc. *New York Yankees owner George Steinbrenner has been criticized for being too meddlesome an owner (as in his frequent disputes with managers).*

"Think about it, Pinocchio," said the fox. "You're turning your back on a **windfall**[1]! Tomorrow your five gold pieces will become two thousand!"

"Two thousand!" repeated the cat.

"But how can they possibly become so many?" asked Pinocchio wonderingly.

"I'll explain," said the fox. "Just outside Dupeland, there's a field called the Field of Wonders, whose soil happens to contain an unusually high **concentration**[2] of microorganisms. What's a microorganism, you ask. That's a **generic**[3] term that **encompasses**[4] all the **infinitesimal**[1] forms of life—bacteria,

---

[1] **windfall** A *windfall* is a sudden, unexpected, large monetary gain or profit (as from an investment, for example). *Saudi Arabia experienced an economic windfall when its crude oil revenues increased from 1.2 billion dollars in 1970 to 22.6 billion dollars in 1974.* Note: The word can also denote an unexpected stroke of good fortune or something (a piece of ripe fruit, for example) blown down by the wind.

[2] **concentration** A *concentration* is a coming or drawing together (of things) into one main body (at a common point or area). Usually when something becomes *concentrated* it becomes more tightly packed (with something). *Miami, Florida, is known for its beaches, hotels, and high concentration of senior citizens.*

[3] **generic** If you refer to something (a name, for example) as *generic*, you mean that it applies to all the members of a group of similar things (as opposed to any specific members). Note: If you're referring to commercial products (drugs, for example), the word means "not protected by a trademark"; thus, *aspirin* is a generic term, but a particular brand of aspirin (*Bayer*, for example) is not. *Today the word* ketchup *refers to a condiment (sauce) made from tomatoes; in the 18th and 19th centuries, however, it was a generic term for all sauces whose only common ingredient was vinegar.*

[4] **encompass (encompasses)** Circles are drawn with an instrument known as a *compass*. Literally, to *encompass* something is to form a circle around it. But people use this word to mean "include" or "contain" (especially comprehensively so, as if encircled). *The continental United States encompasses four time zones: Eastern, Central, Mountain, and Pacific.*

for example—that are impossible to see with the naked eye. Now, as you know, bacteria are usually **detrimental**[2] to animal life. But in soil they cause organic wastes to **decompose**[3] into essential growth nutrients! You know, of course, that if you were to plant an apple seed in **fertile**[4] soil, it would grow into an apple tree with hundreds of **luscious**[5] apples hanging from its branches. Well, it's the same thing with the gold piece you're going to plant. What you do is, you go to the Field of Wonders and you dig a hole. In that hole you bury a gold piece. After covering up the hole with dirt, you sprinkle it with water and then go to bed. During the night, the water

---

[1] **infinitesimal** This word is used to describe anything immeasurably small. *All objects have a gravitational attraction to each other; but since there is a huge difference between the earth's mass and your own, your effect on the planet is infinitesimal while its effect on you is very large.*

[2] **detrimental** If something is *detrimental*, it has a harmful effect; it's damaging, injurious, hurtful, etc. *Industrial pollutants dumped into natural waters have a detrimental effect on fish and other aquatic life.*

[3] **decompose** When a substance *decomposes*, it breaks down or separates into its basic chemical components; it disintegrates, rots, decays, etc. *Environmentalists oppose plastic containers because, unlike natural substances (wood or paper, for example), they don't decompose over time.*

[4] **fertile** This word means "greatly productive." For example, *fertile* soil is soil rich in materials necessary for initiating or sustaining plant growth, a *fertile* animal is one capable of bearing offspring (reproducing), and a *fertile* mind is one rich in ideas. The noun is *fertility*. *Most of Egypt's land is desert, but the Nile Valley and Delta contain extremely fertile farmland.*

[5] **luscious** Something (food, for example) described as *luscious* is pleasing to the senses (especially taste); it's delicious, juicy, delightful, etc. *According to Compton's Encyclopedia, the mango originally tasted like turpentine, but "centuries of cultivation and selection have produced a luscious, often very colorful, fruit with a distinctive spicy flavor."*

and nutrients slowly seep through the **porous**[1] outer layer of the coin. Now, as anyone with even a **rudimentary**[2] knowledge of science knows, when molecules pass through metal — or through a metal's magnetic field — they **induce**[3] a high-voltage electric current. This strong current — combined with **thermal**[4] vibrations, of course — is what actually starts the growth process. The coin blossoms and grows, and the next morning you find a beautiful tree that's loaded with shiny gold pieces."

---

[1] **porous** If a material or substance (skin, bone, soil, charcoal, a sponge, etc.) is *porous*, it has tiny openings through which water, air, etc., can pass. *English writer and critic John Wain (1925–1994) once wrote: "Leather's porous; it lets your skin breathe."*

[2] **rudimentary** The most basic, fundamental elements or principles of a subject are known as *rudiments*. To refer to something as *rudimentary* is to say that it's elementary, or that it's at a beginning stage, or that it's not as yet completely or perfectly developed. *British animal behaviorist Jane Goodall was the first scientist to report that chimpanzees are capable of fashioning rudimentary tools.*

[3] **induce** To *induce* something is to cause it, bring it about, produce it, etc. *People who suffer from insomnia sometimes drink a glass of warm milk before bedtime to induce sleep.* To *induce* a person to do something is to influence or persuade him to do it. *In 1963 clashes between police and demonstrating blacks induced President John F. Kennedy to stress civil rights legislation.*

[4] **thermal** This word means "pertaining to heat or temperature." *Absolute zero is the temperature (about minus 460 degrees Fahrenheit) at which a substance possesses no thermal energy.* Note: Sometimes the word means "designed to help retain body heat," as in *thermal underwear*.

"Wow! So if I were to bury my *five* gold pieces," cried Pinocchio, failing to see the flaw in the fox's apple tree **analogy**[1], "the next morning I would find...how many?"

"It's not hard to calculate your **aggregate**[2] wealth," answered the fox. "Say that each piece gives you five hundred. What you do is, you take five and, in your head, multiply that by five hundred. I know that sounds awfully **cerebral**[3], but the long and short of it is that the next morning you would

---

[1] **analogy** An *analogy* is a comparison between two things that are alike in certain respects but not others. People often offer analogies either as a form of reasoning (to imply that because two things are alike in some respects they will be alike in others) or to make complex ideas more understandable (as when one draws an analogy between the human heart and a pump, for example). *To explain the theory of the expanding universe (which says that galaxies are moving away from each other), the teacher drew an analogy between the universe and a balloon, saying, "If you paint dots on an uninflated balloon and then blow it up, the dots will move away from each other."*

[2] **aggregate** As an adjective this word (pronounced *AG-ruh-git*) means "considered as, or gathered together into, one mass or sum; total, combined, complete, added, entire, etc.," as in *aggregate wealth, aggregate value, aggregate demand*, etc. *Weightlifting competitors must make two successful lifts: the* snatch *(in which the bar is raised above the head in one uninterrupted motion),* and the clean and jerk *(in which the bar is raised to shoulder height, held there briefly, then pushed above the head); the aggregate weight of the two lifts is the competitor's total.* Note: The word can also be used as a noun or verb. As a noun (pronounced the same as the adjective) it denotes an entire mass or sum, and as a verb (pronounced *AG-ruh-gate*) it means "to gather together into one mass or sum."

[3] **cerebral** Your *cerebrum* is the part of your brain that controls thinking. Technically, *cerebral* means "pertaining to the cerebrum" (as in *President Franklin D. Roosevelt died of a cerebral hemorrhage*). But when people describe something as *cerebral*, they usually mean that it appeals to the intellect (as opposed to the emotions) or that it requires concentrated thinking or analyzing. And when they describe a person as *cerebral*, they mean that he's brainy, intelligent, analytical, etc. *Speaking of Johann Sebastian Bach's (1685– 1750) music, which often featured complex counterpoint (interplay between individual melodic lines),* Grolier's Encyclopedia *said, "Combined with its cerebral aspects are exquisite melodies and a sense of passion."*

find twenty-five hundred new, sparkling gold pieces." The fox hesitated a moment, then added, "But I want to be completely honest with you because I like you. Some of the coins may not look as if they sparkle right away."

"How come?"

"Since they grow out of the earth, you might find a slight **residue**[1] of soil on some of them. That can hide their bright metallic **luster**[2]. But if that happens, just wipe off the **extraneous**[3] dirt with your fingers—then you'll see them sparkle. Also, I don't want you to have **inflated**[4] expectations about the number of coins you'll find. The actual number really could range anywhere from about two thousand to three thousand. Of course, you're asking yourself, Why the **dispar-**

---

[1] **residue** A *residue* is what remains after a part or parts are taken away, removed, disposed of, etc.; (often worthless) leavings, scraps, remnants, etc. Sometimes the implication is that what remains is a thin, filmy coating (of something). *In the TV commercial, the housewife became upset because dinner guests were expected shortly and the automatic dishwashing detergent left a white residue on all the glasses.*

[2] **luster** If something has *luster*, it has a shine (from reflected light) on its surface; it glitters, glows, twinkles, sparkles, etc. *From looking at our mother's silverware we knew that silver had a brilliant luster; then in science class we learned that it was the best conductor of heat and electricity of any of the metals.*

[3] **extraneous** Technically, if something is *extraneous*, it comes from without (that is, it doesn't constitute a vital part of something). But people usually use this word to describe anything considered unnecessary or irrelevant (not related to the topic at hand). *When he tried to record his new song at home, he found it impossible to completely eliminate all the extraneous noise (such as ventilation system hum and the ringing of the neighbor's phone).*

[4] **inflated** If a balloon is *inflated*, it's filled with air. But if you say that something that can't be filled with air (expectations, costs, estimates, etc.) is *inflated*, you mean that it's unreasonably increased in size. *In his second inaugural address (January 1973), President Richard Nixon said, "In trusting too much in government, [the American people] have asked of it more than it can deliver; this leads only to inflated expectations [and] reduced individual effort."*

ity[1]? You see, nature is in a constant state of **flux**[2] – and we can't even begin to **fathom**[3] its deep mysteries. But we do know this much: For anything that grows from the ground, including gold, the actual results depend on three **variables**[4]. The first is temperature. Low temperature can **inhibit**[5]

---

[1] **disparity** A *disparity* (between two things) is an inequality or difference (as in age, rank, degree, amount, etc.). *According to* Grolier's Encyclopedia, "*A greater percentage of reports [of UFO sightings] have come from people living in rural areas than from those living in urban areas; the reasons for this disparity are unknown.*"

[2] **flux** If you say that something is in *flux* (or in a state of *flux*), you mean that it constantly changes or that it lacks stability. *In 1690 English philosopher John Locke said, "Things of this world are in so constant a flux that nothing remains long in the same state; thus [thriving] mighty cities come to ruin while other [deserted] places grow into countries filled with wealth and inhabitants."* Note: The word also refers to a flow (the flowing in of the tide, for example) or flood (as in *a flux of words*).

[3] **fathom** Water depth is measured in *fathoms* (units of length equal to six feet), and to *fathom* the depth of water is to measure it. But this word is usually used figuratively to mean "get to the bottom of; understand; figure out" (as in *fathom one's motives*). *According to* Webster's World Encyclopedia, "*the 20th century brought efforts to fathom psychiatric diseases, establish their [classifications], and investigate their causes.*"

[4] **variable (variables)** To *vary* is to undergo change. Something that *varies* or is likely to *vary* (such as the air temperature throughout the day) is known as a *variable*. Also, a factor that may or may not be applicable to a particular problem is informally referred to as a *variable*. *Many doctors say that the relationship between high cholesterol and heart attack is not clear cut because there are many other variables to take into account (such as diet, exercise, alcohol and nicotine consumption, lifestyle, blood pressure, and family history).*

[5] **inhibit** To *inhibit* something is to restrain (hold back, restrict, control, limit, etc.) its progress or development. *Antibacterial soap destroys or inhibits the growth of bacteria.* A person described as *inhibited* is restrained in his actions, impulses, desires, spontaneity, etc. *In 1940 British novelist Virginia Woolf described Nobel Prize–winning poet T. S. Eliot's face as a "great yellow bronze mask all draped upon an iron framework...an inhibited, nerve-drawn, dropped face."*

growth — but it's warm today, so that won't be a problem. The second is the amount of sunlight, which **fluctuates**[1] from day to day." He looked up and declared, "Ah, not a cloud in the sky." Then he continued, "And the third — the one whose role is perhaps most **instrumental**[2] of all — is the actual number of growth nutrients in the soil. Now, this number is not **static**[3], but changes from day to day. It depends on such factors as the rate of decay of fallen leaves and the activity of earthworms and various other **terrestrial**[4] and **subterranean**[5] creatures. Do you understand?" Without waiting for the puppet to respond, he went on, "In the Field of Wonders, we do know that the number of nutrients is extremely high, but, like

---

[1] **fluctuate** If something *fluctuates*, it changes (rises and falls, moves back and forth, varies, etc.) irregularly. *The volume of the oceans fluctuates as water is alternately locked into and released from the polar ice caps.*

[2] **instrumental** If something is *instrumental* in bringing about a certain result or effect, it's contributory, helpful, productive, useful, etc. (in bringing it about). *South African leader Nelson Mandela has been instrumental in ending his country's racist policies.*

[3] **static** If something is *static*, it doesn't change or move; it's fixed, stationary, etc. *Scientists tell us that a molecule is not static, but constantly in motion (that is, its atoms rotate and vibrate around one another).*

[4] **terrestrial** This word means "pertaining to land (as opposed to air or water)" or "pertaining to Earth (as opposed to outer space)." *Frogs and toads are similar in appearance, but frogs are mainly aquatic (live in water) and toads are mainly terrestrial.*

[5] **subterranean** If you remember that the prefix *sub* means "below or under" and that *terra* means "earth or land," it's easy to see that *subterranean* means "existing or operating underground." *Kentucky's Mammoth Cave contains over 330 miles of subterranean passageways at various levels (and visitors can take a boat ride on Echo River in the cave's deepest level).*

anywhere else, it's **indeterminate**[1]. But rest assured that one way or another, you'll end up with a few thousand coins—a **bountiful**[2] supply, guaranteed to make you wealthy beyond your wildest dreams!"

"Wonderful!" cried Pinocchio, dancing about with joy. "And as soon as I have them, I'll give some of them to you—to show my appreciation."

"A gift for us?" cried the fox, pretending to be insulted. "Absolutely not!"

"Absolutely not!" repeated the cat.

"We don't work for ourselves," explained the fox. "As **champions**[3] of the poor, we're here only to help others."

"To help others," repeated the cat.

"And we do that only out of a love of giving—never for the credit. That's why we make all of our charitable donations **anonymously**[4]. And that's why we're always on the lookout

---

[1] **indeterminate** Anything described as *indeterminate* has not been precisely determined; it's inexact, uncertain, vague, approximate, indefinite, etc. *Some percussion instruments (kettledrums, for example) produce sounds of definite pitch while others (cymbals, for example) produce sounds of indeterminate pitch.*

[2] **bountiful** This word means "abundant, plentiful, more than enough," as in *bountiful supply. For its bountiful wheat crops, flour mills, and high rank in butter making, Minnesota is sometimes referred to as the Bread and Butter State.* Note: The word can also mean "generous, giving freely," as in *bountiful friends.*

[3] **champion (champions)** One who fights for or argues in favor of a particular person, group, or cause is known as a *champion* (of that person, group, or cause). *Senator Robert F. Kennedy (1925–1968) was a champion of the civil rights movement.*

[4] **anonymous (anonymously)** If you say that a work of art or a gift is *anonymous,* you mean that the name of the author, composer, etc. (for a work of art) or contributor (for a gift) is either unknown or is intentionally withheld. *Folksinger Woody Guthrie (1912–1967) performed both traditional, anonymous folk songs and songs of his own composition ("This Land Is Your Land," for example).*

46

for **gullible**[1] people — so that we can teach them how to avoid being **bilked**[2] out of their hard-earned money. Call us **cynics**[3] if you like, but there are a lot of selfish, dishonest people in this world who would like nothing better than to cheat you out of your money."

"Really? Gee, I've never heard of anyone as kind and generous as the two of you!"

"Not at all," answered the fox with pretended modesty.

When Pinocchio didn't respond right away, he added, "We're merely two tiny **cogs**[4] in the great big wheel of human kindness."

"What fine people!" thought Pinocchio to himself. And forgetting his father, the new coat, the schoolbook, and all his

---

[1] **gullible** People who are *gullible* tend to believe whatever they're told; as such, they're easily deceived (tricked, fooled, duped). *Some people believe that psychics are legitimate professionals who are truly responsive to supernatural forces; others believe they are merely frauds who like to take advantage of the gullible.*

[2] **bilk (bilked)** To *bilk* someone is to trick him into giving up something valuable (usually money). *In October 1989 former TV evangelist Jim Bakker was convicted of fraud for bilking followers out of $158 million and spending nearly $4 million to supply himself with mansions, an air-conditioned doghouse, and fleets of Mercedes and Rolls-Royce automobiles.*

[3] **cynic (cynics)** A person who tends to doubt or question things, or a person who believes that all people are motivated by selfishness, is known as a *cynic*. The adjective is *cynical*; the attitude of a cynic is known as *cynicism*. *According to Compton's Encyclopedia, the 1980s rock group Guns N' Roses were "often compared to the early Rolling Stones because of their similar cynical style of singing about a hostile world."*

[4] **cog (cogs)** You've probably seen wheels or gears with a series of interlocking teeth (projections) on their rims (as in clocks or machinery). Each of those teeth is known as a *cog*. But people often use this word informally to refer to a person who plays a minor (but often necessary) role in some large organization, activity, etc. *In 1898 American essayist John Jay Chapman said, "Wherever you see a man who gives someone else's [immorality] as a reason for not taking action himself, you see a cog in The Machine that governs us."*

good resolutions, he said to the fox and cat, "I'll go with you. Let's hurry."

Chapter 9 "The Red Lobster Inn"

The cat, fox, and puppet walked and walked. As they traveled, the fox described to Pinocchio—for the puppet's own good, he explained—how swindlers operate. He **embellished**[1] the account with many real-life **anecdotes**[2]. One concerned a real estate **mogul**[3] who sold people nonexistent plots of land! Another concerned a street **vendor**[4] who repeatedly jumped in front of passing horse-drawn carriages so that when he was knocked to the ground he could sue the driver for **negligence**[5]. Still another concerned a **fraudulent**[1] me-

---

[1] **embellish (embellished)** To *embellish* a story or account is to make it more interesting by adding (real or imagined) details. To *embellish* an object (a dress, for example) is to beautify it (by adding ornaments, decorations, etc.). *As the legend of Paul Bunyan (a lumberjack of enormous size and strength) spread through the logging camps of the Midwest, local embellishments (that he dug the Grand Canyon and created the Great Lakes with his footprints, for example) were added.*

[2] **anecdote** An *anecdote* is a short account of a funny or interesting incident. *In October 1776 Benjamin Franklin sailed for France, where, according to Grolier's Encyclopedia, he "was at his best creating the legend of his life among the ladies of Paris, writing witty letters, and telling anecdotes."*

[3] **mogul** A *mogul* is a person of importance, power, influence, etc. (usually in a particular field, as in *film industry mogul*); a big shot, tycoon, etc. *Before building McDonald's into the world's largest hamburger chain, fast food mogul Ray Kroc founded a company to sell a machine that made six milkshakes at once.*

[4] **vendor** A person or company that sells (something) for a living is known as a *vendor*. *One of central New Jersey's major attractions is the Englishtown Auction, a flea market with up to 1,000 vendors on 50 acres.*

[5] **negligent (negligence)** To *neglect* something is to pay no attention (or too little attention) to it. If you're *negligent*, you tend to neglect things. Note: The word *negligence* also has a legal meaning: "failure to exercise the care the law requires for the protection of people's safety, interests, etc." *Many historians believe that the British government mishandled Ireland's food shortage of the late 1840s (when potato crops failed); in 1997 British Prime Minister Tony Blair formally apologized for British negligence during the famine.*

49

dium[2] who charged people an **exorbitant**[3] fee to contact the spirits of their **deceased**[4] pets. The fox finished by saying, "Anyway, I've seen the whole **gamut**[5] of human dishonesty, from counterfeiting to **embezzlement**[6] to **forgery**[1] to **imposture**[2]."

---

[1] **fraudulent** Trickery or deception used to achieve an unfair or unlawful (usually financial) gain is known as *fraud*. A *fraudulent* person is one who uses fraud; he's dishonest, cheating, etc. A *fraudulent* practice or activity is one involving fraud; it's underhanded, illegal, etc. A *fraudulent* object is one that is not genuine or real; its phony, counterfeit, etc. *In 1872 Congress enacted the first U.S. consumer protection law, making it a federal offense to use the mails for fraudulent purposes.*

[2] **medium** A person thought to have the power to communicate with the dead is known as a *medium*. *The 1964 film* Seance on a Wet Afternoon *concerns a mentally unbalanced medium who involves her emotionally weak husband in a kidnapping scheme.*

[3] **exorbitant** An amount (of money, for example) described as *exorbitant* is beyond the limit of what is considered customary or fair; it's excessive, unreasonable, etc. *The most memorable character of Shakespeare's* The Merchant of Venice *is Shylock, a greedy moneylender who charges exorbitant interest rates.*

[4] **deceased** As an adjective, this word describes someone who is no longer living. As a noun, it denotes a person who has died. *In some societies a burial mask is placed on a corpse's face to protect the deceased from evil spirits.*

[5] **gamut** This word denotes the complete or entire range, scale, or extent (of something). The expression *run the gamut* means "cover the whole range." *In 1961 famed photographer/artist Edward Steichen said, "Photography records the gamut of feelings written on the human face."*

[6] **embezzle (embezzlement)** To *embezzle* is to illegally take something (usually money) that has been entrusted to your care; for example, a dishonest bank employee might *embezzle* bank funds. *During the Clinton administration, the head of the White House travel office, who'd transferred $68,000 to a personal account, was charged with embezzlement (but found not guilty when it was revealed that he'd used the money to pay for official expenses).*

"But why would these people risk going to jail?" asked the puppet.

"For one thing, the work is actually rather easy and quite **lucrative**[3]. But the main thing is that they believe they're not really **jeopardizing**[4] their freedom because, in point of fact, swindlers are rarely **foiled**[5] by police. If people stop to figure out the odds—of not getting caught, I mean—then there's a

---

[1] **forgery** The illegal signing of someone else's name (as on a check, for example) or the production of a counterfeit work (a painting, for example) is known as *forgery*. The word can also denote the counterfeit object itself, as in *this painting is a forgery*. The verb is *forge* ("to make or alter fraudulently"), as in *forge a signature*. *In 1994 a famous 1934 photograph of the Loch Ness Monster was revealed to be a forgery.*

[2] **imposture** A person who uses a false name or identity (often in order to deceive for financial gain) is known as an *impostor*. The fraudulent use of an assumed name or identity is known as *imposture*. *In the 2002 based-on-fact film* Catch Me If You Can, *actor Leonardo DiCaprio plays a teenager who is arrested for passing bad checks and imposture (he'd passed himself off as a pilot, doctor, and lawyer).*

[3] **lucrative** If you say that something (a type of employment, for example) is *lucrative*, you mean that it's profitable, well-paying, etc. *Professional tennis has become very lucrative for the top-ranked players, with many earning more than a million dollars a year in prize money.*

[4] **jeopardy (jeopardizing)** Exposure to or risk of possible harm (loss, death, injury, etc.) is known as *jeopardy*. To *jeopardize* something is to put it at risk. *In a March 1947 speech before Congress, President Harry Truman said, "If we wish to inspire the peoples of the world whose freedom is in jeopardy, we must correct the remaining imperfections in our practice of democracy."*

[5] **foil (foiled)** To *foil* someone or something is to prevent it from being successful (in attaining a goal, for example); to defeat it, frustrate it, etc. *In 1980 Larry Holmes foiled Muhammad Ali's try for a fourth heavyweight (boxing) championship.*

very high **incentive**[1] to cheat because they see that the risk is really **negligible**[2]."

"But if the police can't catch them, how can they be stopped?" asked Pinocchio.

"Well, it's really up to the decent, honest members of the **populace**[3] — people like us — to stop them."

"How?"

"Well, usually — especially at the beginning of a deception — you won't have any actual proof of dishonesty. But your **intuition**[4] will tell you that something smells funny, so to speak, and you'll grow **wary**[5]. Once that happens, because you'll be on the alert, you'll be able to recognize swindlers for

---

[1] **incentive** An *incentive* is something that motivates action, usually because of a promise of reward or a threat of punishment; an inducement, enticement, stimulus, etc. *In 1790 Congress established a patent office to protect inventors and give them an incentive to develop new machines and methods.*

[2] **negligible** If you say that something is *negligible*, you mean that it's so small (insignificant, unimportant, etc.) that it's not worth considering; it can be ignored. *In atoms, protons and neutrons each have a weight of 1 (one atomic mass unit); the weight of electrons is negligible.*

[3] **populace** This word denotes the citizens of a community, region, country, etc. (especially the common people, as distinguished from the higher classes). *Paul Revere became a legendary Revolutionary War hero when, on the night of April 18, 1775, he made his "midnight ride" to warn the Massachusetts populace of approaching British troops.*

[4] **intuition** The act of knowing, or the ability to know, something (a fact or truth, for example) without using any reasoning process (study, analysis, logic, etc.) is known as *intuition*. *Intuition* is sometimes informally referred to as a "sixth sense" or a "funny feeling." *According to Grolier's Encyclopedia, the master builders who designed the magnificent cathedrals of 12th-century Europe "proceeded without the insights of science, basing their specifications only on experience, rules of thumb, intuition, and daring."*

[5] **wary** If you're *wary*, you're alert or suspicious in watching for danger; you're cautious, careful, watchful, etc. *Maine moose safari guide Dan Legere once noted, "Some of the big [males] are very wary; others, well, you can't drive 'em away with a brick."*

what they are and it'll be easy to **frustrate**[1] their **devious**[2] schemes."

"Schemes," repeated the cat.

"But," continued the fox, "while it may not be difficult for would-be victims to recognize and stop individual con artists, stopping shady businesses is nearly impossible. Why? Because their **transgressions**[3] — making exaggerated advertising claims or artificially raising prices, for example — aren't technically illegal; they're merely **unethical**[4]. So even if they *are* caught, no **punitive**[5] action will be taken."

"Will be taken," repeated the cat.

---

[1] **frustrate** To *frustrate* something (a plan, effort, goal, purpose, etc.) is to stop it, prevent it, defeat it, etc. *President Richard Nixon's attempts to frustrate the Watergate investigations ultimately failed when his own White House tape recordings revealed that he and his assistants had engaged in an obstruction of justice.*

[2] **devious** Anyone or anything (a plan, for example) *devious* uses unfair methods; it intends to trick or deceive; it's dishonest, underhanded, crooked, etc. *Characters featured in "Peanuts" cartoons include born loser Charlie Brown and the crabby, often devious Lucy.*

[3] **transgression (transgressions)** A *transgression* is a violation of a law, moral code, rule, etc.; a misdeed, wrongdoing, sin, etc. *In basketball, penalties are given for such transgressions as charging, goaltending, walking, and double dribbling.*

[4] **unethical** If you're *unethical*, you lack principles of right or good conduct; you're dishonest, immoral, double dealing, etc. *The Better Business Bureau, an organization established to protect consumers from false advertising and unethical selling practices, was founded in Minneapolis in 1912.*

[5] **punitive** This word means "involving punishment." *In 1935 Soviet leader Joseph Stalin ordered that Soviet children above age 12 be subject to the same punitive laws that apply to adults — eight years in a labor camp for stealing corn or potatoes, for example, or five years for stealing cucumbers.*

"Then you have city government, where **corruption**[1] is **rampant**[2]. You know, without coming right out and admitting it, our government actually **sanctions**[3] all sorts of underhanded practices — bribery, **nepotism**[4], ticket-fixing...you name it."

Pinocchio nodded his head to show that he understood, then shook his head to show that he disapproved.

At last, toward evening, dead tired, they found themselves before a small tavern called the Red Lobster Inn.

"This has been quite a **trek**[5]," said the fox. "Let's stop here to eat something and rest awhile. At midnight we'll start out

---

[1] **corrupt (corruption)** If someone (a government official, for example) is *corrupt*, he's morally bad or dishonest; for example, he can be influenced to take a bribe. The noun is *corruption* ("act or state of being corrupt"). *In his January 1987 State of the City address, New York City mayor Ed Koch, referring to recent government scandals, said, "The knife of corruption endangered the life of New York City; the scalpel of the law is making us well again."*

[2] **rampant** This word describes something (usually something bad or menacing) that's growing or spreading without restraint (weeds or disease, for example), or that's occurring widely and is unchecked (corruption in government, for example). *Cancer is characterized by rampant, abnormal cell growth.*

[3] **sanction (sanctions)** In one sense, to *sanction* something is to regard it as acceptable; to tolerate it. *According to the* Columbia Encyclopedia, *in the 1970s "popular music and such entertainments as rock concerts and movies often glorified and sanctioned drug use."* In another sense, to *sanction* something is to give it official approval or authorization. *The federal government's power to tax personal incomes was sanctioned by the 16th Amendment (1913).*

[4] **nepotism** The showing of favoritism by one in power (in business or politics, for example) to relatives or close friends (by hiring or promoting them without regard to merit, for example) is known as *nepotism*. *When John F. Kennedy selected his younger brother Robert to become the attorney general of the United States (1961), critics charged the President with practicing nepotism.*

[5] **trek** A *trek* is a journey or trip, especially a long, slow, or difficult one. *The 1963 film* The Incredible Journey *concerns two dogs and a cat who make a 200-mile trek across Canada to find their home and family.*

again, for at daybreak tomorrow we must be at the Field of Wonders."

They went into the inn and all three sat down at a round dining table. However, not one of them seemed very hungry.

The poor cat said that he was too tired to eat, but, because he didn't want to become **malnourished**[1], would try. He was able to swallow only thirty-five pieces of fish **garnished**[2] with lemon slices.

The fox, claiming that he, also, was too exhausted to eat, tried his best to force something down. His doctor, he explained, had put him on a special diet that stressed **abstinence**[3] from rich foods. As such, he was trying to **wean**[4] himself from butter, sugar, and eggs. He had to be satisfied with only a small rabbit surrounded by a dozen young, ten-

---

[1] **malnourished** People who are *malnourished* have a lack of proper nutrition (from eating too little food or eating the wrong foods). *According to a 1997 United Nations report, 40 percent of the world's malnourished children live in India.*

[2] **garnish (garnished)** To *garnish* food is to place on top of it something that adds flavor or color (parsley, for example). *In cooking class we learned how to clean and cut fruits and vegetables, garnish dishes, and plan meals.*

[3] **abstinence** The practice of refraining from (giving up) certain pleasures (especially food or drink) is known as *abstinence*. *Doctors say that for heavy smokers, more than ten years of abstinence is necessary before the degree of risk of lung cancer approaches that of those who have never smoked.*

[4] **wean** If you're talking about a baby or small animal, to *wean* it is to get it to give up mother's milk and take other nourishment instead. *Children who are weaned either earlier or later than normal often develop a condition called protein-energy malnutrition.* If you're talking about a particular object or habit that is enjoyable but not good for you, to *wean* yourself from it is to gradually give it up. *Beverly finally agreed that her doctor was right when he said that she should try to wean herself from cigarettes.*

der chickens. That was all. Soothingly patting his **distended**[1] stomach, he said that he felt ill and couldn't eat another bite.

Pinocchio ate least of all. He asked for a little buttered toast but then hardly touched it. With his mind on the Field of Wonders, he was too excited to eat. A waiter who **hovered**[2] nearby suggested sprinkling a bit of cinnamon on the toast to **impart**[3] flavor — but the puppet **declined**[4].

---

[1] **distend (distended)** If something hollow or elastic *distends*, it swells out (as from internal pressure); it expands, inflates, bloats, etc. *In its article on the swift (a type of bird similar to the hummingbird), the* Cambridge Encyclopedia *says that parents feed their baby chicks with "a ball of insects stuck together with saliva and carried back to the nest in a distended throat pouch."*

[2] **hover (hovered)** Technically, if something (a helicopter or hummingbird, for example) *hovers*, it hangs or remains suspended in the air. But if you say that a person *hovers*, you mean that he waits nearby (sometimes annoyingly so). *In 1987 U.S. author and humorist Garrison Keillor said, "[Children] seem not to notice us, hovering, and they seldom offer thanks; but what we do for them is never wasted."* Note: The word can also mean "remain in an uncertain state; waver," as in *hovered between life and death.*

[3] **impart** To *impart* something (flavor, color, mood, energy, motion, character, etc.) to someone or something is to give it. *Writer R. C. Hutchinson once said, "A particular countryside imparts a special character to the men it breeds."* Note: The word can also mean "make known; reveal; tell," as in *impart information.*

[4] **decline (declined)** To *decline* is to (usually politely) refuse something offered to you; to say no. *Concerning the Pulitzer Prize for his novel* Arrowsmith *(1925), Sinclair Lewis (whose views differed from those of the Pulitzer panel) said, "I declined election to the National Institute of Arts and Letters some years ago, and now I must decline the Pulitzer Prize."* Note: The word also means "become less in strength, power, importance, etc." *In 2002 DVD player sales increased and VCR sales declined.*

Because the fox and cat had been so busy stuffing them-selves, very little conversation **transpired¹** during the meal. But after they'd finally put down their knives and forks, the fox **recapitulated²** some of what he'd said earlier, then added, "But anywhere you look in the broad **spectrum³** of criminal behavior, one thing remains the same. All people who com-mit crimes suffer from an emotional disorder. What I mean is that because of a certain psychological **predisposition⁴**, they really can't help their **aberrant⁵** behavior. That's why it's im-

---

¹ **transpire (transpired)** If you say that something *transpired*, you mean that it took place, happened, occurred, etc. *According to* The Written Word III, *"the person preparing the minutes [of a meeting] must be especially careful that summarized information is complete enough to convey what transpired [at the meeting]."*

² **recapitulate (recapitulated)** To *recapitulate* is to repeat or review the main points (of something); to summarize. The noun is *recapitulation. The fifth book of the Old Testament (Deuteronomy) begins with a recapitulation of the noteworthy events of the Israelites' 40-year journey in the wilderness, as described in the fourth book of the Old Testament (Numbers).*

³ **spectrum** Technically, a *spectrum* is a band of rainbow colors produced when sunlight is passed through a prism (a piece of glass with a triangular cross section). But people usually use this word to denote any broad (or entire) range of related ideas, objects, activities, etc. *The smallest adult dino-saurs were only about three feet long; at the other end of the spectrum, the largest were about 140 feet long.*

⁴ **predispose (predisposition)** If you're talking about one's frame of mind, to be *predisposed* toward something is to have a tendency or leaning toward it, as in *predisposed toward fast cars*. If you're talking about one's health, to be *predisposed* to a particular disease or condition is to have a (usually genetic) susceptibility to it, as in *predisposed to asthma*. The noun is *predisposition. In 1988 the first patent was granted for a genetically engineered animal: a cancer-predisposed mouse used in research.*

⁵ **aberrant** If something is *aberrant*, it deviates from what is considered nor-mal or proper; it's abnormal, deviant, unconventional, etc. *Austrian psychia-trist Sigmund Freud (1856–1939) believed that aberrant behavior in children was caused not by genetic factors, but by mishandling on the part of the parents.*

portant for lawbreakers to be **purged**[1] from society once and for all. It's the only way to make the world safe for the rest of us."

"The rest of us," repeated the cat.

"And I'm not talking about **segregating**[2] them from the rest of society by sending them to jail," the fox went on. "I'm actually opposed to that—**adamantly**[3] opposed. Why? Because prisons, instead of **rehabilitating**[4] offenders, generally make them even worse than they already were! I say that all criminals should be sent to a deserted island someplace, where they'd have only each other to hurt."

"Each other to hurt," repeated the cat.

Pinocchio nodded his agreement.

---

[1] **purge (purged)** To *purge* a society is to forcibly remove undesirable people (political enemies of the government, for example) by jailing or killing them. *In the 1930s Soviet leader Joseph Stalin purged his government of thousands of Communist Party officials.* To *purge* one's digestive tract is to forcibly empty it by self-induced vomiting or diarrhea. *An eating disorder known as bulimia is characterized by eating binges followed by purging.*

[2] **segregate (segregating)** To *segregate* something is to separate it (from others or from a main body or group); to set it apart, isolate it, etc. *In order to conserve resources and reduce waste disposal, many American communities have instituted garbage-collection programs that require householders to segregate glass, metal, plastic, and paper for recycling.* Note: The word often refers specifically to the separation of the black and white races, as in *racial segregation. In 1954 the U.S. Supreme Court ruled that segregated schools are unconstitutional.*

[3] **adamant (adamantly)** If you're *adamant* about something (your point of view, for example), you don't give in readily (to urgings, appeals, arguments, etc.); you're unyielding, firm, insistent, etc. *For years, U.S. tobacco companies have adamantly denied that tobacco is an addictive substance.*

[4] **rehabilitate (rehabilitating)** To *rehabilitate* someone (someone sick, injured, or imprisoned, for example) is to restore him to a normal life by improving his health or increasing his usefulness through education, medical treatment, therapy, etc. *Social workers are professionals who try to better the social conditions in a community by caring for abused children, rehabilitating the sick, and extending financial aid to the poor.*

With dinner over, the fox said to the innkeeper, "Give us two good rooms upstairs—one for Pinocchio and the other for my friend and me. Before starting out, we'll take a little nap. Remember to call us at midnight sharp, for we must continue on our journey."

The innkeeper, who seemed to know exactly what the fox and cat were up to, indicated his **tacit**[1] approval by winking and smiling at them.

On the way upstairs, the fox said to Pinocchio, "We'll **rendezvous**[2] at midnight just outside the front door. Don't be late." As the puppet started to enter his bedroom, the fox added, "Have a pleasant nap!"

In his room, Pinocchio got into bed and fell into a **fitful**[3], uneasy sleep. But after a while he began to sleep more deeply

---

[1] **tacit** If something (approval or consent, for example) is *tacit*, it's understood or implied without being spoken out loud; it's silent, unspoken, unstated, etc. *According to Compton's Encyclopedia, at the beginning of World War II "there was almost no organized opposition to [the imprisonment of Jews in concentration camps], even on the part of most churches; this silence meant, to [German dictator Adolf] Hitler, tacit approval of his policies."*

[2] **rendezvous** As a noun, this word (which is borrowed from the French and pronounced *RAHN-day-voo*) denotes a meeting of two or more people at a particular time and place. The word can also signify the meeting place itself. As a verb, to *rendezvous* is to come together or meet at a particular time and place. *In the 18th century, the city of Nassau in the Bahamas (a chain of islands off the east coast of Florida) was a rendezvous for pirates.* Note: The word is also used to describe a meeting, in space, of two spacecraft.

[3] **fitful** If you say that something happens in *fits* (or in *fits and starts*), you mean that it happens or recurs at irregular intervals; it's on and off, intermittent, etc. Anything *fitful* comes, appears, or happens in fits. *According to the second stanza of "The Star-Spangled Banner," as the breeze "fitfully blows, [it] half conceals [and] half discloses [reveals]" the American Flag (as it continues to fly over Fort McHenry, Maryland, after a night of attack by British troops in the War of 1812).*

and he started to dream. He dreamt that he was **sauntering**[1] through a beautiful field filled with trees. From their branches hung a **profusion**[2] of shiny gold coins that twinkled **tantalizingly**[3] in the **dappled**[4] sunlight. They seemed to say: "Let whoever wants us take us!" Just as he pulled down a long, **supple**[5] branch to gather a handful of coins, he was awakened by three loud knocks at the door. It was the innkeeper who had come to tell him that midnight had struck.

---

[1] **saunter (sauntering)** To *saunter* is to walk in a leisurely, relaxed manner; to ramble, stroll, mosey, etc. *In 1842 U.S. naturalist/philosopher/writer Henry David Thoreau said, "The really efficient laborer will·be found not to crowd his day with work, but will saunter to his task surrounded by a wide halo of ease and leisure."*

[2] **profusion** A *profusion* of something is a great amount or abundant supply of it; an outpouring of it. *Historians say that Spanish explorer Ponce de Leon may have named America's southeast peninsula "Florida" (which means "feast of flowers") because when he arrived (1513) he saw a profusion of flowers on its coast.*

[3] **tantalize (tantalizingly)** In Greek mythology, Tantalus was a king who, as punishment for having offended the gods, was forced to suffer everlasting thirst while standing chin deep in water that receded each time he bent to take a drink. Today, to *tantalize* someone is to torment or tease him by exposing him to something that is desirable or fascinating but difficult or impossible to obtain. The adjective *tantalizing* means "tempting, enticing, etc." *In its article on Travel and Tourism, Compton's Encyclopedia says, "Faraway places with strange-sounding names lure the traveler with promises of enchantment, excitement, diverse forms of entertainment, and tantalizing new kinds of food."*

[4] **dappled** Something *dappled* has spots or patches of different colors or shades (from each other or from the background); it's spotted, speckled, dotted, etc. *In December 1981 Town & Country magazine said of New York City's St. John the Divine, "Inside, the cathedral is a Gothic forest dappled in violet twilight and vast with quiet."*

[5] **supple** If something is *supple*, it bends easily (without breaking or losing its shape); it's flexible. *Dance therapy is used not only to enable people who have difficulty talking about their feelings to express their emotions through body movements, but to help the elderly to keep their joints and spines supple.*

"Are my friends ready?" the puppet asked.

"Indeed, yes! They left two hours ago."

"Left? Why in such a hurry?"

"Unfortunately, the cat received a telegram saying that his neighbor's pet goldfish had died. Understandably, he became greatly **perturbed**[1] — that's why he rushed home without saying good-bye to you."

"I see. Did they pay for our dinner and rooms?"

"How could they do such a thing? Being gentlemen of great refinement, they didn't want to offend you by not allowing you the honor of paying the bill."

Pinocchio scratched his head thoughtfully, then asked, "Where did they say they'd meet me?"

"At the Field of Wonders, at sunrise."

Pinocchio paid a gold piece for the dinners and rooms and started on his way toward the field that was to make him rich.

He walked on, not knowing where he was going, for the quiet countryside was dark — so dark that not a thing was visible. Every now and again a **vagrant**[2] leaf, blown by the wind, brushed against his nose and scared him half to death. Once or twice he shouted, "Who goes there?" and the far-away hills echoed back to him, "Who goes there? Who goes there?"

---

[1] **perturb (perturbed)** As a verb, to *perturb* someone is to disturb his peace of mind; to make him uneasy or anxious. The adjective *perturbed* means "uneasy; anxious; upset; troubled." The noun is *perturbation*. *In 1990 British author and comic actor Stephen Fry said of real estate agents, "With their jangling keys, nasty suits, revolting beards, moustaches, and tinted [glasses], [they] roam the land causing perturbation and despair."*

[2] **vagrant** A thing (a leaf, thought, current, etc.) described as *vagrant* is one that's not fixed in place; it moves here and there in a random, unpredictable fashion. A person described as *vagrant* is one who wanders from place to place, especially one with no permanent home or means of support. As a noun, a *vagrant* is such a person (a tramp, hobo, bum, etc.). *In Mark Twain's* The Mysterious Stranger, *Satan says, "Nothing exists but you, and you are but a thought — a vagrant thought, a useless thought, a homeless thought."*

As he walked, Pinocchio noticed a tiny insect glimmering on the trunk of a tree—a small being that glowed with a pale, soft light.

"Who are you?" he asked.

"I'm the ghost of the cricket you killed," answered the little being in a faint voice that sounded as if it came from another world.

"What do you want?" asked the puppet.

"I want to give you some advice. Return home and give the four gold pieces you have left to your poor old father, who's weeping because he hasn't seen you for many days."

"You sound just like your earthly **counterpart**[1]—the one I killed with a hammer. Why are you always **harping**[2] on the idea of my remaining at home? Don't you realize that because I've gone out into the world, tomorrow my father will be a very rich man? You see, these four gold pieces will become thousands!"

"Pinocchio, don't listen to people who promise you wealth overnight. As a rule they're either fools or cheats! Listen to me and go home."

---

[1] **counterpart** A *counterpart* is someone or something that has the same functions or characteristics as another, but in a different place, time, or context. *Canada's Royal Canadian Mounted Police is the counterpart of America's FBI.*

[2] **harp (harping)** To *harp* on something is to talk about it excessively, persistently, tediously, etc.; to dwell on it. *In his January 1941 "Four Freedoms" speech (which called for aid to the Allies during World War II and named the four freedoms worth fighting for as freedom of speech, freedom of worship, freedom from want, and freedom from fear), President Franklin D. Roosevelt said, "We need not overemphasize imperfections in the [treaty that ended World War I, and] we need not harp on failure of the democracies to deal with problems of world destruction."*

"Well, I'm sorry to **curtail**[1] our visit so soon, but I must continue on my way."

"Wait! It's late. Walking alone at night is **hazardous**[2]; the darkness is **fraught**[3] with danger. What if something unexpected happens? This area is so **sparsely**[4] populated that even if you call out for help, no one will hear you."

"I don't care. I have to go."

"Remember that boys who insist on having their own way will be sorry sooner or later."

"Nothing you can say will **dissuade**[5] me. Nothing. Now good-bye."

"Goodnight, Pinocchio, and may you be safe from killers."

---

[1] **curtail** To *curtail* something is to cut it short; reduce or lessen it (in duration, size, amount, etc.). *Under the terms of 1997's multibillion dollar settlement proposal to bring an end to lawsuits filed against them by 40 states, four tobacco companies agreed to place warning labels on packages of cigarettes and to severely curtail advertising.*

[2] **hazardous** If something is *hazardous*, it's filled with danger, risk, peril, etc. *Speaking of cocktail parties, a July 1986 New York Times article said, "You balance the plate between the forefinger and three other fingers, which make a little platform, and with the forefinger and the thumb you grasp the glass — and if you think that isn't hazardous, you haven't done it lately."*

[3] **fraught** This adjective means "filled with (some specified element)," as in *fraught with difficulties*. *In Greek mythology, the voyages of Jason and the Argonauts were fraught with danger and adventure.*

[4] **sparse (sparsely)** If something is *sparse*, it's thinly distributed (that is, it exists or occurs at widely spaced intervals); it's not thick or dense. *Wyoming is sparsely populated; in fact, it has the smallest population of any U.S. state.* Note: The word can also mean "meager; scanty," as in *sparse rainfall* or *sparse meals*.

[5] **dissuade** To *dissuade* someone from doing something is to persuade him not to do it; to discourage him, talk him out of it, etc. *During the Civil War, Charles Francis Adams (son of President John Quincy Adams) helped dissuade Great Britain from officially recognizing the Confederacy.*

There was silence for a moment, and then the cricket's **phosphorescent**[1] light disappeared suddenly, just as if someone had blown out a candle. The road was even darker than before.

---

[1] **phosphorescent** If something is *phosphorescent*, it emits light without emitting any noticeable heat; it glows. *The face of a television's picture tube is coated with a phosphorescent material that gives off light when struck by an electron beam.*

Chapter 10 "Killers"

"Dear, oh, dear! Come to think of it," said the puppet to himself, as he once more set out on his journey, "we boys are really very unlucky. Everybody tells us what to do and then **reprimands**[1] us if we don't do it! Everyone wants to be a **surrogate**[2] father or mother to us, just so they can boss us around; everyone, even that cricket. It wasn't enough for him to stick his nose into my business when he was alive; no, now he wants to **intervene**[3] **posthumously**[4]! Killers indeed! At least I've never believed in them, nor ever will. Aren't they

---

[1] **reprimand (reprimands)** To *reprimand* someone is to criticize or scold him (for a fault or offense). As a noun, a *reprimand* is such an expression of disapproval; a scolding. *According to Dr. R. Brasch's Library of Origins, "We know for certain that even in the late Middle Ages the handkerchief was still unknown by the fact that priests were then reprimanded by their superiors for using their sacred garments for the blowing of their noses."*

[2] **surrogate** As a noun, a *surrogate* is a person who takes the place of or acts for another; a substitute. As an adjective, *surrogate* means "serving as a substitute," as in *surrogate mother*. *When Ronald Reagan was shot and wounded (March 1981), Vice President George H. Bush assumed responsibility as the President's surrogate.*

[3] **intervene** In one sense, to *intervene* is to interfere in the affairs of others; to meddle, intrude, butt in, etc. *In 1904 President Theodore Roosevelt declared that the United States could intervene in the affairs of any Latin American country guilty of misconduct.* In another sense, to *intervene* is to come between two people or groups engaged in a dispute so as to influence the outcome or result; to mediate, intercede, step it, etc. *The U.S. President has the power to intervene in labor-management disputes.*

[4] **posthumous (posthumously)** This word (pronounced *POS-chuh-mus*) means "occurring or continuing after one's death." *In 1992 the National Academy of Recording Arts and Sciences recognized jazz saxophonist John Coltrane (1926–1967) with a posthumous Grammy Lifetime Achievement Award.*

merely **fictitious**[1] characters **concocted**[2] by fathers and mothers just to frighten children who want to run away at night? I'll bet that scientists completely **discount**[3] the existence of bogeymen and other such **deranged**[4] monsters. After all, their existence has never been **verified**[5] by any scientific procedure. But even if killers were real and I did meet some on the road, what difference would it make? I'd just run up to them and say, 'What do you want? Run along and mind your busi-

---

[1] **fictitious** Literature whose content has been produced by the imagination and is not based on fact is known as *fiction* (novels and short stories, for example). To describe something as *fictitious* is to say that it has been invented or created by the mind; it's not real. *No one knows for sure whether legendary English hero Robin Hood was a real person, but many scholars believe that he is a fictitious character.* Note: The word can also mean "used in order to deceive; phony," as in *he checked into the hotel using a fictitious name.*

[2] **concoct (concocted)** To *concoct* something is to create it by using skill or intelligence, especially by bringing together various ingredients or elements in a new or unexpected way. The noun is *concoction. According to* Compton's Encyclopedia, *in the 19th century, "treatments and cures for baldness were concocted of substances as varied as bear's grease, beef marrow, onion juice, butter, and flower water."*

[3] **discount** To *discount* a story, rumor, claim, etc., is to disregard it or to regard it with disbelief. *Although hundreds of people in the northwest U.S. and Canada have reported sighting a large, apelike creature known as Bigfoot (whose footprints, they say, measure 17 inches in length), most scientists discount the existence of such a creature.*

[4] **deranged** If you say that someone is *deranged*, you mean that he's insane, mentally unbalance, crazy, mad, etc. The implication is that his instability has resulted in a (perhaps dangerous) functional disorder. *In December 1980, outside his New York City apartment building, (former Beatles member) John Lennon was shot and killed by a deranged fan.*

[5] **verify (verified)** To *verify* something is to prove the truth of it (as by the presentation of evidence, for example) or to determine the truth of it (as by research or investigation, for example). *Benjamin Franklin's famous kite experiment (1752) verified the presence of electricity in lightning and won him worldwide fame.*

ness.' I can almost see those poor fellows running like the wind. But in case they didn't run away, I could always run myself, and that would be the end of it."

Pinocchio became so **engrossed**[1] in his thoughts that at first he didn't hear the rustling of leaves behind him. But as the sound continued he finally turned, and there in the otherwise **uniform**[2] darkness he saw the barely **perceptible**[3] outline of a slightly different **gradation**[4] of black. All at once, two figures, wrapped from head to toe in black sacks, slid toward him as softly as if they were ghosts.

"Here they come!" Pinocchio said to himself, and, not knowing where to hide the gold pieces, he stuck all four of them under his tongue.

---

[1] **engrossed** If you're *engrossed* in something, your mind or attention is completely occupied by it (often to the point that you lose awareness of everything else). *As a teenager, Austrian composer Alban Berg (1885–1935) became so engrossed in music that he neglected his other studies and failed his high school examinations.*

[2] **uniform** If something (a texture, color, design, pace, etc.) is *uniform*, it's free from variation or change; it's regular, even, consistent, etc. Note: The prefix *uni* means "one" or "single"; thus, *uniform* literally means "having one form." *Some fish change colors to match their background; for example, flounders are uniform in color against a uniformly colored background but become spotted against a spotted background.*

[3] **perceptible** To *perceive* something is to become aware of it (detect it, notice it, observe it, etc.) through the senses (especially sight or hearing). If something is *perceptible*, it's capable of being perceived. *An earthquake that measures less than 2 on the Richter scale is barely perceptible.*

[4] **gradation** This word denotes a process of change that takes place through a series of very small steps, stages, or degrees. It can also denote any one of the individual steps (or stages, degrees) in the series. *According to Compton's Encyclopedia, "in classical Japanese painting, the artist used only black ink, achieving a sense of color in the gradations from deep, [shiny] black to silvery gray."*

He tried to run away, but before he could take a step he felt his arms grasped and heard two horrible, deep voices say to him, "Your money or your life!"

Unable to speak without revealing that the gold pieces were in his mouth, Pinocchio tried with his head, hands, and body to show, as best he could, that he was only a poor puppet without a penny in his pocket.

"Come, come, stop your nonsense and out with your money!" cried the muggers in threatening voices.

Once more, with his head and hands, Pinocchio **pantomimed**[1], "I haven't a penny."

"Out with that money or you're a dead man," said the taller of the two black figures.

"Dead man," repeated the other.

"And after having killed you, we'll kill your father, too."

"Your father, too!"

"No, no, no, not my father!" cried Pinocchio, wild with terror. As he screamed, the gold pieces tinkled together in his mouth.

"Aha! So that's the game! You have the money hidden under your tongue. Out with it!"

But Pinocchio, as stubborn as ever, refused to **relinquish**[2] the coins.

"Are you deaf? Then we'll make you spit it out!"

One of them grabbed the puppet by the nose and the other by the chin, and they pulled him unmercifully from side to side to make him open his mouth. But it was no use. The

---

[1] **pantomime (pantomimed)** As a verb, to *pantomime* is to communicate by means of gestures instead of speech. As a noun, *pantomime* is the technique of using such gestures. *In the party game known as "charades," a participant uses pantomime to convey a well-known phrase (or book title, movie title, etc.) to his teammates.*

[2] **relinquish** To *relinquish* something is to let it go or give it up (especially unwillingly or regretfully). *By terms of the treaty ending the Spanish-American War (1898–1899), Spain relinquished control over Cuba.*

puppet's lips were as tightly closed as if they had been nailed together.

In desperation the smaller of the two figures pulled out a long knife from his pocket and tried to pry Pinocchio's mouth open with it. Quick as a flash, the puppet sank his teeth deep into the brute's hand, bit it off, and spit it out. When he looked down he was amazed to see that it wasn't a hand, but a cat's paw!

Encouraged by this first victory, he violently **wrenched**[1] himself free from the claws of his **assailants**[2] and, leaping over the bushes that lined the road, ran swiftly across the fields. The robbers were after him at once, like hounds after a fox.

After running several miles, Pinocchio was exhausted and lost. He climbed to the top of a tall pine tree and sat there to rest and think. The sack-covered figures arrived soon after. They tried to climb also, but slipped and fell.

Far from giving up the chase, this only spurred them on. They quickly gathered leaves, twigs, and whatever other **combustible**[3] material they could find. They piled it all at the

---

[1] **wrench (wrenched)** To *wrench* something is to give it a sudden, forceful twist or turn (as when you try to force something free by pulling at it). *With its long neck, long tongue, and long upper lip, the giraffe can easily wrench loose mouthfuls of leaves from trees.* Note: If you say that something is emotionally *wrenching*, you mean that it pulls at your heart; it's distressing.

[2] **assailant (assailants)** To *assail* someone is to attack him, especially violently or with repeated blows. An *assailant* is one who assails; that is, an attacker, aggressor, mugger, etc. *In 1984, speaking of his visit with the imprisoned Turkish terrorist who'd wounded him in an assassination attempt three years earlier, Pope John Paul II said, "Today I was able to meet my assailant and repeat to him the pardon [I'd given] him."*

[3] **combustible** If you say that something (a particular material or substance) is *combustible*, you mean that it's capable of catching fire and burning — or, more especially, that it tends to catch fire and burn easily and rapidly. *An automobile's carburetor or fuel injection system produces a combustible mixture of fuel and air.*

69

foot of the tree and set fire to it. In an instant the tree began to burn. Pinocchio saw the flames climb higher and higher. Not wanting to end his life like a roasted duck, he jumped quickly to the ground and ran off. The muggers followed close behind.

Dawn was breaking when, without any warning, Pinocchio found his path blocked by a deep pool of **stagnant**[1] water covered with green slime. It was about five feet in length, and its **breadth**[2] was equal to the width of the path. What was there to do? With a "One, two, three!" he jumped clear across it. The robbers jumped also, but, not having judged the distance properly, fell right into the middle of the pool. Pinocchio, who heard the splash and felt it, too, cried out, laughing, but never stopping in his race, "Have a nice bath!"

He thought they must surely be drowned and turned his head to see. But two **somber**[3] figures were still following him, though their black sacks were drenched and dripping with slimy water.

---

[1] **stagnant** If a liquid or gas (especially water or air) is *stagnant*, it's not flowing or running; it's motionless, still, etc. The implication is that as a result it's likely to be stale and foul-smelling. *Mosquitoes usually lay their eggs in stagnant water.* Anything else (the economy, one's mind, etc.) described as *stagnant* is sluggish, inactive, dull, etc. *In his first inaugural address (January 1993), President Bill Clinton said, "We inherit an economy that is the world's strongest, but is weakened by business failure [and] stagnant wages."*

[2] **breadth** The *breadth* of something is its size or extent, especially its distance from side to side (its width). *A notice posted (late 1950s) at the University of Wisconsin library read: "Books are quiet; they do not dissolve into wavy lines or snowstorm effects; they do not pause to deliver commercials; they are three-dimensional, having length, breadth, and depth; they are convenient to handle and completely portable."*

[3] **somber** People described as *somber* are serious (businesslike, practical, etc.) and gloomy (grim, cheerless, etc.). Things (clothing, paintings, etc.) described as *somber* are dark or dull in color or mood. *Arthur Miller's* The Crucible *(1953) — a play concerning the Salem witch trials of 1692 — is set against the somber background of Puritan New England.*

Chapter 11 *"The Blue-Haired Fairy"*

As he ran, Pinocchio felt more and more certain that he would have to give himself up into the hands of his attackers. Suddenly he saw a little cottage gleaming white as the snow among the trees of the forest.

"If I have enough breath left to reach that little house, I may be saved," he said to himself. Not waiting another moment, he darted swiftly through the woods, with the robbers still after him.

After a hard race of almost an hour, tired and out of breath, Pinocchio finally reached the door of the cottage and knocked. No one answered.

He knocked again, harder than before, for behind him he heard the steps and the labored breathing of his **persecutors**[1]. The same silence followed.

As knocking was of no use, Pinocchio began to kick and bang against the door, as if he wanted to break it. At the noise, a window opened and a lovely young girl appeared. She had blue hair and a face as white as wax. Her eyes were softly closed and her hands were gently crossed before her chest. The **chaste**[2] simplicity of her pure white dress **en-**

---

[1] **persecute (persecutors)** In one sense, to *persecute* someone is to mistreat him (by unfairly imprisoning him or causing him pain or injury, for example) because of his race, religion, principles, etc. In another sense, to *persecute* someone is to persistently or repeatedly annoy (harass, pester, torment, etc.) him (for any reason). The noun is *persecution*. *Anne Frank was a teenaged Jewish girl who kept a diary while hiding from Nazi persecution in the Netherlands during World War II.*

[2] **chaste** If a person is *chaste* (rhymes with *taste*), she's pure in thought or conduct; she's moral, innocent, decent, modest, etc. If a thing (a painting or an article of clothing, for example) is *chaste*, it's simple or pure in design or style. *In Shakespeare's* Hamlet *(1603), the young prince tells his mother, Queen Ophelia, that even if she is "as chaste as ice [and] as pure as snow," she will not escape scandal (for having married Claudius, her husband's brother and murderer).*

hanced[1] her air of peacefulness. With a voice so weak that it hardly could be heard, she whispered, "No one lives in this house. Everyone is dead."

"Won't you at least open the door for me?" cried Pinocchio in a pleading voice.

"I also am dead," whispered the girl paradoxically[2].

"Dead? What are you doing at the window, then?"

"I'm waiting for the coffin to come and take me away."

After these words, the little girl disappeared and the window closed without a sound.

"Oh, beautiful blue-haired child," cried Pinocchio, "open, I beg of you. Take pity on a poor boy who's being chased by two kill—"

He didn't finish, for two powerful hands grasped him by the neck and the same two horrible voices growled threateningly, "Now we have you!"

The puppet, sensing that death was near, trembled so hard that the joints of his legs rattled and the gold coins tinkled in his mouth.

"Well," the bandits asked, "will you open your mouth now or not?"

With the clanking coins restricting the mobility[1] of his tongue, Pinocchio said nothing.

---

[1] **enhance (enhanced)** To *enhance* something is to raise it to a higher degree; to increase it, intensify it, etc. (in value, beauty, reputation, etc.). *In May 1985 violinist (and then-president of New York City's Carnegie Hall) Isaac Stern said, "Everywhere in the world, music enhances a hall, with one exception: Carnegie Hall enhances the music."*

[2] **paradox (paradoxically)** A statement that seems as though it can't be true (such as "sometimes we must be cruel to be kind") but nevertheless is (or might be) true is known as a *paradox. In the movie, the car was moving forward, but its wheels, paradoxically, looked as though they were spinning backwards!*

"Ah! You don't answer? Very well, this time we'll make you open it."

Taking out two long, sharp knives, they struck two heavy blows on the puppet's back.

Luckily for him, Pinocchio was made of very hard wood and the knives broke into a thousand pieces. In shocked disbelief the muggers stared down at the remnants[2] of the shattered knives. Then they looked at each other in dismay[3].

"I think," said one of them to the other, "that there's nothing left to do now but hang him."

"Hang him," repeated the other.

Through closed lips the terrified puppet screamed, "Don't hang me!" But with the gold coins stuck under his tongue, the words came out as a muffled "oh-ay-ee."

"What's that you say?" asked the bandits. "We can't understand you. You must learn to enunciate[4]!"

---

[1] **mobility** If something is *mobile*, it's movable (or, especially, readily movable). *Mobility* is the condition of being mobile (that is, it's the ability or readiness to move). *A jeep — a motor vehicle that combines the ruggedness of a truck with the mobility of a car — was first used by the U.S. Army during World War II.* Note: The word also refers to the movement of people from one social class to another (as in *upward mobility*).

[2] **remnant (remnants)** A *remnant* (of something that no longer exists) is a small, remaining part (of it); a fragment, scrap, trace, etc. *In 1937 aviation pioneer Amelia Earhart set out to fly around the world, but her plane mysteriously disappeared; 55 years later, a search party reported finding remnants of the plane on a Pacific island.*

[3] **dismay** As a noun, *dismay* is a loss of courage (as from an inability to cope with trouble or danger) or a feeling of sad disappointment (as from a hopeless situation). As a verb, to *dismay* someone is to break down his courage, disappoint him, or alarm him. *In 1970, to the dismay of their intensely devoted fans, the Beatles disbanded.*

[4] **enunciate** To *enunciate* is to pronounce words clearly and distinctly. *In his 1980 book* Homesickness, *author Murray Bail said, "The British [must] enunciate clearly in order to [pierce] the humidity and hedges, the moist walls and alleyways."*

They tied Pinocchio's hands behind his shoulders and slipped a noose around his neck. Throwing a rope over the **gnarled**[1] top branch of a tall oak tree, they pulled till the poor puppet hung far up in space.

Satisfied with their work, they sat on the grass waiting for Pinocchio to give his last gasp. But after three hours the puppet's eyes were still open and his mouth was still shut. And his legs kicked harder than ever.

Tired of waiting, the killers stood up and called to him mockingly, "We'll be back tomorrow morning. During the night, please be so kind as to drop dead—with your mouth wide open." With these words they turned and left.

A few minutes went by and then a cold, stormy wind began to blow. As it shrieked and moaned, the poor little puppet was blown violently back and forth. The rocking made him sick, and the noose, becoming tighter and tighter, choked him. A thick film of tears covered his eyes.

Death was creeping nearer and nearer, and the puppet still hoped for some good soul to come to his rescue, but no one appeared. As he was about to die, he thought of his poor old father, and, hardly conscious of what he was saying, murmured to himself: "Oh, Father, if you were only here!"

These were his last words. He closed his eyes, opened his mouth, stretched out his legs, and hung there, lifeless.

---

[1] **gnarled** If wood is *gnarled*, it's knotty and twisted. If a person (or his skin, hands, etc.) is *gnarled*, he has a rough, rugged, weather-beaten appearance (as from hard outdoor work or age). *Japanese bonsai trees are cultivated indoors in small containers and stand only about a foot tall — but they have the proportions and gnarled appearance of large outdoor trees.*

Chapter 12 "The Doctors"

If the poor puppet had dangled there much longer, all hope would have been lost. Luckily for him, the pretty girl with blue hair once again looked out her window. Filled with pity at the sight of the poor little fellow being knocked helplessly about by the wind, she clapped her hands sharply together three times.

At this signal, a loud rustling of wings was heard and a large bird came and settled itself on the window ledge.

"What do you command, beautiful fairy?" asked the bird, bending his beak in homage[1] (for the child with blue hair was none other than a very kind fairy who had lived, for more than a thousand years, in that forest).

"Do you see that puppet hanging from the limb of that big oak tree?"

"I see him."

"Very well. Fly immediately to him. With your strong beak, break the knot that holds him, take him down, and lay him softly on the grass at the foot of the tree."

The bird flew away and after two minutes returned, saying, "I've done what you've commanded."

"How did you find him? Alive or dead?"

"Looking at him, I thought he was dead. But that assumption proved erroneous[2], for as soon as I loosened the knot

---

[1] **homage** Respect or honor shown to another (especially publicly) is known as *homage* (sometimes pronounced with a silent *h*). *Bronze plaques on the walls of the Baseball Hall of Fame pay homage to the greats of the game.*

[2] **erroneous** If something is *erroneous*, it contains (or is based on) an error or mistake; it's incorrect, faulty, untrue, wrong, etc. *The milk snake gets its name from the erroneous notion that it sucks milk from cows.*

75

around his neck, he **expelled**[1] a long sigh, then mumbled, 'Thank you. Now I feel better!'"

The fairy clapped her hands twice. A magnificent poodle in an **immaculate**[2] coachman's uniform appeared. He walked on his hind legs, just like a man.

"Come," said the fairy to him. "Get my best coach ready and set out toward the forest. On reaching the oak tree, you'll find a poor, half-dead puppet stretched out on the grass. Lift him up tenderly, place him on the silken cushions of the coach, and bring him here to me."

The dog, to show that he fully understood the fairy's **explicit**[3] instructions, wagged his tail two or three times, then set off at a quick pace.

In a few minutes, a lovely little coach pulled out of the stable. It was drawn by a hundred pairs of white mice, and the poodle sat on the coachman's seat and snapped his whip gaily in the air, as if he were a real coachman in a hurry to get to his destination.

In fifteen minutes the coach was back. The fairy, who was waiting at the door of the house, lifted the poor little puppet in her arms, took him to a small room, put him to bed, and sent immediately for the best doctors of the neighborhood.

One after another the doctors came: a crow, an owl, and a glowing cricket. They gathered around Pinocchio's bed.

---

[1] **expel (expelled)** To *expel* something is to force it out or drive it away, as in *expel air from the lungs* or *expel a student from college*. *In the 1973 film* The Exorcist, *a priest tries to expel a demon from a young girl.*

[2] **immaculate** If something is *immaculate*, it's spotlessly clean. *As a stand-up comic in the mid-1970s, Steve Martin often wore an immaculate white suit and an arrow through his head.*

[3] **explicit** If something is *explicit*, it's clearly and definitely expressed; it's precise, specific, etc. *The U.S. Constitution does not explicitly mention a right of privacy; however, the Fourth Amendment guarantees against "unreasonable searches and seizures."*

"I'd like to **canvass**[1] your expert opinions, gentlemen," said the fairy, turning to the three doctors. "Is this poor puppet dead or alive? And if he's alive, what's wrong with him?" The crow stepped out and felt Pinocchio's pulse. Then he **solemnly**[2] pronounced the following words: "To my mind he's dead and gone. But if by any chance he's not, then that would be a sure sign that he's still alive!"

"At the risk of **alienating**[3] my good friend the crow," said the owl, in a cool, **detached**[4] manner, "I must say that I can't **endorse**[5] his opinion. As you know, the traditional **criteria**[1]

---

[1] **canvass** To *canvass* a group of people is to ask for their opinions; to take a survey or poll. *The first U.S. newspaper to canvass public opinion during a presidential election was the* Harrisburg Pennsylvanian *(during the election of 1824, in which John Quincy Adams defeated Andrew Jackson).* Note: In another sense, to *canvass* is to go through a neighborhood (or city, district, etc.) asking for votes, sales orders, or donations.

[2] **solemn (solemnly)** If a person (or his facial expression, eyes, tone of voice, mood, etc.) is *solemn*, he's serious or cheerless (as from serious or weighty concerns, for example). If a thing (a vow, document, event, etc.) is *solemn* it has a serious, formal, dignified, or ceremonious character. The noun is *solemnity*. *Rosh Hashanah (the Jewish New Year) is mark by solemnity as well as festivity.*

[3] **alienate (alienating)** To *alienate* someone is to cause him to become unfriendly, hostile, etc., or to cause him to become withdrawn, indifferent, etc. *In 1824 English essayist William Hazlitt said, "Few things tend more to alienate friendship than a [lack] of punctuality in our engagements."*

[4] **detached** If you say that someone is *detached*, you mean that he's not emotionally involved; he's impersonal, distant, etc. *In memoirs published by his former aides, President Ronald Reagan was described as detached and uninformed.*

[5] **endorse** To *endorse* something (a theory or philosophy, for example) is to express approval of it; support it. *President Bill Clinton endorsed the "three strikes and you're out" provision of the Federal Crime Act of 1994. In politics, to endorse a candidate is to publicly support him. Republican New York City Mayor Rudolph Giuliani crossed party lines during the November 1994 New York gubernatorial election by endorsing Democrat Mario Cuomo.*

for determining death are...how can I put this without using any medical **jargon**[2] or scientific **nomenclature**[3]?...well, you know that a person's dead if his heart and lungs stop working. But because we're dealing with a puppet, not a human, those factors might not be **relevant**[4] — so it's difficult to make an accurate **diagnosis**[5]. To my mind he's alive. But if by any chance he's not, then that would be a sure sign that he's dead!"

Hoping to **authenticate**[6] the puppet's condition one way or the other, the fairy asked the cricket, "And what's your opinion?"

---

[1] **criteria** A *criterion* is a standard, rule, or norm upon which a judgment or decision can be based. The word is usually used in the plural: *criteria*. *Show dogs are judged by various criteria, including the shape of the head, the placement of the ears, and the color and texture of the coat.*

[2] **jargon** The specialized or technical language or vocabulary of a particular group (profession, class, region, etc.) is known as *jargon*. *In CB radio jargon, "smokey" means "highway patrolman" (from the resemblance of state troopers' hats to that of Smokey the Bear).*

[3] **nomenclature** A set or system of technical names used in a particular science (or other discipline) is known as *nomenclature*. *What is known in common English as a chimpanzee is known in zoological nomenclature as* Pan troglodytes.

[4] **relevant** If you say that something is *relevant*, you mean that it has a bearing on (is connected to or related to) the matter at hand; it's pertinent, applicable, etc. *In a trial, information is admitted as evidence only if it is relevant and firsthand.* Note: The opposite is *irrelevant* (not relevant).

[5] **diagnosis** A *diagnosis* is an opinion or conclusion about what disease a person (or animal) suffers from. Such an opinion or conclusion is generally expressed by a doctor as the result of a physical examination, a review of laboratory tests, an evaluation of patient history, etc. *Biopsy (the removal and microscopic examination of a sample of living tissue) is the only conclusive method for the diagnosis of cancer.*

[6] **authenticate** To *authenticate* something is to establish that it's true or genuine; to confirm it, substantiate it, etc. *Although people have reported seeing the abominable snowman (a hairy, humanlike creature) in Asia's Himalaya Mountains, its existence has never been authenticated.*

"Puppet medicine is not my area of **expertise**[1]; in fact, I'm barely **conversant**[2] with it. What little I do know I **gleaned**[3] from a few short articles I read years ago as a medical student. So, because, as I say, my knowledge of it is **superficial**[4] and **scanty**[5], I can't give you any **definitive**[6] answers. Whatever I might say would be nothing more than a purely **sub-**

---

[1] **expertise** Expert skill or knowledge in a particular area or field is known as *expertise* (pronounced *eks-per-TEEZ*). *World War II general George Patton was known for his expertise at warfare using tanks and other vehicles.*

[2] **conversant** To be *conversant* with something (a particular subject or topic, for example) is to be familiar with it or knowledgeable about it, as from study or experience. *If you're conversant with Mary Shelley's 1818 novel* Frankenstein, *you know that "Frankenstein" is not the name of the monster, but of the doctor who created him.*

[3] **glean (gleaned)** To *glean* something (information or evidence, for example) is to collect or gather it little by little or bit by bit. *One of the ways researchers glean information about ancient peoples is by X-raying and dissecting mummies.*

[4] **superficial** Anything described as *superficial* is concerned only with what's obvious or on the surface; it's shallow, trivial, insubstantial, insignificant, etc. *Until scuba gear was invented (1943), divers had to be satisfied with only a superficial exploration of the ocean.*

[5] **scanty** If you say that the amount or quantity of something is *scanty*, you mean that it's barely adequate, small, limited, etc. *Extreme cold in the north and scanty rainfall in the south greatly limit the output of crops in Siberia (a region of central and eastern Russia).*

[6] **definitive** This word means either "authoritative; complete; reliable," as in *a definitive biography*, or "serving to supply a final decision or answer," as in *a definitive verdict. Most film critics agree that the 1935 version of* Mutiny on the Bounty *(starring Charles Laughton and Clark Gable) remains the definitive version, in spite of excellent remakes in 1962 (with Trevor Howard and Marlon Brando) and 1984 (with Anthony Hopkins and Mel Gibson).*

jective[1] interpretation. But I do know one thing: that good doctors, when they don't know something, rather than make **ambiguous**[2] remarks, should know enough to keep quiet. Actually, this puppet here is no stranger to me. I've known him for a long time; in fact, I'm something of a **confidant**[3] of his."

Pinocchio, who until then had been very quiet, shuddered so hard that the bed shook.

"That wooden boy," continued the cricket, "has had a **checkered**[4] past—some good, but mostly bad. I could **cite**[1]

---

[1] **subjective** People's opinions can be either *objective* or *subjective*. An *objective* opinion is one based on fact, logic, etc. A *subjective* opinion is one based on one's personal feelings, gut instincts, etc. *During a radio interview a well-known orchestra conductor said, "There are two kinds of music: good music and bad music; if you like it, it's good, and if you don't like it, it's bad" — in other words, judgments about music are subjective.*

[2] **ambiguous** If something (a statement, a set of instructions, etc.) is *ambiguous*, it has more than one possible meaning or interpretation; it lacks clarity; it causes confusion. *As a geographical label, "America" is ambiguous — to some it means the United States; to others it means all of North America; and to still others it means all of the Western Hemisphere.*

[3] **confidant** To *confide* in someone is to reveal private information to him and to trust him to keep it secret. A *confidant* is a person (usually a close friend) in whom you confide. A female confidant is a *confidante*. To tell something in *confidence* — or, to use the adverb, to tell something *confidentially* — is to tell it with the understanding that it will be kept secret. *American financier Bernard Baruch (1870–1965) was an advisor and confidant of every U.S. President from Woodrow Wilson to John F. Kennedy.*

[4] **checkered** If you say that an object (a piece of fabric, for example) is *checkered*, you mean that it's marked with squares (like a checkerboard). But if you say that someone's career, life, past, etc., is *checkered*, you mean that it's marked by alternating periods of good and bad fortune, ups and downs, etc. *With his foreign successes (visit to the People's Republic of China, end of the Vietnam War) and failures at home (high inflation, Watergate scandal) you might say that Richard Nixon had a checkered Presidency (interestingly, his dog's name was Checkers!).*

many instances of **unconscionable**[2] behavior—but let's just say that he's a rascal of the worst sort."
Pinocchio opened his eyes and closed them again.
"He's **rebellious**[3] and lazy. He's a runaway."
Pinocchio hid his face under the sheets.
"He's a disobedient boy who's breaking his father's heart!"
Long, shuddering sobs were heard. When they lifted the sheets a little, they discovered Pinocchio was crying uncontrollably, like a baby!
"If a rascal cries like a baby," said the cricket thoughtfully, "that can be **construed**[4] to mean that he's learned his lesson the hard way and that he's taken his first step on the road to becoming a good boy."

---

[1] **cite** To *cite* something is to mention it (out loud or in writing) as an example in order to support, prove, or illustrate something. *People who believe that ordinary citizens should be allowed to own guns often cite the Second Amendment to the Constitution, which guarantees "the right of the people to keep and bear arms."*

[2] **unconscionable** Any act described as *unconscionable* is one not guided by conscience; that is, it's not guided by what is just, right, or reasonable (it's unprincipled, immoral, dishonest, etc.). *American author Washington Irving (1783-1859) apparently didn't enjoy having his works edited, for he is known for having said, "Sometimes the unconscionable editors will clip our paragraphs."*

[3] **rebellious** To *rebel* against something (an authority or government, for example) is to show or express (sometimes by force) opposition to it; to defy it, rise up against it, resist it, etc. A person described as *rebellious* is one who tends to rebel; that is, he's defiant, resistant, unruly, etc. *J. D. Salinger's novel* The Catcher in the Rye *(1951) concerns a sensitive but rebellious boarding school student named Holden Caulfield.*

[4] **construe (construed)** To *construe* something (an action, condition, or statement whose meaning is indefinite, for example) is to interpret it to mean a particular thing. *In the 17th and 18th centuries poverty was regarded as a natural, normal condition; beginning in the 19th century, however, it was generally construed as a sign of individual failure.*

Chapter 13 "Medicine"

As soon as the three doctors had left the room, the fairy went to Pinocchio's bed and felt his pulse for herself. It was racing, and the fairy, knowing that a quick pulse often **denotes**[1] fever, touched his forehead. It was burning up.

"How do you feel?" she asked.

"I feel hot, weak, and achy," he mumbled.

She filled a glass with **tepid**[2] water and then poured some yellow powder into it. Then she stirred it with a spoon, creating a **homogeneous**[3] mixture. Holding it to his lips, she said lovingly, "Drink this, and soon you'll be up and well."

Pinocchio looked at the glass, made a face, and asked in a whining voice, "Is it sweet or sour?"

"It's sour, but it's good for you."

"If it's sour, I don't want it."

---

[1] **denote (denotes)** To *denote* something is (1) to indicate or signify it (as in *a falling barometer denotes an approaching storm*), (2) to be a name for it (as in *the word "palette" denotes the roof of the mouth*), or (3) to stand as a symbol for it (as in *the character "+" denotes addition*). *To some people the term "rock 'n' roll" denotes music in the style of Chuck Berry; to others it denotes pop music in general (as distinguished from classical music, for example).*

[2] **tepid** If you say that the temperature of something (water, for example) is *tepid,* you mean that it's lukewarm (that is, it's neither hot nor cold). If you say that a person's reaction or response to something is *tepid,* you mean that it's lukewarm (that is, it lacks emotion or enthusiasm). *In March 1965 Time magazine referred to contemporary English drama as "the measuring out of life in tepid teacups."*

[3] **homogeneous** If you're talking about a substance (a liquid, for example), then this word means "uniform and consistent in structure or composition." *A milkshake is a homogeneous mixture of milk and ice cream.* If you're talking about a group of people or things, then the word means "all of the same or similar type or kind." *In 1958 novelist William Faulkner said, "If we Americans are to survive, it will have to be because we choose to be first of all Americans; to present to the world one homogeneous and unbroken front, whether of white Americans or black ones or purple or blue or green."*

"The powder I put in is only a small **component**[1] of the medicine. It's mostly just water. Drink it!"

"But it's sour. I don't like anything sour."

"Drink it and I'll give you a lump of sugar to take the sour taste from your mouth."

"Where's the sugar?"

"Here it is," said the fairy, taking a lump from a golden bowl.

"I want the sugar first, then I'll drink it."

"Do you promise?"

"Yes."

The fairy gave him the sugar and Pinocchio, after chewing and swallowing it in a second, said, smacking his lips, "If only sugar were medicine! I would take it every day."

"Now keep your promise and drink this. It'll be good for you."

Pinocchio took the glass in both hands and stuck his long nose into it. He **winced**[2] and said, "It's too sour, much too sour! I can't drink it."

"How do you know, when you haven't even tasted it?"

"I can tell. I can smell it. It's **repulsive**[3]. It smells like rotten lemons and stale vinegar mixed together. It **reeks**[1]!" Then,

---

[1] **component** A *component* is something used with other things to make something; or, to put it another way, it's one of the parts into which something can be divided (as in *automobile components*). *A sundae is usually made of three components: ice cream, syrup, and whipped cream.*

[2] **wince (winced)** To *wince* is to draw back involuntarily, as from pain or disgust; to flinch. *English author Samuel Johnson (1709–1784) once said, "A fly may sting a stately horse and make him wince; but one is but an insect, and the other is a horse still."*

[3] **repulsive** If something is *repulsive* it arouses feelings of disgust and extreme dislike; it's horrid, sickening, etc. *In September 1985, speaking of a new perfume designed to protect against muggers, journalist Jack Scaff explained, "The idea is to make the woman so repulsive that the attacker runs away. It sounds funny until you smell it."*

astute² negotiator that he was, Pinocchio said, "I want another lump of sugar, then I'll drink it."

The fairy, with all the patience of a good mother, gave him more sugar.

"I still can't drink it," Pinocchio said, making more faces.

"Why?"

"Because the pillow near my feet is lying on an angle."

The fairy straightened the pillow.

"It's no use. I can't drink it even now."

"What's the matter now?"

"I don't like the way the door looks. It's half open."

The fairy closed the door.

"I won't drink it," cried Pinocchio, bursting out crying. "I won't drink this awful stuff. I won't, I won't! No, no, no, no!"

"But you're sick. Very, very sick."

"If I drink that, I'll probably get even sicker. Anything that smells that bad is bound to have an **adverse³** effect."

---

¹ **reek (reeks)** If a substance *reeks*, it gives off (or becomes filled with) a strong, unpleasant odor; it stinks. If something immaterial *reeks*, it's filled with something unpleasant (as in *the autobiography reeked with self-pity*). As a noun, a *reek* is a strong, unpleasant odor. *According to* Compton's Encyclopedia, *English novelist Charles Dickens' (1812–1870) vision of the American Midwest was that it "contained nothing but foul and reeking canal boats, swamps, bullfrogs, and tobacco juice."*

² **astute** People who are *astute* have keen insight and perception; they're wise and shrewd (especially with regard to their own affairs); they have good judgment; they're difficult to mislead or fool. *In literature, Sherlock Holmes is an astute English detective whose powers of reasoning enable him to solve crimes that leave all other crime fighters stumped.*

³ **adverse** If something is *adverse*, it's contrary to (acts against) one's interests or welfare; it has a harmful effect; it's damaging, injurious, hurtful, etc. *Excessive alcohol consumption can adversely affect the liver; for example, it can cause cirrhosis (degeneration of liver tissue) or liver cancer.* Note: The word can also mean "unfriendly or opposing in purpose or effect," as in *adverse criticism.*

"That's not true. Now listen to me. I'm not giving you this medicine simply to relieve your aches and **malaise**[1]. You need it to stay alive! I didn't want to tell you this because I didn't want to frighten you, but you have a **terminal**[2] illness. In a few hours it will take you far away to another world."

"I don't care," answered the puppet **nonchalantly**[3].

"That's an awfully **blasé**[4] attitude. Aren't you afraid of the unknown, of eternity?"

"No. Those are just **abstract**[5] ideas. A sour taste is real. I'd rather die than drink that awful medicine."

At that moment, the door of the room flew open and in came four black rabbits.

"What do you want?" asked Pinocchio.

---

[1] **malaise** A general or vague feeling of bodily discomfort and weakness (as at the onset of or during an illness) is known as *malaise* (pronounce *muh-LAIZ*). *Chickenpox — a contagious disease, primarily of children — is caused by a virus and is characterized by skin eruptions, fever, and malaise.*

[2] **terminal** If an illness is *terminal*, it causes death; it's fatal. *By signing a document known as a "living will," person with a terminal illness can instruct his doctors and relatives not to prolong his life artificially (with life-support systems, for example).*

[3] **nonchalant (nonchalantly)** If you're *nonchalant* (pronounced with the accent on the third syllable) you have a cool, casual manner; you appear to be unconcerned, carefree, indifferent, etc. *The funny thing about jazz musicians is that they maintain the same nonchalant attitude whether the music is calm or intense.*

[4] **blasé** If you're *blasé* about something, you're indifferent or unconcerned about it; you're bored or unimpressed by it. *It has been pointed out that men don't notice dust — which may explain why most of them have a blasé attitude about housecleaning!*

[5] **abstract** Things that are *abstract* are conceptual or theoretical; that is, they are thought of apart from material objects. For example, a piece of candy is a material object, but the concept of sweetness is said to be *abstract*. *In literature, the abstract idea of time sometimes takes human form in the character Father Time.*

"We've come for your body," said the largest rabbit **gravely**[1].

"But I'm not dead yet!"

"No, not yet. But a sickness has invaded you, and the invading cells **replicate**[2] themselves very quickly. Since you've refused to take the medicine that would have made you well, you'll be dead in no time. Once you're dead...how can I put this without being too **graphic**[3]?...well, once you're dead we'll take your corpse to the puppet medical school, where your **dismembered**[4] body parts will be **dissected**[5] for study."

---

[1] **grave (gravely)** People described as *grave* are serious, thoughtful, and dignified. Matters described as *grave* are important, weighty, critical. Situations described as *grave* threaten a seriously bad outcome. *In January 1987 journalist Richard Gilman said, "Being a sports fan is a complex matter – a relief from the seriousness of the real world, with its unending pressures and often grave obligations."*

[2] **replicate** To *replicate* something is to duplicate or copy it. *A synthesizer is a (usually keyboard) musical instrument that can electronically replicate the sound of any other instrument.* Note: In biology, when an organism *replicates* itself, it reproduces to make an exact copy (or copies) of itself.

[3] **graphic** If you say that a narrative (account, recital, story, etc.) is *graphic*, you mean that it's described in realistic detail. Sometimes the implication is that the detail is too realistic and is thus unsettling or disturbing. *Upton Sinclair's novel* The Jungle *(1906) exposed unsanitary conditions in the meat-packing industry with its graphic descriptions of the grinding up of poisoned rats and of workers falling into vats.*

[4] **dismember (dismembered)** To *dismember* a person or animal is to cut or tear off its limbs (arms, legs, wing, tail, etc.). *When crocodiles feed on large animals (antelope, deer, and hogs, for example), they first drown them, then dismember them.* To *dismember* a thing (a country, for example) is to divide or separate it into pieces. *During the World War I (1914–1918) the British and the French developed plans for the dismemberment of the Ottoman Empire.*

[5] **dissect (dissect)** To *dissect* something (animal tissue, for example) is to cut it apart to examine or study its structure. *Thanks to the Internet, students no longer have to dissect dead frogs in biology class; today, using the Interactive Frog Dissection Kit, they can perform a virtual dissection online.*

Pinocchio, envisioning that **grisly**[1] scene, cried out in horror, "Oh, fairy, my fairy...give me that glass! Quick, please! I don't want to die! No, no, not yet...not yet!"

Holding the glass in both hands, and still seeing in his mind's eye the **gruesome**[2] image of his **cadaver**[3] being horribly **mutilated**[4], he swallowed the medicine in one gulp.

"Well," said the four rabbits, "this time we've made the trip for nothing." And turning on their heels, they marched out of the room, muttering and grumbling between their teeth.

In a moment, Pinocchio felt fine. With one leap he was out of bed and into his clothes.

The fairy, seeing him run and jump around the room, said to him, "The medicine was good for you, after all, wasn't it?"

"Yes! It's given me new life."

"Why, then, did I have to beg you so hard to make you drink it?"

---

[1] **grisly** This word describes things (especially instances of violence or cruelty) that arouse horror or disgust. *Jack the Ripper conducted a series of grisly murders in London in 1888.*

[2] **gruesome** If something is *gruesome* it causes feelings of horror or disgust (especially as a result of its crudity or inhumanity); it's hideous, frightful, shocking, etc. *When World War II ended (1945), some of the pictures of Nazi death camps were too gruesome to be published.*

[3] **cadaver** A dead body, especially one intended for medical study, is known as a *cadaver* (pronounced with the accent on the second syllable). *In human organ transplantation, whereas some organs (kidneys, for example) can be obtained from either a living donor or a cadaver, others (the heart, for example) can be obtained only from cadavers.* Note: To describe a living person as *cadaverous* is to say that he is extremely thin and pale.

[4] **mutilate (mutilated)** To *mutilate* something (an object or a living thing) is to (sometimes violently) injure or disfigure it by removing or irreversibly damaging parts of it. *In a report describing wounded soldiers (observed in 1863 when he worked as a Civil War nurse), poet Walt Whitman wrote, "Some have their legs blown off; some [have] indescribably horrid wounds in the face or head; all [are] mutilated, torn."*

"I'm a boy, you see, and all boys find medicine even more **repellent**[1] than sickness."

"What a shame! Boys ought to know, after all, that medicine, taken in time, can save them from pain and even from death. I admit the medicine tasted sour, but if you think about it, the momentary unpleasantness is **trivial**[2] when looked at in a larger **context**[3]."

"You're right. Next time I won't have to be begged so hard. I'll remember those black rabbits — and the **phobic**[4] reaction I had to what would have happened to me at the puppet medical school — and I'll take the medicine at once!"

---

[1] **repellent** If something is *repellent*, it causes distaste or extreme dislike (sometimes causing one to back away); it's disgusting, offensive, obnoxious, hateful, etc. *The 1991 Oscar-winning film* The Silence of the Lambs *(which concerns a cannibalistic serial killer) contains scenes too repellent for many moviegoers.*

[2] **trivial** If you refer to something as *trivial*, you mean that it's unimportant or insignificant. *In August 1989, 51-year-old U.S. author Joyce Carol Oates said, "I used to think getting old was about [concern for your appearance], but it's actually about losing people you love; getting wrinkles is trivial."*

[3] **context** The surrounding conditions or circumstances in which a particular event occurs, or the parts of a written or spoken statement that surround a particular passage and help reveal its meaning, is known as *context*. *Deaf people who interpret a speaker's words by "reading lips" rely not only on lip movements, but also on facial expressions and context.* Sometimes *context* refers to any meaningful frame of reference, overall picture, backdrop, etc., in which events or words exist. *"Pluto" exists in three well-known contexts: astronomy (ninth planet from the Sun), mythology (god of the underworld), and Walt Disney cartoons (a pet dog).*

[4] **phobia (phobic)** A *phobia* is an intense but irrational fear of a particular object or situation. Sometimes the word is used informally to refer to any strong dislike or fear (whether irrational or not). The adjective is *phobic*. *In her autobiography, award-winning actress Tallulah Bankhead (1903–1968) wrote, "I have three phobias which, could I [silence] them, would make my life as slick as a sonnet but as dull as ditch water: I hate to go to bed, I hate to get up, and I hate to be alone."*

"Good. Now, even though you feel fine, it's not a good idea for you to be running around so much. You need time to **recuperate**[1] after such a serious illness. Come sit here beside me and tell me how it came about that you found yourself in the hands of killers."

"Well, it's a long story," said Pinocchio, sitting down, "but I'll try to make it as **concise**[2] as I can. Anyway, here's what happened: Fire-Eater gave me five gold pieces to give to my father, but on the way home I met a fox and a cat, who asked me, 'Do you want the five pieces to become two thousand?' And I said, 'Yes.' And they said, 'Come with us to the Field of Wonders.' And I said, 'Let's go.' Then they said, 'Let's stop at the Red Lobster Inn to rest, and after midnight we'll set out again.' We ate and went to sleep. When I woke up they were gone and I started out in the darkness all alone. On the road I met two killers dressed in black sacks, who said to me, 'Your money or your life.' I said, 'I haven't any money' — for, you see, I had put the money under my tongue. One of them tried to put his hand in my mouth, but I bit it off and spit it out. But it wasn't a hand; it was a cat's paw. And they ran after me and I ran and ran, till at last they caught me and tied my neck with a rope and hung me from a tree branch. They said they'd come back the next morning to find me dead with my mouth —"

---

[1] **recuperate** To *recuperate* is to recover from an illness; to regain health or strength (as by resting, staying in bed, etc.). *Journalist Margaret Mitchell began the Pulitzer Prize–winning novel* Gone with the Wind *while recuperating from an ankle injury (1926).*

[2] **concise** If you say that writing or speech is *concise*, you mean that it's brief and compact (expressed in few words) but nevertheless clear and meaningful. *A concise sentence that uses all 26 letters of the alphabet (such as "The quick red fox jumps over the lazy brown dog") is known as a* **pangram** *and is often used to quickly test the keys of a typewriter.*

Here the fairy interrupted the **monologue**[1] to ask, "Where are the gold pieces now?"

"I lost them," answered Pinocchio. But he was lying, for he had them in his pocket.

As he spoke, his nose, long as it was, became at least two inches longer.

"Where did you lose them?"

"In the nearby woods," the puppet answered, with a slight upward **inflection**[2].

At this second lie, his nose grew a few more inches.

"If you lost them in the nearby woods," said the fairy, "we'll look for them and find them, for everything that's lost there is always found."

"No, wait! That's not it. I must have had **amnesia**[3] for a second. Now I remember. I didn't lose the gold pieces. I swallowed them when I drank the medicine."

At this third lie, his nose became so long that he couldn't even move in any direction. If he turned to the right, he'd knock it against the bed or into the windowpane; if he turned to the left, he'd strike the wall or door; and if he raised his head a bit, he'd risk poking out the fairy's eyes.

---

[1] **monologue** A *monologue* is a long speech by a single speaker (as distinguished from a *dialogue*, which is a conversation between two or more people). A person who delivers a *monologue* in company or during a conversation is generally accused of monopolizing the conversation. *In May 1985, speaking of arms negotiations with the Soviet Union, chief U.S. arms negotiator Max Kampelman said, "A dialogue is more than two monologues."*

[2] **inflection** This word denotes a change of pitch or tone of the voice. *In the Chinese language, inflection affects a word's meaning; that is, the same sound can mean one thing if the voice rises but something else if it falls.*

[3] **amnesia** A loss of memory—especially one brought on by shock, disease, or injury—is known as *amnesia*. *After the car crash (August 1997) that killed Diana, Princess of Wales, police sources said that her bodyguard, the sole survivor of the crash, had amnesia and couldn't remember anything about the circumstances of the accident.*

Then, instead of further trying to **elicit**[1] the truth from him, the fairy sat staring at him, laughing.

"Why are you laughing?" the puppet asked.

"I'm laughing at your lies."

"How do you know I'm lying?"

"For a long time," she said with a serious expression, "doctors have **speculated**[2] that, where puppets are concerned, there's a direct **correlation**[3] between the telling of lies and sudden nose growth. Now, through **extensive**[4] experimentation and the use of highly **sophisticated**[5] scientific equipment,

---

[1] **elicit** To *elicit* something (the truth, a response, etc.) is to draw it out (of someone). *In the U.S. Supreme Court, the chief justice presents his view of a case first, then elicits the opinions of the other justices in order of seniority.*

[2] **speculate (speculated)** When you *speculate* about something, you imagine it to be true without conclusive evidence; you theorize, presume, suspect, suppose, etc. *Some scientists speculate that Saturn's outermost moon, Phoebe, is an asteroid that was captured by the planet.*

[3] **correlate (correlation)** To *correlate* two or more things (facts, ideas, etc.) is to show that they have a meaningful connection or relationship. The noun is *correlation. Scientists have discovered that there is a correlation between exposure to the sun's ultraviolet rays and the occurrence of skin cancer in humans; that's why it's important to wear sunscreen when you go to the beach.*

[4] **extensive** If something is *extensive*, it's large in size or amount (that is, it's spacious, expansive, long, wide, etc.), or it's great in scope or degree (that is, it's far-reaching, comprehensive, thorough, etc.). *President Herbert Hoover (1874–1964) once joked, "The President differs from other men in that he has a more extensive wardrobe."*

[5] **sophisticated** A person who is *sophisticated* is (as a result of education and experience) worldly-wise, mature, cultivated, refined, etc. A thing that is *sophisticated* is either one that appeals to sophisticated people (as in *sophisticated humor*) or one that is complex, intricate, or advanced in design (as in *sophisticated machinery*). *In October 1961 British Prime Minister Harold Macmillan said that Communism "is a strange, perverted [system] that has a queer attraction both for the most primitive and for the most sophisticated societies."*

their theories have been **substantiated**[1]. They've discovered that when a puppet tells a lie, the part of its brain that controls nose growth becomes **hyperactive**[2]; that is, it produces an **abundance**[3] of chemicals that **incite**[4] swelling. And they've **disseminated**[5] the results of their **painstaking**[6] research to fairies all around the world. That's how I know."

---

[1] **substantiate (substantiated)** To *substantiate* something is to establish its truth by providing evidence; to verify it, confirm it, prove it, etc. *English physician William Harvey described blood circulation in 1628, but his theory was not fully substantiated until 1827.*

[2] **hyperactive** People or things that are *hyperactive* are overly, highly, or abnormally active. If a person is *hyperactive*, he's constantly active; he's unable to relax or be quiet. The noun is *hyperactivity*. *A high-sugar diet was once thought to cause hyperactivity in children (but recent studies do not support this idea).*

[3] **abundant (abundance)** If a supply or amount of something (crops or wildlife, for example) is *abundant*, it's more than enough; it's plentiful. *Danish author Isak Dinesen once said, "I don't believe in evil; I believe only in horror. In nature there is no evil, only an abundance of horror."*

[4] **incite** To *incite* is to provoke, prompt, or urge on (some particular action). *The Chicago Seven were seven political extremists accused of inciting a riot at the 1968 Democratic National Convention in Chicago.*

[5] **disseminate (disseminated)** To *disseminate* something (information, ideas, statistics, schoolbooks, etc.) is to spread it widely; to make it widely known or widely available. *After adopting and proclaiming the Universal Declaration of Human Rights (December 1948), the United Nations asked that the text of the Declaration be "disseminated, displayed, read, and [explained]" in schools throughout the world.*

[6] **painstaking** If you divide this word into "pains" and "taking," you can see that if you do something in a *painstaking* way, you "take pains" when doing it; that is, you're extremely careful and thorough. *Speaking of TWA Fight 800 (which in July 1996 exploded and crashed into the Atlantic Ocean off the coast of Long Island, killing all 230 people aboard) the* World Almanac and Book of Facts *said, "During a long and painstaking process of retrieving and analyzing wreckage, authorities investigated whether the explosion had been caused by mechanical failure, a terrorist bomb, or a missile."*

Pinocchio didn't know whether or not the fairy was kidding with him. But mostly, he didn't know where to hide his shame. He tried to escape from the room, but his nose had grown so long that he couldn't get through the door!

Chapter 14 "The Field of Wonders"

Crying as if his heart would break, Pinocchio **mourned**[1] for hours over the length of his nose. No matter how he tried, it wouldn't go through the door. The fairy showed no pity toward him, for she was trying to teach him a lesson that would put an end to his **habitual**[2] lying once and for all. But when she saw him pale with fright and with his eyes half out of his head from terror, she weakened. Perhaps the circumstances didn't **warrant**[3] such drastic measures after all. Feeling sorry for him, she clapped her hands together and a thousand woodpeckers flew in through the window and settled themselves on Pinocchio's nose. They pecked and pecked so hard at his nose that in a few moments it was the same size as before.

"How good you are, my fairy," said Pinocchio, drying his eyes, "and how much I love you!"

"I love you, too," answered the fairy, "and if you wish to stay with me, you may be my brother and I'll be your good sister."

"I would like to stay...but what about my poor father?"

"I've thought of everything. Your father has been sent for, and before nightfall he'll be here."

---

[1] **mourn (mourned)** To *mourn* is to feel or express grief or sorrow (about something). *When President John F. Kennedy was assassinated (November 1963), his death was mourned throughout the world.*

[2] **habitual** This is the adjective form of the word *habit*. Anything (a behavior, action, etc.) done *habitually* is done in the nature of a habit; that is, it's done regularly, frequently, repeatedly, etc. (as in *the English are habitual tea drinkers*). *The cuckoo bird habitually flips its tail in all directions.*

[3] **warrant** If you say that something *warrants* a particular course of action, you mean that it provides sufficient grounds for (or justifies) that course of action. *President Theodore Roosevelt believed that weakness or wrongdoing in Latin American countries warranted U.S. intervention into the affairs of those countries.*

"Really?" cried Pinocchio joyfully. "Then, my good sister, if you're willing, I'd like to go to meet him. I can't wait to kiss that dear old man, who has suffered so much for my sake."

"How do you feel?"

"I feel fine. More than fine. Really."

"Okay, go ahead. But be careful not to lose your way — and don't run! Take the path through the woods and you'll surely meet him."

Pinocchio set out and soon found himself in the woods. When he reached the tall oak tree he stopped, for he thought he heard a rustle in the bushes. He was right. There stood the fox and the cat, the two traveling companions with whom he'd eaten at the Red Lobster Inn.

"Here comes our dear Pinocchio!" cried the fox, hugging and kissing him. "What are you doing here?"

"Doing here?" repeated the cat.

"It's a long story," said the puppet. "The other night, when you left me alone at the inn, I met killers on the road."

"Killers? Oh, you poor thing! How **traumatic**[1] for you! What did they want?"

"They wanted my gold pieces."

"Scoundrels!" said the fox.

"The worst sort of scoundrels!" added the cat.

"But I began to run," continued the puppet, "and they followed after me, until they overtook me and hung me to the branch of that oak tree." Pinocchio pointed to the tall oak nearby.

---

[1] **traumatic** Any extreme, lasting emotional wound (as from violence or childhood abuse, for example) is known as a *trauma*. If something is *traumatic*, it results from or is in the nature of a trauma; that is, it's frightful, alarming, tragic, awful, etc. *In October 1984, speaking of the opening of St. Mary's Hospital (New York City's first facility for terminally ill children), Executive Director Dr. Burton Grebin said, "The death of a child is the single most traumatic event in medicine; to lose a child is to lose a piece of yourself."*

"Could anything be worse?" said the fox. "What an awful world to live in! Where can gentlemen like us find a safe place?"

As the fox talked, Pinocchio noticed that the cat carried his right paw in a sling.

"What happened to your paw?" he asked.

The cat began to answer, but his stammering explanation became so **garbled**[1] that the fox jumped in to help him out.

"Please excuse my friend's **disjointed**[2] **narrative**[3], but the truth is, he's much too **unassuming**[4] to **articulate**[5] what really

---

[1] **garbled** This word is used to describe speech or writing that's mixed up, distorted, hard to understand, etc. *Because Neil Armstrong's first words from the moon's surface (July 1969) were slightly garbled by static, they were understood to be "One small step for man, one giant leap for mankind"; what he actually said (quoted the following day in the* New York Times*) was "That's one small step for a man, one giant leap for mankind."*

[2] **disjointed** If you say that speech or writing is *disjointed*, you mean that it's not properly connected; that is, it's out of order, broken up, jumbled, etc. *In his novel* Ulysses *(1922), Irish author James Joyce employed a technique known as "stream of consciousness," in which he used disjointed language to reflect the rambling, fragmentary thoughts of the human mind.*

[3] **narrative** A *narrative* is a spoken (or sometimes written) story or account (whether true or fictitious) of events, experiences, etc. *Most religious narratives involve some kind of miracle.*

[4] **unassuming** This word describes people who are not self-important, bossy, boastful, or showy; they are modest, quiet, simple, plain, etc. *Speaking of First Lady Martha Washington, Abigail Adams (wife of Vice President John Adams) once said, "Her manners are modest and unassuming, dignified and feminine."*

[5] **articulate** As a verb, to *articulate* (pronounced ar-TIK-u-late) is either to express (oneself) in words, as in *articulate one's emotions*, or to pronounce (one's) words clearly and distinctly. *When he arrived, he was too out of breath and upset to articulate a single word.* As an adjective, if you say that someone is *articulate* (pronounced ar-TIK-u-lit), you mean that he uses language (or puts his thoughts into words) easily, fluently, and effectively. *An articulate speaker, conductor Leonard Bernstein (1918–1990) won fame for his ability to explain music clearly to people with little musical knowledge.*

happened. What he tried to say — if I may **paraphrase**[1] — is that about an hour ago we met an old wolf on the road. He was starving and begged for help. Having nothing to give him, my good friend here, out of the kindness of his heart, bit off his own front paw and gave it to the poor beast, so that he might have something to eat."

As he spoke, the fox wiped away a tear.

Pinocchio, almost in tears himself, whispered into the cat's ear, "If all cats were like you, how lucky mice would be!"

"What are you doing now?" the fox asked.

"I'm waiting for my good father, who'll be here any minute."

"And your gold pieces?"

"I still have them in my pocket, except one that I spent at the Red Lobster Inn."

"To think," said the fox, "that those four gold pieces might become about two thousand tomorrow. Why don't you listen to me? Why don't you **sow**[2] them in the Field of Wonders? Do that and you'll be living on easy street."

"Where's that?"

---

[1] **paraphrase** When you *paraphrase* something written or spoken, you restate it using different words. The implication is that the new statement is more easily understood and perhaps shorter than the original. As a noun, a *paraphrase* is such a restatement. *The so-called Golden Rule ("Do unto others as you would have them do unto you") is actually a paraphrase of a passage from the New Testament: "All things whatsoever ye would that men should do to you, do ye even so to them."*

[2] **sow** To *sow* (rhymes with *go*) seeds is to scatter or plant them (so that they will grow into crops). The word is sometimes used figuratively to refer to the planting, introduction, or spreading of anything (as in *sow distrust* or *sow rumors*). *In Greek mythology, a prince named Cadmus killed a dragon and sowed its teeth; from them sprang an army of men.*

"Ha, ha! No, it's not a real street. "Easy street" is a just a **colloquialism**[1]. When I used that phrase I meant to **imply**[2] that you'll be rich and you'll have a life of ease!"

"Oh. Well, today it's impossible. I'll go with you some other time."

"But another day will be too late," said the fox.

"Why?"

"Because the field has been sold. You know, of course, that the government keeps a list of fields that are open to the public. Tomorrow, sad to say, the Field of Wonders will be **deleted**[3] from the **roster**[1]."

---

[1] **colloquial (colloquialism)** This word describes speech or writing that is informal, conversational, familiar, everyday (rather than formal). A *colloquialism* is a colloquial word or phrase. *In her written report, the teacher indicated that the new student had become "extremely upset"; but later, when she told her husband about it, she said, colloquially, that the student had "freaked out."*

[2] **imply** If you say that a person *implies* something (a thought or meaning, for example), you mean that he express it indirectly; he hints at it, suggests it, etc. *Austrian-born American psychologist Bruno Bettelheim (1903–1990) once said, "Translators need to be very sensitive to not only what is written but also to what is implied."* If you say that an idea or thing *implies* something, you mean that it indirectly conveys the truth or existence of something (a certain understood meaning or consequence, for example). *In 1984 Princeton University professor George Kennan said, "The very concept of history implies the scholar and the reader; without a generation of civilized people to study history, to absorb its lessons and relate them to its own problems, history, too, would lose its meaning."* The noun is *implication.*

[3] **delete (deleted)** To *delete* something (a written or printed word, passage, or symbol, for example) is to remove it, take it out, erase it, omit it, etc. *English editor Thomas Bowdler is famous for his 1818 edition of Shakespeare's plays (called* The Family Shakespeare*), in which he deleted words and expressions he considered improper for family reading.*

"Well, how far is this Field of Wonders?"

"Only two miles away. Will you come with us? We'll be there in half an hour. You can plant the money, and, after a few minutes, you'll **reap²** your two thousand coins and return home rich. Are you coming?"

Pinocchio was still **reluctant³**, for he remembered the good fairy, old Geppetto, and the advice of the cricket. If he was aware that today the fox claimed that it takes only a few minutes for gold coins to blossom, whereas earlier he'd said that it takes all night, he didn't mention the **discrepancy⁴**.

"Have you ever heard the expression 'He who hesitates is lost'?" asked the fox.

"I think so. What does it mean?"

---

¹ **roster** A *roster* is a list. Although it especially refers to a list of names (as members of a sports team, for example), it can refer to any type of list (as in *a roster of coming events*). *According to* Compton's Encyclopedia, *"When [Massachusetts] was the literary and cultural center of the nation, its roster of writers and philosophers included such names as Ralph Waldo Emerson, Nathaniel Hawthorne, Henry David Thoreau, Robert Frost, Emily Dickinson, and Herman Melville."*

² **reap** To *reap* a crop is to cut it, gather it, collect it, etc. *Thanksgiving is a U.S. national holiday that honors the memory of the harvest reaped by the Pilgrim colonists in 1621.* Note: The word can also be used to refer to the taking or gaining of anything at all, as in *reap profits* or *reap rewards*.

³ **reluctant** If you say that you're *reluctant* to do some particular thing, you mean that you hesitate or hold back because to some extent you're opposed to it. The implication is that you may go ahead and do it, even though it may be against your better judgment. The noun is *reluctance*. *In his first inaugural address (January 1981), President Ronald Reagan said, "Our reluctance for conflict [with other nations] should not be misjudged as a failure of will; when action is required to preserve our national security, we will act."*

⁴ **discrepancy** A *discrepancy* is a lack of agreement between two things (facts or claims, for example) that should match; a difference, inconsistency, etc. *A slight discrepancy exists between the length of a year as measured by our calendar (365.2425 days) and the length of a year as measured by one complete revolution of the earth around the sun (365.2422 days).*

"It means that if you spend too much time **deliberating**[1] about what to do, you lose the chance to act altogether."

"Yes, but—"

"Do you mean" interrupted the fox, "to stand there and tell me that you're content with being poor, that you don't care about enjoying the **niceties**[2] of civilized life—fine dining, stylish clothes, silk sheets?"

"Well, I—"

"And what about your education? You don't want to **skimp**[3] on that, do you? Once you become rich, you'll be able

---

[1] **deliberate (deliberating)** When you *deliberate* (pronounced *dih-LIB-er-ate*) about something (a choice to be made, for example), you consider it carefully and often slowly; you weigh it (in your mind), think it through, etc. When a group of people *deliberate*, they consult with each other in order to reach a decision (as in *the jury deliberated for three hours*). The noun is *deliberation*. *In a July 1965 press conference concerning the Vietnam War, President Lyndon Johnson said, "After this past week of deliberations, I have concluded that it is not essential to order Reserve units into service now."* Note: As an adjective, the word (pronounced *dih-LIB-er-it*) means "intentional; on purpose" (as in *deliberate dishonesty* or *deliberate misspelling*).

[2] **niceties** If you're talking about style of living, *niceties* are refined, elegant, choice, or sometimes dainty features. *According to the* Washington Post, *Los Angeles's Westwood Marquis hotel features "such niceties as real coat hangers and feather pillows."* If you're talking about objects, actions, ideas, etc., *niceties* are fine points (small details, subtle distinctions, etc.). *In February 1989 journalist Joan Reinthaler said that the members of the Smithson String Quartet "are schooled in the niceties if 18th-century performance practices."* If you're talking about etiquette or manners, *niceties* are social courtesies, pleasantries. *Author A. T. Ellis once wrote of a character: "She could no more be bothered with the niceties of drawing-room small talk than could a fox."*

[3] **skimp** To skimp is to scrimp; that is, it's to economize, to avoid waste or unnecessary expense, to be thrifty or stingy. *Author Jacques Pepin once wrote of a "deceitful cook who skimps on ingredients and shortchanges guests."*

to attend one of those **prestigious**[1] private schools out in the country."

"Yes, but—"

Just then the fox turned to the cat and, loudly enough so that the puppet would overhear, and with a slight space between each word for dramatic effect, mock-whispered into his ear, "This **demented**[2] **lunatic**[3] actually *likes* being poor!" Then the fox and cat both burst out laughing.

And Pinocchio ended up doing what most boys do when they don't have much inner strength or common sense. He shrugged his shoulders and said to the fox and cat, "Let's go!"

And they went.

They walked and walked for at least half a day and at last they came to a place called Fool's Trap. As soon as they entered the town, Pinocchio saw that all the houses were **di-**

---

[1] **prestige (prestigious)** *Prestige* refers to someone or something's high standing or importance among others, as in *a position of great prestige,* or to the level of respect at which someone or something is regarded by others (whether high or not), as in *his prestige rose when he was elected class president.* The adjective is *prestigious,* which means "having a high reputation," as in *the Oscar is the film industry's most prestigious award. In August 1980, speaking of office workers, the* New York Times *said that "windows [in one's office] are as essential to prestige as Christmas is to retailing."*

[2] **demented** In psychiatry, *dementia* is a loss of intellectual faculties (such as memory, concentration, judgment, etc.). If someone is *demented,* he suffers from dementia; in other words, he's mentally ill, insane, mad, crazy, nuts, etc. *In his 1855 poem "Song of Myself," Walt Whitman said of animals: "Not one is dissatisfied; not one is demented [by an obsession with] owning things."*

[3] **lunatic** It was once believed that the changing phases of the moon could cause insanity. The Latin word for *moon* is *luna.* A *lunatic* is a person who is insane or one whose behavior is highly abnormal; a madman, maniac, nut, etc. *According to the* Dictionary of Cultural Literacy, *"In his story 'The Tell-Tale Heart,' Edgar Allan Poe makes his narrator a raving lunatic."*

lapidated[1] and all the stores were closed. Peering through the grimy window of one store he noticed that everything inside was dusty and in **disarray**[2]. Looking into another he saw nothing but piles of **rubble**[3].

In the streets he saw **mangy**[4] dogs whose mouths were wide open from hunger. He saw large butterflies who couldn't fly because they'd had to sell their colorful wings. He saw peacocks who were ashamed to be seen because they'd had to sell their beautiful tails.

---

[1] **dilapidated** If something (a building or automobile, for example) is *dilapidated*, it's in a state of disrepair or decay (as from age, wear, misuse, etc.); it's broken-down, shabby, etc. *In 1205 Italian Roman Catholic monk Saint Francis of Assisi began treating lepers and restoring dilapidated churches.*

[2] **disarray** If something (a person's clothing or hair, or a country's government or economy, for example) is in *disarray*, it's in a state of disorder or confusion; it's disorganized, mixed up, messed up, etc. *In July 1975, Boston University President John Silber said, "The younger generation finds a special value in the costumes of poverty and disarray simply because these aspects of life have become far scarcer for children of the middle class than good clothes and [attractiveness]."*

[3] **rubble** Technically, *rubble* denotes broken or crumbled pieces of stone or brick. But people generally use this word to refer to the worthless remains or remnants of anything that has been destroyed, whether by natural or human forces (wreckage, debris, ruins, etc.). Or sometimes they simply use it as a synonym for "rubbish" (garbage, trash, etc.). *Entire sections of London were reduced to rubble during 1940's Battle of Britain (in which German planes bombed the city for 57 nights).*

[4] **mangy** Technically, if an animal is *mangy*, it suffers from *mange* (a skin disease caused by mites and characterized by infected patches of skin, itching, and hair loss). But in general usage, if you say that something is *mangy*, you mean that it's worn out, shabby, filthy, moth-eaten, etc. (as in *a mangy carpet*), or that it looks sickly, scabby, scaly, etc. *U.S. author John Steinbeck (1902–1968) once said, "A book is like a man – clever and dull, brave and cowardly, beautiful and ugly; for every flowering thought there will be a page like a wet and mangy [dog]."*

The fox lightly elbowed Pinocchio in the ribs, cocked his chin toward these poor souls, and whispered, "The **dregs**[1] of society."

Through this crowd of **paupers**[2], a **lavishly**[3] decorated coach passed now and then. Within each one sat an **elegantly**[4] dressed fox or hawk.

"Where is the Field of Wonders?" asked Pinocchio, growing tired of waiting.

"Be patient. It's only a few more steps away."

They passed through the city and its little, **ramshackle**[1] homes, and Pinocchio wondered how people could live in such **hovels**[2].

---

[1] **dregs** Small pieces of solid matter that naturally settle at the bottom of a liquid (wine, for example) are known as *dregs*. By extension, the word can be used to refer to any tiny bits of worthless matter, or to people who are considered undesirable, low-class, coarse, etc. *According to the* Reader's Companion to American History, *Gerald Ford will be remembered as a President "whose historic role it was to mop up the dregs of the two most damaging episodes in the history of the modern White House: the Watergate affair and the Vietnam War."*

[2] **pauper (paupers)** A *pauper* is a person who is extremely poor, especially one with no means of support who depends on the charity of others. *In ancient Greece, citizenship was denied to women, slaves, paupers, and foreigners.*

[3] **lavish (lavishly)** A person described as *lavish* is either very free or overly free in spending or giving (as in *the millionaire was lavish with his money*). A thing described as *lavish* is either very great or overly great in amount, number, quantity, quality, etc. (as in *lavish helpings of dessert*). *In 1967 actor Richard Burton said of his wife, actress Elizabeth Taylor, "She is an extremely beautiful woman, lavishly endowed by nature"; then he added that "she has a double chin, her legs are too short, and she has a slight potbelly."*

[4] **elegant (elegantly)** Things (art objects, clothing, one's handwriting, etc.) that are *elegant* exhibit graceful, tasteful, or refined beauty. People who are *elegant* are refined, sophisticated, well-dressed, well-spoken, polished, etc. *According to the* Dictionary of Cultural Literacy, *the Presidency of John F. Kennedy "was known for its dazzling, stylish quality, partly because of his elegant wife, Jacqueline."*

"Why don't these people fix their broken-down homes?" the puppet asked the fox.

"You know, when these **sordid**[3] little houses were brand-new, they really looked rather pretty. But because they were made of **shoddy**[4] materials, they quickly fell into disrepair. Of course, the owners would like to fix them up, but they just don't have the money for the **renovations**[5]." Then, shaking his head: "It's a curse to be poor. A curse!"

---

[1] **ramshackle** If something (a house, for example) is *ramshackle*, it's poorly constructed, loosely held together, or in a state of disrepair; that is, it's rickety, shaky, flimsy, shabby, etc. *In olden times, traveling theater groups often performed in ramshackle buildings and barns; if, after a performance, the audience clapped loudly enough, they'd literally "bring down the house."*

[2] **hovel (hovels)** A *hovel* is a small, miserable, dirty, ugly house; a shack, slum, dump, etc. *On pre–Civil War Southern plantations, slaves lived in hovels while their masters lived in beautiful mansions.*

[3] **sordid** If a physical thing (a shack, for example) is *sordid*, it's dirty, filthy, etc., especially depressingly or miserably so. *The 1948 anti-apartheid novel* Cry, the Beloved Country *depicts sordid living conditions in the slums of Johannesburg, South Africa.* If a non-physical thing (one's behavior, a situation, etc.) is *sordid*, it's morally shameful, degraded, depraved, etc. *Speaking of sentencing 12 men convicted of Britain's 1963 Great Train Robbery, judge Edmund Davies said, "Let us clear any romantic notion of daredeviltry from our minds; [the robbery] is nothing less than a sordid crime of violence inspired by vast greed."*

[4] **shoddy** Things (houses, cars, furniture, etc.) that are *shoddy* are made of inferior materials (though sometimes they falsely appear as if they're made of superior materials); they're cheap, cheesy, flimsy, poorly made, etc. *The June 1995 collapse of a Seoul, South Korea, department store (in which hundreds of shoppers were killed) was blamed on shoddy construction.*

[5] **renovate (renovations)** To *renovate* something (a building, for example) is to restore it to good condition (by repairing it, replacing broken or worn parts, etc.); to make it look new (or as if new) again. *In 1902 First Lady Edith Roosevelt (wife of President Theodore Roosevelt) oversaw a major renovation of the White House.*

"Can't they get money by planting coins in the Field of Wonders?"

"They're not as lucky as you. They earn a bare **subsistence**[1] and no more. They have no coins to plant—not even a penny."

"Not even a penny," repeated the cat.

Just outside the walls of the town, they stepped into a **bleak**[2] field that looked pretty much like any other field.

"Here we are!" exclaimed the fox. He pointed down at a spot near the center of the field and said to the puppet, "Dig a hole right there and put the gold pieces into it."

The puppet eagerly obeyed. He dug the hole, put the four gold pieces into it, and covered them up very carefully. In his

---

[1] **subsistence** To *subsist* is to remain alive (especially to remain alive by having access to food and other items necessary for life), as in *hamsters subsist mostly on cereal grains.* The noun *subsistence* refers to the condition (or fact) of being or staying alive, or to a means (especially a barely sufficient means) of staying alive (as in *coconuts and crabs provided a subsistence for the shipwrecked sailor*). *In his second inaugural address (January 1937), President Franklin D. Roosevelt said, "I see a United States which can demonstrate that, under democratic methods of government, the lowest standard of living can be raised far above the level of mere subsistence."*

[2] **bleak** If you say that a physical thing or place (a landscape, for example) is *bleak*, you mean that it's barren, empty, bare, without ornamentation, etc. *Before going "over the rainbow" to the Land of Oz, Dorothy lived on a bleak Kansas farm.* If you say that a non-physical thing (one's future, one's prospects, one's outlook, etc.) is *bleak*, you mean that it provides no encouragement; it's depressing, gloomy, disheartening, etc. *In January 1973 President Richard Nixon began his second inaugural address as follows: "When we met here four years ago, America was bleak in spirit, depressed by the prospect of seemingly endless war abroad and of destructive conflict at home. As we meet here today, we stand on the threshold of a new era of peace in the world."*

excitement he forgot all about the unfortunate **inhabitants**[1] of Fool's Trap.

"Now," said the fox, "go to that brook that runs **adjacent**[2] to the field, bring back a pail full of water, and sprinkle it over the spot."

Pinocchio followed the directions closely, but, as he had no pail, he was forced to **improvise**[3]. He pulled off a shoe and filled it with water. Then, carefully carrying the shoe so that no water would spill, he returned to the spot where the coins were buried and sprinkled the ground. "Anything else?" he asked.

"Nothing else," answered the fox. He scanned the skies and then stuck out his paw as if to feel the air temperature.

---

[1] **inhabitant (inhabitants)** To *inhabit* a particular place is to live in that place (as in *small animals inhabit the woods*). To refer to someone as an *inhabitant* of a particular place is to say that he inhabits (lives in) that place; he's a resident, dweller, occupant, etc. *According to* The Columbia Dictionary of Quotations, *in (French author) Cyrano de Bergerac's* The Other World: States and Empires of the Moon *(1656), "the inhabitants of the moon tell time by using a natural sundial formed by their long noses, which project their shadows onto the 'dial' of their teeth."*

[2] **adjacent** If two things are *adjacent* to each other, they're lying next to each other; they're touching, bordering, adjoining, neighboring, etc. *Minnesota's "twin cities" are Minneapolis (the state's largest city) and the adjacent St. Paul (the state's capital).*

[3] **improvise** If you're talking about performing arts (music, dance, acting, etc.), to *improvise* is to create or make up parts (melodies, steps, dialogue, etc.) on the spur of the moment, as you perform (as in *improvise a jazz solo*). If you're talking about a particular problematic situation, to *improvise* is to quickly or offhandedly prepare or provide something by creatively making do with whatever materials happen to be available. *During the boring train ride we improvised a checkers set by using nickels, pennies, and a piece of paper with squares drawn on it.*

"With today's **optimal**[1] weather conditions, the tree should sprout in no time. Now go for a walk, but return here in twenty minutes. By then the tree will have grown and its branches will be loaded with gold coins!"

Pinocchio, beside himself with joy, thanked the fox and the cat many times as they all began to walk from the field. Finally, he promised them each a beautiful gift.

"As we've said before, we don't want any gifts," answered the fox. "Even to take a single coin as a mere **memento**[2] would be unthinkable. We're here only to help others, and it's more than enough for us to have shown you how to become rich with little or no trouble. For this we are as happy as can be."

"Happy as can be," repeated the cat.

They said good-bye to Pinocchio and, wishing him luck, went on their way.

---

[1] **optimal** If you say that something (a set of circumstances, a condition, etc.) is *optimal*, you mean that it's the best that it can be; it's the most favorable or desirable; it's ideal, choice, excellent, etc. *An automobile's fuel injection system produces an optimal mixture of gasoline and air (for combustion in the engine).*

[2] **memento** A *memento* is anything (an object, for example) that serves as a reminder of something (a past event, an absent person, something that once existed, etc.); a souvenir, keepsake, etc. Note: Be careful to spell and pronounce the second letter of this word with an "e" *(memento)*, not an "o" *(momento)*. *In his will, Johnny Weissmuller — who in the 1920s won five Olympic gold medals for swimming and in the 1930s and '40s portrayed Tarzan in films — donated his collection of mementos to a foundation to help disadvantaged children.*

Chapter 15 "Pinocchio Goes to Jail"

If Pinocchio had been told to wait a day instead of twenty minutes, the time could not have seemed longer to him. He walked some distance from the field, then impatiently paced back and forth for about ten minutes. Finally he turned his nose back toward the Field of Wonders.

As he walked with hurried steps, his heart pounded and his busy brain kept thinking: "What if, instead of two thousand, I find five thousand—or one hundred thousand? First I'll buy myself a **palatial**[1] mansion. Then I'll dress myself from head to toe in **regal**[2] splendor. Then I'll buy hundreds of ponies to play with, and then I'll fill my kitchen with lollipops, ice cream, and candy."

---

[1] **palatial** This word (pronounced *puh-LAY-shul*) is the adjective form of the word *palace*. If you say that something is *palatial*, you mean that its size or fanciness is suggestive of or suitable for a palace; that is, it's stately, magnificent, luxurious, splendid, etc. *The city of Newport, Rhode Island, is famous for its jazz festivals, yacht races, and palatial mansions.*

[2] **regal** If you describe something (clothing, a banquet, a parade, etc.) as *regal*, you mean that it pertains to, is befitting of, or resembles a king or queen; it's majestic, stately, splendid, etc. *According to Compton's Encyclopedia, a dog named Saur was the "king" of Norway for three years during the 11th century (the real king, angry because his subjects had once removed him from power, placed Saur on the throne and demanded that he be treated regally).*

He amused himself with this **fanciful**[1] **reverie**[2] until he arrived back at the edge of the field. There he stopped to see if, by any chance, a tree filled with gold coins was in sight. When he saw nothing, his daydreams of **sumptuous**[3] living came to an abrupt halt. He took a few steps forward but still saw nothing! He ran to the place where he had dug the hole and buried the gold pieces. He stared down at the ground. Again nothing! He got down on his hands and knees and **scrutinized**[4] the earth inch by inch. Again nothing. Pinocchio became very thoughtful and scratched his head.

---

[1] **fanciful** A *fancy* is a mental image, especially one that is strange or fantastic. If something is *fanciful*, it's characterized by or exhibits fancy; that is, it's imaginary, unreal, make-believe, etc., and at the same time often curious, queer, odd, etc. *Long before man traveled by rocket to the moon, science fiction writers suggested all sorts of fanciful methods of getting there.* Note: The word can also mean "showing creativity or originality in design; imaginative," as in *fanciful Halloween costumes.*

[2] **reverie** A *reverie* is a state of dreamy thought (of pleasant things). If you're "in a reverie," you're lost in thought; you're daydreaming. *In 1769 future President Thomas Jefferson said that if a story we read is "lively and a [fairly good] picture of nature, we are thrown into a reverie, from which if we awaken it is the fault of the writer."*

[3] **sumptuous** If something (a residence, a banquet, etc.) is *sumptuous*, it's characterized by great expense or luxury; it's extravagant, magnificent, splendid, costly, etc. *On Thanksgiving Day, many Americans enjoy a sumptuous dinner of roast turkey, stuffing, cranberry sauce, pumpkin pie, and other treats.* Note: Sometimes the word means "rich in detail," as in *sumptuous theatrical sets* or *a sumptuous orchestral score.*

[4] **scrutinize (scrutinized)** To *scrutinize* something is to look at it or examine it with great care or in great detail; to inspect it, study it, etc. The noun is *scrutiny. In August 1897, Ronald Ross (the British physician who discovered that mosquitoes transmit malaria) wrote in his journal: "[The mosquito] stomach tissues still remained to be examined — lying there before me on the glass slide, a great white expanse of cells like a great courtyard of flagstones, each of which must be scrutinized."*

As he did so, he heard a hearty burst of laughter. He stood and turned sharply, and there on the branch of a tree sat a large parrot, busily grooming his feathers.

"What are you laughing at?" Pinocchio asked **peevishly**[1].

"I'm laughing because, while I was cleaning myself, I tickled myself under my wing."

The puppet didn't answer. He walked to the brook, filled his shoe with water, and once more sprinkled the ground that covered the gold pieces.

Another burst of laughter, even louder than the first, was heard in the quiet field.

"Well," cried the puppet, angrily this time, "will you tell me what's so funny?"

"I'm laughing at those fools who believe everything they hear and allow themselves to be **deluded**[2]."

"Are you **insinuating**[1], perhaps, that I'm one of those fools?"

---

[1] **peevish (peevishly)** People who are *peevish* tend to complain a lot; they are easily exasperated; they're grouchy, irritable, disagreeable, etc. *According-ing to* Compton's Encyclopedia, *when English novelist Charles Dickens (1812–1870) visited Illinois (during his 1942 tour of the U.S.), "he became peevish, impa-tient of small discomforts, resenting the fact that hotelkeepers dared to talk to him."*

[2] **delude (deluded)** To *delude* someone is to thoroughly deceive him; to fool him or trick him into believing that something false is true; to dupe him, bamboozle him, etc. *In 1958 newscaster Edward R. Murrow said, "Don't be deluded into believing that the heads of [radio and TV] networks control what ap-pears on their [network's news programs]; they all have better taste."* The noun *delusion* can refer to either an act or instance of deluding (someone) or to any strongly held false belief (as when a mental patient suffers from the delusion that he is Napoleon, for example). *In 1991 journalist P. J. O'Rourke joked, "It is a popular delusion that the [American] government wastes vast amounts of money through inefficiency and [laziness]; enormous effort and elabo-rate planning are required to waste this much money."*

"I certainly am, poor Pinocchio. The notion that gold coins can be **harvested**[2] from a field is **fallacious**[3] — and you're a fool to believe it. I, too, once believed that it's possible to **amass**[4] a great fortune without doing any work, and today I'm very sorry for it. I've discovered, but too late, one of the

---

[1] **insinuate (insinuating)** To *insinuate* a thought or idea is to state it indirectly; to hint at it, suggest it, imply it, etc. *In February 2000 a* Washington Post *editorial noted that Republican Presidential candidate John McCain "has insinuated that George W. Bush lacks the experience and knowledge to be President."* To *insinuate* yourself into something or someplace where you're not necessarily wanted (a group of people, one's good graces, etc.) is to introduce or force yourself into it, especially by indirect or subtle means. *In 1903 Russian self-proclaimed holy man Rasputin insinuated himself into Russia's royal family (Czar Ncholas II and his wife Alexandra).* The noun *insinuation* refers either to an act or instance of insinuating or to a particular (usually unfavorable) suggestion. *In his first inaugural address (January 1953), President Dwight D. Eisenhower said, "We reject any insinuation that one race or another, one people or another, is in any sense inferior or expendable."*

[2] **harvest (harvested)** As a verb, to *harvest* crops is to gather them. By extension, the word can be used informally to refer to the receiving or gathering of any kind of benefits from any particular action (as in *harvest rich rewards*). As a noun, a *harvest* is a crop that has ripened and been gathered. By extension, the word can be used informally to refer to a supply of anything gathered or obtained (as in *a harvest of perpetual peace*). *In 1859 English playwright Douglas Jerrold said of Australia, "Earth is here so kind, that just tickle her with a hoe and she laughs with a harvest."*

[3] **fallacious** If you say that something (a concept, statement, etc.) is *fallacious*, you mean that it contains a falsehood or that it's logically unsound; it's erroneous, misleading, untrue, etc. Note: The noun *fallacy* refers to any false or mistaken notion. *The idea that eating meat makes one hostile and aggressive whereas eating a vegetarian diet makes one peaceful and mellow is fallacious —both Hitler and Mussolini were vegetarians.*

[4] **amass** To *amass* something (money, a collection of valuable or useful items, information, etc.) is to gather or accumulate it into a large quantity (for profit, pleasure, future use, etc.). *In the board game Monopoly, the player who amasses the most wealth is the winner.*

111

cardinal[1] rules of life: that in order to get money honestly, you must work for it—with your hands or brain."

"I don't know what you're talking about," said the puppet, who was beginning to tremble with fear.

"Have you ever noticed that in fables and **parables**[2] foxes are always portrayed as clever, **crafty**[3] creatures whose motives are always **suspect**[4]? That's because usually they really do have **ulterior**[5] motives."

"What do you mean?"

---

[1] **cardinal** If you describe something (a rule, principle, event, etc.) as *cardinal*, you mean that it's of primary (first, foremost) importance; that is, it's crucial, essential, fundamental, key, etc. The implication is that other things (future events, for example) depend or "hinge" on it (in fact, the word *cardinal* derives from the Latin word for *hinge*). *Austrian writer Franz Kafka (1883–1924) once said, "There are two cardinal sins from which all the others spring: impatience and laziness."*

[2] **parable (parables)** A *parable* is a short, simple story that conveys a moral lesson, religious principle, or universal truth. For example, two well-known biblical parables are the stories of the Good Samaritan and the Prodigal Son. *In 1978 English writer Malcolm Muggeridge (1903–1990) said, "Every happening, great and small, is a parable whereby God speaks to us, and the art of life is to get the message."*

[3] **crafty** People who are *crafty* cleverly use underhanded or sneaky methods or schemes to get what they want; they're shrewd, slick, sly, etc. *In Charles Dickens' Oliver Twist (1838), the crafty villain Fagin teaches young Oliver and other orphaned boys to pick pockets and steal for him.*

[4] **suspect** If you describe something (someone's motive, statement, or opinion, for example) as *suspect*, you mean that it should be regarded with suspicion, doubt, or mistrust. *You should never tell a lie because if you're caught, then everything else you say becomes suspect.*

[5] **ulterior** If something (a motive, purpose, meaning, etc.) is *ulterior*, it's intentionally kept secret or hidden—often so as to deceive. *In August 1998, when the U.S. conducted missile strikes against targets in Afghanistan, several critics of Bill Clinton raised the issue of possible ulterior motives on the part of the President (they questioned whether the attack had been launched to turn public attention from ongoing scandals concerning the President's personal life).*

"I mean that you've been **hoodwinked**[1]! I mean that you're the victim of a carefully calculated **hoax**[2]! Let me spell it out for you. First the fox and his **accomplice**[3] — that **despicable**[4] little **parasite**[5] — **beguiled**[1] you with fantastic stories of over-

---

[1] **hoodwink (hoodwinked)** To *hoodwink* someone is to fool or trick him; to pull the wool over his eyes; to dupe him, bamboozle him, etc. *In 1982 the New York Times was hoodwinked into unknowingly rerunning one of their old crossword puzzles (a California man took an old puzzle, switched the "across" with the "down" clues and answers, and sent it in).*

[2] **hoax** A *hoax* is either an act that is intended to trick or fool someone (especially a mischievous or playful one, such as a practical joke), or a thing (a photograph, a story, evidence, etc.) that is passed off as true but is actually false. *While some people believe that crop circles are created by aliens from outer space, others believe they are a hoax perpetrated by mischievous humans.*

[3] **accomplice** An *accomplice* is a person who helps another person commit a wrongdoing or criminal act. *On the same day that President Abraham Lincoln was assassinated by John Wilkes Booth (April 14, 1865), several of Booth's accomplices tried (unsuccessfully) to kill Secretary of State William Seward.*

[4] **despicable** If you say that someone or something is *despicable*, you mean that it deserves to be regarded with hate or disgust; it's awful, wicked, vile, miserable, etc. Note: This is the adjective form of the verb *despise* (see *despise*). *The day after the September 11th (2001) terrorist attacks, President George W. Bush said that the search for those behind the "evil, despicable acts of terror" was underway.*

[5] **parasite** Technically, a *parasite* is an animal or plant that lives in or on an organism of another species (for example, a tapeworm is a parasite that lives in human intestines). But when you refer to a person as a *parasite*, you mean that he's someone who lives on the hospitality of others (he takes money and free meals, for example) and gives nothing in return. *In her November 1964* Movie World *magazine article on actress Sandra Dee, journalist Carol Ardman wrote: "Every famous person meets up with many individuals who are nothing but parasites, but every famous person isn't lucky enough to be able to separate the parasites from those who are sincere."*

113

night wealth. Then, while you were taking a walk, they returned here in a great hurry. They took the four gold pieces you'd buried and **absconded**[2]."

Pinocchio's mouth opened wide. He refused to believe what the parrot said and began to claw **maniacally**[3] at the earth. But if he really expected to find sprouting gold coins buried in the soil, he was soon **disabused**[4] of that notion. He dug and dug until the hole was as big as he was, but no coins were found.

In desperation, he ran to the city and went straight to the courthouse to report the theft. But he had to wait thirty minutes on a hard bench before he could see the judge. He found a law book that someone had neglected to put away sitting on the bench next to him, and he busied himself by thumbing

---

[1] **beguile (beguiled)** To *beguile* someone is to trick or mislead him, especially by means of charm, flattery, or persuasion. *In the biblical story of Adam and Eve, a serpent (snake) beguiles Eve into eating the forbidden fruit of the tree of knowledge.* Note: The word can also mean simply "greatly amuse, charm, entertain, etc." *During the mid-20th century, Sammy Davis, Jr., beguiled audiences with his spirited singing and dancing.*

[2] **abscond (absconded)** To *abscond* is to leave (someplace) quickly, suddenly, and secretly, so as to avoid capture or arrest (for having committed a crime, for example); to flee from justice, escape, run off, etc. *In the 1960 horror classic* Psycho, *an employee, entrusted to deposit a large sum of cash at her company's bank, instead absconds with it to an isolated motel.*

[3] **maniacal (maniacally)** The adjective form of the noun *maniac* is *maniacal* (pronounced *muh-NIGH-uh-kul*). If you do something in a *maniacal* way, you do it as one who is a maniac might; that is, you do it with frenzy, franticness, wildness, violence, excessive excitement, etc. *During the 1950s and '60s, actor Vincent Price specialized in portraying horror film villains with deep, long, maniacal laughs.*

[4] **disabuse (disabused)** To *disabuse* someone is to rid him of a false notion or mistaken conception (that he holds); to set him straight, show him the truth, undeceive him, etc. *If, in 1765, the British government expected the American colonists to willingly pay a new stamp tax, they were disabused of that notion when the colonists angrily rose in protest.*

through it. But he couldn't make sense of its **convoluted**[1] legal language. He finally found himself standing before the judge, who had a flowing white beard and wore gold-rimmed glasses. Pinocchio **recounted**[2] the deception **perpetrated**[3] against him without leaving out a single detail. For a while the judge listened with great patience and seemed very interested in the strange **saga**[4]. Every so often he stroked his beard or removed his glasses. Then suddenly he put his glasses back on and

---

[1] **convoluted** Technically, if something (a seashell, a leaf, a human organ, etc.) is *convoluted*, it has overlapping folds (or coils, swirls, curls, etc.). But if you say that a non-physical thing (reasoning, language, a lawsuit, a plot, etc.) is *convoluted*, you mean that it's complicated, intricate, involved, etc. *The novels of William Faulkner (1929's* The Sound and the Fury, *for example) are known for their convoluted time sequences and their seemingly endless, convoluted sentences.*

[2] **recount (recounted)** To *recount* is to tell (either verbally or in writing) the facts or details of something that happened. The Iliad *is an epic poem by (ancient Greek poet) Homer that recounts the story of the Trojan War.*

[3] **perpetrate (perpetrated)** To *perpetrate* a crime or error (or wrongdoing, fraud, deception, practical joke, etc.) is to carry it out, commit it, perform it, execute it, etc. One who commits such an unwelcome or damaging act is known as a *perpetrator*. *In 1963 author Lesley Conger said, "Every act of dishonesty has at least two victims: the one we think of as the victim, and the perpetrator as well; each little dishonesty makes another little rotten spot somewhere in the perpetrator's psyche [mental makeup]."*

[4] **saga** A *saga* is a story or tale, especially a long, complicated one. *American filmmaker George Lucas wrote and directed the science fiction adventure* Star Wars *(1977); soon after, he wrote and produced two further episodes in the saga:* The Empire Strikes Back *(1980) and* Return of the Jedi *(1983).* Note: Sometimes the word refers specifically to a novel (1972's *The Godfather*, for example) that chronicles the history of several generations of a particular family.

said loudly and stiffly, "Don't **elaborate**[1] so much; just present those facts that are **pertinent**[2] to the actual crime." Pinocchio, flustered by the judge's harsh tone, quickly finished by mumbling, "The fox and the cat were the thieves."

"**Alleged**[3] thieves," answered the judge **brusquely**[4], reaching out and ringing a bell.

At the sound, two large work dogs appeared, dressed like policemen. Pointing to Pinocchio, the judge said, "The **gist**[5] of this puppet's story is that a fox and cat robbed him of four gold pieces—or so he claims. While there's no legal **prece-**

---

[1] **elaborate** When telling a story or explaining something, to *elaborate* (pronounced *ih-LAB-uh-rate*) is to give a longer or fuller treatment (by adding details, for example). The word is often followed by the preposition *on* or *upon*. *English scientist Sir Isaac Newton (1642–1727) elaborated on his theory of light in his book* Opticks *(1704).* Note: As an adjective, the word (pronounced *ih-LAB-uh-rit*) means "intricate; detailed; complicated," as in *an elaborate plan* or *elaborate machinery.*

[2] **pertinent** If you describe something as *pertinent*, you mean that it directly relates to the matter at hand; it's relevant, applicable, etc. *Before arguing a case in court, an attorney files a document called a brief, which outlines the pertinent facts of the case and the laws that apply to it.*

[3] **allege (alleged)** To *allege* something is to state or declare it to be true without proof. As an adjective, if you refer to something as *alleged* (as in *alleged murderer*, for example), you mean that it has been declared to be as described or designated, but without proof. *During the mid-20th century, the U.S. House of Representatives maintained a Committee on Un-American Activities, which was especially known for its investigation of alleged Communists.*

[4] **brusque (brusquely)** People who are *brusque* (in manner or speech) are rudely abrupt or brief; that is, they're blunt, ungracious, impatient, discourteous, etc. *In March 2000, journalist Mary McGrory described New York City mayor Rudolph Giuliani as "a tiger of a mayor, who, like his [fellow New Yorkers], is brusque, hostile, and given to communicating in insults."*

[5] **gist** The *gist* (pronounced *jist*) of something (an argument, explanation, story, speech, etc.) is the central or essential idea of it; the heart, substance, or essence of it. *The 1807 children's book* Tales from Shakespeare, *by Charles and Mary Lamb, contains the gist of many of the playwright's best-known works.*

dent[1] for a case concerning a victimized puppet, I do know that a case like this—where there's no **preponderance**[2] of evidence for either side—can be tied up in **litigation**[3] for years. We don't want that, do we? Luckily, as an officer of the court,

---

[1] **precedent** A *precedent* is an instance or case (of something) that may serve as an example or model for dealing with future similar instances or cases. *During the Revolutionary War, the Daughters of Liberty raised money for the colonists' army, setting a precedent that would be followed by future generations in wartime.* In law, the word refers specifically to a legal decision that may serve as an authoritative rule or model for future similar cases. *In 1734 the John Peter Zenger "freedom of the press" case (in which publisher Zenger was arrested for using his newspaper to publicly accuse the governor of New York of wrongdoing) established the precedent that printing criticism that is true is not illegal.* Note: If something happens that has never happened before, it is said to be *unprecedented. In 1940 Franklin D. Roosevelt won an unprecedented third term as President.*

[2] **preponderance** A *preponderance* is a greater number (or weight, power, influence, importance, etc.) of one thing, as compared to another (as in *a preponderance of women in the nursing field* or *the preponderance of matter over antimatter in the universe*). *Between 1900 and 1915 more than 13 million people immigrated to the United States, with the preponderance from southern and eastern Europe.*

[3] **litigation** To *litigate* is to bring about or carry on a lawsuit. The noun *litigation* (pronounced with the accent on the third syllable) is used to signify an act or instance of litigating, or to signify a particular lawsuit itself. *Before becoming (1967) the first black member of the U.S. Supreme Court, Thurgood Marshall practiced law, specializing in civil rights litigation.* Note: A person involved in a lawsuit (a plaintiff or defendant) is known as a *litigant* (pronounced with the accent on the first syllable). *The TV show* The People's Court *features real litigants arguing real cases before a real judge.* Also note: People who tend to initiate lawsuits or people who tend to dispute (things) or argue are said to be *litigious* (pronounced *lih-TIJ-us*).

it's my **prerogative**[1] to settle this case here and now—and that's what I intend to do." He scratched his head thoughtfully for a few moments, then continued, "This fellow here has made a number of **scandalous**[2] accusations. The way I see it is that while we don't know if he's actually **perjured**[3] himself, we do know that he's **defamed**[4] some worthy citizens

---

[1] **prerogative** A *prerogative* (pronounced with the accent on the second syllable) is an exclusive right, power, or privilege (to decide, judge, make rules, etc., or to behave in a certain way) granted a particular person by virtue of his position, office, rank, title, etc. (as in *the prerogative of a school principle to suspend a student* or *the prerogative of a parent to set a bedtime*). *In 1987 the* London Times *said that it is the "prerogative of [a politician's] wife to cough noisily when [her husband] goes on too long at the [speaker's platform]."*

[2] **scandalous** A *scandal* is a publicized incident about a person who has disgraced himself (as a result of illegal or immoral behavior, for example), or a publicized account of an event or situation that is offensive to the morals of society (the Watergate scandal, for example). If you refer to a statement as *scandalous*, you mean that it can cause scandal; that is, it's damaging to one's reputation. If you refer to an action as *scandalous*, you mean that it is deserving of scandal; that is, it's disgraceful, shameful, improper, shocking, outrageous, etc. *When Elvis Presley appeared on* The Ed Sullivan Show *in 1956, his hip swirling was considered so scandalous that he was shown only from the waist up.*

[3] **perjury (perjured)** The illegal act of telling a lie under oath (on the witness stand in court, for example) is known as *perjury*. As a verb, to *perjure* yourself is to commit this illegal act (that is, to tell a lie under oath). *In 1950 U.S. diplomat Alger Hiss was convicted of perjury for having denied he passed State Department secrets to a Communist agent.*

[4] **defame (defamed)** To *defame* someone is to attack his good name or reputation by making (often untrue) evil, harmful statements about him. As a noun, *defamation* (often heard in the phrase *defamation of character*) is an act or instance of (someone) defaming (another). *During the 1950s, many American actors, writers, and musicians were defamed (and their careers were destroyed) when they were falsely accused of being Communists or Communist Party sympathizers.*

and is guilty of **slander**[1]. Take him, therefore, and throw him in jail."

The puppet, on hearing this sentence passed upon him, was flabbergasted. "But the parrot will **corroborate**[2] my story!" he screamed in desperation. "Ask him!" But the **canine**[3] officers clapped their paws over his mouth and carried him off to jail.

Pinocchio had to remain in jail for four long, weary months. In the beginning, he spent all his time pacing his cell and thinking about how he might **extricate**[4] himself from this crazy mess. But he didn't merely want to be released from

---

[1] **slander** The illegal act of publicly making false oral (as opposed to written) statements hurtful or damaging to one's reputation is known as *slander*. Note: The illegal writing of such statements is known as *libel*. As a verb, to *slander* someone is to make such statement about him. Sometimes the word (whether noun or verb) is used informally to refer to any evil, hurtful talk (whether false or not and whether illegal or not). *In his book* Following the Equator *(1897), Mark Twain wrote: "It takes your enemy and your friend, working together, to hurt you to the heart: the one to slander you and the other to get the news to you."*

[2] **corroborate** To *corroborate* something (for example, a person's claim, story, account, testimony, etc., or an experiment's results, data, etc.) is to establish it as true or genuine (as by swearing to it under oath, providing additional evidence supporting it, etc.); to confirm it, verify it, prove it, back it up, etc. *In 1973 former White House counsel John Dean testified that President Richard Nixon knew of the Watergate cover-up; the subsequent release of taped conversations in which Nixon discussed the matter corroborated Dean's testimony.*

[3] **canine** As an adjective, this word means "pertaining to or characteristic of dogs; like a dog." As a noun, a *canine* is a dog. Note: Technically, the noun refers to any animal of the dog family (including wolves, coyotes, hyenas, foxes, etc.). *Lassie, the world's most famous canine movie and TV star, first appeared in the 1942 film* Lassie Come Home.

[4] **extricate** To *extricate* something (yourself, another person, an object, etc.) from something else (a tight spot, confinement, a difficult situation, etc.) is to free or release it; to disengage it, untangle it, etc. *In 1987 18-month-old Texas toddler Jessica McClure fell to the bottom of an 8-inch-wide, 22-foot-long abandoned well pipe; it took rescue crews 58 hours to extricate her.*

jail; he also wanted his honor **vindicated**[1]. At first he considered asking to speak to the judge again in order to **reiterate**[2] his innocence and to point out that an **objective**[3] analysis of the facts would prove that the fox and cat were indeed guilty. Failing that, he'd ask the judge to **extradite**[4] him back to his home town, where he knew he'd be able to convince any reasonable-minded authority of his innocence. But he was afraid to approach the judge for fear of an even worse punishment.

---

[1] **vindicate (vindicated)** To *vindicate* someone is to clear him of guilt, blame, accusation, or suspicion (by providing evidence that proves his innocence, for example). The implication is that his good name or reputation is restored. The noun is *vindication*. *In his resignation speech (August 1974), President Richard Nixon (who'd been accused of covering-up the Watergate affair) explained, "America needs a full-time President and a full-time Congress; to continue to fight through the months ahead for my personal vindication would almost totally absorb the time and attention of both."*

[2] **reiterate** To *reiterate* something (a statement, opinion, etc.) is to say it or state it again; to repeat it. *German-born American physicist Albert Einstein (1879–1955) once said, "Too many of us look upon Americans as dollar chasers; this is a cruel [accusation], even if it is reiterated thoughtlessly by the Americans themselves."*

[3] **objective** People's opinions can be either *objective* or *subjective*. An *objective* opinion is one based on fact, logic, etc. A *subjective* opinion is one based on one's personal feelings, gut instincts, etc. *In 1978 Russian writer Alexander Solzhenitsyn said, "I have spent all my life under a Communist regime, and I will tell you that a society without any objective legal scale is a terrible one indeed."*

[4] **extradite** To *extradite* someone (a lawbreaker or prisoner in a foreign land, for example) is to surrender him to another country or authority for trial or punishment. *In June 1968 James Earl Ray (assassin of Martin Luther King, Jr.) was captured in London and extradited to the U.S. for trial.*

After **methodically**[1] examining every **facet**[2] of the entire situation, he decided that the best idea would be to present his case to a higher authority here in Fool's Trap—an authority of unquestioned **integrity**[3], of course—who had the power to **countermand**[4] the judge's **edict**[5].

---

[1] **methodical (methodically)** To do something in a *methodical* way is to do it in a series of carefully planned, orderly steps; to do it systematically, logically, step by step, etc. *According to the* Reader's Companion to American History, *bird expert and naturalist artist John J. Audubon "was single-minded and methodical in his working methods; he traveled all over the United States to observe and collect birds, measured and dissected them, made careful field sketches."*

[2] **facet** Technically, a *facet* is one of the small, flat, smooth surfaces on a crystal, cut gemstone, rock, etc. But if you're referring to something non-physical (an idea, plan, argument, one's personality or career, etc.), a *facet* is one of numerous aspects (or parts, details, elements, etc.) of it. *In 1863 French composer Hector Berlioz wrote in a letter: "Music is the greatest of the arts; it is also the one which brings the greatest misery to those who understand it in all its facets."*

[3] **integrity** *Integrity* is an aspect of a person's character. People who have *integrity* are honest, moral, ethical, upright, etc. They do the right thing because it is part of their nature to do so (even when no one is watching!). *Baseball manager Leo Durocher once said, "I never question the integrity of an umpire; their eyesight, yes."* Note: If you're talking about a thing rather than a person, then *integrity* refers to the condition of being complete and perfect in every respect; the condition of being whole, sound, consistent throughout, etc. (for example, a letter written with the same pen throughout has integrity; a letter written with two dissimilar pens doesn't have integrity).

[4] **countermand** To *countermand* something (an order, rule, law, command, etc.) is to cancel or reverse it; to retract it, revoke it, etc. *In 1989, after the U.S. Supreme Court decided that burning the American flag in public to protest government policies is a right protected by the First Amendment, President George H. Bush asked that the decision be countermanded by a new constitutional amendment (but his idea was rejected by the Senate).*

[5] **edict** An *edict* is a command or regulation (a law, for example) put into effect by a ruler (a king, for example) or other lawful authority. *In 1616 the Roman Catholic Church issued an edict that one may never defend or teach (Polish astronomer) Copernicus's theory that the earth revolves around the sun.*

He began thinking about what he would say. He worked on his presentation **obsessively**[1] until it was perfectly formed in his mind. First he'd point out that a judge is seen by the public as a **bulwark**[2] against injustice and as such is expected to ensure the **equitable**[3] treatment of all citizens within his **jurisdiction**[4] by making fair, **disinterested**[1] decisions. Then

---

[1] **obsession (obsessively)** An *obsession* is an abnormal preoccupation with a particular thought or idea. In other words, if you can't stop thinking about a certain thing, you have an *obsession* about that thing. To do something *obsessively* is to do it in the nature of an obsession; that is, to do it continuously, compulsively, single-mindedly, etc. *In 1976 writer Gore Vidal said, "I am an obsessive rewriter, doing one draft and then another and another, usually five; in a way, I have nothing to say, but a great deal to add."* As a verb, to be *obsessed* by something is to have your thoughts dominated or preoccupied by it. *Columnist Dave Barry points out that many foods "are marketed as being low-fat or fat-free [because] Americans are obsessed with fat content."*

[2] **bulwark** Technically, a *bulwark* is a structure (a mound of earth, a wall, etc.) used as a defense against attack (as at a fort, for example). But in general usage, a *bulwark* is anything that offers any kind of protection (against danger, injury, etc.) or anyone who provides support or encouragement in time of need. *President Franklin D. Roosevelt once said, "The only sure bulwark of continuing liberty is a government strong enough to protect the interests of the people, and a people strong enough and well enough informed to maintain its control over its government."*

[3] **equitable** If you say that something (a settlement, deal, arrangement, etc.) is *equitable*, you mean that it's fair, impartial, just, right, etc. (as in *equitable distribution of wealth*). *Film star Lauren Bacall (born 1924) once said, "In Hollywood, an equitable divorce settlement means each party getting fifty percent of [the] publicity."*

[4] **jurisdiction** This word can signify either (1) the authority or power (of a person, court, etc.) to interpret and apply laws (as in *on a naval vessel the captain has jurisdiction*) or (2) the things or geographical areas over which such authority extends (as in *all districts south of the river are his jurisdiction*). *In the United States, the federal government has jurisdiction over some matters (the age at which one may vote, for example) and state governments have jurisdiction over others (the age at which one may drive, for example).*

he'd say that in this particular case, this judge demonstrated a **flagrant**[2] disregard for the truth. Next he'd claim that the judge is **bigoted**[3] against puppets and that his attitude, as evidenced by the unfair prison sentence, promotes a philosophy suggesting that **discrimination**[4] is acceptable. Then he'd

---

[1] **disinterested** If you refer to someone as *disinterested* (as in *a disinterested outsider*), you don't mean that he's not interested. You mean that he's fair, impartial, unbiased, etc. (because he is not swayed by his own interests). The implication is that he would thus be good at settling disputes between others in a fair, just manner. Likewise, a thing (a report, study, experiment, etc.) that is *disinterested* is one that is fair, objective, unbiased, etc. *Famed trial lawyer and author Louis Nizer once said, "Books are standing counselors and preachers, always at hand and always disinterested; having this advantage over oral instructors, that they are ready to repeat their lesson as often as we please."*

[2] **flagrant** If you describe something bad or objectionable (an error or evildoing, for example) as *flagrant*, you mean that it's outrageously noticeable or glaring (as in *a flagrant lie* or *a flagrant miscarriage of justice*). The implication is that the wrongdoing can't be missed and can't be forgiven. *In 1970 Supreme Court justice Hugo Black said, "The flagrant disregard in the courtroom of elementary standards of proper conduct should not and cannot be tolerated."*

[3] **bigot (bigoted)** A *bigot* is a person who looks down on or dislikes anyone who is not a member of his own race, religion, country, political party, etc. To be *bigoted* (toward a person or group) is to have such negative feelings (toward that person or group). The attitude of a bigot is known as *bigotry*. *African-American author Maya Angelou once said, "Perhaps travel cannot prevent bigotry, but by demonstrating that all peoples cry, laugh, eat, worry, and die, it can introduce the idea that if we try [to] understand each other, we may even become friends."*

[4] **discriminate (discrimination)** To *discriminate* against a person or group is to treat that person or group poorly or unjustly (in matters of education or employment, for example) because of their race, gender, religion, class, nationality, etc. The noun is *discrimination*. *New York Yankee great Lou Gehrig once said, "There is no room in baseball for discrimination; it is our national pastime and a game for all."* Note: In another sense, to *discriminate* is to be able to recognize fine distinctions between things (see *discriminating*).

try to further **discredit**[1] the judge by pointing out that he'd completely ignored every known legal **doctrine**[2], such as the right of the accused to speak to an attorney and to be given a trial before an **impartial**[3] jury. After that he'd claim that, with his **perverse**[4] **conception**[5] of justice, the judge had actually

---

[1] **discredit** To *discredit* someone is to cause him to lose his good name or reputation (by showing him to be untrustworthy, corrupt, etc.). *Senator Joseph McCarthy (who in the early 1950s wrongly accused many public figures of being Communists) was discredited in 1954 when the Senate said that his actions were "contrary to senatorial traditions."*

[2] **doctrine** A *doctrine* is a particular principle (or idea, belief, policy, etc.) taught or accepted by a particular group, especially a religious, political, scientific, or philosophic one (as in *the doctrine that all men are created equal* or *the doctrine of survival of the fittest*, for example). *In 1954, speaking of the unanimous U.S. Supreme Court decision that declared segregated schools unconstitutional, Chief Justice Earl Warren said, "In the field of public education, the doctrine of 'separate but equal' has no place."*

[3] **impartial** To be *impartial* (when making a determination about a dispute, for example) is to be fair and just; to favor neither side; to be evenhanded, unprejudiced, unbiased, etc. *Speaking of his attempts at painting, (British prime minister) Winston Churchill once said, "I cannot pretend to be impartial about colors; I rejoice with the brilliant ones and am genuinely sorry for the poor browns."*

[4] **perverse** If you say that someone or something is *perverse*, you mean that it's contrary to what is right or good; it's immoral, indecent, naughty, unwholesome, sinful, unnatural, etc. The noun is *perversion*. *Assassinated U.S. politician Harvey Milk (1931–1978) once said, "More people have been slaughtered in the name of religion than for any other single reason; that, my friends, is true perversion."*

[5] **conception** A *conception* is something that exists in the mind; that is, it's an idea (or thought, notion, understanding, plan, design, etc.), as in *a blind man with no conception of color* or *the popular conception that accountants have dull personalities*. The word often applies to a person's individual or peculiar idea about something (rather than a widely held idea), as in *Richard Nixon's conception of the role of the President*. *In 1923 Spanish artist Pablo Picasso said, "Through art we express our conception of what nature is not."*

defiled[1] the **sanctity**[2] of the entire justice system and, to pay for this **sacrilege**[3], should permanently remove himself from the bench. He'd finish by suggesting that if, in case, the judge failed to **renounce**[4] his judgeship, he should be forced to co-operate with an official **inquisition**[5] into all his past rulings —

---

[1] **defile (defiled)** To *defile* something is to make it unclean, make it morally impure, or spoil whatever holiness or sacredness it possesses; to degrade it, violate it, blacken it, etc. *In 1883 South African feminist writer Olive Schreiner said, "Marriage for love is the [most beautiful] symbol of the union of souls; marriage without [love] defiles the world."*

[2] **sanctity** The *sanctity* of something is the holiness or sacredness of it (as in *the sanctity of marriage, the sanctity of home, the sanctity of the ballot*, etc.). *Utah Republican senator Orrin Hatch once said that the death penalty is "our society's recognition of the sanctity of human life."*

[3] **sacrilege** Any act of disrespect (insult, injury, theft, etc.) toward anything (or anyone) sacred (or considered sacred) is known as *sacrilege*. The adjective is *sacrilegious*. *To Muslims, the text of the Koran (the sacred book of Islam) is holy, and it is a sacrilege to imitate its literary style.*

[4] **renounce** To *renounce* something (a title, position, right, claim, possession, belief, etc.) is to give it up; to relinquish it, abandon it, etc. The noun is *renunciation*. *As a 16-year-old student in Switzerland, Albert Einstein became so impressed with that country's democratic atmosphere that he formally renounced his German citizenship.*

[5] **inquisition** An *inquisition* is any (often official) prolonged questioning or investigation of someone. Sometimes the word implies that the rights of the person being questioned are ignored, the questions are harsh, and the punishments for wrongdoing are cruel (as in the religious and political Inquisitions of 13th–19th century Europe). *In the 1991 film* Guilty by Suspicion, *Robert De Niro plays a 1950s Hollywood director and suspected Communist who loses his home and career after he refuses to cooperate with the House Un-American Activity Committee's inquisition into his political affairs.*

and then be **impeached**[1] for any wrongful punishments the **probe**[2] might uncover.

And if, Pinocchio decided, when he voiced these many **recriminations**[3] he sounded like an annoying, **disputatious**[4] lawyer, too bad. And if he sounded like some **militant**[5] politi-

---

[1] **impeach (impeached)** If a public official is *impeached*, he is accused of misconduct (while in office) and placed on trial; if found guilty, he is removed from office. The noun is *impeachment*. *In 1998 the House of Representatives impeached Bill Clinton (for perjury and obstruction of justice); the Senate conducted a trial and found the President not guilty.*

[2] **probe** As a noun, a *probe* is a thorough examination or exploration of something. The word often refers specifically to an investigation (by a government committee, for example) of suspected wrongdoing by a public official. *President Richard Nixon halted an FBI probe of the Watergate burglary (June 1972) six days after it occurred.* Note: The word also designates (1) a slender surgical instrument used to explore wounds or body cavities and (2) an unmanned space vehicle that explores various aspects of the solar system (as in *space probe*). As a verb, to *probe* (into something) is to thoroughly investigate or explore (it). The adjective is *probing*, meaning "investigative; exploratory."

[3] **recrimination (recriminations)** To *incriminate* someone is to accuse him of a crime or other wrongful act. To *recriminate* is to accuse an accuser in return; to bring a countercharge against an accuser. A *recrimination* is an act or instance of recriminating; a counter-accusation. *Irish-born British statesman and author Edmund Burke (1729–1797) once said, "To [incriminate] and recriminate never yet was the road to [the settlement of] differences among men."*

[4] **disputatious** People who are *disputation* tend to engage in argument or debate (they tend to *dispute* things); they're argumentative, quarrelsome, disagreeable, combative, etc. *In his* Autobiography, *after describing his own "disputatious turn" as a youth, Benjamin Franklin (1706–1790) said that disputatious people "are generally unfortunate in their affairs; they get victory, sometimes, but they never get good will, which would be of more use to them."*

[5] **militant** Notice the similarity of this word to the word *military*. People who are *militant* are either likely to quarrel or fight, or they are aggressive in serving a cause or spreading a belief (as in *militant feminist* or *militant anti-abortionist*). *Rock singer Ani DiFranco once complained, "Men make angry music and it's called rock-and-roll; women include anger in their vocabulary and suddenly they're angry and militant."*

cal **activist**[1], all the better—because, after all, serious wrongs had been committed and they needed to be **rectified**[2] as soon as possible.

But Pinocchio soon learned that he'd be unable to present his case to anyone. According to the jailer, the court of appeals, the only body **empowered**[3] to **invalidate**[4] a judge's decision, was **defunct**[5]. And since Fool's Trap was an

---

[1] **activist** An *activist* is a person who aggressively supports or promotes a particular (usually controversial) political cause or goal (as in *civil rights activist* or *anti-war activist*). *After retiring from acting, (1950s and '60s film star) Doris Day became an animal rights activist.*

[2] **rectify (rectified)** To *rectify* something that's wrong (an error, an inaccuracy, unfairness, etc.) is to make it right or set it right: to fix it, correct it, remedy it, etc. *According to the* Internet Directory, *"Many UFO-related websites fail to deliver what most viewers want: pictures. The Skywatch International site, however, rectifies that common oversight and offers links to pictures galore."*

[3] **empower (empowered)** To *empower* someone is to give him power or authority. Sometimes the power is general in nature (as in *empowered by his new-found confidence*); other times it refers to some particular, often legal, action (as in *an agent empowered to sign contracts for his client*). *The Federal Food and Drugs Act (1938) empowered the FDA (Food and Drug Administration) to test the safety of new drugs and to prevent unsafe ones from being sold.*

[4] **invalidate** If something legal (a contract or ruling, for example) is *valid*, it's sound and binding; it has the force of law. If you *invalidate* something, you make it no longer valid; you cancel it, nullify it, undo it, etc. *In 1973 the U.S. Supreme Court invalidated state laws that prohibited abortion.*

[5] **defunct** If you say that something (a practice, a political organization, a business, a law, etc.) is *defunct*, you mean that it's no longer in effect or that it no longer operates or functions. If you say that a person is *defunct*, you mean that he's dead. *The brand name Frisbee (for a dinner-plate-sized plastic disk thrown through the air) is said to have derived from the defunct Frisbie Baking Company, which produced Mother Frisbie's Pies.*

autonomous[1] region, there was no **recourse**[2] outside the area either.

Poor Pinocchio probably would have remained **incarcerated**[3] indefinitely had it not happened that, by a narrow margin, the mayor of Fool's Trap had just been elected to a second term. After the losing candidate **grudgingly**[4] con-

---

[1] **autonomous** This word (pronounced with the accent on the second syllable) derives from the Greek words for "self" *(auto)* and "law" *(nomos)*. If a government, organization, geographic region, etc., is *autonomous*, it's self-governing; it's independent; it's not controlled by outside forces. *During World War II the U.S. Air Force operated as a part of the U.S. Army; in 1947 it became an autonomous military force.*

[2] **recourse** Sometimes you need to turn to someone or something authoritative or powerful for help or protection, or to solve a problem. Access to, or the act of turning or resorting to, a person or thing for such help is known as *recourse* (as in *the accused had recourse to a trial by jury*). The word also signifies the person or thing so turned to (or resorted to, appealed to) for such help (as in *when he lost all his money, his only recourse was his father*). *In his second inaugural address (January 1885), after pointing out that the U.S. and the USSR were capable of destroying each other with nuclear weapons, President Ronald Reagan asked, "Is there either logic or morality in believing that if [they threaten] to kill tens of millions of our people, our only recourse is to threaten killing tens of millions of theirs?"*

[3] **incarcerate (incarcerated)** To *incarcerate* someone is to imprison him; to put him in jail. The noun is *incarceration* ("imprisonment"). *In a June 1975 Supreme Court ruling that non-dangerous mental patients cannot be confined in institutions against their will, Justice Stewart Potter said, "May the state fence in the harmless mentally ill solely to save its citizens from exposure to those whose ways are different? One might as well ask if the state, to avoid public unease, could incarcerate all who are physically unattractive or socially [odd]."*

[4] **grudgingly** As a noun, a *grudge* is an (especially long-standing) feeling of resentment or ill will (toward someone). But as a verb, to *grudge* (or *begrudge*) is to give (something to someone) reluctantly or unwillingly, or to resent the good fortune of (someone). To do something *grudgingly* is to do it reluctantly or unwillingly. *In the 1985 book* Dear America: Letters Home from Vietnam, *Bernard Edelman is quoted as having written: "They were called grunts, and many of them, however grudgingly, were proud of the name. They were the infantrymen, the foot soldiers of the war."*

ceded[1], the mayor quietly **gloated**[2] for a few days. Then he suddenly **convened**[3] a special government meeting to announce that, in order to celebrate the extension of his **regime**[4],

---

[1] **concede (conceded)** To *concede* is to (often reluctantly) acknowledge or recognize (something) as being true (or valid, just, proper, etc.); to admit. Note: Often what is acknowledged or admitted is an opponent's victory before it has been officially established, in which case to *concede* is to admit defeat, to give up (as in an election or chess match, for example). *American showman and circus owner P. T. Barnum (1810–1891), famous for the phrase "There's a sucker born every minute," doubted that he'd ever uttered those words – but he did concede that he may have once said, "The people like to be humbugged."*

[2] **gloat (gloated)** To *gloat* over something (that has happened) is to think about it with great or excessive (and often spiteful or triumphant) self-satisfaction or pleasure (as in *he gloated over his enemy's misfortune*). *In the circus, after one clown plays a practical joke on another (such as dumping water on his head), the jokester usually smiles, struts, and gloats while the victim sits in glum silence.*

[3] **convene (convened)** When this verb doesn't take an object (as in *we will convene at two o'clock*), it means "to come together or assemble (usually for some official public purpose)." When it takes an object (as in *convene a meeting*), it means "to cause (individuals) to come together or assemble formally." *When the 104th Congress convened in January 1994, Newt Gingrich of Georgia became the first Republican Speaker of the House in 40 years.*

[4] **regime** This word signifies a particular type of government or ruling system (as in *the Nazi regime*). It also signifies a period (of time) in which a particular government or ruling system is in power (for example, in China the Chiang Kai-shek regime followed the Sun Yat-sen regime). Note: The term of office of an American President may be referred to as a *regime (the Nixon regime)*, but is more often called an *administration (the Kennedy administration)*. *In 1986, referring to life in Czechoslovakia under a Communist regime, Czech playwright (and future president) Václav Havel said, "True enough, the country is calm – calm as a morgue or grave, would you not say?"*

he was ordering fireworks displays and granting **amnesty**[1] to all rascals.

On learning the news, Pinocchio immediately said to the jailer, "Let me out, please."

Although the jailer had the authority to **implement**[2] the mayor's order, he wasn't sure if Pinocchio really fell under the category of rascal. He said, "But you're not a rascal, you're a pup—"

"I beg your pardon," interrupted Pinocchio, "but I am a rascal."

"Do you have any written evidence to **document**[3] that?"

"No, but I've always been a very bad—"

"Just a minute. Let me think."

---

[1] **amnesty** *Amnesty* is a pardon (a freedom from prosecution; a granting of immunity) given by a government to one who has committed a criminal act (especially a political criminal act). *Whereas President Richard Nixon denied amnesty to Vietnam draft evaders, President Gerald Ford granted amnesty (1974) to those who were willing to do public service work.*

[2] **implement** As a verb, to *implement* something (a plan, policy, etc.) is to put it into effect; to carry it out (as in *the IRS has implemented programs for the electronic filing of tax returns*). *In 1984 White House counsel Edwin Meese sarcastically defined an expert as "somebody who is more than 50 miles from home, has no responsibility for implementing the advice he gives, and shows slides."*

[3] **document** As a verb, to *document* something (a claim, for example) is to support it or prove it with evidence or decisive information (sometimes by presenting official papers or legal documents); to authenticate, certify, or substantiate it. *After writing the anti-slavery novel* Uncle Tom's Cabin *(1852), Harriet Beecher Stowe wrote* A Key to Uncle Tom's Cabin *(1853), which documented her case against slavery.*

As a low-level **bureaucrat**[1], the jailer was expected to rigidly followed the letter of the law. But he'd often longed for some **leeway**[2] to exercise independent judgment, however **fallible**[3] that judgment might prove. Finally he answered, "Well, thank you for **apprising**[4] me of your true status. Far be it from me to deny the rights of a rascal." Then he added, "But I have to warn you: Leaving here won't be easy. Once

---

[1] **bureaucrat** A government in which power is concentrated in administrative bureaus (divisions, units) is known as a *bureaucracy*. The implication is that in this type of government a rigidity of routine leads to inefficiency, delays in making decisions, lack of intelligent thought, etc. A *bureaucrat* is a non-elected official in such a government (and as such he's not accountable to the public). The word is also sometimes used to describe any petty, narrow-minded person. *After Japan's 1995 earthquake (in which 5,100 people were killed and 26,800 were injured), bureaucrats held up the entry of emergency supplies and rescue dogs flown from Europe.*

[2] **leeway** This word signifies a degree of freedom of action (within some set limits); latitude. It can also signify the room (adequate or extra time, space, opportunity, etc.) allowed for this; elbowroom. *Many federal programs (such as Medicaid, Aid to Families with Dependent Children, and unemployment insurance) give individual states considerable leeway in establishing eligibility requirements and benefits.*

[3] **fallible** If you're talking about people, to be *fallible* is to be liable (likely) to make (or capable of making) a mistake. All humans, by nature, are *fallible*. If you're talking about a report, judgment, idea, or the like, *fallible* means "liable to be in error, false, inaccurate, etc." The noun is *fallibility*. *In 1992 British actress and author Eleanor Bron said, "Both men and women are fallible; the difference is, women know it."*

[4] **apprise (apprising)** To *apprise* someone of something is to give him notice of it; make him aware of it; inform or advise him of it. *When he was apprised (1946) of lynchings and other forms of mob violence still practiced in the South, President Harry Truman appointed a committee on civil rights to investigate.*

you're out, you'll have to live with the **stigma**[1] of having served jail time. You'll be treated like a second-class citizen."

"I don't care."

"All right, then. Now sign this legal document that states that you're a **bona fide**[2] rascal, and I'll stamp it with the official seal. Then you can go."

At this **juncture**[3] Pinocchio hesitated.

"Don't worry. It's just a **formality**[4]," explained the jailer. "Go ahead and sign."

Pinocchio signed his name, and the jailer, after stamping the document, took off his cap, bowed low, and opened the door of the prison. Pinocchio ran out and away, with never a look back.

---

[1] **stigma** A *stigma* is a mark of discredit or disgrace (as on one's reputation); a blot on one's record; a stain. *For women, until the 1960s a stigma was attached to remaining single; in fact, unmarried women (especially older ones) were insultingly referred to as "old maids."*

[2] **bona fide** This phrase (which in Latin means "in good faith") describes anything that is genuine, authentic, real, not fake, not phony, etc., as in *a bona fide Picasso* or *a bona fide member of the group. Taxpayers can deduct travel expenses paid for another person with them on a business trip if the person has a bona fide business purpose for the travel.*

[3] **juncture** A *juncture* is a point in time, especially an important, critical, or crucial point (as when circumstances come to a head or when a decision must be made). *According to Pulitzer Prize–winning journalist Frances Fitzgerald, "The United States came to Vietnam at a critical juncture of Vietnam history."* Note: The word can also be used as a synonym for *junction* ("place where two things meet"), as in *the juncture of the Missouri and Mississippi rivers.*

[4] **formality** Technically, a *formality* is an established method of doing something (as required by law, custom, etiquette, etc.). But people usually use this word to imply that the requirement in question is carried out merely for the sake of form and lacks any real importance. *If you've hit the ball over the fence, you've made a home run; the running of the bases is merely a formality.* Note: The word also means *formalness* ("state or condition of being formal"), as in *let's do away with formality and address each other by our first names.*

Chapter 16 "The Snake"

Without losing a moment, Pinocchio fled from the city and set out on the road that led back to the house of the lovely fairy.

It had been raining on and off for a **fortnight**[1], and the road was now so muddy that, at times, Pinocchio sank down almost to his knees. He was so eager to see his father and blue-haired fairy sister that he ran and jumped like a dog, and mud splashed all over him.

"How unhappy I've been," he said to himself. "And yet I deserve everything, for I'm certainly very stubborn and stupid! I always have to have my own way. I won't listen to those who love me and who have more sense than I do. But from now on, I'll be different and I'll try to be good. I've found out, beyond any doubt, that bad boys are far from happy, and that, in the long run, they wind up as **unequivocal**[2] failures. I wonder if Father is waiting for me. Will I find him at the fairy's house? It's been so long since I've seen him, and I do so want his love and his kisses. And will the fairy ever forgive me for all I've done? She who's been so good to me and to whom I owe my life! Can there be a worse or more heartless son than—"

---

[1] **fortnight** A *fortnight* is a period of two weeks. Note: The word is a contraction of "fourteen nights." *According to the* Cambridge Encyclopedia, *during the 16th century, "the English [government] discovered a welcome source of revenue [income] in beards; anyone sprouting a beard of more than a fortnight's growth was taxed."*

[2] **unequivocal** If something (a refusal, a success, an indication, evidence, etc.) is *unequivocal*, it's clear and unambiguous (in its meaning or purpose); it's specifically stated and leaves no trace of doubt or misunderstanding; it's definite, explicit, unmistakable, etc. *In delivering the opinion of the Supreme Court in 1966's* Miranda *case, Chief Justice Earl Warren said, "If a person in custody is to be subjected to [questioning], he must first be informed in clear and unequivocal terms that he has the right to remain silent."*

In the middle of thus **berating**[1] himself, he stopped suddenly, frozen with terror. A huge snake lay stretched across the road. It had green skin, fiery eyes, and a pointed tail that smoked like a chimney.

Knowing that snake bites were **potentially**[2] deadly, Pinocchio ran back wildly, then settled himself on a pile of stones to wait for the snake to go on his way and leave the road clear for him. He waited an hour; two hours; three hours; but the snake was always there. He occupied himself by occasionally scraping off splotches of dried mud that had **adhered**[3] to his clothes and then dropping them into the **crevices**[4] that lay between the stones he sat upon.

---

[1] **berate (berating)** To *berate* someone is to (often angrily and at length) scold or criticize him (for a wrongdoing or fault); to bawl him out, tell him off, etc. *Speaking of late-19th-century social reformer Carry Nation (who strongly believed that the drinking of alcoholic beverages should be illegal),* Compton's Encyclopedia *said that she "would appear at a saloon, berate the customers, and proceed to damage as much of the place as she could with her hatchet."*

[2] **potential (potentially)** As an adjective, this word means "possible (as opposed to actual); capable of being or becoming," as in *potential danger, potential usefulness, potential enemies, potential customers,* etc. *In 1928 British author Aldous Huxley said, "Silence is as full of potential wisdom and wit as [is] the [uncut] marble of great sculpture."* As a noun, one's *potential* is his hidden (or undeveloped, untapped) ability or excellence that may or may not be developed. *In 1976 the president of California's Mills College said, "The basic purpose of a liberal arts education is to [free] the human being to exercise his or her potential to the fullest."*

[3] **adhere (adhered)** If something (a substance, for example) *adheres* to something else, it sticks or clings to it (by or as if by glue, suction, molecular forces, etc.). The noun is *adherence. Doctors say that if you are severely burned, you should cut away loose clothing, but you should not remove clothing adhered to your skin.* In another sense, if a person *adheres* to a rule, principle, or manner of doing something, he follows it, supports, it, carries it out, etc. *In 1860 presidential candidate Abraham Lincoln asked, "What is conservatism? Is it not adherence to the old and tried, against the new and untried?"*

[4] **crevice (crevices)** A *crevice* is a narrow crack or opening. *Birds build their nests not only in tree branches, but also in shrubs, on the ground, in holes in trees, and in crevices in rocks.*

Finally, trying to feel very brave, he walked toward the snake. Standing at a safe distance, he said in a sweet, soothing voice, "I beg your pardon. Would you be so kind as to step aside to let me pass?"

But he might as well have been talking to a wall. The snake never moved.

Once more, in the same sweet voice, he said, "I'm going home where my father is waiting for me. It's been so long since I've seen him! Would you mind very much if I passed?"

He waited for some sign of an answer, but none came. On the contrary, the snake, who had seemed, until then, wide awake and full of life, became suddenly very quiet and still. His eyes closed and his tail stopped smoking.

"Is he asleep, I wonder?" thought Pinocchio. "Maybe I can jump over him."

Tingling with **apprehension**[1], the puppet slowly inched forward until he was **precariously**[2] close to the **quiescent**[3]

---

[1] **apprehension** A fearful, nervous, or anxious anticipation (about something difficult or scary that you have to do) is known as *apprehension*. The adjective is *apprehensive*. *Many people are apprehensive about going to the doctor — especially if they think they might get an injection.*

[2] **precarious (precariously)** If something (a situation, a condition, a living, a footing, etc.) is *precarious*, it's dangerously lacking in stability or security (generally as a result of forces beyond one's control); it's risky, perilous, hazardous, unsafe, uncertain, etc. *At the end of the 1997 film* Breakdown, *a large truck dangles precariously from the edge of a high bridge.*

[3] **quiescent** If something (especially something once active) is *quiescent* (pronounced *kwee-ESS-int*) it's (often temporarily) at rest, quiet, still, inactive, motionless, etc. *In 1980, after having been quiescent for 123 years, Washington State's volcanic Mount Saint Helens violently erupted, causing death and destruction.*

green form. Just as he bent his knees to give **impetus**[1] to the jump, the snake, sensing the puppet's **proximity**[2], suddenly shot up like a spring. **Recoiling**[3] in terror, Pinocchio tumbled backwards, head over heels. He fell so awkwardly that his head stuck in the mud, and there he remained with his legs straight up in the air.

At the sight of the puppet kicking and squirming, the snake laughed so hard that he burst a blood vessel. All at

---

[1] **impetus** This word signifies anything (an impulse, stimulus, incentive, etc.) that causes or increases motion, action, or effort. It can also signify the increased activity itself. *The civil rights movement gained impetus when the Supreme Court eliminated (1954) segregation in schools.* Note: The word can also signify the physical energy or force associated with motion. *If you wear a glove when playing handball, you'll notice that the glove not only protects the hand from injury, but gives the ball greater impetus.*

[2] **proximity** If two things are close to each other (as in place, time, order, relation, etc.), they are said to be in *proximity*. *Colorado and Wyoming are in proximity on a map, but they are not in proximity in an alphabetical listing of states.* Sometimes the word signifies the degree of nearness of two things, whether close together or not (as in *climate is determined by proximity to the oceans*). *When landing a plane, a pilot must be aware of his speed and altitude, of weather conditions, and of the proximity of other planes.*

[3] **recoil (recoiling)** When a person *recoils*, he springs back (or draws back, shrinks back, pulls back, etc.) involuntarily (either physically or emotionally), as from fear, alarm, disgust, etc.; he flinches, winces, etc. *When the matador stabbed the bull in the neck we recoiled in disgust.* Note: When a gun *recoils*, it springs back after firing. Also note: When an object (an atomic particle, for example) *recoils*, it rebounds or springs back (as from a collision or elasticity, for example).

once his body began to jerk **spasmodically**[1]. When the **convulsive**[2] motions finally **subsided**[3], he was dead.

Pinocchio, having freed himself from his awkward position, once more began to run so as to reach the fairy's house before dark. But as he ran, pangs of hunger grew so strong that, unable to withstand them, he jumped into a field that **abutted**[4] a farmhouse to pick some grapes.

But getting up close, Pinocchio noticed that the grapes were **withering**[5] on the vine. As he was trying to decide

---

[1] **spasmodic (spasmodically)** In medicine, a *spasm* is an (especially sudden or abnormal) involuntary muscle contraction. To describe a motion as *spasmodic* is to say that it resembles a spasm or spasms; that is, it's marked by quick abrupt movements (it's jerky, twitchy, etc.). But to describe a pursuit, action, activity, etc., as *spasmodic* is to say that it's marked by sudden outbursts of energy or that it occurs at irregular intervals (it's intermittent). *In 1987, speaking of the romance between John F. Kennedy and Jacqueline Kennedy, author Doris Kearns Goodwin said, "It was a very spasmodic courtship, conducted mainly at long distance with a great clanking of coins in dozens of phone booths."*

[2] **convulsive** In medicine, *convulsions* are violent, involuntary muscle contractions (as caused by high fever, poisoning, hysteria, etc.). A motion described as *convulsive* is marked by quick, abrupt movements (it's jerky, spasmodic, sudden, etc.). *Epilepsy is caused by uncontrolled electrical activity in the brain and is characterized by periodic convulsive seizures.*

[3] **subside (subsided)** When something (an activity, feeling, motion, etc.) *subsides*, it becomes less intense, active, or violent; it dies down, lessens, decreases, etc. (usually to a more normal level). *The symptoms of a cold (sore throat, nasal congestion, coughing) usually subside in about a week.*

[4] **abut (abutted)** Things that *abut* each other are directly next to each other; they're adjacent; they touch; they share an edge or border. *Lake Michigan (one of the Great Lakes) abuts four states: Michigan, Indiana, Illinois, and Wisconsin.*

[5] **wither (withering)** If something (a woman's beauty, a plant, etc.) *withers*, it dries up, shrivels, loses freshness, droops, fades, decays, etc. (from age, loss of moisture, etc.). *In 1984, speaking of London hotels, Harper's magazine said, "Nothing makes you feel that you've overstayed your welcome like a flower arrangement that has withered and died."*

whether or not to eat them, he heard a loud cracking sound and his legs were caught in an iron trap. It had been placed there by a farmer to catch some weasels who'd been attacking his chickens.

Chapter 17 "The Watchdog"

Pinocchio began to scream and weep and beg. But all was of no use, for no houses were in sight and not a soul passed by on the road.

Night came.

Partly because of the sharp pain in his legs, and partly because he was afraid to be alone in the dark, the puppet was about to faint. But just then he saw a tiny firefly flickering by. He called to it, "Dear little firefly, will you set me free?"

"Poor little fellow!" replied the firefly, stopping to look at him with pity. "How did you get caught in that trap?"

"I was hungry so I stepped into this field to take a few grapes and—"

"Are the grapes yours?"

"No."

"Who taught you to take things that aren't yours?"

"But I was hungry."

"Hunger doesn't excuse stealing."

"That's true, that's true!" cried Pinocchio in tears. "I won't do it again."

Just then, the conversation was interrupted by approaching footsteps. It was the farmer, who was walking on tiptoes to see if, by chance, he'd caught one of the weasels who'd been eating his chickens.

He was greatly surprised when, on holding up his lantern, he saw that, instead of a weasel, he'd caught a boy!

"Ah, you little thief!" said the farmer in an angry voice. "So you're the one who steals my chickens!"

"No, no!" cried Pinocchio, sobbing bitterly. "I came here only to take a very few grapes."

"Someone who steals grapes may very easily steal chickens as well. Tell me, are you aware of the laws—and penalties—concerning stealing in this town?"

"Well—"

"Take my word for it, I'll teach you a lesson you'll never forget."

He opened the trap, **seized**[1] the puppet by the neck, and carried him to his farmhouse as if he were a sack of corn. When he reached the yard in front of the house, he flung Pinocchio to the ground, put a foot on his neck, and said to him roughly, "It's late now and it's time for bed. First thing tomorrow we'll settle matters. In the **interim**[2], since my watchdog died today, you'll take his place and guard my chicken coop."

He **shackled**[3] Pinocchio's neck with a thick metal dog collar. Then he **tethered**[4] him with a long iron chain.

---

[1] **seize (seized)** To *seize* is to (1) grab hold of (as in *he seized him by the collar*), (2) capture (as in *the police seized the escaped prisoner*), or (3) take possession of (as in *Germany seized Poland*). *In 1979 Spanish abstract artist Joan Miró (1893–1983) said, "My way is to seize an image the moment it has formed in my mind, to trap it as a bird and to pin it at once to canvas."*

[2] **interim** As a noun, an *interim* is an intervening period of time (as between one event or situation and another); meantime. As an adjective, if something (a government, agreement, etc.) is *interim*, it takes place during an intervening period of time; it's for the time being; it's temporary. *Grover Cleveland was elected to nonconsecutive presidential terms (1885–1889 and 1893–1897); in the interim he moved to New York City and practiced law.*

[3] **shackle (shackled)** As a noun, a *shackle* is a metal ring or similar device (often one of a pair) used to encircle and confine the wrist, ankle, etc. of someone (a prisoner, for example). As a verb, to *shackle* someone is either to restrict his motion by literally putting shackles on him, or to limit or restrict his freedom of action, thought, etc. (by any means). *Magician and escape artist Harry Houdini (1874–1926) frequently jumped from bridges in shackles and released himself underwater.*

[4] **tether (tethered)** As a noun, a *tether* is a rope or chain that holds an animal in place (one end is attached to the animal and the other to a fixed object, such as a stake). As a verb, to *tether* is to fasten or confine an animal or restrict its motion with a tether or the like. The word is often used figuratively to refer to the limiting or restricting of anyone by anything (as in *the matrimonial tether*). *In 1986 the research submarine* Alvin *used a mobile, tethered robot equipped with a television camera to explore the wreck of the sunken ocean liner* Titanic.

"If it happens to rain tonight," said the farmer, "you can sleep in that little doghouse there. It was my old dog's bed for three years, and it's a fit **abode**[1] for a lowly thief like you. And if, by chance, any weasels come around, be sure to bark!" After this last instruction, the farmer went into his house, closed the door, and locked it.

Poor Pinocchio huddled close to the doghouse more dead than alive from cold, hunger, and fright. Now and then he pulled and tugged at the collar that nearly choked him and thought to himself: "I deserve it! Yes, I deserve it! I've been nothing but a **truant**[2] and a **vagabond**[3]. I've never obeyed anyone and I've always done as I pleased. If I'd studied and worked and stayed with my poor old father, I wouldn't find myself in this **demeaning**[4] **predicament**[1]. Oh, if only I could

---

[1] **abode** An *abode* is the place where one lives; a dwelling place, house, home, etc. For example, in Greek mythology Olympus was the *abode* of the gods. *In 1764 French philosopher Voltaire (1694–1778) said, "It is not known precisely where angels dwell — whether in the air, the void, or the planets; it has not been God's pleasure that we should be informed of their abode."*

[2] **truant** A *truant* is a person who is absent without permission (especially a student who skips school). As an adjective, to be *truant* is to be absent without permission or to be idle, neglectful of duty, lazy, etc. *Beginning in the late 1980s, parents could be fined or imprisoned for allowing their child to participate in a gang, be truant from school, use drugs, or have access to a gun.*

[3] **vagabond** A *vagabond* is a person (usually with no permanent home) who wanders from place to place; a tramp, drifter, hobo, etc. The implication is that such a person is aimless, worthless, irresponsible, etc. *According to the Articles of Confederation (an early form of the U.S. Constitution), "paupers, vagabonds, and fugitives from justice [are not] entitled to all privileges of free citizens."*

[4] **demeaning** If something (a hurtful nickname, unskilled work, an embarrassing situation, etc.) is *demeaning*, it lowers one's social standing, or it lowers one's level of dignity or self-worth; it's degrading. As a verb, to *demean* someone is to cause his status or dignity to be lowered. *In March 2002 a petition was created to encourage Target Department Stores to stop selling a Halloween costume that demeans the mentally ill by portraying a mental patient as an individual in a straight jacket and a "Hannibal Lecter" face mask.*

start all over again! But what's done can't be undone, and I must be patient!"

After this **introspective**[2] little speech, which came from the very depths of his being, Pinocchio went into the doghouse, gathered the straw into a bed, and lay down.

---

[1] **predicament** A *predicament* is any problematic (or unpleasant, embarrassing, puzzling, worrisome, troublesome, dangerous, etc.) situation from which it is difficult to free oneself; a fix, a jam, a tight spot, a "pickle." *In the 1975 film* Jaws, *the police chief was faced with the predicament of whether or not to close the beach (where a shark may or may not have been seen).*

[2] **introspective** If you're *introspective*, you tend to observe or examine your own thoughts and feelings; you're thoughtful, meditative, self-aware, inner-directed, etc. The noun is *introspection. Speaking of getting older, writer and botanist Janice Emily Bowers once said, "Forty is about the age for unexpected developments: [outgoing people] turn introspective, [shy people] become sociable, and everyone, without regard to type, acquires grey hairs and philosophies of life; many also acquire gardens."*

Chapter 18 "The Weasels"

Even though a boy may be deep in the **doldrums**[1], he rarely loses sleep over his unhappiness. Pinocchio, being no exception to this rule, soon drifted off. But about midnight he was awakened by strange whisperings coming from the yard. He stuck his nose out of the doghouse, and, in the dim light provided by a **crescent**[2] moon, saw four small, dark, furry animals. They were weasels! One of them left his companions and, coming to the door of the doghouse, said in a sweet voice, "Good evening, Fido."

"My name isn't Fido," answered Pinocchio.

"Who are you, then?"

"I'm Pinocchio."

"What kind of name is that?"

"I'm the **namesake**[3] of a very lucky family my father once knew."

"Oh. But what are you doing here?"

"I've been **relegated**[1] to the doghouse."

---

[1] **doldrums** If you're "in the *doldrums*," you feel sad, depressed, sluggish, spiritless, etc. Note: The word comes from a region of the ocean near the equator, known as the *doldrums*, where, because there is sometimes no wind (though at other times there are violent winds), sailing ships can become stranded for weeks at a time. *Pulitzer Prize–winning poet Phyllis McGinley (1905-1978) once said, "A hobby a day keeps the doldrums away."*

[2] **crescent** As a noun, a *crescent* is a figure (or shape) like that of the moon when it is less than half full; that is, one side is convex (curves outward) and the other concave (curves inward), and it tapers to points at the ends. As an adjective, the word means "shaped like a crescent," as in *crescent roll* (croissant). *In geography class we learned that Nantucket (an island off southeast Massachusetts) and Lake Geneva (a lake on the border of France and Switzerland) are both roughly crescent shaped.*

[3] **namesake** A *namesake* (from the phrase "for the name's sake") is a person or thing having the same name as (or named after) another. *Like its namesake in Italy, the city of Rome, Georgia, was built on seven hills.*

"The doghouse? But where's Fido? Where's the old dog who used to live here?"

"He died."

"Died? Poor thing! He was so good! Still, judging by your face, I think you, too, are a good dog."

"I beg your pardon, but I'm not a dog!"

"What are you, then?"

"Can't you see? I'm a puppet."

"Are you taking the place of the watchdog?"

"I'm sorry to say that I am. I'm being punished."

"That's a strange punishment."

"The farmer **imposed**[2] it on me as a **penance**[3] for something I did wrong."

"Well, this might be your lucky night...I think your father was right to give you that lucky name! You see, I'll make the same deal with you that we made with Fido. I'm sure you'll be glad to hear it."

"What is it?"

---

[1] **relegate (relegated)** To *relegate* (someone or something) is to send or dismiss (him or it) to an inferior, unimportant, or out-of-the way place, position, or condition (as in *relegated to the attic, relegated to second-class status, relegated to kitchen duty,* etc.). *In ancient Greece, while men participated in government, women, along with slaves and children, were relegated to the household.*

[2] **impose (imposed)** To *impose* something (that must be obeyed, endured, paid, etc.) is to put it into effect with authority (as in *impose a sales tax*). *In 1974 the U.S. government, to reduce the amount of gasoline Americans used, imposed a national speed limit of 55 miles per hour.* Note: When this verb doesn't take an object, to *impose* is to take unfair advantage by (sometimes improperly) forcing yourself in where you may not be wanted (as in *I didn't stay for dinner because I didn't want to impose*).

[3] **penance** A *penance* is a punishment undergone to make up for or show sorrow for a sin or wrongdoing. *According to Greek mythology, as a penance for killing his wife and children in a fit of madness, the mighty Hercules undertook a series of seemingly impossible tasks known as the "twelve labors" (which included the killing of the many-headed monster Hydra and the cleaning of the filthy Augean stables).*

"We'll come once in a while, as in the past, to pay a visit to this chicken coop, and we'll take away eight chickens. Of these, seven are for us, and one for you, provided, of course, that you'll make believe you're sleeping and won't bark for the farmer."

"Did Fido really agree to that?" asked Pinocchio.

"Indeed he did! And because of that we were the best of friends. Now, sleep away peacefully, and remember that before we go we'll leave you a nice fat chicken all ready for your breakfast in the morning. In fact, because this is your first time, I'll **amend**[1] the deal this once and leave you two chickens. Understood?"

"Only too well," answered Pinocchio. And shaking his head in a threatening manner, he seemed to say, "We'll see about that."

As soon as the weasels had talked things over, they went straight to the chicken coop, which stood close to the doghouse. Digging busily with teeth and claws, they opened the little door and slipped in. But they were no sooner in than they heard the door close with a sharp bang.

The one who had shut it was Pinocchio, who, not satisfied with that, dragged a heavy stone in front of it. That done, he started to bark. And he barked as if he were a real watchdog: "Bow-wow! Bow-wow-wow!"

The farmer heard the loud barks and jumped out of bed. Taking his gun, he leaped to the window and shouted, "What's the matter?"

"The thieves are here," called Pinocchio.

"Where are they?"

---

[1] **amend** To *amend* something (a proposal, motion, law, policy, etc.) is to change or modify it (by adding to it, subtracting from it, rephrasing it, etc.), so as to improve it, make it more accurate, etc. The noun is *amendment*. *The U.S. Constitution has been amended a number of time, as when, for example, 18-year-olds were given the right to vote (1971).* Note: To *amend* one's behavior is to change it for the better; to correct it, improve it.

"In the chicken coop."

"I'm coming."

And, in fact, the farmer was down in the yard in an instant and running toward the chicken coop.

He opened the door, pulled out the weasels one by one, and, after tying them in a bag, said to them, "I've got you at last! I could kill you right now, but instead I'll give you a **reprieve**[1]. Why? Because I have a **lenient**[2] spirit. I'll let you stay safe in this bag all night. Tomorrow morning I'll take you to the inn, where you'll make a fine meal for some hungry soul. It's really too great an honor for you, one you don't deserve. But, you see, I'm very kind and forgiving—so I'm going to do this for you!"

Then he went up to Pinocchio and began to pet him.

"How did you ever find them out so quickly? And to think that my dear Fido, my faithful Fido, never saw them in all these years!"

---

[1] **reprieve** A *reprieve* is a postponement or cancellation of a punishment (as in *the governor granted the condemned man a reprieve*), or the time period during which the postponement takes place. Note: The word can also be used loosely to signify any type of temporary relief from any kind of danger, pain, etc. (as in *a reprieve from a headache*). *In 1849 Russian novelist Fyodor Dostoyevsky was arrested for membership is a secret political group and sentenced to be shot; he was granted a last-minute reprieve from execution but instead was sentenced to four years of hard labor in Siberia.*

[2] **lenient** If you're *lenient*, you tend not to be harsh or strict (in establishing or enforcing punishments, for example); you're tolerant, easygoing, mild, permissive, merciful, etc. The noun is *leniency*. *In his second inaugural address (March 1865, when the Union victory in the Civil War was in sight), President Abraham Lincoln urged leniency toward the South when he said, "With malice [ill will] toward none, with charity for all…let us strive on to finish the work we are in; to bind up the Nation's wounds."*

The puppet could have told him, then and there, all he knew about the **ignoble¹ collaboration²** between the dog and the weasels, but thinking of the dead dog, he said to himself: "Why **desecrate³** the dead? They can't defend themselves, so the best thing to do is to leave them in peace!"

"Were you awake or asleep when they came?" continued the farmer.

"I was asleep," answered Pinocchio, "but they woke me with their whisperings. One of them even came to the door of the doghouse and tried to talk me into making a secret **pact⁴** with them. He said, 'If you promise not to bark, we'll promise to give you one of the chickens for your breakfast.' Can you

---

¹ **ignoble** If something (an activity or thought, for example) is *ignoble* (pronounced with the accent on the second syllable), it's marked by low moral character; it's dishonorable. *Speaking of the Vietnam War, baby doctor, best-selling author, and political activist Benjamin Spock (1903–1998) said, "What is the use of physicians like myself trying to help parents to bring up children healthy and happy, to have them killed in such numbers for a cause that is ignoble?"*

² **collaborate (collaboration)** To *collaborate* (with another person or persons) is to work together (with him or them) toward a common goal; to join forces, act jointly, cooperate, etc. (as in *Gilbert and Sullivan collaborated to write many operettas*). The noun is *collaboration*. *Nobel Prize–winning French writer André Gide (1869–1951) once remarked, "Art is a collaboration between God and the artist, and the less the artist does the better."*

³ **desecrate** To *desecrate* something is to violate or spoil the sacredness (or sacred nature) of it (as in *desecrate a church by covering it with graffiti*). *A 1968 federal law made it illegal to publicly burn or otherwise desecrate the American flag (but in 1989 the Supreme Court ruled that that law violated the free speech guarantee of the First Amendment).*

⁴ **pact** A *pact* is an (often formal) agreement between two or more nations, individuals, etc.; a deal, bargain, bond, contract, treaty, etc. *The 1928 Pact of Paris (also known as the Kellogg-Briand Pact) was an agreement reached by 15 major countries who pledged to settle all conflicts by peaceful means rather than by war (but the pact proved meaningless because it failed to provide any means of enforcement).*

believe that? Those **depraved**[1] criminals had the nerve to make that proposition to me! I may be full of faults, but I do know that what they asked me to do — to accept a share of stolen property — is **equivalent**[2] to out-and-out stealing!"

"Fine boy!" cried the farmer, slapping him on the shoulder in a friendly way. "You ought to be proud of yourself. And to show you what I think of you, I'm setting you free!"

And he removed the dog collar from his neck.

---

[1] **depraved** If something (a person, idea, concept, etc.) is *depraved*, it's morally corrupt; that is, it's perverted, indecent, unnatural, evil, sinful, etc. *In his first annual message to Congress (December 1901), President Theodore Roosevelt wrote of his assassinated predecessor, "President McKinley was killed by an utterly depraved criminal belonging to that body of criminals who object to all governments, good and bad alike."*

[2] **equivalent** If two things are *equivalent*, they are equal (in amount, degree, value, effect, significance, meaning, etc.), or they are basically the same as each other in that they have similar or identical effects, consequences, etc. *Writer and naturalist Henry David Thoreau (1817–1862) once said, "A kitten is so flexible that she is almost double; the hind parts are equivalent to another kitten with which the forepart plays; she does not discover that her tail belongs to her until you [step] on it."*

Chapter 19 "The Pigeon"

As soon as he no longer felt the **oppressive**[1] weight of the thick metal collar, the **emancipated**[2] puppet started to run across fields and meadows. And he never stopped till he came to the path that led to the fairy's house.

When he reached it, he looked into a valley far below him, and there he saw the woods where he'd unluckily met the fox and the cat, and the tall oak tree where he'd been hung. But though he searched far and near, he couldn't see the house where the blue-haired fairy lived.

He became terribly frightened and, running as fast as he could, he finally came to the spot where the house had once stood. It was no longer there. In its place lay a small marble slab, which bore this sad **inscription**[3]: "Here lies the beautiful

---

[1] **oppressive** Anything *oppressive* weighs down on you, pushes you down. More specifically, if a burden, task, weight, or the like is *oppressive*, it calls for or requires great effort or exertion; it's difficult to carry out or support. But if a government, ruler, law, or the like is *oppressive*, it's characterized by a cruel or unjust exercise of authority or power; it's dictatorial, controlling, unreasonably harsh, heavy-handed, etc. And if weather (hot, humid air, for example) is *oppressive*, it weighs heavily on the senses or spirit; it causes sluggishness, depression, etc. The verb is *oppress* ("weigh down" or "treat unjustly" or "make gloomy"); the noun is *oppression*. *In 1990 Russian author Tatyana Tolstaya, speaking of writers and society, said, "The worse your daily life, the better your art; if you have to be careful because of oppression and censorship, this pressure produces diamonds."*

[2] **emancipate (emancipated)** To *emancipate* someone is to release him from (especially legal or political) bondage or restraint; to set him free. *President Abraham Lincoln led the Union during the Civil War (1861–1865) and emancipated slaves in the South (1863).*

[3] **inscription** To *inscribe* is to mark or engrave words on a surface (as by writing a dedication on the first page of a book or by carving a phrase on a marble gravestone, for example). An *inscription* is such a marking or engraving. *Two well-known inscriptions are those on the Liberty Bell ("Proclaim liberty throughout all the land unto all the inhabitants thereof") and the Statue of Liberty (which includes the words "Give me your tired, your poor, your huddled masses yearning to breathe free").*

149

fairy who died of grief when abandoned by her brother, Pinocchio."

The poor puppet was overcome with anguish at reading those words. He fell to the ground and, covering the cold marble with kisses, burst into bitter tears. He cried all night, and dawn found him still there, though his tears had dried and only hard, dry sobs shook his wooden frame. But these were so loud that they echoed from the faraway hills.

As he sobbed he said to himself: "Oh, my fairy, my dear, dear fairy, why did you die? They say that our existence on earth is **finite**[1], that no one is **immortal**[2]. But as a magical fairy you had the ability to **manipulate**[3] the course of nature

---

[1] **finite** If something (a number or amount of something, for example) is *finite*, it's capable of being completely counted; it has bounds or limits. The opposite is *infinite* (pronounced *IN-fuh-nit*), which means "without bounds or limits; uncountable." *In our discussion about stars, we couldn't agree on whether the number of stars in the universe was finite or infinite, but we did agree that the life span of any individual star was finite.*

[2] **immortal** To be *mortal* is to be subject to death; to have a limited life span. Someone who is *immortal* is not mortal; he's not subject to death (for example, in Greek mythology, the gods — Zeus, Poseidon, Apollo, etc. — were said to be immortal). The noun is *immortality*. *In 1943 author and lecturer Anne Smedley said, "The belief in immortality has always seemed cowardly to me; when I was very young I learned that all things die, and [anything] good must be won [while we are alive] or not at all.* Also, a person (who has died) might be called *immortal* if his reputation or memory lives forever. To *immortalize* someone (or something) is to cause him or his memory to live forever (or seemingly forever). *Medieval Swiss archer William Tell was immortalized in an 1829 opera by Gioacchino Rossini.*

[3] **manipulate** This word has two senses, depending on the context. To *manipulate* something with your hands is to skillfully control or operate it; handle it (as in *manipulate the dials of a machine*). *The pitch of a kettledrum can be changed by manipulating screws (with T-shaped handles) at the edge of the head.* In another sense, to *manipulate* something is to shrewdly, deviously, or falsely influence it to one's own advantage (as in *manipulate public opinion* or *manipulate stock prices*). *In 1955 journalist Walter Lippmann said, "Successful politicians advance only as [long as they satisfy], bribe, seduce, bamboozle, or otherwise manage to manipulate the demanding and threatening elements in [the population]."*

by calling upon forces that exist beyond the **realm**[1] of the **material**[2] world. You could have **invoked**[3] the **occult**[4]. You weren't supposed to die. Oh, why didn't I die instead of you,

---

[1] **realm** A *realm* is a particular field of interest, study, thought, or activity (as in *the realm of physics*). *Some well-known singers (Tony Bennett, Joni Mitchell, and Cat Stevens, for example) have achieved success in the realm of painting.* The word also signifies a figurative place (region, domain) in which particular things exist or occur (as in *the realm of dreams*). According to the Reader's Companion to American History, *"Baseball has always been such a difficult game that those few who play it well and joyfully and gracefully – players such as Babe Ruth and Willie Mays – are lifted by fans into the realm of myth."* And sometimes the word simply signifies a particular kingdom or geographical area (as in *the realm of England*).

[2] **material** As an adjective, this word is used to describe anything pertaining to the physical rather than the spiritual (as in *material objects*), or to anything pertaining to this world as opposed to heaven, the afterlife, or the like (as in *material existence*). *American writer and philosopher Ralph Waldo Emerson (1803–1882) once said, "Great men are they who see that spiritual is stronger than any material force, that thoughts rule the world."*

[3] **invoke (invoked)** To *invoke* a higher power (God, for example) is to call upon it (for help, aid, support, etc.). *The last sentence of President Abraham Lincoln's Emancipation Proclamation (1863), which declared that all persons held as slaves shall be forever free, reads: "And upon this act, sincerely believed to be an act of justice…I invoke the considerate judgment of mankind and the gracious favor of Almighty God."* Note: The word has two other meanings. To *invoke* a law, rule, treaty, strategy, etc., is to apply it or enforce it (as in *invoke the Fifth Amendment*). And the word can also mean "cite (mention) as an authority or an authoritative example in order to support or justify something (as in *invoke the U.S. Constitution*)."

[4] **occult** As a noun, the *occult* is anything considered supernatural; that is, anything outside the natural world or beyond the range of ordinary understanding. Some specific arts and practices that fall under the category of "the occult" are magic, witchcraft, sorcery, spiritualism (communication with the dead), fortune-telling, ESP, and numerology. As an adjective, the word means "pertaining to the occult; that is, supernatural, magical, out-of-body, etc." *English writer Daniel Defoe, best known for his 1719 novel* Robinson Crusoe, *had a continuing interest in the occult, as evidenced by his 1726 work,* The Political History of the Devil.

when I am so bad and you are so good? And my father—where can he be? Please, dear fairy, tell me where he is and I'll never, never leave him again! You're not really dead, are you? If you love me, you'll come back, alive as before. Don't you feel sorry for me? I'm so lonely. What will I do alone in the world? Will I have to spend the rest of my life roaming the streets like a poor **waif**[1]? Where will I eat? Where will I sleep? Who will make my clothes?"

Poor Pinocchio! All these **vexing**[2] concerns swirled around in his mind until he could no longer stand it. Losing all control, he tried to tear out his hair, but as it was only painted on his wooden head, he couldn't even pull it.

Just then a pigeon flew far above him. Seeing the puppet, he called to him, "Tell me, little boy, what are you doing there?"

"Can't you see? I'm crying," sobbed Pinocchio, lifting his head toward the voice and rubbing his eyes with his sleeve. "My lovely sister has died."

---

[1] **waif** A *waif* is a person (often a neglected or orphaned child) who has no home or friends. Such a person is often thin from lack of nourishment. As a result, the word is sometimes used to signify any person (especially a girl or young woman, whether homeless and friendless or not) with a thin appearance (as when a thin fashion model is called a *waif*, for example). *The 1964 film* My Fair Lady *concerns a professor in England (played by Rex Harrison) who teaches a waif with a cockney accent (played by Audrey Hepburn) how to speak and act like a member of the upper class.*

[2] **vex (vexing)** To *vex* someone is to annoy or bother him (or irritate him, disturb him, pester him, etc.). Anything described as *vexing* (a difficult problem or grouchy neighbor, for example) is bothersome, annoying, irritating, etc. *One of English novelist Jane Austen's (1775–1817) fictional characters (Catherine Morland in* Northanger Abbey*), says of history, "I read it a little as a duty, but it tells me nothing that does not either vex or weary me; the quarrels of popes and kings [fill] every page."*

"My deepest **condolences**[1]," said the pigeon respectfully. Then, to try to soften the puppet's grief—but being careful to avoid such unpleasant words as *death* and *dying*—he added **euphemistically**[2], "It's especially difficult when a **sibling**[3] passes, but take **solace**[4] in knowing that she sleeps in peace."

"Thank you," muttered Pinocchio, still weeping.

"Tell me, do you by chance know of a boy named Pinocchio?"

"Pinocchio! Did you say Pinocchio?" replied the puppet, jumping to his feet. "Why, I'm Pinocchio!"

At this answer, the pigeon flew swiftly to the ground.

"Then you know Geppetto also?"

---

[1] **condolence (condolences)** A *condolence* is an (often formal) expression of sympathy to someone who is suffering grief, sorrow, misfortune, etc. (especially to a relative of one who has died). The word is often used in the plural. *After the assassination (November 1995) of Israeli Prime Minister Itzhak Rabin, Palestinian leader Yasser Arafat visited Israel and extended his personal condolences to Rabin's widow, Leah.*

[2] **euphemism (euphemistically)** Because words and phrases pertaining to such topics as death, sex, and bathroom functions may be considered offensive, people sometimes substitute inoffensive words or phrases in their place. Such a substituted word or phrase is known as a *euphemism* (pronounced with the accent on the first syllable). For example, "pass away" is a euphemism for "die," and "bathroom tissue" is a euphemism for "toilet paper." *Some scholars believe that the answer to how the phrase "the birds and the bees" became a euphemism for "sex education" lies in a few lines from English poet Samuel Coleridge (1772-1834): "All nature seems at work...the bees are stirring, birds are on the wing."*

[3] **sibling** A *sibling* is each of two or more individuals born to the same parents; or, to put it simply, a brother or sister. *According to the Bible, Moses's siblings, Aaron and Miriam, helped their younger brother lead the Israelites out of Egypt.*

[4] **solace** Comfort (or consolation, relief, etc.) at a time of sorrow (or misfortune, distress, trouble, etc.) is known as *solace*. *In Edgar Allan Poe's most famous poem, "The Raven" (1845), the narrator seeks solace from the death of his beloved, Lenore, by devoting himself to a study of ancient literature (until he is distracted by a tapping at his chamber door).*

"Do I know him? He's my father, my poor, dear father! Has he, perhaps, spoken to you of me? Will you take me to him? Is he still alive? Answer me, please! Is he still alive?"

"I can't **affirm**[1] that. All I know is that I saw him three days ago on the seacoast."

"What was he doing?"

"He was building a little boat and studying **nautical**[2] charts. For the past four months, that poor man has been looking for you. Not having found you after an **exhaustive**[3] search, he's made up his mind to **embark**[4] on a sea voyage to look for you in distant lands."

---

[1] **affirm** To *affirm* something is to state or declare it to be true; to state it as a fact. *Although many people claim to have seen UFOs, scientists cannot affirm their existence.* The noun is *affirmation. In his inaugural address (1977), President Jimmy Carter said of his goals of justice, equality, and world peace, "They will not be my accomplishments, but the affirmation of our nation's continuing moral strength."* Note: In law, to *affirm* something is to confirm it (as in *the higher court affirmed the opinion of the lower court*) or to ratify it (as in *a vote was taken and the amendment was affirmed*).

[2] **nautical** This word (derived from the Greek word for "sailor," *naut*) is used to describe anything pertaining to ships, sailors, the sea, or navigation. *The seafood restaurant was decorated with nautical touches, including an anchor, a ship's steering wheel, and a ship's clock.*

[3] **exhaustive** If something (a search, investigation, study, etc.) is *exhaustive,* it's thoroughly carried out; no part of it is left unexamined or unconsidered; it's comprehensive, complete, etc. *After an exhaustive investigation of the assassination (1963) of John F. Kennedy, the Warren Commission (a committee headed by Supreme Court chief justice Earl Warren) concluded that 24-year-old Lee Harvey Oswald, acting alone, had killed the President.*

[4] **embark** If you're talking about a vessel (a ship or aircraft, for example), to *embark* is to go aboard (as at the start of a journey). Note: To get off a vessel is to *disembark.* If you're talking about a venture (or enterprise, undertaking, journey, etc.) to *embark* is to set out on it; take the initial step of it; begin it. *When he was six years old, Austrian composer/pianist Wolfgang Amadeus Mozart (1756–1791), along with his older sister, Maria Anna, embarked on a series of concert tours to Europe's courts and major cities.*

"How far is it from here to the shore?" asked Pinocchio anxiously.

"About fifty miles."

"Fifty miles? Oh, dear pigeon, how I wish I had your wings!"

"If you want to come, I'll take you with me," said the pigeon, who was **atypically**[1] large.

"How?"

"On my back. Are you very heavy?"

"Heavy? Not at all. I'm as light as a feather."

"Okay, then."

Saying nothing more, Pinocchio jumped on the pigeon's back. He was delighted to discover that its **plumage**[2] was comfortably soft and thick.

The bird began its flight, and in a few minutes they'd reached the clouds. The puppet looked down to enjoy the scenic **panorama**[3] just as they happened to be angling over a

---

[1] **atypical (atypically)** If something (an object or living thing, for example) is *atypical*, it's not typical; that is, it departs from what is normal (for its type); it's irregular, nonstandard, uncharacteristic, etc. *According to the* Columbia Encyclopedia, *"Unlike normal cells, cancer cells are atypical in structure and do not have specialized functions; they compete with normal cells for nutrients, eventually killing normal tissue."*

[2] **plumage** A bird's *plumage* is its entire covering of feathers; its feathers collectively. From bird to bird, it varies in color, thickness, etc. It protects from the cold, provides camouflage, attracts a mate, etc. *As its name implies, the blue jay has a mostly blue plumage.*

[3] **panorama** A *panorama* is a wide, unobstructed view of an extensive area, particularly a natural setting (as in *the mountaintop provided a scenic panorama of the valley*). A planetarium reproduces a panorama of the sky as seen at a particular time from a particular location. Note: Sometimes the word is used figuratively to signify a wide view of anything or a comprehensive survey (as by a series of changing scenes or unfolding events) of anything (as in *a panorama of American history*).

deep, rocky **chasm**[1]. Suddenly losing his **equilibrium**[2], he clutched wildly at the pigeon's neck to keep himself from falling.

They flew all day without any further **mishaps**[3]. Toward evening the pigeon said, "I'm very thirsty!"

"And I'm very hungry!" answered Pinocchio.

"Let's stop a few minutes at that big birdhouse down there. Then we can go on and be at the seashore in the morning."

They flew down to the birdhouse, where they found nothing but a bowl of water and a small basket filled with sesame seeds.

Pinocchio had always hated sesame seeds. According to him, their **pungent**[1] flavor made him sick. But that night he

---

[1] **chasm** A *chasm* is a deep, steep-sided opening (a wide crack) in the Earth's (or another planet's) surface; a pit, canyon, gulf, etc. *According to the* Information Please Almanac, *"Mars is a rugged planet with huge volcanoes and deep chasms."* Note: The word is also used figuratively to refer to any type of wide or large break or split (as in *the chasm between the American Dream and middle-class reality*).

[2] **equilibrium** In physics, *equilibrium* is a state of rest or balance that occurs when opposing forces (such as gravity, inertia, centrifugal force, etc.) cancel each other out or equalize each other. But the word also can be used to signify any type of balance. For example, in psychology, it refers to emotional balance; in economics, to a balance between supply and demand; in ecology, to a balance of nature; and so on. *According to* Compton's Encyclopedia, *"Due to the uneven heating of the Earth's surface, the atmosphere is in a constant state of imbalance; weather conditions are the result of the atmosphere's attempt to gain equilibrium — a state it never achieves."*

[3] **mishap (mishaps)** A *mishap* (pronounced *MISS-hap*) is an unfortunate accident (especially a minor one or one whose consequences are not serious). *In 1986* Newsweek *magazine said that the real-life cases tried on the TV show* The People's Court *"are likely to swirl around botched paint jobs, unshoveled sidewalks, defective toasters, and every conceivable — and sometimes inconceivable — mishap involving a dry cleaner."*

ate them eagerly. As he finished them, he turned to the pigeon and said, "I'd never have thought that sesame seeds could taste so good!"

"You must remember," answered the pigeon, "that hunger is the **ultimate**[2] sauce!"

After resting a few more minutes, they set out again. As they flew it became darker and darker until they could see nothing but blackness on the ground below. But by doing what **migratory**[3] birds do — that is, relying on **olfactory**[4] cues and noting **lunar**[5] and **stellar**[1] positions — the pigeon was able

---

[1] **pungent** If a food or odor is *pungent*, it sharply affects the sense of taste or smell (whether agreeably or disagreeably); it's spicy, tart, strong, etc. Similarly, if a non-physical thing (a remark, memory, concept, etc.) is *pungent*, it sharply affects the mind or feelings; it's penetrating, biting, stimulating, etc. *The skunk is known for its black-and-white-striped fur and the pungent, offensive odor it sprays for defense.*

[2] **ultimate** If you describe something as *ultimate*, you mean that it's of the greatest extreme; the maximum; the most perfect, etc. (as in *the ultimate insult* or *the ultimate weapon*). *In 1977 rock music journalist Lester Bangs said, "The ultimate sin of any performer is [disrespect] for the audience."* Note: The word can also mean "final; last in a series" (as in *ultimate destination*) or "eventual" (as in *ultimate extinction*).

[3] **migrate (migratory)** When animals (certain birds, for example) *migrate*, they travel (usually when the seasons change) from one location (region, country, etc.) to another. The noun is *migration*. The adjective *migratory* means "migrating" or "pertaining to migration." *In 1975, speaking of women who attend matinee performances of Broadway shows, journalist Deirdre Carmody said, "Like an immense flock of chattering birds observing precise migratory habits, every Wednesday, just a few minutes before noon, they swoop down upon the midtown area."*

[4] **olfactory** This word means "pertaining to the sense of smell." *Ants have a complex system of communication, which includes visual, auditory, and olfactory signals.*

[5] **lunar** This word means "pertaining to the moon." *A plaque planted on the lunar surface by astronauts Neil Armstrong and Edwin "Buzz" Aldrin reads: "Here men from the planet Earth first set foot upon the moon, July 1969 A.D. We came in peace for all mankind."*

to stay firmly on course. Early the next morning they arrived safely at the seashore.

Pinocchio jumped off the pigeon's back, and the pigeon, not wanting any thanks for a kind deed, flew away swiftly and disappeared.

The shore was full of people who were shrieking and tearing their hair as they looked toward the sea.

"What's happened?" Pinocchio asked a little old woman.

"A poor old father lost his only son some time ago and today he built a tiny boat for himself to go in search of him across the sea. Considering the **immensity**[2] of the ocean, I don't think he'll ever make it across. Right now the water's very rough and we're afraid the boat will turn over and he'll drown."

"Where's the boat?"

"There. Straight out there," answered the little old woman, pointing to a tiny boat floating on the sea.

---

[1] **stellar** This word means "pertaining to the stars." *In 1609 Italian astronomer Galileo constructed the first astronomical telescope, which he used to discover the four largest moons of Jupiter and the stellar composition of our galaxy, the Milky Way.* Note: In another sense the word means "having the quality of a star performer; outstanding, brilliant, etc." *Center fielder and switch hitter Mickey Mantle was a stellar performer for the New York Yankees for 18 years.*

[2] **immensity** The adjective *immense* means "(sometimes immeasurably) vast, huge, enormous, etc." The noun *immensity* means "the state or condition of being immense; in other words, vastness, enormity, boundlessness, infiniteness, etc." *In 1960 German-American rocket engineer Wernher von Braun said, "Our sun is one of 100 billion stars in our galaxy; our galaxy is one of billions of galaxies populating the universe. It would be [rudely bold] to think that we are the only living things in that enormous immensity."*

Pinocchio looked closely for a few seconds. At first the misty waves **obscured**[1] his view and he saw nothing. Then suddenly he gave a sharp cry: "It's my father! It's my father!" The little boat, which from the shore looked no bigger than a nutshell, was tossed about by the angry waters. It alternately appeared and disappeared in the waves. Pinocchio, standing on a high rock, waved toward the boat with hand and cap.

It looked as if Geppetto, though far away from shore, recognized his son, for he took off his cap and waved also. He seemed to be trying to make everyone understand that he would come back if he were able, but the sea was so heavy that he couldn't control the **careening**[2] craft. Suddenly a huge wave came and the boat disappeared.

They waited and waited for it to reappear, but it was gone.

---

[1] **obscure (obscured)** As a verb, this word has two senses. If you're talking about an object, to *obscure* it is either to cut it off from sight or to make it difficult to see, as in *clouds obscured the mountaintop*. If you're talking about the meaning of something (language, life, reality, history, etc), to *obscure* it is to make it difficult to know or understand, as in *myths and legends obscured the true story*. *The* National Review *once noted: "Unlike the origins of most nations, America's origins are not obscured in the mists of time."* As an adjective, the word also has two senses. If you're talking about language, meaning, etc., it means "unclear, ambiguous, uncertain, etc.," as in *obscure references*. If you're talking about a person or place, it means "little known; unimportant; far from the center of activities," as in *an obscure Dutch painter* or *an obscure little town*. *In 1981 French film director François Truffaut said, "All film directors, whether famous or obscure, regard themselves as misunderstood or underrated."*

[2] **careen (careening)** When a vessel, such as a boat or plane, *careens*, it leans, sways, or tips to one side while in motion. When a vehicle, such as a car or bus, *careens*, it either leans to one side while in motion (as when speeding around a corner, for example), or it lurches or swerves. *According to the* Encarta Encyclopedia, *"BMX racing, or motocross, takes place on indoor or outdoor dirt tracks [on which] packs of riders careen around tight turns and jump over ramps and hills."*

"Poor man!" said a fishermen on the shore, as they turned to go home.

Just then they heard a desperate cry and, looking back, they saw Pinocchio dive into the sea and heard him cry out, "I'll save him! I'll save my father!"

The puppet, being made of wood, floated easily and swam like a fish in the rough water. Now and again he disappeared only to reappear once more. In an instant, he was far away from land. At last he was completely lost to view.

Chapter 20 "The Land of the Busy Bees"

Hoping to find his father in time to save him, Pinocchio swam all night.

And what a horrible night it was! It poured rain, it hailed, it thundered, and the lightning was so bright that it turned the night into day.

At dawn, he saw, not far away, a long stretch of sand. It was an island in the middle of the sea.

Pinocchio tried his best to get there, but he couldn't. The waves tossed him about as if he were a twig or a bit of straw. At last, luckily, a tremendous wave tossed him directly onto the shore. The blow from the wave was so strong that, as he fell to the ground, his joints rattled and almost broke. Nevertheless, he jumped to his feet and cried, "Once more I've escaped with my life!"

Little by little the sky cleared. The sun came out in full splendor and the sea became as sedate[1] as a county pond.

The puppet took off his clothes and laid them on the sand to dry. He looked out over the water to see if he could see a little boat with a man in it. He searched and searched, but he saw nothing except sea and sky.

The idea of finding himself in so lonesome a spot made him so sad that he was about to cry, but just then he saw a dolphin swimming nearby, with his head far out of the water.

Not knowing what to call him, the puppet shouted, "Hey there, may I have a word with you?"

---

[1] **sedate** A thing (a lake, for example) described as *sedate* is peaceful, quiet, calm, steady, motionless, etc. A person (or social gathering, work of art, pastime, etc.) described as *sedate* is quiet, calm, dignified, composed, cool, collected, unemotional, etc. *A suggestion to change the social studies curriculum suddenly changed the sedate PTA meeting into a free-for-all.* Note: As a verb, to *sedate* someone is to calm him by means of a drug (as in *the dentist sedated the patient*).

"Certainly," answered the dolphin, who happened to be very friendly.

"Will you please tell me if, on this island, there are places where one can eat without fear of being eaten?"

"Yes, there are," answered the dolphin. "In fact, you'll find one not far from this spot."

"Is it **accessible**[1] on foot?"

"Certainly. Take that path right there. When it **diverges**[2], stay to your left and then follow your nose. You can't go wrong."

"Tell me another thing. You travel day and night through the sea. Did you see, perhaps, a little boat with my father in it?"

"Who's your father?"

"He's the best father in the world, even though I'm the worst son."

"Last night's storm didn't **bode**[1] well for small craft," answered the dolphin. "The little boat must have sunk."

---

[1] **accessible** If something is *accessible*, it's easy to reach or enter (as a place), easy to get at (as an object), easy to approach or talk to (as a person), easy to understand (as a concept), or easy to obtain (as information). *In 1984 President Ronald Reagan's daughter Maureen said, "We are an ideal political family, as accessible as Disneyland."* Note: When people say that a particular place is *accessible*, they often mean simply that it's reachable, whether easily or not (as in *a mountaintop accessible only by helicopter*). *Yellowstone Park became accessible to vacationers when the Northern Pacific Railroad was completed in 1883.*

[2] **diverge (diverges)** When something (a road, for example) *diverges*, it lies, extends, or proceeds in different directions from a common point; it branches off. Note: The opposite is *converge* ("come together at a common point"). *In his poem "The Road Not Taken," Robert Frost (1874–1963) said, "Two roads diverged in a wood, and I/I took the one less traveled by/And that has made all the difference."* In another sense, if people's opinions or interests *diverge*, they differ. *The teaching of religious leader Martin Luther (1483–1546) diverged from the traditional beliefs of the Roman Catholic Church.*

"And my father?"

"For the last few days a **colossally**[2] large shark has been **dominating**[3] the depths around here. Like other sharks, he attacks without **provocation**[4]. He eats everything in sight—

---

[1] **bode** To *bode* is to suggest or indicate (a future possibility) beforehand; to be a sign or omen of; to forecast, foreshadow, foretell, etc. If something "bodes well," the outcome is likely to be favorable; if something "bodes ill," the outcome is likely to be unfavorable. *In 1577 Taqi al-Din, chief astronomer of the Ottoman Empire, interpreted the appearance of a bright comet as boding well for Sultan Murad III in his fight against the Persians.*

[2] **colossal (colossally)** As a noun, a *colossus* is a gigantic statue (such as the Statue of Liberty, for example), and technically, if something is *colossal*, it resembles a colossus. *Egypt's Great Sphinx is a colossal stone figure with the head of a man and the body of a lion.* However, most people use this word to mean simply "gigantic, huge, enormous, etc." (when describing anything of gigantic size). *According to* Compton's Encyclopedia, *"the blue whale is the largest animal to have ever lived; whalers have reported colossal specimens over 100 feet long and weighing up to 150 tons."*

[3] **dominate (dominating)** In one sense, to *dominate* something is to (sometimes in a bossy manner) exert a commanding or controlling influence over it; to rule it, lord over it, etc. *While President (1953–1961), Dwight D. Eisenhower claimed that if the Communists succeeded in controlling Vietnam, they would eventually dominate all of Southeast Asia.* In another sense, to *dominate* something is to be the most important, conspicuous, or influential person or thing present. *In the late 1970s, disco music dominated the pop charts.*

[4] **provoke (provocation)** To *provoke* a person is to (sometimes intentionally) anger him, annoy him, aggravate him, stir him up, etc. (especially so as to move him to action). *In the South in the 1960s, African-Americans involved in the civil rights movement, to draw attention to their cause, often sat at segregated lunch counters in order to provoke police into arresting them.* To *provoke* a particular incident or reaction (criticism, controversy, hysteria, etc.) is to bring it about, give rise to it, cause it, etc. *President Richard Nixon's April 1970 announcement that the U.S. needed to draft 150,000 additional soldiers for an expansion of the Vietnam War effort provoked massive protests on college campuses throughout the nation.* The noun is *provocation*.

swimmers, fish, ships. Your father may have been one of the **casualties**[1]."

"Exactly how big is this shark?" asked Pinocchio, who was beginning to tremble with fright.

"How big?" replied the dolphin. "Just to give you an **inkling**[2], I can tell you that he's as big as a mountain and that he has a mouth so wide that he could easily swallow an entire railroad train."

"Good gracious!" cried the puppet, scared to death.

By this time, the sun's **torrid**[3] rays had completely dried Pinocchio's clothes. Dressing himself as fast as he could, he turned to the dolphin and said, "Good-bye, and thank you."

This said, he took the path at so swift a pace that he seemed to fly, and at every small sound he heard, he turned in fear to see whether the shark was following him.

After walking a half hour, he came to a small country called the Land of the Busy Bees. The streets were filled with

---

[1] **casualties** People killed or injured in war or as the result of an unfortunate accident, incident, or natural catastrophe (plane crash, riot, earthquake, etc.) are referred to as *casualties. Iraqi military casualties in the 1991 Persian Gulf War numbered about 100,000 killed and 300,000 wounded.* Note: Things (businesses, for example) lost, destroyed, harmed, or eliminated (as the result of some act or event) can also be referred to as *casualties.*

[2] **inkling** To be given an *inkling* of something is to be given a slight hint or suggestion of it (as in *she wasn't given an inkling of what was in the box*). To have an *inkling* of something is to have a slight understanding of it or vague notion about it (as in *she had only an inkling of how to operate a computer*). *In August 1986, speaking of President Ronald Reagan's proposed Strategic Defense Initiative ("Star Wars"), Soviet military chief of staff Sergei Akhromeyev warned, "If the United States [installs] a shield in space, the Soviet Union will very quickly respond in a way which the United States has no inkling of as yet."*

[3] **torrid** If a physical substance, object, etc., is *torrid,* it's intensely hot. *The temperature of the Venus's torrid surface (over 800 degrees Fahrenheit) is hot enough to melt lead.* If something non-physical (a love song, a romance, etc.) is *torrid,* it's fiercely passionate. *William Shakespeare's* Antony and Cleopatra *(1606) dramatizes the torrid but ill-fated love affair of (Roman general) Mark Antony and (Egyptian queen) Cleopatra.*

people running back and forth, on business. Everyone worked; no one was **idle**[1].

"I understand," said Pinocchio to himself wearily, "that this is no place for me! I was not born for work."

But in the meantime, he began to feel hungry, for it had been a full day since he'd last eaten. What could he do? He knew that there were only two ways of **averting**[2] hunger. He'd have to either work or beg.

He was ashamed to beg, because his good father had **indoctrinated**[3] him with certain principles, one of which was that begging should be done only by the sick or the old. He

---

[1] **idle** If you're *idle*, you're not engaged in activity; you're not working; you're doing nothing. *In 1901 President Theodore Roosevelt said, "Men who are idle, men who seek gains not by genuine work but by gambling, are always a source of menace not only to themselves but to others."* Note: If you say that a thing is *idle*, you mean that it's not being used; it's not in operation (as in *idle machinery* or *idle hands*).

[2] **avert (averting)** To *avert* something is to prevent it (from happening); to stop it, ward it off, etc. *In November 1990 environmental ministers meeting at Geneva, Switzerland, demanded that all nations burn less oil to avert global warming.* Note: In another sense, to *avert* something is to turn it away or aside (as in *avert one's eyes*).

[3] **indoctrinate (indoctrinated)** To *indoctrinate* someone is to teach or instruct him (in a particular subject, principle, belief, idea, etc.). The noun is *indoctrination*. *According to* Grolier's Encyclopedia, *American playwright Eugene O'Neill's (1888–1953) "indoctrination to the [principles] of Irish Catholicism, in his home and while attending a Catholic boarding school and high school, left him with a deep spirituality that is [evident] in his work."* Sometimes the implication is that when a person is *indoctrinated*, he is taught or encouraged to accept one particular side of an issue without criticism; that he is, in effect, brainwashed. *While in power (1933-1945), the Nazis indoctrinated the German people with their ideas.*

had said that the **impoverished**[1] in this world deserve our pity and help only if, through either sickness or **senility**[2], they've become **incapacitated**[3]. All others should work, and if they didn't, and went hungry, too bad for them.

Just then a man passed by. He was worn out and wet with perspiration. He was pulling, with great difficulty, two heavy carts filled with coal. Pinocchio looked at him and, judging him by his looks to be a kind man, said with shame-filled eyes, "Will you be so good as to give me a penny, for I'm faint from hunger?"

"Not only one penny," answered the man. "I'll give you four if you'll help me pull these two wagons."

"I'm surprised!" answered the puppet, very much offended. "I'd like you to know that I've never been a donkey, nor have I ever pulled a wagon."

"Good for you!" answered the man. "Then, my boy, if you're really faint from hunger, eat two pieces of your pride. And I hope they don't give you a tummy ache."

A few minutes after, a bricklayer passed by, carrying a pail full of plaster on his shoulders.

---

[1] **impoverished** If you're *impoverished*, you've been reduced to poverty; you have no money; you're poverty-stricken, poor, broke, etc. *In his "War on Poverty" speech (1964), President Lyndon Johnson said, "Through a new community-action program, we intend to strike at poverty at its source — in the streets of our cities and on the farms of our countryside among the very young and the impoverished old."*

[2] **senile (senility)** If you say that an old person is *senile*, you mean that he exhibits the loss of mental faculties associated with old age; he's forgetful, feeble-minded, disoriented, etc. The noun is *senility*. *In 1987, after 30 years in office, the president of (the African country of) Tunisia, 84-year-old Habib Bourguiba, was declared senile and removed from office.*

[3] **incapacitated** If you're *incapacitated*, you have no strength or ability to perform (usually as the result of a physical disability or handicap); you're disabled, helpless, incapable, unfit, etc. *Although in 1919 President Woodrow Wilson suffered a stroke that left him incapacitated, his condition was not made public.*

"Good man, will you be kind enough to give a penny to a poor boy who's starving?"

"Gladly," answered the bricklayer. "Come with me and carry some plaster, and instead of one penny, I'll give you five."

"But plaster's heavy," answered Pinocchio, "and the work is too hard for me."

"If the work is too hard for you, my boy, enjoy your hunger, and may it bring you luck!"

In less than a half hour, at least twenty people passed and Pinocchio begged of each one. But they all answered, "Aren't you ashamed to beg? Don't you realize that by **dint**[1] of hard work and **perseverance**[2] you can earn your own bread?"

In spite of all his failures thus far, Pinocchio refused to allow himself to become **disheartened**[3]. Finally, there passed

---

[1] **dint** This word is usually heard in the phrase "by dint of," which means "through the application of," "by means of," "by force of," etc. *By dint of such dramatic strategies as mass marches and hunger strikes, the National Woman's Party helped win women the right to vote (1920).*

[2] **persevere (perseverance)** To *persevere* is to steadily persist in (stick to, continue with) a particular course of action, undertaking, or purpose, often in spite of difficulties; to "keep on keeping on," so to speak. The noun is *perseverance*, which is what some people informally call "stick-to-itiveness." *To describe the perseverance of U.S. Postal Service mail carriers, people often say that "neither snow, nor rain, nor heat, nor gloom of night" shall stop them from completing their rounds (interestingly, that phrase was actually written by ancient Greek historian Herodotus to describe the perseverance of Persian messengers of his day).*

[3] **disheartened** To become *disheartened* is to lose heart; in other words, to lose hope, courage, spirit, enthusiasm, etc. People who become *disheartened* feel depressed, discouraged, sad, broken, crushed, etc. *After his 1851 novel* Moby Dick *was misunderstood and poorly received, Herman Melville became disheartened; however, he continued to produce important works, including the novella* Billy Budd.

before him a little woman **encumbered**[1] with two heavy water buckets.

"Good woman," said the puppet, whose wooden tongue was suddenly **parched**[2] by thirst, "will you allow me to have a drink from one of your buckets?"

"With pleasure, my boy!" she answered, setting the two buckets on the ground before him.

Pinocchio could hardly believe his good fortune. When he had had his fill, he wiped his mouth and said, "My thirst is gone. Now if I could only get rid of my hunger!"

On hearing these words, the good little woman said, "If you help me carry one of these buckets home, I'll give you a slice of bread."

Pinocchio looked at the buckets and said neither yes nor no.

"And with the bread, I'll give you a bowl of soup."

Pinocchio gave the buckets another look but continued to **balk**[3] at the idea of having to carry one.

---

[1] **encumber (encumbered)** To *encumber* someone is (1) to burden him (weigh him down) with something heavy, as in *a hiker encumbered with a 30-pound backpack*, (2) to burden him with debts, responsibilities, obligations, or the like, as in *a man encumbered with child support payments*, or (3) to restrict or limit his progress or freedom of movement, as in *political action encumbered by red tape (time-consuming governmental procedures)*. *According to the* Encarta Encyclopedia, "*Eighteenth-century [French] dancers were encumbered by elaborate costumes, masks, wigs or large headdresses, and heeled shoes.*"

[2] **parch (parched)** When something (land, grain, or one's throat, for example) becomes *parched*, it becomes extremely or overly dry (especially from exposure to heat). *The Sahara was not always a parched desert as it is today; during the Ice Age it was a rich grassland.*

[3] **balk** To *balk* (rhymes with *talk*) is to hesitate or stop (before doing or continuing a particular action or activity). *All the tenants agreed that the apartment building should hire a 24-hour security guard; then, most balked when they found out that doing so would result in a rent increase of $150 a month!* Note: In baseball a *balk* is a failure to complete a pitch once it's been started; it's an illegal motion resulting in a penalty advancing the runner(s) one base.

"And after the soup, some cookies."

At this last **enticement**[1], Pinocchio could no longer resist and said firmly, "Very well. I'll carry one home for you."

The bucket was very heavy, and the puppet, not being strong enough to carry it with his hands, had to put it on his head.

When they arrived at the woman's house, she sat Pinocchio down at a small table and placed before him the bread, the soup, and the cookies, all of which Pinocchio ate with **gusto**[2].

His hunger finally satisfied, he raised his head to thank his kind **benefactress**[3]. But he hadn't looked at her long when he gave a cry of surprise and sat there with his eyes and mouth wide open.

"Why all the surprise?" asked the good woman, laughing.

"Because," answered Pinocchio, stammering and stuttering, "because...you look like...you remind me of...yes, yes, the same voice, the same eyes, the same hair...yes, yes, yes, you also have the same blue hair she had. Oh, my little fairy,

---

[1] **entice (enticement)** To *entice* someone is to attract him to (or sometimes lure him into) some particular thing (a situation, place, course of action, etc.) by arousing his hope or desire. The noun *enticement* refers either to the act of enticing or to the actual thing (an object, a promise, etc.) by which one is enticed. *According to* Grolier's Encyclopedia, "*[Brazilian soccer great] Pele retired in 1974 but was enticed to return to play in 1975 when the New York Cosmos offered him a multimillion-dollar contract.*"

[2] **gusto** To do something (eat, drink, perform, speak, etc.) with *gusto* is to do it with hearty enjoyment or with enthusiasm and energy. *In 1985, speaking of the U.S. Marine Band, journalist Dana Kleiman said, "A sea of red coats and white trousers, in perfect step, the [melodies] of the [Nation] blasted with gusto, the kind of sing-along oom pah pah of which patriotism is made.*"

[3] **benefactor (benefactress)** A *benefactor* is a person (male or female) who gives kindly aid or help (especially one who gives money to a person, organization, charity, or cause). If such a person is female, she also may be called a *benefactress. Harvard University (Cambridge, Massachusetts) was named in honor of its first benefactor, clergyman John Harvard (1607–1638), who left the school half his estate and his 400-volume library.*

my little fairy! Tell me that it's you! Don't make me cry any longer! If you only knew! I have cried so much, I have suffered so!"

And Pinocchio threw himself onto the floor and clasped the knees of the mysterious little woman and began to cry.

Chapter 21 "Pinocchio's Mother"

Afraid that Pinocchio might melt away if he cried much longer, the woman finally **acknowledged**[1] that she was indeed the little fairy with blue hair.

"You rascal! How did you know it was I?" she asked, laughing.

"My love for you told me who you were."

"Do you remember? You left me when I was a little girl and now you find me a grown woman. I'm so old, I could be your mother!"

"For a long time I've wanted a mother, just like other boys. But how did you grow so quickly?"

"That's a secret!"

"Tell it to me."

"It's a secret only fairies are permitted to know. I'm afraid I'm not at liberty to **disclose**[2] it."

"But I also want to grow a little. Look at me! I've never grown taller than three feet."

"But you can't grow," answered the fairy.

"Why? What's wrong with me? Did I suffer some kind of **natal**[3] injury? Did the part of my brain that controls growth **malfunction**[1]? Did—"

---

[1] **acknowledge (acknowledged)** To *acknowledge* something is to admit or recognize (sometimes reluctantly or under pressure) that it's true or that it exists. *In the 1783 Treaty of Paris, which ended the Revolutionary War, Great Britain formally acknowledged American independence.*

[2] **disclose** To *disclose* something (a secret or anything that has been or ought to be kept from the knowledge of others) is to make it known, reveal it, tell it, etc. *In 1994 former President Ronald Reagan disclosed that he had Alzheimer's disease in the hope of increasing public awareness of the illness.*

[3] **natal** This word is used to describe anything pertaining to (or accompanying, dating from, or present at) one's birth, as in *natal influences*. *In astrology, your natal chart is determined by the position of all the planets at the exact moment of your birth.*

"No, no. Of course not. There's nothing wrong with you. It's just that puppets never grow. They're born puppets, they live as puppets, and they die as puppets."

"But I'm tired of always being a little puppet!" cried Pinocchio disgustedly. "People speak of the **brevity**[2] of childhood — but for me it feels **interminable**[3]. It's time for me to grow up and become a man, as everyone else does."

"There's another secret that all adults know, and this one I can **divulge**[4]."

"What is it?"

"Every child thinks that when he grows up, he'll become a different person. But the child-adult **dichotomy**[1] is a false one.

---

[1] **malfunction** If something (a machine or bodily organ, for example) *malfunctions*, it fails to function properly; it breaks down, acts up, stalls, quits, "goes on the fritz," etc. *In November 1996 a Russian spacecraft headed for Mars malfunctioned and crashed into the Pacific Ocean.*

[2] **brevity** This word, the noun form of the word *brief*, has two senses. If a particular event (or situation, circumstance, activity, etc.) has *brevity*, it's short in duration; it's brief. *Not much is remembered about the Presidency of James Garfield, perhaps because of the brevity of his term of office — only 200 days from his inauguration (March 1881) to his death at the hands of an assassin.* If one's speech or writing has *brevity*, it uses few words; it's compact, concise, short, etc. *Abraham Lincoln's Gettysburg Address (November 1863) is noted for its definition of democracy (government of the people, by the people, and for the people) and its brevity (less than 300 words, which took less than three minutes to deliver).*

[3] **interminable** If something is *interminable*, either it lasts, or seems to last, forever (as in *an interminable wait on a stalled train*), or it's annoyingly, tiresomely, or monotonously long (as in *an interminable list of rules and regulations*). *In 1976 journalist Anatole Broyand said, "The tension between yes and no, between I can and I cannot, makes us feel that, in so many instances, human life is an interminable debate with one's self."*

[4] **divulge** To *divulge* something (a secret or anything private or previously unknown) is to reveal it (or report it, tell it, show it, etc.). *According to the International Treaty at the Hague Conference of 1899, prisoners of war must not be forced to divulge military information other than name, rank, and serial number.*

After children grow up, they find that their thoughts and feelings are pretty much the same as they always were."
"Well, then what I want is to change from a puppet into a real boy — and then grow up."
"And you will if you deserve it."
"Really? Will I be **transformed**[2] **instantaneously**[3]? Or will it be a gradual **transition**[4]?" .

---

[1] **dichotomy** Technically, a *dichotomy* (pronounced *die-KOT-uh-me*) is a division (of something) into two parts. But people usually use this word to refer to a division into two parts which are (in concept, opinion, idea, meaning, quality, etc.) somehow sharply contrasting (as in *the dichotomy between theory and practice* or the *dichotomy between words and action*). *In 1993 TV producer Ellen Lewis said, "There is a striking dichotomy between the behavior of many women in their lives at work [where they battle assumptions about the roles of men and women] and in their lives as mothers [where they accept and reinforce these roles]."*

[2] **transform (transformed)** To *transform* something is to (usually markedly) change it from one form (or structure, appearance, type, condition, nature, character, substance, function, etc.) into another (as in *a prince transformed into a frog by a witch's spell*). *In 1965 Spanish painter Pablo Picasso (1881–1973) said, "There are painters who transform the sun into a yellow spot, but there are others who, thanks to their art and intelligence, transform a yellow spot into the sun."*

[3] **instantaneous (instantaneously)** If something (a particular action, for example) is *instantaneous*, it happens (or occurs, or is done, or is completed) in an instant; that is, it happens in an almost imperceptibly short amount of time (or, to use other words, it happens in a split second, in a moment, lightning quick, immediately, spontaneously, etc.). *In May 1844, with his telegraph and "Morse code," American inventor Samuel Morse demonstrated the possibility of almost instantaneous communication between cities by sending an electrical message ("What hath God wrought!") from Washington, D.C., to Baltimore, Maryland.*

[4] **transition** A *transition* is a passage (or movement or change) from one state (or form, style, position, stage, etc.) to another (as in *the transition from an agricultural to an industrial economy*). *Sylvia Plath's novel* The Bell Jar *(1963) concerns a schoolgirl whose transition to adulthood is marked by periodic mental breakdowns.*

173

"You're not going to **evolve**[1] little by little through a series of **incremental**[2] steps, if that's what you mean. Rather, the change will happen all at once — but not until you deserve it."

"What can I do to deserve it?"

"It's very simple. Just behave like a good boy."

"Don't you think I do?"

The fairy thought for a moment and then said, "How can I say this **tactfully**[3]? Let's just say that you can do better. For example, good boys do as they're told. You, on the other hand — "

"And I never obey."

"Good boys do their homework, but you — "

---

[1] **evolve** When something (an idea, an art form, an invention, etc.) *evolves*, it gradually takes shape, develops, or changes (often by becoming more complex or organized). *According to the* Columbia Encyclopedia, *singer/song-writer Bob Dylan "exercised a profound influence on folk and rock music, his style evolving from folk to folk-rock to country."* Note: In biology, to *evolve* is to come into being through evolutionary development (as in *man evolved from apes*).

[2] **increment (incremental)** An *increment* is something added (or the amount of something added), especially as one of a regular or uniform series of such additions. If you describe something (increases, gains, steps, progress, improvements, shifts, etc.) as *incremental,* you mean that they advance in increments; that is, they advance in (often small) regular amounts or as a series of (often small) steps. *A January 1999 editorial in the* Washington Post *said that President Bill Clinton "continues to propose incremental health care reforms as [opposed to the large-scale] kind that [failed] at such great political cost in 1994."*

[3] **tact (tactfully)** If you have *tact,* you have a keen sense of what is appropriate and proper in dealing with others or in handling delicate situations; in particular, you know how to say things without being insulting or giving offense. *Comedian Steve Allen (1921–2000) once told a story about a fan proudly showing off her new baby; Allen, thinking the baby the ugliest he had ever seen, tactfully remarked, "Now, that's a baby!"*

"And I use any **pretext**[1] to get out of it."

"Good boys do their chores."

"And I **procrastinate**[2] or don't do them at all."

"Good boys always tell the truth."

"And I'm a **chronic**[3] liar."

"Good boys go to school."

"And I get sick if I go to school. But from now on I'll be different."

"Do you promise?"

"I promise. I want to be a good boy and to be a comfort to my father. Where's my poor father now?"

"I don't know."

"Will I ever be lucky enough to find him and hug him again?"

"I think so. Indeed, I'm sure of it."

At this answer, Pinocchio became very happy. He grasped the fairy's hands and kissed them. Then, lifting his face, he

---

[1] **pretext** A *pretext* is a false reason (or purpose, motive, appearance, etc.) put forward to conceal a real reason (or intention, condition, etc.); a misleading excuse. For example, if you don't feel like cleaning your room, you might use an imaginary illness as a *pretext* for not doing so. *In 1774 French philosopher Denis Diderot said, "Disturbances in society are never more fearful than when those who are stirring up the trouble can use the pretext of religion to mask their true designs."*

[2] **procrastinate** To *procrastinate* is to put off doing something that ought to be done (generally out of laziness); to postpone or delay needlessly. *Comedienne Judy Tenuta once joked, "My mother always told me I wouldn't amount to anything because I procrastinate; I said 'Just wait.'"*

[3] **chronic** If you describe a behavior as *chronic* you mean that it's habitual or constant (as in *chronic smoker*). If you describe a situation or medical condition as *chronic* you mean that it has lasted a long time and that it's marked by frequent recurrences (as in *chronic warfare* or *chronic pain*). *According to Grolier's Encyclopedia, "Many baseball authorities believe that [Sandy Koufax] might have established himself as the greatest pitcher ever had not chronic arthritis in his left elbow forced his early retirement in 1966."*

175

looked at her lovingly and asked, "Tell me, it isn't true that you're dead, is it?"

"It doesn't seem so," answered the fairy, smiling.

"If you only knew how I suffered and how I wept when I read 'Here lies—'"

"I know it, and for that I've forgiven you. The depth of your sorrow made me see that you have a kind heart. There's always hope for boys with hearts such as yours. Do you know why I've come so far to look for you? It's because of my **conviction**[1] that there's a good boy somewhere deep down inside of you. That's why. And from now on, I'm going to be your mother."

"Oh, how lovely!" cried Pinocchio, jumping with joy.

"You will obey me always and do as I wish?"

"Gladly, very gladly; more than gladly!"

"Beginning tomorrow," said the fairy, "you'll go to school every day."

Pinocchio's face fell a little.

"Then you'll choose the trade or profession you like best."

Pinocchio became more serious.

"What are you mumbling to yourself?" asked the fairy.

"I was just saying," whined the puppet, "that it seems too late for me to go to school now."

"No, my child. Remember that it's never too late to learn."

"But I don't want to learn a trade or profession."

"Why?"

"Because work tires me out!"

"My dear son," said the fairy, "laziness is a serious illness, and it must be eliminated in early childhood, while it's still in

---

[1] **conviction** A *conviction* is a fixed, firm, or strong belief (in something); a feeling of certainty (about something). *American writer Owen Wister (1860-1938) once said, "Every good man in this world has convictions about right and wrong."*

an **embryonic**[1] stage; otherwise, it will destroy you. On the other hand, a love of work promotes well being and **longevity**[2]. No one can find happiness without it."

These words touched Pinocchio's heart. He lifted his eyes to his mother and said seriously, "I'll work; I'll study; I'll do everything you say. After all, the life of a puppet has grown very tiresome to me and I want to become a real boy, no matter how hard it is. You promise that, don't you?"

"Yes, I promise. And now it's all up to you."

---

[1] **embryonic** In biology an *embryo* is a plant or animal that is not yet fully developed (such as a developing baby within the womb). By extension, people sometimes use the word *embryo* figuratively to signify any new or developing project, concept, idea, etc. The adjective *embryonic* (whether referring to living organisms or to concepts) is used to describe what is in an early stage; what is just beginning; what is immature, undeveloped, etc. *The first Australian railroad (which linked Sydney with a town about 100 miles to the southwest) was built in 1869; by the 1880s, all six of the colonies that made up the continent had at least an embryonic rail network.*

[2] **longevity** This word means either "long life; great duration of life," as in *exercise increases longevity*, or "length of life; life span (whether long or not)," as in *the average longevity of a chipmunk is six years. Two actor/comedians known for their longevity (in fact, each lived to 100) are George Burns (1896–1996) and Bob Hope (1903–2003).*

Chapter 22 *"Pinocchio Goes to School"*

Bright and early the next morning, Pinocchio started for school.

When the other children saw a puppet enter the classroom, they laughed until they cried. All the boys played tricks on him. One pulled his hat off, another tugged at his coat, and a third tried to paint a mustache under his nose. One even tried to tie strings to his hands and feet to make him dance. The teacher finally put an end to the **mayhem**[1] by ordering the children to their seats.

For a while, by sitting very still and forcing himself to wear a **deadpan**[2] expression, Pinocchio managed to maintain his **composure**[3]. But behind him he could hear the other boys whispering to each other about him and quietly laughing. Any remark that wasn't **blatantly**[4] cruel was filled with **innu-**

---

[1] **mayhem** This word signifies a state of (often violent or noisy) commotion, confusion, or disorder; havoc, disruption, chaos, pandemonium, etc. (as in *the mayhem of the Marx Brothers*). *According to* Compton's Encyclopedia, *in the early days of radio (1920s), "because there was very limited regulation, radio stations interfered with each other, creating mayhem on the air."*

[2] **deadpan** If something (a facial expression or manner of speech, for example) is *deadpan*, it's totally without expression or emotion; it's blank, wooden, etc. Such an expression or manner is sometimes "put on" by performers for comic effect. *Comedian Jack Benny (1894-1974) was known for his deadpan stares and for his image as the world's stingiest man and world's worst violin player.*

[3] **composure** A person's *composure* is his calmness of mind; his self-control; his coolness, poise, etc. *First Lady Jacqueline Kennedy was admired for her elegance in fashion and for her composure following the 1963 assassination of her husband (President John F. Kennedy).*

[4] **blatant (blatantly)** Anything described as *blatant* is completely and unashamedly (and often offensively) obvious or conspicuous; it's glaring, barefaced, etc. (as in *blatant lie* or *blatant exaggeration*). *If you walk through various neighborhoods of New York City, you'll see blatant differences in levels of wealth.*

endo[1]. At first he ignored their insults; but as they continued, he found it harder and harder to remain **impassive**[2]. Then, when they started trading **jocular**[3] remarks — "Is that a nose or a flagpole?" for example — he lost his patience and, turning around, said threateningly, "Careful, boys; I haven't come here to be **harassed**[4] or made fun of. I'll respect you and I want you to respect me."

"Good for you!" **jeered**[5] the boys, bursting with laughter.

---

[1] **innuendo** If you express something (usually negative) about someone or something without actually coming right out and saying it — that is, if you say it indirectly by merely hinting at it or by making a remark with a double meaning — you're using *innuendo*. *During the 1980 presidential election campaign, Republican vice presidential candidate George H. Bush said that while he was taking "the high road" (in conducting his campaign), his Democratic opponents (Jimmy Carter and Walter Mondale) were guilty of "innuendo and low-road politics."*

[2] **impassive** If you're *impassive*, you experience no emotion or you show none; you are (or act as though you are) calm, unmoved, undisturbed, unaffected, indifferent, etc. *When he drew four aces on the first deal, he kept his face impassive, though his heart was filled with glee.*

[3] **jocular** People who are *jocular* speak or act in a joking manner; they're funny, witty, playful, tongue-in-cheek, etc. Speech or action described as *jocular* is in the nature of (or contains) a joke. *In 2001 journalist Rich Lowry said that whenever President George W. Bush is first introduced to someone, his routine is "a firm handshake, a look in the eye, [and] a jocular exchange of words."*

[4] **harass (harassed)** To *harass* someone is to (usually persistently or repeatedly) bother him (or disturb, pester, or irritate him) with demands, threats, annoyances, or the like. *According to Compton's Encyclopedia, before she was burned at the stake, (15th-century teenaged French military leader and heroine) Joan of Arc "had been held for many months in chains, threatened with torture, and harassed by thousands of questions."*

[5] **jeer (jeered)** To *jeer* is to speak or call out in a mocking, insulting, or teasing manner; to make fun of or poke fun at (someone), especially in a rude or unkind way; to tease, insult, ridicule, etc. As a noun, a *jeer* is a mocking, insulting, or teasing remark or shout; a sarcastic wisecrack. *Baseball umpire Tom Gorman once said (of his profession)," It's a strange business: all jeers and no cheers."*

179

Just then, the teacher, who'd been writing on the blackboard, spun around and said sharply, "What's going on here?"

"Sorry, sir," said the boy who'd made the flagpole remark. "Just trying to inject a moment of **levity**[1] to make our new classmate feel more comfortable. We were just kidding with him—all in fun, of course—and he **misconstrued**[2] our innocent jokes for insults. But we won't do it again." Then the boy lowered his head, as if in shame.

"Very well," said the teacher. "But don't let it happen again. I won't **tolerate**[3] that kind of behavior. Does everyone understand that?"

"Yes, sir," all the children chanted in **unison**[1].

---

[1] **levity** Technically, this word signifies lightness of mind, manner, character, behavior, etc. But people generally use this word to signify a lack of seriousness; an instance of (sometimes inappropriate) merriment; undignified behavior, etc. *In 1973 writer Michael Lesy said that if you've ever had pictures taken by a professional photographer, "you seldom smiled, since levity was not the mark you wanted put across your face forever."*

[2] **misconstrue (misconstrued)** To *misconstrue* something (a statement or one's motives, for example) is to mistake the meaning of it; misinterpret it; take it in the wrong sense. *If you omit the hyphen in the following, your meaning may be misconstrued: "100-odd teachers attended the educator's conference."*

[3] **tolerate** To *tolerate* something (bad behavior, a bad situation, an opposing point of view, etc.) is to put up with it; to allow it, permit it, accept it, endure it, etc. *In 1961 British philosopher and mathematician Bertrand Russell said, "[Nuclear weapons are] utterly horrible [and] no one with one spark of humanity [should] tolerate [them]."* The adjective is *tolerant* (as in *a nation tolerant toward all religious beliefs*). The noun is *tolerance* (as in *zero tolerance for guns and drugs in school*). Note: Speaking medically, to *tolerate* something is to endure it with no ill effects (as in *tolerate a strong medicine* or *tolerate intense heat*).

But none of this caused the boys to **desist**[2] from their she-nanigans. As soon as the teacher's back was turned, the boy across from Pinocchio put out his hand and pulled the puppet's nose. This time Pinocchio **retaliated**[3]. In one **deft**[4] motion, he extended his leg under the desk and kicked the boy hard on the shin.

"Oh, what hard feet!" cried the boy, rubbing the spot where the puppet had kicked him.

"And what elbows! They're even harder than the feet!" shouted another one, who'd thrown a spitball and received a blow in the ribs in **reprisal**[5].

---

[1] **unison** When a group (of people, animals, etc.) does something in *unison*, they do it all at the same time, in the same way; they do it together; they act as one (as can be seen in synchronized swimming or competitive rowing, for example). *According to* Grolier's Encyclopedia, *"In flight, a line of pelicans may move as choreographed dancers, beating their wings, gliding, and dipping in unison."* Note: In music, a *unison* is the sounding of notes at the same pitch (by different voices or instruments together).

[2] **desist** To *desist* is to stop or discontinue some (sometimes harmful or illegal) action or activity. *The U.S. government prohibits false or deceptive advertising, and violators are ordered to desist from running such ads.*

[3] **retaliate (retaliated)** To *retaliate* is to pay back an injury (or insult, wrong, etc.) with another; to get even, settle the score, get revenge, etc. *In his second inaugural address (January 1985), President Ronald Reagan said, "For decades, if either [the U.S. or the Soviet Union] resorted to the use of nuclear weapons, the other could retaliate and destroy the one who had started it."*

[4] **deft** If you're *deft* in action, you're quick, skillful, neat, light, etc. *Former basketball great "Magic" Johnson was known for his height, speed, and deft ball handing.* If you're *deft* in thought or expression, you're quick, clever, practiced, accomplished, etc. *Comedian and actor Billy Crystal has earned praise for his deft hosting of the Academy Awards.*

[5] **reprisal** A *reprisal* is an act or instance of retaliation (a getting even or getting back for an injury or wrong). Note: Military *reprisal* is the inflicting of equal or greater injuries (than those received) on an enemy. *In April 1986 President Ronald Reagan ordered an air attack on the headquarters of Libyan leader Muammar Qaddafi in reprisal for a terrorist bombing of a Berlin nightclub in which American lives were lost.*

With that kick and that blow Pinocchio won everybody's respect. Everyone admired him and wanted to be his friend.

As the days passed into weeks, even the teacher praised him, for he had an **acquisitive**[1] mind and a **retentive**[2] memory. He was always the first to arrive in the morning and the last to leave when school was over.

If Pinocchio had any fault, it was that, because he was now near the top of the school's social **hierarchy**[3], he had too many friends. Among these were the members of a **notorious**[4]

---

[1] **acquisitive** Anything (one's mind, a nation, a corporation, a person, etc.) described as *acquisitive* has a strong desire to acquire (gain, possess) things. An *acquisitive* mind wants to acquire ideas, information, knowledge, etc. An *acquisitive* nation wants to acquire other territories by force. An *acquisitive* corporation wants to acquire other companies by buying them out. An *acquisitive* person is either one with an acquisitive mind or one who strongly wants to acquire wealth, land, possessions, etc. *In 1982 journalist and humorist Andy Rooney said, "[Republicans] think that if we [the American people] admit that we have selfish, acquisitive natures and then set out to get all we can for ourselves by working hard for it, that things will be better for everyone."*

[2] **retentive** This is the adjective form of the word *retain*. If your mind is *retentive*, you have the power or ability to retain information (facts, knowledge, etc.) with ease; you have a good memory. *Spanish-born American philosopher George Santayana (1863–1952) once said, "Progress, far from consisting in change, depends on retentiveness; those who cannot remember the past are [doomed] to repeat it."*

[3] **hierarchy** A *hierarchy* is any system of people or things (as in an organization, social group, scientific classification, set of values, etc.) ranked one above the other. For example, in the *hierarchy* of the U.S. army, a corporal is above a private but below a sergeant, and in the *hierarchy* of biological classification, a genus is above a species but below a family. *Champion bridge player Ely Culbertson (1893–1955) once said, "A deck of cards [is] built like the purest of hierarchies, with every card a master to those below it, a [servant] to those above it."*

[4] **notorious** People or things described as *notorious* are famous for something bad; they're widely but unfavorably known (as in *the notorious gangster Al Capone*). *Established as a prison in the 1850s, Devil's Island (a Caribbean island off the northern coast of South America) became notorious for its severe tropical climate and for the cruel treatment of prisoners.*

clique[1] of **rowdy**[2] troublemakers who cared not a bit for study or for success. In Pinocchio's mind their naughty behavior was **deplorable**[3], but at the same time it added to their **allure**[4]. The teacher, noticing that Pinocchio tended to **gravitate**[5] toward these boys, one day warned him, "Be careful,

---

[1] **clique** A *clique* (pronounced *click*) is a small group of people (often within a larger group) who are friends (or who share an interest, activity, or attitude) and who tend to exclude others (from their group). *The high school lunchroom, table by table, was divided into various cliques: a clique of athletes, a clique of nerds, a clique of drama club members, and so on.*

[2] **rowdy** A person or group described as *rowdy* is rough, disorderly, and noisy. *In the 1978 film* Animal House, *a college's rowdiest fraternity, Delta House, engages in partying, rock 'n' roll, and food fights.*

[3] **deplore (deplorable)** In one sense, to *deplore* something is to feel or express strong disapproval of it. *Many parents deplore violence on television because of the harmful influence it may have on children.* In another sense, to *deplore* something is to feel or express sorrow, regret, or grief over it. *In 1958, speaking of Arkansas's refusal to enforce the Supreme Court's 1954 school desegregation ruling, President Dwight D. Eisenhower said, "I deplore the need or the use of troops anywhere to get American citizens to obey the orders of [the] courts."*

[4] **allure** If a person or thing has *allure* it has a quality that draws one's interest, attention, admiration, or enthusiasm; it has the power to attract, entice, charm, or fascinate. For example, women sometimes wear jewelry, perfume, or makeup to add to their *allure*. *In 1981 French artist Paul Gauguin (1848–1903) moved to (the South Pacific island of) Tahiti and expressed its romantic allure through his paintings.*

[5] **gravitate** As you learned in science class, the force of gravity causes physical objects to be attracted to (move toward) each other. But if you say that a person *gravitates* toward something (another person, a particular location, a field of interest, etc.), you mean that he has a natural tendency to move toward it (as if attracted by gravity). *In 1977 U.S. architect Christopher Alexander said, "When they have a choice, people will always gravitate to those rooms [that] have light on two sides, and leave the rooms [that] are lit only from one side unused and empty."*

Pinocchio! Good boys who associate with **ruffians**[1] will sooner or later lose their love for study. Some day they'll be led astray."

"That's just a **generality**[2]," answered the puppet, shaking his head. "There's no danger of that happening to me because I'm too wise and my moral **caliber**[3] is too high. I'd never allow their bad values to **impinge**[4] upon my good ones."

But it happened that one day, as he was walking to school, one of these boys ran up to him and said, "Have you heard the news?"

"No!"

---

[1] **ruffian (ruffians)** A ruffian is a rough, tough, disorderly (sometimes lawless) person; a roughneck, hooligan, thug, bully, etc. *In his February 1776 pamphlet "Common Sense," American patriot and political philosopher Thomas Paine said that if one were to trace the line of "kings in the world" to its origins, he would probably "find the first of them nothing better than the principle ruffian of some restless gang, whose savage manners obtained him the title of chief of [thieves]."*

[2] **generality** A *generality* is a statement or principle that applies to a whole class of instances, rather than to a particular instance. The implication is that such a statement or principle is not always true. For example, the well-known phrase "blondes have more fun" is a generality. *While campaigning against Richard Nixon in the 1960 presidential election, John F. Kennedy complained that his opponent's speeches contained nothing but "generalities from Poor Richard's Almanac."*

[3] **caliber** The *caliber* of someone or something is its degree of worth, excellence, merit, etc.; its quality. *Leadership expert Dennis A. Peer once said, "One measure of leadership is the caliber of people who choose to follow you."* Note: When speaking of a firearm, the word refers to the diameter of the barrel (usually expressed in hundredths of an inch), as in *a .22-caliber rifle.*

[4] **impinge** When one thing *impinges* on (or upon) another, it has a (usually unwanted) effect on it; it intrudes, infringes, or trespasses on it. *According to the* Cambridge Biographical Encyclopedia, *Boris Pasternak's novel* Dr. Zhivago *(1957) "describes with intense feeling the Russian Revolution as it impinged upon one individual [a Russian doctor and poet]."* Note: If you're speaking of physical objects, to *impinge* is to strike, collide, hit against, etc., as in *a bone impinging on a nerve.*

"A shark as big as a mountain has been seen near the shore."

The **simile**[1] struck a chord deep within the puppet and he felt his wooden heart skip a beat. He gazed thoughtfully at the boy, then mumbled **meditatively**[2], "Hmm...I wonder if it could be the same shark I heard about when my father was drowned."

"I'm going to see it. Are you coming?"

"I can't. I have to go to school."

"So go to school tomorrow. What difference does one lesson more or less make?" the boy **rationalized**[3].

"But I thought that attending class every day was **obligatory**[4]. What will our teacher say?"

---

[1] **simile** A *simile* (pronounced *SIM-uh-lee*) is a figure of speech or literary device that compares unlike things by using the word "like" or "as" (for example, "slept like a log" or "dead as a doornail"). Note: Such a comparison that does not use the word "like" or "as" is known as a *metaphor* (for example, "heart of stone"). *One of English poet William Wordsworth's (1770– 1850) most famous similes is the opening line of his poem "Daffodils": "I wandered lonely as a cloud."*

[2] **meditate (meditatively)** To *meditate* is to consider (think about) something carefully or at length; to ponder, reflect, study, etc. The noun is *meditation* ("the act of meditating") and the adjective is *meditative* ("characterized by or inclined toward meditation"). *Zen Buddhists (members of a religious sect popular in China and Japan) believe that enlightenment (spiritual or intellectual insight) can be attained through meditation rather than through faith or devotion.*

[3] **rationalize (rationalized)** To *rationalize* is to justify one's (often undesirable) actions or opinions by offering reasonable-sounding but incorrect explanations for them. *Some men who never find the "right girl" to marry rationalize their failure by calling themselves "confirmed bachelors."*

[4] **obligatory** This word is the adjective form of the word *obligation* ("a course of action demanded of a person"). If something is *obligatory*, it's required (as a matter of obligation) by law, society, or one's conscience; it's mandatory, compulsory, etc. *The Pledge of Allegiance was once an obligatory public school ritual (but state laws no longer require students to recite it).*

"Let him say whatever he wants. He's paid to complain all day."

"And my mother?"

"Mothers don't know everything."

"Do you know what I'll do?" said Pinocchio. "For certain reasons of my own, I, too, want to see that shark. But I'll go after school. I can see him then as well as now."

"You fool!" cried the boy. "Do you think that a fish of that **magnitude**[1] will stand there waiting for you?"

The puppet was in a **quandary**[2]. On the one hand, he knew he should go to school. On the other, he couldn't pass up an opportunity to find his father.

"How long does it take to get from here to the shore?" he asked.

"An hour there and back."

"All right, then. Let's see who gets there first!" cried Pinocchio.

---

[1] **magnitude** Depending on the context, this word means either "greatness in size, rank, or significance," as in *the magnitude of the Great Depression*, or simply "size, extent, dimensions (whether great or not)," as in *angles of similar magnitude*. *In his second inaugural address (March 1865), President Abraham Lincoln said, "Neither party expected, for the [Civil War], the magnitude or the duration which it has already attained."*

[2] **quandary** A *quandary* is a state of uncertainty or puzzlement, especially about what course of action to take; a difficult or worrisome situation or problem. *President Theodore Roosevelt once remarked: "Having captured our men, we were in a quandary how to keep them."*

Chapter 23 "The Fight"

Running like the wind, Pinocchio reached the shore in a very short time. He put down his schoolbooks and then glanced all around. But there was no sign of a shark. The sea was as smooth as glass.

"Hey, where's that shark?" he asked, turning to his schoolmate.

"He may have gone for breakfast," he answered, putting down his books. "Or perhaps he went to bed for a little nap." From the silly **banter**[1], Pinocchio knew that the boy had played a trick on him.

"What's the idea?" he said angrily to him. "What's the joke?"

"Oh, the joke's on you!" cried the rascal, dancing about.

"And that is —?"

"That I've made you stay out of school to come with me! Ha, ha!"

"But—"

"Don't you know that everyone thinks you've officially **defected**[2] from our fun-loving, mischief-making gang? Tell me, why don't you join us anymore when we go on our afternoon

---

[1] **banter** This word signifies light, playful, good-natured conversation (often including teasing, joking, ribbing, joshing, etc.). *TV sitcoms sometimes have no real plot, but consist instead of misunderstandings, embarrassing situations, slapstick, and lively banter.*

[2] **defect (defected)** As a verb, to *defect* (pronounced with the accent on the second syllable) is to abandon or desert a particular cause, party, country, position, association, etc. (often to join another). *Romanian gymnast Nadia Comaneci, who at age 14 won three gold medals in the 1976 Olympics at Montreal, defected to the U.S. in 1989.*

escapades[1] — it's to study, isn't it? You should be ashamed of yourself for being such a goody-goody. If you spent half as much time and energy on having fun as you now **expend**[2] on studying, you'd be much happier. Can't you see that?"

"Gee, thanks for that wonderfully **incisive**[3] **critique**[4]," said the puppet sarcastically.

"Look, we've all talked it over, and we've agreed **unanimously**[5] to give you one more chance to join us again. What do you say?"

"I don't know. Anyway, what's it to you if I study?"

---

[1] **escapade (escapades)** An *escapade* is an exciting, reckless, or wild (not necessarily lawful) undertaking or adventure; a caper, prank, fling, stunt, etc. *According to the* Encarta Encyclopedia, *Cyrano de Bergerac was a 17th-century "French writer whose many duels and other escapades gained him a reputation as a romantic hero [in spite of his oversized nose]."*

[2] **expend** To *expend* something (energy, time, etc.) is to use it up, consume it, exhaust it. *French writer and philosopher Albert Camus (1913-1960) once said, "Nobody realizes that some people expend tremendous energy merely to be normal."* Note: To *expend* money is to spend it, pay it out, etc. *Sixteenth-century Spanish explorers expended vast sums in unsuccessfully searching for El Dorado (a kingdom of northern South America fabled for its wealth of gold and precious jewels).*

[3] **incisive** If something (a comment, a judgment, an analysis, an investigation, a person's mind, etc.) is *incisive*, it clearly and sharply penetrates to the heart of a subject; it's cutting, keen, piercing, etc. *Ted Koppel and Mike Wallace are two television newsmen known for their incisive interviews.*

[4] **critique** A *critique* is a critical review or discussion of some subject or problem (especially one dealing with a work of literature or art). *Speaking of the unkind movie reviews (French filmmaker) François Truffaut had written before he began directing,* Compton's Encyclopedia *said, "[He] wrote of the established French cinema, making enemies with each new harshly worded critique."*

[5] **unanimous (unanimously)** If something (a vote or group decision, for example) is *unanimous*, it shows compete agreement; all concerned share the same opinion or view. *In January 1789 the Electoral College unanimously chose George Washington as first President of the United States.*

"Don't you see? If you study and receive high marks, you establish a **benchmark**[1]. It makes my grades look bad to the teacher. It makes me look stupid. If I had my way, I'd **abolish**[2] studying entirely. Better yet, I'd **demolish**[3] every schoolhouse."

"I don't agree. For one thing, my study habits don't **detract**[4] from your academic record, which is based solely on your test scores. For another, you don't have to remain a **mediocre**[5] student. You can do what I do—spend most of your time studying instead of trying to have fun all the time."

---

[1] **benchmark** A *benchmark* is something that serves as (or is taken as) a measure by which other similar things can be compared, evaluated, judged, etc.; a yardstick. *For many years baseball experts considered Babe Ruth's record of 60 home runs in a single season (1927) a benchmark against which future home run hitters would be judged.*

[2] **abolish** To *abolish* something (a practice, regulation, condition, etc.) is to do away with it; put an end to it (as in *abolish slavery, abolish the Stamp Act,* or *abolish poverty*). *Some lawmakers would like to abolish the Electoral College in favor of direct popular vote for President.*

[3] **demolish** To *demolish* something (a run-down building, for example) is to destroy it (especially on purpose); tear it down, dismantle it, level it. *In 1990 the Berlin Wall was demolished and East and West Germany were formally reunited for the first time since World War II.*

[4] **detract** If one thing *detracts* from another, it negatively interferes with it; in other words, the first thing somehow (usually unintentionally) reduces the second's level of quality, value, reputation, importance, beauty, believability, etc. *Although many Flamenco dancers use castanets (hand-held percussion instruments that make a snapping sound), some fans believe that these actually detract from the music and the dancing.*

[5] **mediocre** To describe something (a performance, a book, a student, etc.) as *mediocre* is to say that it ranks around the middle of a scale of evaluation; it's neither good nor bad; it's average, ordinary, undistinguished, unremarkable, etc. Note: People sometimes use the word to mean "barely adequate; rather poor; inferior; second-rate." *The* London Observer *once said, "Television – all it has ever done is to teach people how to tolerate mediocre entertainment."*

"And have everyone think I'm a **puritanical**[1] spoilsport like you? I don't think so. I have more important things to do with my life."

"Like what? You're just being lazy."

"Lazy? Don't call me that! Don't ever call me that! You better take that back right now!"

"Make me!" said Pinocchio, with a **defiant**[2] forward thrust of his chin.

"Take it back, I said, or you'll be sorry!"

When the puppet still refused to **retract**[3] the statement, the boy gave Pinocchio's shoulder a poke. The puppet, to show that he was not the least bit **intimidated**[4] by the other, imme-

---

[1] **puritanical** In the 1600s, *Puritans* were English Protestants or New England colonists who urged a strict moral code, placed a high value on hard work, and believed that pleasure and luxury were sinful. Today, if you say that someone is *puritanical*, you mean that he's extremely (sometimes excessively) strict about moral or religious matters, or that he doesn't approve of people having a good time. *When puritanical Boston missionaries first visited Hawaii (1861), they told the Hawaiians that surfing was contrary to the laws of God and that the practice should be discontinued.*

[2] **defiant** To *defy* something (authority, an order, a regulation, etc.) is to boldly or openly resist or challenge it; to refuse to go along with it. If you're *defiant*, you tend to defy; you're resistant, disobedient, hostile, etc. *Actor James Dean (1931–1955) specialized in portraying defiant youths in such films as 1955's* Rebel Without a Cause.

[3] **retract** To *retract* something (a statement, accusation, opinion, etc.) is to withdraw it or take it back as being unjustified or incorrect. *In an 1820 letter, English poet Lord Byron said that the works of rival English poet John Keats were "neither poetry nor anything else"; he later retracted his attack, limiting his criticism to Keats' earliest works.*

[4] **intimidate (intimidated)** Depending on the context, to *intimidate* someone is to (1) make him feel afraid (by threats, for example), (2) influence or force him (by threats or fear) to carry out (or not carry out) some particular action, or (3) make him feel inferior by displaying superiority (of wealth, fame, importance, intelligence, etc.). *Concerning the 1973 Supreme Court decision legalizing abortion (Roe v. Wade), Justice Harry Blackmun said, "The states are not free, under the [pretense] of protecting [the mother's] health or [an unborn] life, to intimidate women into continuing pregnancies."*

190

diately answered that with a shove. That was the **catalyst**[1] that triggered the beginning of an all-out fight. In a few moments, it raged hot and heavy.

Pinocchio was so **dexterous**[2] with his hard wooden hands and feet that his opponent was forced to **recede**[3]. Wherever on the other boy those hands and feet landed, they left a painful mark. The most **vulnerable**[4] part of his body proved to be

---

[1] **catalyst** In chemistry, a *catalyst* is a substance that causes some kind of chemical reaction. *In nuclear reactions, carbon acts as a catalyst to convert hydrogen into helium and gamma rays.* By extension, the word is used to refer to anything (a person, situation, event, occurrence, etc.) that causes or sparks any type of reaction or change. *The Japanese surprise air attack (December 1941) on Pearl Harbor served as the catalyst that brought the United States into World War II.*

[2] **dexterous** If you're *dexterous*, you have skill and ease in physical movement, especially in the use of your hands; you have good physical coordination. The noun is *dexterity*. *In 1986 the New York Times said of Seattle chef Kathy Pavletich Casey, "When she goes about her kitchen duties, chopping, carving, mixing, [and] whisking, she moves with the grace of a ballet dancer, her fingers [working] the food with the dexterity of a [Las Vegas card dealer].* Note: The would can also refer to mental skill and ease (as in *the President's dexterous use of his cabinet*).

[3] **recede** When something *recedes*, it moves back or away from a particular point; it retreats, withdraws, etc. *According to the expanding universe theory, all galaxies are receding from each other at great speeds.* Note: In another sense, when something *recedes* it becomes (or seems to become) less, fainter, or more distant. *In 1964 Alfred Barr, Director of Collections at New York City's Museum of Modern Art, said, "This museum is a torpedo moving through time, its head the ever-advancing present, its tail the ever-receding past of 50 to 100 years ago."*

[4] **vulnerable** If something is *vulnerable*, it's able or likely to be damaged or harmed (as in *a territory vulnerable to military attack, a plant vulnerable to disease,* or *a narrow skyscraper vulnerable to high winds*), or it's able or likely to suffer something undesirable (as in *a species vulnerable to extinction*). If a person is *vulnerable*, he's able to be physically or emotionally hurt (as in *a sensitive child vulnerable to criticism*). The opposite is *invulnerable* ("impossible to injure, hurt, or wound"). *In Greek mythology, Achilles' mother tried to make him invulnerable by dipping him into the magical waters of the River Styx; however, the heel by which she held him remained vulnerable.*

his shins, which had already been kicked several times, causing him to howl.

Because he was unable to get close to Pinocchio without being kicked, the boy picked up his schoolbooks and starting hurling them at the puppet. A **barrage**[1] of reading books, history books, and science books flew threw the air. But the **onslaught**[2] accomplished nothing. With his sharp eyes and **agile**[3] movements, Pinocchio was able to predict their **trajectories**[4] and then jump to the side or duck to avoid being struck.

---

[1] **barrage** Technically, a *barrage* is a bombardment (concentrated discharge) of artillery fire (bullets, bombs, missiles, rockets, etc.). But the word is also used to signify an overwhelming quantity or outpouring of anything (as in *a barrage of questions*). *In her 1962 book* Silent Spring, *biologist and environmentalist Rachel Carson said of America's widespread use of chemical insecticides, "As crude a weapon as a cave man's club, the chemical barrage has been hurled against the fabric of life."*

[2] **onslaught** An *onslaught* is a (usually violent) assault or attack; a raid, strike, etc. *According to* Grolier's Encyclopedia, *"The fall of France [June 1940] was an extraordinary victory for Hitler [in World War II]; the supposedly unbeatable French army had melted away before the onslaught of his mobile units with their convincing display of mechanized power."* Note: In another sense, an *onslaught* is an overwhelming outpouring or quantity (of something), as in *an onslaught of foreign-made goods.*

[3] **agile** If you're *agile*, you're quick and well-coordinated in movement. *Mountain goats are agile rock climbers.* The noun is *agility. In 1961* Time *magazine said that a baseball umpire "should combine the [righteousness] of a Supreme Court justice [with] the physical agility of an acrobat."*

[4] **trajectory (trajectories)** The path that an object (a comet, UFO, missile, bullet, baseball, football, etc.) takes when hurled or thrown through space or the air is known as its *trajectory*. Because of the force of gravity, trajectories are often smoothly curved. *According to* Compton's Encyclopedia, *"Much technological effort before and during World War II went into aiming [aerial] bombs; this challenging task involves choosing the point at which to release a bomb from a moving aircraft so that its trajectory intersects a target on the ground."*

Now the boy looked around for new ammunition. Seeing Pinocchio's bundle of books lying nearby, he ran to it and snatched it up.

One of the books, a **compilation**[1] of hundreds of mathematical tables, was very large and heavily bound in leather. Of all his books, Pinocchio loved that one best, for he had an unusual **aptitude**[2] for mathematics.

Thinking it would make a fine weapon, the boy took hold of it and threw it at the puppet with all his strength. But Pinocchio ducked and the **projectile**[3] struck the head of another classmate who'd just run up to watch the excitement. The thrower then screamed a **belated**[4] "Watch out!" and the vic-

---

[1] **compilation** To *compile* is to bring together (materials from various sources) into one place, especially to collect various writings into a single book (as in *compile an anthology of short stories*). A *compilation* is something compiled, such as a book, list, report, set of data, etc. *The* Nautical Almanac *is a yearly compilation of the predicted daily positions of the Sun, Moon, planets, and certain stars; these positions enable the longitude of a ship at sea to be determined.*

[2] **aptitude** If you have an *aptitude* for something (a subject of study, a sport or game, an artistic or mechanical skill, etc.) you're naturally good at it; you have the capacity to learn it easily or excel in it; you're gifted or talented in it. *When he was a child living on a Michigan farm, (automobile manufacturer) Henry Ford (1863–1947) expressed a dislike for farming and displayed an aptitude for machinery.*

[3] **projectile** A *projectile* is an object fired, thrown, or otherwise propelled through air or water. The word often refers to weapons, whether explosive (missiles, grenades, bombs, torpedoes) or non-explosive (stones, spears, darts, arrows), but it also refers to non-weapons (meteorites, experimental rockets, etc.). *Scientists sometimes capture fast-moving lizards by stunning them with a "lizard blowgun," a four-foot aluminum tube with corks (or olives!) as projectiles.*

[4] **belated** Notice the similarity of this word to the word *late*. If something (a birthday greeting, for example) is *belated*, it comes or happens after the customary or expected time; it's late, too late, overdue, after the fact, etc. *The Vietnam Veterans Memorial in Washington, D.C., was built (1982) as a belated tribute to the more than 58,000 Americans killed or missing during the Vietnam War (1954–1975).*

tim, pale as a ghost, cried out, "Help! I'm dying!" and fell senseless to the ground. Pinocchio heard his head crack against the hard dirt.

At the sight of that pale little body, the boy who'd thrown the book suddenly became so **distraught**[1] that he turned and ran. In a few moments he was gone.

Although scared to death by the **ghastly**[2] accident, Pinocchio ran to the sea and **saturated**[3] his handkerchief with cool ocean water. Then he ran back and gently patted the forehead of his poor little schoolmate with it. Sobbing bitterly, he said to him, "Open your eyes and look at me! Why don't you answer? I wasn't the one who hit you, you know. Open your eyes. If you keep them shut, then I'll die, too."

Then the puppet thought to himself: "Oh dear, how will I ever go home now? How will I ever face my mother again? What will happen to me? Where will I go? Where will I hide?

---

[1] **distraught** If you're *distraught* (pronounced *dis-TRAWT*), you're deeply worried and upset (as from emotional conflict, feelings of hopelessness, etc.); you're troubled, tormented, distressed, etc. *According to the* Cambridge Encyclopedia, *on the day (November 22, 1963) President Kennedy was assassinated in Dallas, TX, astrologer Jeane Dixon was "lunching with friends at the Mayflower Hotel in Washington [when] she suddenly became so distraught that she couldn't touch her food. 'Something dreadful is going to happen to the President today!' she declared."*

[2] **ghastly** If something (a crime, a person's appearance, an injury, a scream, etc.) is *ghastly*, it arouses feelings of shock, horror, fright, dread, etc., especially because it suggests death or ghosts; it's gruesome, hideous, nightmarish, monstrous, etc. *Jack the Ripper, who was responsible for seven ghastly murders in London in 1888, was never captured.*

[3] **saturate (saturated)** To *saturate* an object with a substance is to thoroughly fill it with that substance; to soak it (as in *a sponge saturated with water*). *Frost forms on objects (grass and windowpanes, for example) when the air is saturated with water vapor and the temperature is below freezing.* Note: The word can also pertain to the non-physical (as in *words saturated with lies*). *In 1944 British critic Cyril Connolly said that American novelist Ernest Hemingway (1899–1961) "saturated his work with sunshine and salt water, with food [and] wine."*

Oh, how much better it would have been, a thousand times better, if only I'd gone to school! Why did I listen to that boy? He was a bad influence! And to think that the teacher had told me—and my mother, too!—'Beware of bad company!' That's what they said. But I'm stubborn and selfish. I listen, but I always do as I please. And then I pay. I've never had a moment's peace since I've been born! Oh, dear! What will become of me? What will become of me?"

Pinocchio went on crying and moaning. Then he said to the lifeless body of his little friend, "You came here to try to **mediate**[1] a truce between me and that other boy, didn't you? You did nothing wrong. You don't deserve to die. Open your eyes. Please open your—" Suddenly he heard heavy steps approaching.

He looked up and saw two tall police officers near him.

"What are you doing on the ground?" they asked Pinocchio.

"I'm helping this schoolmate of mine."

"Is anything wrong with him?"

"I think so," answered Pinocchio weakly.

One of the officers bent down for a closer look. Right away he noticed the boy's shallow breathing and pale, moist skin. When he pulled up the child's drooping eyelids he found that

---

[1] **mediate** If two people (or groups, countries, etc.) are in dispute about something, to *mediate* is to help them settle their differences (by acting as an impartial but helpful third party). One who mediates is a *mediator*. The process of mediating is *mediation*. *President Theodore Roosevelt won the 1906 Nobel Peace Prize for mediating the agreement that ended the Russo-Japanese War (1904–1905).*

the eyes were **glazed**[1] and the pupils were **dilated**[2]. Then, seeing angry bruises and **coagulated**[3] blood above the boy's ear, he said, "His temple's been **lacerated**[4] and he's in shock." Then to Pinocchio: "All right, what happened? Who did this?"

"Not I," stammered the puppet, who had hardly a breath left in his whole body.

---

[1] **glaze (glazed)** As a noun, a *glaze* is a thin, smooth, shiny (often glassy) coating (as on certain ceramics, furniture, foods, paintings, etc.). As a verb, to *glaze* something is to give it such a coating. The adjective *glazed* (as in *glazed eyes*) means "having a glassy coating." Note: Glazed eyes are usually associated with an absence of thought (as from boredom, shock, a coma, etc.). *In 1867 Prussian premier Otto von Bismarck said, "Anyone who has ever looked into the glazed eyes of a soldier dying on the battlefield will think hard before starting a war."*

[2] **dilate (dilated)** When something *dilates*, it becomes wider or larger; it expands. For example, the pupils of your eyes *dilate* in dim light (to allow more light to pass through) and contract in bright light (to limit the amount passing through). *In 1987 French author Jean Baudrillard said, "Boredom is like a pitiless zooming in on the skin of time; every instant is dilated like the magnified pores of the face."*

[3] **coagulate (coagulated)** When something (blood or milk, for example) *coagulates*, it changes from a fluid to a thickened mass; it thickens, jells, clots, etc. *Rubber plants yield a milky, white sap that can be coagulated with an acid to form crude rubber.*

[4] **lacerate (lacerated)** To *lacerate* something (your skin, for example) is to rip, cut, or tear it. A *laceration* is a cut or wound, especially a rough or jagged one. *According the* World Almanac and Book of Facts, *people visit hospital emergency rooms for lacerations of the face more often than they do for skin rashes but less often than they do for earaches.*

"Come now. Would you have us believe that he was mauled[1] by a wild animal? Or that he fell off a roof? Now tell the truth. Who did it."

"Not I," he repeated.

"What was he wounded with?"

"With this book," answered the puppet, holding up the math book to show it to the officer.

"Whose book is it?" asked the officer, noticing a bit of congealed[2] blood on the book's corner.

"Mine."

"I see. Then how do you reconcile[3] your claim of innocence with the fact that your book has this poor boy's blood on it and you're the only one here?"

Pinocchio could have told the officers all about the troublemaker who'd instigated[1] the fight, but he was no tattletale.

---

[1] **maul (mauled)** To *maul* an object (a package, for example) is to damage or mangle it by rough or careless handling. To *maul* a person is to injure, bruise, or disfigure him by beating him, shoving him, biting him, knocking him about, etc. *The campers lay in their sleeping bags frozen in fear, wondering whether they'd be mauled to shreds by the grizzly bear that was snooping around just outside their tent.*

[2] **congeal (congealed)** When a liquid *congeals*, it hardens or thickens; it becomes solid or semi-solid (often by cooling or freezing). *To make Jell-O, first dissolve the powder in hot water, then place the solution in the refrigerator to congeal.*

[3] **reconcile** When two things (such as contradictory statements or opinions) are (or seem to be) opposed or different, to *reconcile* them is to bring them into agreement (usually by showing how they are actually alike, compatible, or consistent). *Italian monk and philosopher Thomas Aquinas (1225–1275) tried to reconcile religion and science by showing that elements of the teachings of (ancient Greek philosopher) Aristotle were compatible with Christianity.* Note: In another sense, to *reconcile* yourself to something is to bring yourself to accept it. *Before California became a state (1850), American trappers and traders living there had a hard time reconciling themselves to Mexican rule.*

At the risk of being made the **scapegoat**[2] for a crime he didn't commit, he said nothing.

"Okay, that's enough." said the officer, taking the book. "Come along with us."

"But I—"

"Come with us!"

"But I'm innocent."

"Innocent? The **incriminating**[3] evidence is right here!" shouted the officer, thrusting the book an inch in front of Pinocchio's nose. "There's no question that you'll be **indicted**[4]

---

[1] **instigate (instigated)** To *instigate* something (a fight or riot, for example) is to start it; bring it about; provoke it. *The Boston Tea Party (in which in 1773 a band of colonists disguised as Mohawk Indians boarded three anchored British ships and dumped 342 chests of tea into Boston harbor in order to protest the British tea tax) was instigated by American patriot Samuel Adams.*

[2] **scapegoat** A *scapegoat* is a person who is made to take the blame for another (or others). *In 1932, the third year of the Great Depression, American voters made President Herbert Hoover the scapegoat for all their economic troubles; he was overwhelmingly defeated in that year's presidential election by New York Democrat Franklin D. Roosevelt.*

[3] **incriminate (incriminating)** If something (evidence or testimony, for example) is *incriminating*, it tends to prove guilt (of a person accused of a crime or wrongdoing, for example). *In 1776 American Revolutionary War soldier Nathan Hale spied on British soldiers on Long Island but was captured carrying incriminating papers and sentenced to die by hanging; at his execution he declared, "I only regret that I have but one life to lose for my country."*

[4] **indict (indicted)** To *indict* (pronounced *in-DITE*) someone is to, through legal process, formally charge him with a crime. Once *indicted* (by a grand jury), a person must stand trial. *In 1967 heavyweight boxing champion Muhammad Ali was indicted for refusing induction into the army (at trial he was found guilty but the verdict was later overturned by the Supreme Court).*

for this crime. And if the judge **unearths**[1] any evidence that shows that your attack was **premeditated**[2], you'll serve jail time. Now come with us!"

Before starting out, the officer called out to several fishermen passing by in a boat, "Fishermen! Hey! This is an emergency! I hereby appoint you temporary, **auxiliary**[3] police officers. Do your best to **resuscitate**[4] this injured little boy.

---

[1] **unearth (unearths)** This word literally means "dig up (from the earth)," as in *archaeologists unearthed King Tut's tomb*. But when people say that something (previously hidden or unknown) has been *unearthed*, they mean that it has been discovered or brought to public notice through investigation. *In 1965, when consumer activist Ralph Nader publicly accused General Motors of producing an unsafe car, GM hired a private detective to unearth information or materials that might be used to blackmail Nader (but the private eye found nothing and GM was forced to apologize).*

[2] **premeditated** To *meditate* is to think (about something); to consider (it). If you say that something (a crime, for example) is *premeditated*, you mean that it had been thought about beforehand; it had been planned (as opposed to its having happened merely by impulse, on the spur of the moment). *In his speech (December 8, 1941) to Congress the day after the Japanese attack of Pearl Harbor, President Franklin D. Roosevelt said, "No matter how long it may take us to overcome this premeditated invasion, the American people in their righteous might will win through to absolute victory."*

[3] **auxiliary** As an adjective, this word means (1) "giving assistance or support," as in *auxiliary health-care workers*, (2) "acting as a supplement," as in *auxiliary engine*, or (3) "held or used in reserve," as in *auxiliary military units*. *Each of the skydivers carried a small auxiliary parachute (in case the main chute failed to open).*

[4] **resuscitate** To *resuscitate* someone who is unconscious or apparently dead is to revive him; bring him back to consciousness or life (as by using smelling salts, forcing air into his lungs, injecting drugs, or the like). *In September 1996 a team of South African research scientists successfully resuscitated a rat's heart after it had been frozen, with liquid nitrogen, at minus 320 degrees Fahrenheit.* Note: The word can also be used figuratively to mean "give renewed vitality or strength to." *In 1977 legalized gambling resuscitated Atlantic City's depressed tourism industry.*

Take him home with you, put him to bed, and treat his wounds. Tomorrow we'll come back for him." The two officers took hold of Pinocchio and put him between them. Then one said to him in a **gruff**[1] voice, "Now march! And go quickly, or it'll be even worse for you!" They didn't have to say it again. Pinocchio silently allowed himself to be escorted between the officers along the road to the village. But the poor puppet was in a daze. He felt like he was in a horrible dream. Everything looked **distorted**[2]. He felt **queasy**[3] and feverish. His legs trembled and his tongue was

---

[1] **gruff** If something (a person's voice or manner, for example) is *gruff*, it's harsh, rough, unfriendly, abrupt, blunt, impolite, etc. *Actor Lee J. Cobb (1911–1976) is known for his gruff characterizations in such films as* On the Waterfront *(1954) and* 12 Angry Men *(1957).*

[2] **distorted** If a physical object is *distorted*, it gives a false or inaccurate view; that is, its shape or form appears warped, deformed, out of proportion, etc. *Greek-born Spanish painter El Greco (1541–1614) is known for his intense contrasting colors and for his distorted, elongated human figures.* If something nonphysical (facts, ideas, etc.) is *distorted*, it gives a false or inaccurate impression of the truth; it's misleading, exaggerated, skewed, etc. *Although the Warren Commission concluded (1964) that assassin Lee Harvey Oswald had acted alone in the shooting (1963) of President John F. Kennedy, many people believe there is evidence to suggest that the truth had been distorted by cover-ups and lies.*

[3] **queasy** If you're *queasy*, you feel somewhat nauseated; that is, you feel a bit sick to your stomach. *Dennis discovered that the motion sickness pill he swallowed before boarding the sightseeing helicopter not only prevented him from becoming queasy, it also relaxed him (in fact, he fell asleep)!*

dry. And his throat felt so **constricted**[1] that, try as he might, he couldn't utter a single word. Yet, in spite of this **delirium**[2], one thought continually tormented him—the thought of passing under the window of the good fairy's house. What would she say on seeing him **embroiled**[3] in legal difficulties? What would she say on hearing the **gory**[4] details of what had just

---

[1] **constrict (constricted)** To *constrict* an opening or passageway (one of living tissue, for example) is to make it smaller or narrower, as by binding, squeezing, or other (often encircling) pressure. *Asthma is a respiratory disorder characterized by labored breathing resulting from constricted air passages.* To *constrict* one's growth, development, freedom, spontaneity, etc., is to limit or restrict it. *According to the* Cambridge Dictionary of American Biography, *"In 1925 [opera singer Marian Anderson (1902–1993)] won a major vocal competition that gained her a career as a [soloist], but [she] was always constricted by the limitations placed on African-American artists."* To *constrict* the flow of a liquid is to slow or restrict it. *Certain drugs are particularly dangerous if taken during pregnancy because they constrict the blood flow to the developing fetus.*

[2] **delirium** If you suffer from *delirium*, you have (as a result of high fever, shock, drugs, alcohol, or the like) a temporary disorder of the mind characterized by confusion, disorientation, hallucinations, delusions, trembling, etc. *Recovery from a coma proceeds in stages – before regaining normal brain function the patient goes through a state of restless delirium followed by a state of quiet confusion.* Note: The word can also signify a state of uncontrolled emotion (especially joy), as in, to use the adjective, *delirious Yankee fans.*

[3] **embroil (embroiled)** If you're speaking of a situation or circumstance marked by conflict, controversy, hostile actions, etc. (such as a lawsuit, scandal, war, etc.), to be *embroiled* (in it) is to be involved (in it), especially deeply or intimately so. *In 1948 the newly created State of Israel became embroiled in war with its Arab neighbors (Egypt, Syria, Jordan, Lebanon, and Iraq), who opposed the formation of a Jewish state in Palestine (the Holy Land).*

[4] **gory** As a noun, *gore* is blood that has been shed (as from violence or surgery), especially clotted blood from a wound. If you say that something (a movie, a description, etc.) is *gory*, you mean that it involves or is characterized by much bloodshed or violence (and that therefore it is, to many people, disagreeable, disturbing, gruesome, disgusting, etc.). *The shower scene in Alfred Hitchcock's 1960 black-and-white horror classic* Psycho *(in which a woman is stabbed to death in a cheap motel shower) is the goriest, and most memorable, scene of the film (interestingly, the "blood" is actually chocolate syrup!).*

happened to his schoolmate's head? What would she say on thinking he'd **blundered**[1] yet again? Then another thought entered his head. What would his teacher say on learning that his math book had been **confiscated**[2] as evidence?

They had just reached the village when a sudden gust of wind sent Pinocchio's cap sailing far down the street.

"Would you allow me," the puppet asked the officers, "to run after my cap?"

"Very well, but hurry."

After a few seconds the puppet had reached his cap and picked it up—but instead of putting it on his head, he stuck it between his teeth and then, looking like a bullet shot from a gun, raced toward the sea.

---

[1] **blunder (blundered)** As a noun, a *blunder* is a (sometimes serious) mistake, typically caused by stupidity, ignorance, carelessness, confusion, etc. As a verb, to *blunder* is to make such a mistake. *In 1948 the* Chicago Tribune *blundered when it reported Harry Truman's defeat in that year's presidential election (in fact, Truman defeated Republican candidate Thomas E. Dewey).*

[2] **confiscate (confiscated)** To *confiscate* something owned by another (property, money, a possession) is to take it with (sometimes legal) authority and usually without ceremony or delay. The implication is that the person (or group, country, etc.) who confiscates something believes that what is being taken is wrongfully owned by the other. *After taking power in 1959, Cuban leader Fidel Castro confiscated all foreign-owned property.*

The officers judged from his **initial**[1] **velocity**[2] and rate of **acceleration**[3] that it would be impossible to catch him. One of them pulled from his pocket a long, silver whistle and blew on it. Although its super-high pitch was **inaudible**[4] to humans and puppets, dogs responded to it. In a moment a large police dog, one that had won first prize in all the dog races,

---

[1] **initial** As an adjective, this word describes anything that relates to, exists at, or occurs at the beginning (of something); to anything that is first (of several or many parts, steps, stages, repetitions, etc.). *The Wright brothers made their initial (airplane) flight at Kitty Hawk, North Carolina, in 1903.* Note: The word is often used when a first impression or reaction (to something) ultimately changes (as in *the medical profession's initial hostility toward birth control*).

[2] **velocity** This word means "the rate at which something travels or moves; speed." For example, thing that move fast (bullets, rockets, etc.) are said to travel at a high velocity, and things that move slow (snails, caterpillars, etc.) are said to move at a low velocity. The word is often used instead of the word "speed" if the context is scientific. *Italian scientist Galileo (1564–1642) found experimentally that objects with different weights fall at the same velocity (interestingly, this finding was received with hostility because it contradicted the accepted teaching of ancient Greek philosopher Aristotle).*

[3] **acceleration** In physics, *acceleration* is the rate of increase of velocity (speed). For example, if you drop a ball from a tall building, the ball doesn't fall at a steady rate; rather, it gains speed as it falls. The rate at which its speed increases is known as *acceleration*. *Downhill skiers use a pair of poles to aid in accelerating, turning, and balancing.* If you're not speaking of physics, the verb *accelerate* means simply to move or cause to move (or proceed, develop, happen, etc.) faster; to speed up. *During adolescence, the body's growth rate accelerates.*

[4] **inaudible** If a sound is *inaudible*, it can't be heard (because its volume is too soft, its frequency is overly high or low, its source is too far away, etc.). The opposite is *audible*, which means "capable of being heard." *Ancient Greek philosopher and mathematician Pythagoras believed that the movement of the stars and planets created "music of the spheres," a beautiful sound inaudible on Earth.*

came running up. The officers sent him after the wooden **fugitive**[1].

---

[1] **fugitive** A *fugitive* is a person who is fleeing (especially from the law); a runaway. *Belle Starr (1848–1889) was an American outlaw whose Oklahoma cabin became a hideout for fugitives from justice.*

Chapter 24 "The Fisherman"

Pinocchio heard, close behind him, the heavy panting of the beast who was fast on his trail, and now and then even felt his hot breath on him. But luckily, by this time the shore was only a few short steps away.

As soon as he set foot on the beach, Pinocchio gave a leap and fell into the water. The dog tried to stop, but as he was running very fast, couldn't, and he, too, landed in the sea. Strange though it may seem, the dog couldn't swim. He beat the water with his paws to hold himself up, but the harder he tried, the deeper he sank. As he stuck his head out once more, his eyes were bulging and he barked out wildly, "I'm drowning! I'm drowning!"

"Then drown!" answered Pinocchio from afar, happy at his escape.

"Please help me! Save me! Oh! Oh!"

At those **frenzied**[1] cries of suffering, the puppet, who, after all, had a **humane**[2] spirit, was moved to compassion. He turned toward the poor animal and said to him, "If I save you, do you promise not to bother me again or run after me?"

"I promise! I promise! Only hurry, for if you wait any longer, I'll be dead and gone!"

---

[1] **frenzied** The noun *frenzy* means "a state of violent emotion or wild excitement." Anything described as *frenzied* is characterized by frenzy; that is, it's frantic, wild, violent, raving, crazy, etc. *In 1952 Democratic presidential nominee Adlai Stevenson said, "Patriotism is not short, frenzied outbursts of emotion, but the [calm] and steady dedication of a lifetime."*

[2] **humane** If you're *humane*, you show compassion and sympathy to others; you're concerned with ending or minimizing pain or suffering (for people and animals); you're kind, merciful, charitable, etc. *Benjamin Rush (1745–1813) was an American doctor and politician who signed the Declaration of Independence, spoke out against slavery and capital punishment (the death penalty), and urged the humane treatment of the mentally handicapped.*

Pinocchio hesitated still another moment. Then, remembering how his father had often told him that no one ever loses by doing a kind deed, he swam to the dog and, catching hold of his tail, dragged him to shore.

The poor dog was so weak that he couldn't stand up. He had swallowed, in spite of himself, so much water that he was as **bloated**[1] as a balloon. Pinocchio, however, still not trusting the dog, jumped once again into the sea. As he swam away, he called out, "Good-bye, and I wish you well."

"Good-bye and thank you," answered the dog. "I'll always be **beholden**[2] to you for saving my life. If the chance ever comes, I'd like to **reciprocate**[3] by doing something for you."

Pinocchio waved good-bye, then went on swimming close to shore. At last he thought he'd reached a safe place. Glancing up and down the beach from the water, he saw a long column of smoke coming from an **orifice**[4] in the rocks.

---

[1] **bloated** If something is *bloated*, it's enlarged or swollen beyond normal size (from internal liquid or gas); it's puffy, inflated, etc. *Leeches are blood-sucking worms with slightly flattened bodies (but they become bloated after a large meal).*

[2] **beholden** To be *beholden* to someone is to owe him your gratitude or to owe him a favor (usually for some favor or kindness he has done for you); to be indebted or obligated to him. *One problem with our democratic system is that an elected official might feel beholden to a special interest group (the tobacco industry or the National Rifle Association, for example) that contributed money to his campaign.*

[3] **reciprocate** To *reciprocate* is to give or do something in return (for something given or done by another). *In November 1977, as a move toward permanent peace between Israel and the Arab states, Egyptian president Anwar Sadat visited Israel; a month later Israeli prime minister Menachem Begin reciprocated by visiting Egypt.*

[4] **orifice** An *orifice* (pronounced *OR-uh-fiss*) is an opening or hole; a vent, crack, etc. Note: The word is often used to refer specifically to an opening in the human body, such as the mouth or ear, for example. *Germs enter the body through breaks in the skin (cuts, wounds, insect bites) or through natural bodily orifices.*

"That must be a cave," he said to himself. "And in that cave there must be a fire. I'll dry my clothes and warm myself, and then...well, then we'll see."

His mind made up, Pinocchio swam to the shore. But as he started to climb the rocks, he felt something under him lifting him up higher and higher. He tried to escape, but it was too late. To his great surprise, he found himself in a large net, among a huge number of fish of all kinds and sizes, who were fighting and struggling desperately to free themselves.

At the same time, he saw a fisherman come out of the cave—a fisherman so **grotesque**[1] that Pinocchio thought he was a monster. His head was covered by a **disheveled**[2] growth of stringy, wet, green seaweed. His body and eyes were also green, as was the long, tangled beard that reached down to his feet. He looked like a gigantic slimy lizard with legs and arms.

When the fisherman pulled the net out of the sea, he cried out joyfully, "Wonderful! Once more I'll have a fine meal of fish!"

"It's lucky I'm not a fish!" said Pinocchio to himself, trying with these words to find a little courage.

The fisherman took the net to the cave—a dark, **dank**[3], smoky place. In the middle of it, a pan full of oil and **aromatic**[1] herbs sizzled over a fire.

---

[1] **grotesque** If something is *grotesque*, it's fantastically ugly or odd in appearance or manner; it's monstrous, hideous, nightmarish, deformed, abnormal, etc. *The 1980 film* The Elephant Man *concerns a man whose grotesque appearance forces him to wear a bag over his head.*

[2] **disheveled** If something (one's hair or clothing, for example) is *disheveled*, it's hanging or thrown about in loose disorder; it's untidy, disarranged, messy, sloppy, unkempt, etc. *A disheveled appearance can be either unintentional (as with mad scientists, for example) or intentional (as with grunge musicians, for example).*

[3] **dank** A place (a cave or tropical forest, for example) described as *dank* is disagreeably or unhealthily damp or humid. *In the Middle Ages peasants lived in dank huts made of wood covered with mud.*

"Now, let's see what kind of fish I've caught today," said the fisherman. He put a hand as big as a shovel into the net and pulled out a handful of tuna.

"Fine fish, these tuna!" he said, after looking at them and smelling them with pleasure. After that, he threw them into a large, empty tub.

Many times he repeated this operation. As he pulled each fish out of the net, his mouth watered with the thought of the **delectable**[2] dinner to come.

"Fine fish, these bass!"

"Very tasty, these mackerel!"

"Delicious flounders, these!"

"What splendid cod!"

"And look at this **bevy**[3] of cute, little sardines! They'll **complement**[1] the larger fish beautifully!"

---

[1] **aromatic** As a noun, an *aroma* is a (usually pleasant or sweet) odor or smell (as from a food or spice). To describe something as *aromatic* is to say that it gives off an aroma; that is, it's fragrant, sweet-smelling, etc. *Perfumes are made from both natural substances (plant oil, for example) and aromatic synthetic chemicals.*

[2] **delectable** If something is *delectable*, it's greatly pleasing, especially to the taste; it's delicious, scrumptious, delightful, enjoyable, etc. *In 1968 British TV journalist Alistair Cooke complained that all Americans mistakenly believe that cranberry sauce "is a delectable necessity of Thanksgiving and that turkey in uneatable without it."*

[3] **bevy** A *bevy* is a (usually small) group of animals or people (or anything else), especially of birds, girls, or women (as in *a bevy of swans* or *a bevy of bathing beauties*). *According to the* Information Please Almanac, *Miami, Florida, is home to "over 170 multinational companies and a bevy of Fortune 500 companies [companies on* Fortune *magazine's list of the 500 largest U.S. corporations]."*

The bass, mackerel, flounders, cod, and sardines all went together into the tub to keep the tuna company. The last to come out of the net was Pinocchio.

Just as the fisherman was about to add him to the **pot-pourri**[2], his green eyes opened wide with surprise and he cried out, "What kind of fish is this? I don't remember ever eating anything like it."

He looked at it closely and, after turning it over and over, said at last, "It must be a crab!"

Pinocchio, hurt at being mistaken for a crab, said angrily, "What nonsense! A crab indeed! I'll have you know that I'm a puppet!"

"A puppet?" asked the fisherman. "I must admit that a puppet fish is, for me, a completely new experience. All the better. I'll **savor**[3] every mouthful."

"But can't you see that I'm not a fish? Can't you hear that I speak and think as you do?"

---

[1] **complement** Notice the similarity of this word to the word *complete*. When one thing *complements* another, it adds something lacking in the other; it makes the other more complete or more perfect. *France's magnificent Palace of Versailles is complemented by the beautiful formal gardens that lie before it.* Often two things *complement* each other equally; they go or work well together (as a particular shirt and pair of pants, for example). Note: Be careful to spell the sixth letter of this word with an *e*, not an *i*. The verb *compliment* has a different mean ("to express praise or admiration").

[2] **potpourri** Originally, this word (pronounced *poh-por-EE*) signified a mixture of dried flowers and spices used to scent the air. But today the word denotes any mixture or combination of various items; an assortment, mixed bag, stew, blend, etc. Reader's Digest, *a monthly magazine whose circulation is the world's highest, is a potpourri of inspirational, humorous, patriotic, and educational articles.*

[3] **savor** To *savor* something (tasty food, beautiful music, lovely scenery, etc.) is to enjoy or appreciate it fully. *American writer and humorist E. B. White (1899–1995) once said, "I arise in the morning torn between a desire to save the world and a desire to savor the world; this makes it hard to plan the day."*

"That's true," answered the fisherman. "And now, seeing that you can speak and think, I'll treat you with special consideration."

"And that is —"

"That, as a sign of my **esteem**[1], I'll allow you to choose the manner in which you'll be cooked. Do you want to be fried in a pan, or do you prefer to be boiled in water?"

"If I must choose," answered Pinocchio, "I'd rather go free so I can return home!"

"You must be joking! Do you think that I, with my **discriminating**[2] taste in food, would want to lose the opportunity to sample such a **sublime**[3] piece of fish? A puppet fish doesn't come to these waters very often. I may never get another chance. Leave it to me. I'll fry you in the pan with the others. I know you'll like it. It's always a comfort to be in good company."

---

[1] **esteem** A feeling of positive regard, admiration, or respect for someone or something is known as *esteem*. *Baseball great Stan Musial, who between 1943 and 1957 won the National League batting title seven times, was held is such high esteem that he was affectionately called "Stan the Man."* Note: Such a feeling for oneself is known as *self-esteem*. *Studies have shown that exercise is likely to reduce the risk of heart attack, help weight loss, improve sleep, and increase self-esteem.*

[2] **discriminating** If you have *discriminating* taste or a *discriminating* mind, you're able to recognize fine differences or distinctions between things (for example, you can easily tell the difference between cheap and fine wine, inferior and superior works of art, valid and faulty arguments, etc.). *The jazz saxophonist was so good at covering up his mistakes that only a few discriminating listeners knew that he'd started his solo in the wrong key.*

[3] **sublime** If something is *sublime*, it's outstanding or excellent, especially if it produces a sense of awe, grandeur, or power (as in *Switzerland's sublime scenery*) or if it's of a high moral, spiritual, or intellectual worth (as in *the sublime music of J. S. Bach*); it's heavenly, grand, supreme, etc. *In 1937 Canadian artist Emily Carr said, "It is wonderful to feel the grandness of Canada in the raw, not because she is Canada but because she's something sublime that you were born into, some great rugged power that you are a part of."*

The unlucky puppet, hearing this, began to cry and wail and beg. With tears streaming down his cheeks, he said, "How much better it would have been if I had gone to school! I didn't do the right thing, and now I'm paying for it! Oh! Oh! Oh!"

And because Pinocchio wriggled like an eel to escape from him, the fisherman took a long cord, tied him up, and threw him into the bottom of the tub with all the others.

Then he took a wooden bowl full of flour and started to roll the fish into it, one by one. When they were white with it, he threw them into the pan. Pinocchio's turn came last. The fisherman, without even looking at him, turned him over and over in the flour until he looked like a puppet made of chalk.

Chapter 25 "The Snail"

Suddenly, a large dog came running into the cave. "Get out!" cried the fisherman threateningly, still holding onto the puppet, who was covered with flour.

But the poor dog was starving, and he howled, "Give me a bite of fish and I'll go in peace."

"Get out, I say!" repeated the fisherman. And he drew back his foot to give the dog a kick.

Then the dog, who was far too hungry to care about being kicked, turned in a rage toward the fisherman and bared his terrible fangs. Pinocchio, terrified though he was, recognized the dog as the one he'd saved from drowning. In a pitiful little voice the puppet called out, "Save me! Save me!"

The dog immediately recognized Pinocchio's voice and was amazed to see that it came from the little flour-covered bundle that the fisherman held in his hand. With one great leap, the dog grasped that bundle in his mouth and, holding it carefully between his teeth, raced through the door.

The fisherman, angry at seeing his precious meal snatched from under his nose, ran after the dog, but a bad fit of coughing made him stop and turn back.

Meanwhile, the dog, as soon as he'd found the road that led to the village, stopped and dropped Pinocchio softly to the ground.

"How can I thank you, " asked the puppet.

"It's not necessary," answered the dog. "You saved me once, and what's given is always returned. We all must help each other in this world."

"But how did you get in that cave?"

"I was lying here on the sand more dead than alive, when the aroma of sizzling oil and fresh fish came to me and **whet-**

ted[1] my appetite. I followed it into the cave. Oh, if I had come a moment later!"

"Don't speak of it," wailed Pinocchio, still trembling with fright. "Don't say a word. If you'd come a moment later, I would have been fried and eaten. It makes me shiver just to think of it."

The dog held out his paw to the puppet, who shook it heartily, feeling that now he and the dog were good friends. Then they said good-bye and the dog went home.

Pinocchio, left alone, now looked around and saw a little cabin built of logs and roofed with **corrugated**[2] metal. An old man sat at the door sunning himself. Walking up to him, the puppet said, "Excuse me, sir, but have you heard anything of a poor schoolboy with a wounded temple?"

"Yes, the boy was brought to this cabin and now –"

"Now he's dead?" Pinocchio interrupted sorrowfully.

"No, he's alive and he's already returned home. He's fine."

"Really? Really?" cried the puppet, jumping with joy. "Then the **abrasions**[3] weren't really serious?"

---

[1] **whet (whetted)** To *whet* something (one's appetite, curiosity, desire, interest, etc.) is to stimulate it; arouse it. For example, people often eat appetizers before a meal to *whet* their appetites. *The rise of sports in 16th-century England whetted people's appetites for more sports; in fact, Mary, Queen of Scots, became interested in golf and helped popularized the game during her reign (1542–1567).*

[2] **corrugated** If you say that something (metal or cardboard, for example) is *corrugated*, you mean that it has been shaped or bent into folds or alternating, parallel ridges and grooves (usually to strengthen or stiffen it). *A washboard, a metal board with a corrugated surface, can be used either to wash clothes or play music.*

[3] **abrasion (abrasions)** As a verb, to *abrade* is to wear down by friction or rubbing. And as a noun, *abrasion* is the processes of *abrading*. But if you're speaking specifically of someone's skin, an *abrasion* is a scraped area (as from an injury). *A Band-Aid is an adhesive bandage with a gauze pad in the center used to cover minor cuts, insect bites, and abrasions.* Note: People often use this word informally to refer to any type of minor skin wound (cut, scratch, bruise, etc.).

"But they might have been," answered the old man, "for a heavy book was thrown at his head."

"Who threw it?"

"A schoolmate of his named Pinocchio."

"And who is this Pinocchio?" asked the puppet, pretending ignorance.

"They say that he's a mischief-maker. And they say that he has no **qualms**[1] about telling lies."

"That's not true!"

"Do you know this Pinocchio?"

"Only by sight!" answered the puppet.

"And what do you think of him?" asked the old man.

"I think he's a very good boy, eager to study, kind to his father, and respectful of his mother."

As he was telling these lies about himself, Pinocchio touched his nose and found it twice as long as it should be. Scared out of his wits, he cried out, "Don't listen to me! All the wonderful things I've just said are **fabrications**[2]. I know Pinocchio well and he's a very bad boy who, instead of going to school, runs away with his friends to have a good time."

At this speech, his nose returned to its normal size.

"Why are you so white?" the old man asked.

"I accidentally rubbed myself against a newly painted wall," he said, ashamed to admit that he'd been covered with flour for the frying pan.

---

[1] **qualm (qualms)** This word, often used in the plural and in the negative (as in *has no qualms about*) refers to the uneasy, disturbing, or guilty feeling you get when you do (or are thinking about doing) something considered wrong or bad (such as lying, cheating, stealing, breaking rules, being nasty, etc.). *Radio talk show hosts like to talk about politics and have no qualms about criticizing elected officials.*

[2] **fabricate (fabrications)** To *fabricate* something (a story, excuse, lie, etc.) is to make it up; invent it; devise it (especially in order to deceive). A *fabrication* is something fabricated, especially an untrue story; a lie. *We can't help but think that most supermarket tabloid headlines (such as "Scientists Clone Dinosaurs to Use as Weapons against Russia") are mere fabrications.*

"What have you done with your coat and your hat and your pants?"

"I met bandits on the road and they robbed me. Tell me, my good man, do you have, perhaps, a little suit to give me, so that I can go home?"

"My boy, as for clothes, I have only a bag that I keep beans in. If you want it, take it. There it is."

Pinocchio didn't wait for him to repeat his words. He took the bag, which happened to be empty, and after cutting a big hole at the top and two at the sides, he slipped into it as if it were an oversized shirt. Strangely dressed as he was, he started out toward the village.

Along the way he felt very uneasy and he said to himself: "How will I ever face my good fairy? What will she say when she sees me? Will she forgive this last mischief of mine? I'm sure she won't. Oh, no, she won't. And I deserve it, as usual! For I'm a wicked boy—always making promises I don't keep!"

He came to the village late at night. It was dark and raining heavily, and he could see nothing. He went straight to the fairy's house and knocked on the door.

He waited and waited. Finally, after a full thirty minutes, the fourth-floor window opened and Pinocchio saw a snail look down. A tiny light glowed on top of its head. "Who knocks at this late hour?" it called.

"Is the fairy home?" asked the puppet.

"The fairy's asleep and doesn't wish to be disturbed. Who are you?"

"It's Pinocchio."

"Who is Pinocchio?"

"The puppet; the one who lives in the fairy's house."

"Oh, I understand," said the snail. "Wait for me there. I'll come down to open the door for you."

"Hurry, I beg of you, for I'm dying of cold."

"My boy, I am a snail, and snails never hurry."

An hour passed; then two hours; the door was still closed. Pinocchio, who was trembling with fear and shivering from the cold rain on his back, knocked a second time, this time louder than before.

At that second knock, a window on the third floor opened and the same snail looked out.

"Dear little snail," cried Pinocchio, "I've been waiting two hours for you! And two hours on a dreadful night like this is as long as two years. Hurry, please!"

"My boy," answered the snail in a calm, peaceful voice, "I am a snail, and snails never hurry." And the window closed.

A few minutes later midnight struck; then one o'clock; then two o'clock; the door still remained closed!

The many hours of discomfort and fear finally **culminated**[1] in Pinocchio losing all control. **Seething**[2] with frustration, he drew back his leg and gave a violent kick against the door. He kicked so hard that his foot went straight through the wood and his leg followed almost to the knee. No matter how he pulled and yanked, he couldn't get it out. There he stayed as if nailed to the door.

---

[1] **culminate (culminated)** When something *culminates*, it ends (often in some particular way or with some particular result or event); it concludes; it reaches its final stage. *The institution of slavery led to a bitter political struggle between the North and South that culminated in the Civil War (1861–1865).* The noun is *culmination*. *The Wright brothers' first successful flight (1903) of a motor-driven aircraft was the culmination of years of experimentation with kites and gliders.*

[2] **seethe (seething)** When liquid (such as water in a teakettle or a river during a storm) *seethes*, it bubbles, churns, surges, or foams (from boiling or as if from boiling). If a person *seethes*, his emotions seem to boil; that is, he's in a state of agitation, especially a state of intense but unexpressed anger (as in *seething with resentment*). If a group (a nation, society, organization, etc.) *seethes*, it's in a state of turmoil (struggle, disorder, commotion, etc.). *In 1986 Secretary of State George Shultz, speaking of Washington, D.C., said, "Nothing ever gets settled in this town, a seething debating society in which the debate never stops."*

Poor Pinocchio! The rest of the night he had to spend with one foot through the door and the other on the ground.

As dawn was breaking, the door finally opened. That little snail had taken exactly nine hours to go from the fourth floor to the first!

"What are you doing with your foot through the door?" it asked the puppet.

"It was an accident. Won't you try to free me from this torture?"

"My boy, this is a job for a carpenter."

"Ask the fairy to help me!"

"The fairy's asleep and doesn't wish to be disturbed."

"Bring me something to eat, at least, for I'm faint from hunger."

"Right away!" said the snail.

In fact, after three and a half hours, Pinocchio saw him return with a tray of bread, roast chicken, and fruit.

"Here's the breakfast the fairy sends you," said the snail.

At the sight of all these good things, the puppet felt much better.

But upon tasting the food, he was disgusted to find that the bread was made of chalk, the chicken of cardboard, and the fruit of plaster!

He wanted to cry; he wanted to throw away the tray and all that was on it. Instead, from pain and weakness, he fainted.

When he regained his senses, he found himself stretched out on a sofa and the good fairy was seated near him.

"This time also I forgive you," said the fairy to him. "But be careful not to get into trouble again."

Receiving the fairy's forgiveness so easily made Pinocchio feel very guilty. But while his guilt troubled him deeply, it also had the effect of **rekindling**[1] his sense of purpose. He suddenly sat up straight and with eyes gleaming vowed to study hard and to behave himself. And he kept his word for the rest of that year!

The most **climactic**[2] event of the school year was the announcement of the Student of the Year award, which was based on both scholastic achievement and conduct. Pinocchio had scored highest in every one of his final examinations! With that remarkable feat and his excellent behavior, he easily won the award. As the **recipient**[3], he was given five gold stars and was the subject of a flattering speech by his teacher.

---

[1] **rekindle (rekindling)** If you're talking about a fire, a flame, firewood, etc., to *rekindle* it is to re-light it (as in *dying embers rekindled by the wind*). If you're talking about something immaterial (such as one's interests, one's ambitions, a debate, etc.), to *rekindle* it is to revive or renew it; to newly awaken, stimulate, or arouse it. *In his inaugural address (January 1965), President Lyndon Johnson said, "Let us reject any among us who seek to reopen old wounds and to rekindle old hatreds; they stand in the way of a [unified] nation."*

[2] **climactic** In a true or made-up literary or dramatic work (history, novel, play, film, etc.), a *climax* is an intense, decisive moment that serves as a turning point or as the conclusion of some crisis. The adjective *climactic* means "pertaining to or in the nature of a climax." *The climactic Battle of Gettysburg (July 1863) marked the beginning of the Union army's advantage in the Civil War — but nearly two years of heavy fighting would follow before the South was finally forced to surrender (April 1865).* Note: Be careful to spell the word with a *c* after the *a*; the word *climatic* has a different meaning: "pertaining to climate (weather conditions)."

[3] **recipient** A *recipient* is a person who receives something. The word is often used to signify one who has received an award, prize, medal, diploma, inheritance, or the like. *In 1964 clergyman and civil rights leader Martin Luther King, Jr., became the youngest recipient of the Nobel Peace Prize.* Note: The word is also often used to signify a medical patient who has received blood, tissue, or an organ (as from a donor). *In 1985 artificial heart recipient Murray Haydon joked from his hospital bed, "Would you please turn on the television; I'd like to see if I'm still alive and how I'm doing."*

In spite of himself, Pinocchio **basked**[1] in the high praise **bestowed**[2] on him—especially when it was announced that on the mathematics exam, he'd successfully solved a difficult problem that had **stymied**[3] every other student in the class.

The next day the fairy said to him lovingly, "It **gratifies**[4] me to see that you've worked so hard and behaved so well. Tomorrow your wish will be granted."

"What do you mean?"

"Don't you see? Your bad record has been **annulled**[1] by your hard work and good behavior. Tomorrow you will **cease**[2] to be a puppet and will become a real live boy."

---

[1] **bask (basked)** To *bask* in something (a pleasant situation) is to take great pleasure or satisfaction in it; to enjoy it. *According to the* Reader's Companion to American History, *"Boys idolized [home run champ Babe Ruth, who] basked in their admiration."* Note: The word often refers specifically to enjoying or lying in pleasant warmth (as in *bask in the sunshine*). *In 1958 British historian Arnold Toynbee said of Australia, "The immense cities [Sidney, Melbourne, Brisbane, Perth] lie basking on the beaches of the continent like whales that have taken to the land."*

[2] **bestow (bestowed)** To *bestow* something (a prize, award, trophy, diploma, etc.) is to present it (as an honor or gift). *In 1996 Southampton College of the University of Long Island bestowed an honorary degree on Sesame Street's Kermit the Frog to publicize the school's marine studies program.* Note: Sometimes the word means simply "give." *President Benjamin Harrison's (1833–1901) nickname, "Little Ben," was originally bestowed upon him by his soldiers (he'd commanded an Indiana volunteer regiment during the Civil War), perhaps because of his short stature.*

[3] **stymie (stymied)** To *stymie* something (one's efforts, a plan, an undertaking, etc.) is to block, halt, or stop it (by presenting difficulties or problems that can't be overcome or resolved). *People searching for (18th-century French Queen) Marie Antoinette in the encyclopedia will be stymied until they discover that she is alphabetized under "M" for Marie, not under "A" for Antoinette.*

[4] **gratify (gratified)** If something *gratifies* you, it pleases you, especially by satisfying your desires, wishes, expectations, etc. *In 1901, speaking to the Young People's Society in New York City, author Mark Twain said, "Always do right – this will gratify some and astonish the rest."*

Pinocchio was beside himself with joy. All his friends and schoolmates were to help him celebrate the **momentous**[3] occasion the next day! The fairy promised that the party would include a chocolate cake and **festive**[4] decorations in many bright colors.

---

[1] **annul (annulled)** To *annul* something (a marriage or law, for example) is to put an official (often legal) end to it; to cancel it, make it void, declare it invalid, etc. *Eleanor of Aquitaine, the beautiful and intelligent heiress of the duchy of Aquitaine (historical region of southwest France), became queen of France when she married King Louis VII (1137); when the marriage was annulled (1152) she married King Henry II of England and became queen of that country!*

[2] **cease** When something (a particular condition, the performance of an action or activity, etc.) *ceases*, it comes to an end; it stops. *The first mass-produced automobile, the Model T Ford, was introduced in 1908; production ceased in 1927, after more than fifteen million had rolled off the assembly line.*

[3] **momentous** If something (a decision, an occasion, etc.) is *momentous*, it's of great or far-reaching importance or significance; it's eventful, weighty, fateful, earthshaking, etc. *Japan's surprise attack on Pearl Harbor (December 1941) was a momentous event, for it marked the beginning of the Untied States' involvement in World War II.*

[4] **festive** If something (food, activities, decorations, etc.) is *festive*, it's suitable for a feast or festival; that is, it's cheery, merry, celebratory, etc. *In 1983, speaking of campaigning for political office, author Ralph Martin said, "Handshaking is friendly until your hands bleed, [and] confetti looks festive until you're forced to spit out mouthfuls hurled directly into your face."*

Chapter 26 "Lampwick"

Late that afternoon Pinocchio asked for permission to hand out the invitations.

"Indeed, you may go and invite your friends to tomorrow's party. But once you've handed out all the invitations, don't **dawdle**[1]; come right home. You must be back before dark. Do you promise?"

"Yes. I'll be back in an hour without fail."

"Be careful, Pinocchio! Boys make promises very easily, but they just as easily **default**[2] on them. Can I trust you?"

"Yes, **implicitly**[1]. You see, I'm not like other boys—when I give my word, I keep it."

---

[1] **dawdle** To *dawdle* is to waste time or move slowly; to dilly-dally, loiter, delay, etc. *Novelist Henry Miller (1891–1980) once wrote: "Breakfast was the one ceremony of the day over which she dawdled and lingered."*

[2] **default** As a verb, to *default* on something (a loan, a promise, an obligation, etc.) is to fail to fulfil or deliver it (as by not paying back money, not performing a particular task, not appearing at a required appointment, etc.). *With the authority of Congress, the IRS (Internal Revenue Service) shares information with other government agencies; in most cases the information is used in the attempt to find people who have defaulted on child-support payments or student loans.* As a noun, a *default* is an instance of such a failure, often in particular the failure of a competitor or team to participate in a contest or sporting event. *In 1975 Russian chess master Anatoly Karpov was declared world champion by default when American Bobby Fischer, the title-holder, refused to agree to terms for a match.*

"We'll see. But in case you do disobey, you'll be the one who suffers—not anyone else."

"Why?"

"Because boys who don't listen to their parents and teachers are always sorry in the end."

"But I've learned my lesson," said Pinocchio.

"And what lesson is that?"

Pinocchio thought for a moment, then said, "It's hard to **verbalize**[2] what it is exactly...but I guess the **crux**[3] of it is that children who lie or steal or who are lazy always end up unhappy. From now on I'll be good."

"We'll see if that's true. I hope it is."

Without adding another word, the puppet said good-bye to his mother, and, singing and dancing, left the house.

---

[1] **implicit (implicitly)** This word has several meanings, depending on the context. If you describe trust, faith, obedience, or the like, as *implicit*, you mean that there are no doubts or reservations connected with it; it's absolute, unquestioning, etc. *Eleanor Roosevelt once said of her husband, President Franklin D. Roosevelt, "I had implicit confidence in his ability to help the country in a crisis."* If you say that an agreement, acceptance, guarantee, or the like, is *implicit*, you mean that it's implied or understood rather than directly expressed; it's unspoken. *In loading passengers of the sinking* Titanic *into lifeboats, the crew followed the implicit rule of "women and children first."* And if you say that something is *implicit* in something else, you mean that it's contained in the very nature of it but not readily apparent. *In 1987 Supreme Court justice Sandra Day O'Connor said, "[A] reckless disregard for human life [is] implicit in knowingly engaging in criminal activity known to carry a risk of death."*

[2] **verbalize** To *verbalize* something (a thought, an idea, a visual image, etc.) is to express it in words (often out loud). *In 1985 American composer Virgil Thomson (1996–1989) said, "I never learned to verbalize an abstract musical concept. No thank you. The whole point of being a serious musician is to avoid verbalization whenever you can."*

[3] **crux** The *crux* of a matter (or issue, argument, etc.) is its most basic, central, or decisive point. *In her 1954 book* Let's Eat Right to Keep Fit, *nutritionist Adelle Davis emphasized proper diet as the crux of both physical and emotional well-being.*

In a little more than an hour, all his friends were invited. Some had accepted quickly and gladly. Others had to be **coaxed**[1] with the promise of chocolate cake.

Among his schoolmates, Pinocchio had one whom he liked best of all—the tall, thin, bright one whose nickname, fittingly, was "Lampwick." As the laziest boy in the school and the biggest troublemaker, his values were the **antithesis**[2] of Pinocchio's. Nevertheless, an **affinity**[3] existed between them.

That day, Pinocchio went straight to his friend's house to invite him to the party, but Lampwick wasn't home. He went a second time, and again a third, but still without luck.

Where could he be? Pinocchio searched everywhere and finally found him standing near a farmer's wagon.

"What are you doing here?" asked Pinocchio, running up to him.

"I'm waiting for midnight to strike to go—"

"Where?"

"Far, far away!"

---

[1] **coax (coaxed)** To *coax* someone is to try to persuade him (to perform some action, agree to something, etc.) by gentle urging, flattery, sweet-talk, promises, etc. *We coaxed our cat out of its hiding place by offering it food and speaking to it in a higher-than-normal voice.*

[2] **antithesis** The *antithesis* (pronounced *an-TITH-i-sis*) of something (a concept, style, philosophy, policy, personality, etc.) is its direct or exact opposite. For example, stinginess is the *antithesis* of generosity; capitalism is the *antithesis* of communism. *German religious philosopher Jakob Boehme (1575–1624) believed that evil was a necessary antithesis to good.*

[3] **affinity** In one sense, an *affinity* is a natural liking for (or attraction to) a particular person or thing. *As a conductor, Leonard Bernstein (1918–1990) had a special affinity for the works of (Austrian composer) Gustav Mahler (1860–1911).* In another sense, an *affinity* is a similarity or likeness (of character, nature, structure, appearance, etc.) between people or things (languages, plants, or animals, for example), suggestive of a relationship or common type. *In 1786 English linguist Sir William Jones noted an affinity between Sanskrit, Latin, and Greek, and argued that all descended from an earlier, extinct language.*

"And I've gone to your house three times looking for you!"

"What did you want?"

"Haven't you heard? Don't you know about my good luck?"

"What?"

"Tomorrow I end my days as a puppet and become a real boy—like you and all my other friends."

"That's great!"

"Will you come to my party tomorrow?"

"But I'm telling you that I'm going away tonight."

"What time?"

"Midnight."

"Where are you going?"

"To another country—the best in the world—a wonderful place!"

"What is it?"

"It's called Playland. Why don't you come with me?"

"Me? Oh, no!"

"You're making a big mistake, Pinocchio. Believe me, if you don't come, you'll be sorry. Where can you find a place that's better? No schools, no teachers, no books! And no homework either! You find homework as **irksome**[1] as I do, right? Well, in that heavenly place there's no such thing as homework! And here, it's only on weekends that we have no school. In Playland, every day is like the weekend. Vacation begins on the first day of January and ends on the last day of December. Oh, that's the place for me! All countries should be like it! We'll be so happy there!"

"But how do you spend your time in Playland?"

---

[1] **irksome** If something (performing a difficult or time-consuming task, for example) is *irksome*, it's annoying, bothersome, irritating, etc., and at the same time (because it may involve dull or unrewarding work) tedious, tiresome, wearisome, etc. *When the bride and groom returned from their honeymoon, they were faced with the irksome task of writing 250 thank-you notes.*

"That's the best part. Here, we have to suffer the **monotony**[1] of our daily school routine. There, you play all day long. At night you go to bed, and the next morning, the fun begins all over again. What do you think of that?"

"Hmm..." said Pinocchio, nodding his wooden head as if to say, "That sounds pretty good."

"Do you want to go with me, then? Yes or no?"

"But what if something bad happens?"

"Don't be such a **pessimist**[2]. Nothing is going to happen. So is it yes or no? Make up your mind."

"No, no, and again no! I've promised my kind fairy to be a good boy and to be home before dark. Anything else would be a **breach**[3] of trust. Look, the sun's already setting and the moon's beginning to rise. I must leave right now."

---

[1] **monotony** This word signifies a tedious sameness or repetitiousness in something (such as in music, a landscape, the sound of one's voice, one's work, one's diet, etc.). The adjective is *monotonous* ("tediously repetitious or unvarying"). Note: The noun and adjective are both pronounced with the accent on the second syllable. *In 1879 Scottish writer Robert Louis Stevenson (1850–1894) said, "Night is a dead, monotonous period under a roof; but out in the open world it passes lightly, with its stars and dews and perfumes, and the hours are marked by changes in the face of Nature."*

[2] **pessimist** A *pessimist* is a person who expects the worst (or who expects bad things to happen, or who stresses the negative). The noun is *pessimism;* the adjective is *pessimistic. Journalist George Will once said, "The nice part about being a pessimist is that you are constantly being either proven right or pleasantly surprised."*

[3] **breach** In a general sense, a *breach* is a break; more specifically, it can be (1) a break, gap, opening, etc., in a structure or line of defense, as in *a breach in the wall,* (2) a break in friendly relations, as in *a breach between the President and Congress,* or (3) the breaking of, or failure to meet the requirements of, a law, regulation, obligation, contract, promise, trust, etc., as in *a breach of the treaty. In 1962 the Supreme Court ruled that required prayer in public schools is a breach of the First Amendment (which prohibits establishing a religion).*

"Wait two more minutes," replied Lampwick, not bothering to check the progress of the **celestial**[1] spheres.

"It's too late!"

"Only two minutes!"

"Don't you understand? My mother was good enough to allow me some **latitude**[2] with my schedule today—so that I could hand out my party invitations. But her letting me out of the house was **contingent**[3] on my promise to return home before dark! What if she scolds me?"

"Scolds you? What are you, a sissy? She won't scold you. She'll overlook anything you do by reminding herself that boys will...I mean...puppets will be puppets," explained

---

[1] **celestial** This word means "pertaining to the sky or heaven (whether material or spiritual)." For example, the sun, moon, planets, and stars are *celestial* bodies, and angels are *celestial* beings. *According to the New Testament, the Star of Bethlehem was a bright celestial object that led the three gift-bearing Wise Men of the East to the infant Jesus.*

[2] **latitude** In geography, lines of *latitude* are imaginary horizontal lines on a map or globe by which distances (expressed in degrees) north or south of the equator can be measured. For example, the city of New Orleans lies at 30 degrees north. Similar vertical imaginary lines are known as lines of *longitude* (which are expressed in degrees east or west of the prime meridian, which runs through Greenwich, England). However, when you speak of having *latitude* in a particular situation, you mean that you have a certain amount of freedom (of action, opinion, etc.); you're not unduly restricted or limited. *In the Supreme Court's 1966* Miranda vs. Arizona *ruling (which requires police officers to advise a suspect of his right to remain silent and to have a lawyer present during questioning), chief justice Earl Warren pointed out, "This Court has always given ample latitude to law enforcement agencies in the legitimate exercise of their duties."*

[3] **contingent** If something (a particular desired course of action, for example) is *contingent* on something else (someone else's approval, for instance), it's dependent on it. For example, proposed tax cuts are *contingent* on the approval of Congress. *In the Supreme Court's 1973* Roe vs. Wade *decision (which legalized abortion), justice Harry Blackmun noted, "The law has been reluctant to [give] legal rights to the unborn except in narrowly defined situations and except when the rights are contingent upon live birth."*

Lampwick, **alluding**[1] to the old **adage**[2]. "And even if she does scold you, let her. So what? Are you afraid it will injure your fragile **ego**[3]?"

Ignoring the question, Pinocchio asked, "Are you going alone or with friends?"

"Alone? Are you kidding? There will be more than a hundred of us!"

Pinocchio thought for a moment, then said, "Let me ask you a **hypothetical**[1] question: If, by chance, I did decide to go

---

[1] **allude (alluding)** To *allude* to something is to make an indirect or casual mention of it; to refer to it. Usage Note: Whereas some people use the words *allude* and *refer* synonymously, others distinguish between them as follows: *allude* applies to indirect references in which the source is not specifically identified (for example, if you were to say "I don't think we're in Kansas anymore," you'd be *alluding* to the film *The Wizard of Oz*); *refer* applies to a specific mention of a source (for example, if you were to say "They're debating the issue on the Hill today," you'd be *referring* to Capitol Hill in Washington, D.C., where Congress meets). *When, in an 1858 speech, Abraham Lincoln said, "A house divided against itself cannot stand," he was alluding to both the Bible and the intensifying conflict between the North and South over slavery.*

[2] **adage** An *adage* is a traditional or familiar saying that expresses a general truth; a proverb. *When we opened our fortune cookies we couldn't help but laugh when we saw that the first predicted "You will inherit a large sum of money" and the second contained the adage "A fool and his money are soon parted."*

[3] **ego** Your *ego* is your sense of self-importance; your self-image. People who are said to have a large ego are usually self-centered and (often unjustifiably) think very highly of themselves. People with a fragile ego tend to have their feelings hurt easily. Note: An *alter ego* is another side (or aspect) of yourself (or of your personality); for example, Superman's *alter ego* is Clark Kent. *Actress Billie Burke (who played the Good Witch of the North in the 1939 film* The Wizard of Oz) *once said of Hollywood: "To survive there, you need the ambition of a Latin-American revolutionary, the ego of a grand opera tenor, and the [endurance] of a cow pony."*

with you—and I don't want you to **infer**[2] from this question that I have any intention of going—how would we get there?"

"At midnight a wagon passes here that takes us there."

"Listen, Lampwick," said the puppet, "are you really sure that there are no schools in Playland?"

"Not even the shadow of one."

"Not even one teacher?"

"Not one."

"And you don't have to study?"

"Never, never, never!"

"What a great land!" said Pinocchio. "Of course, I've never been there, but I can imagine what it would be like."

"Why don't you come, too?"

"I told you I promised my good fairy that I'd behave myself, and I'm going to keep my word—and that's that." When Lampwick didn't answer right away, Pinocchio added, "Listen, I'm a puppet, so I'm not **susceptible**[3] to human **frailties**[1] like you are. It's useless for you to even try to tempt me."

---

[1] **hypothetical** A *hypothetical* situation or object is one based on (or relating to or restricted to) what is theoretical, supposed, or assumed, rather than on what is real, true, or proven. A *hypothetical* question is one asked in the nature of "what if..." or "let's say that...," rather than one asked with purposeful or sincere intent. *A time machine is a hypothetical device by means of which one can travel into the future and the past.*

[2] **infer** When you *infer* something (the truth about some matter, for example), you use your reasoning to draw a conclusion about it based on indirect information (related evidence, premises, suggestions, implications, etc.), as in *infer one's personality from his handwriting* or *infer the sun's future from theoretical models. In the 1887 novel* A Study in Scarlet, *(fictional English detective) Sherlock Holmes says: "From a drop of water a logician could infer the possibility of an Atlantic or Niagara without having seen or heard of one or the other."*

[3] **susceptible** If you're *susceptible* to something (a disease or an influence, for example) you're easily or readily affected by it; you're vulnerable to it (as in *susceptible to colds, susceptible to extreme heat,* or *susceptible to flattery*). *In 1988 research scientists Philip Leder and Timothy Steward received a patent for the "Harvard mouse," a mouse genetically altered to be susceptible to cancer.*

"Have it your way. I hope you enjoy your **humdrum**[2] existence. And send my regards to all the schoolhouses and teachers you meet along your way."

"Good-bye, Lampwick. Have a good time."

With these words, Pinocchio started on his way home. Turning once more to his friend, he asked, "But are you sure that in that country each day is like the weekend?"

"Very sure!"

"And that vacation begins on the first of January and ends on the thirty-first of December?"

"Very, very sure!"

"What a great country!" repeated Pinocchio, indecisively.

Then, in sudden determination, the puppet said hurriedly, "Good-bye for the last time, and good luck."

"Have it your way, then. Good-bye."

"How soon will you go?"

"In about two hours."

"What a pity! If it were only one hour, I might wait with you."

"And the fairy?"

"By this time I'm late, and one hour more or less wouldn't make any difference."

"And if the fairy yells at you?"

---

[1] **frailty (frailties)** The adjective *frail* means "weak," and a *frailty* is a physical or moral weakness. But when people speak of "human frailties," they're talking about faults that arise from the imperfections of human nature (such as a tendency to yield to temptation, for example). *In her 1980 biography of French-born American religious writer, poet, priest, and monk Thomas Merton (1915–1968), author Monica Furlong said, "I have avoided the [devotional] approach, have tried to see him as the normal man he was, with his fair share, perhaps more than his fair share, of human frailties."*

[2] **humdrum** If something (one's life, for example) is *humdrum*, it lacks variety or excitement; it's uninteresting, boring, dull, etc. *President William Howard Taft (who served immediately after the dynamic Theodore Roosevelt) once said of his own term of office (1909–1913), "It is a very humdrum, uninteresting administration, and it does not attract the attention or enthusiasm of anybody."*

"Don't worry. It's not as if she's some kind of **shrew**[1] or something. She's the nicest mother in the world! The worst she'll do is lecture me a little about how I should always do the right thing. I can handle it."

In the meantime, the night became darker and darker, and one by one the stars came out. While the flickering **astral**[2] lights looked down upon the two boys, all at once, far down the road, another light flickered and a bell tinkled.

"There it is!" cried Lampwick, jumping to his feet.

"What?" whispered Pinocchio.

"The wagon that's coming to take me to Playland. For the last time, are you coming or not?"

"But is it really true that in that country boys never have to study?"

"Never, never, never!"

"What a wonderful, beautiful, marvelous country! Oh! Oh!"

---

[1] **shrew** A *shrew* is a bad-tempered, scolding, or nagging woman. The adjective is *shrewish*. *Fifth century B.C. Greek philosopher Socrates once said of his shrewish wife, Xanthippe (who nagged and scolded him for not being a better provider), "As I thought about associating with all kinds of people, I thought nothing they could do would disturb me, once I had accustomed myself to endure my wife's temperament."*

[2] **astral** This word means "pertaining to the stars" or "resembling a star; star-shaped." *According to the* Oxford Encyclopedia, *"[Astrology was] developed in Mesopotamia in the second millennium B.C.; it interpreted astronomical [events] as astral omens, the [events] being indications of the gods' intentions for kings and kingdoms."*

Chapter 27 "Playland"

Finally the wagon arrived. It made no noise, for its wheels were covered with straw and rags. It was drawn by twelve pairs of donkeys, all of the same size, but of different colors. Some were gray, others white, and still others a mixture of brown and black. But what was most **bizarre**[1] was that all the donkeys, instead of iron horseshoes, wore laced shoes made of leather, just like ones boys wear.

The wagon was so closely packed with boys of all ages that it looked like a can of sardines. They were uncomfortably piled one on top of another and could hardly breathe, yet no one complained. The thought that in a few hours they'd reach a country where there were no schools, no books, and no teachers made the boys so happy that they felt no discomfort.

No sooner had the wagon stopped than the driver—a short, **obese**[2] fellow with greasy hair and small eyes—turned to Lampwick. With a handshake and smile, he asked, "Tell me, my fine boy, do you also want to come to my wonderful country?"

"Indeed, I do."

"But I must tell you that there's no more room in the wagon. It's full."

---

[1] **bizarre** If something is *bizarre*, it's strikingly unusual or strange (as in style or appearance); it's weird, odd, peculiar, abnormal, fantastic, grotesque, etc. (as in *the punk rocker's bizarre clothing*). *In 1965 Spanish artist Pablo Picasso (who represented human forms as abstract geometric shapes) said, "People seek the new, the extraordinary, the extravagant [in art]... I have [satisfied them] with all the many bizarre things that have come into my head—and the less they understand, the more they admire it."*

[2] **obese** People who are *obese* (pronounced *oh-BEESS*) are extremely fat; they're grossly overweight. The noun is *obesity* (pronounced *oh-BEE-si-tee*). *According to Grolier's Encyclopedia, 20th-century psychologist Stanley Schachter "contributed to the understanding of obesity, showing that hunger in obese people is driven by external causes—for example, the sight of food—rather than by bodily sensations."*

"Never mind," answered Lampwick. "If there's no room inside, I can sit on the top of the coach." And with one leap, he perched himself there.

Then the man turned to Pinocchio and, in an overly polite, **servile**[1] manner, bowed and asked, "And what about you, my handsome young lad? Will you also come with us to my glorious country?"

"I'll stay here," answered Pinocchio. "I want to return home. I'm going to study and succeed in life."

"Pinocchio!" Lampwick called out. "Listen to me. I know you think that good study habits are **conducive**[2] to success, but ask yourself—is it really worth it? Come with us and we'll always be happy."

"No, I can't!"

"Come with us and we'll always be happy," cried four other voices from the wagon.

"Come with us and we'll always be happy," shouted the more than one hundred boys in the wagon, all together.

"And if I go with you, what will my good fairy say?" asked the puppet, who was beginning to weaken in his good intentions.

---

[1] **servile** If you're *servile*, you act in the manner of a servant or slave; that is, you're submissive and courteously yielding to others' wishes, demands, etc. Note: The word also means "of or suitable to a servant or slave," as in *servile labor* or *servile class. Twentieth-century English detective novelist P. D. James once wrote of one of her characters: "In his attitude to senior officers [he was] respectful without being servile."*

[2] **conducive** If something is *conducive* (usually followed by the word *to*), it tends to cause or bring about some particular end or result (by somehow contributing to, allowing, promoting, or encouraging that end or result), as in *soil conditions conducive to farming* or *weather conducive to outdoor sports. In a 1990 speech, South African political leader Nelson Mandela said of the armed struggle of South African blacks against apartheid (strict racial segregation), "We express the hope that a climate conducive to a negotiated settlement will be created soon."*

"Don't worry about that so much. You're such a baby!" Then Lampwick shouted down to the other boys, "Isn't he a baby?" Then, using a tactic that almost never fails, he called to Pinocchio, "Do you know what? On second thought, go back home to your mother. We shouldn't twist your arm if you're really too afraid to come with us." Then to the other boys: "We shouldn't twist his arm if he's really too afraid, should we?"

Pinocchio didn't answer. He sighed deeply once; a second time; a third time. Finally, he said, "Okay, make room for me! I'm coming, too!"

"The seats are all filled," answered the little man, "but to show you how much I think of you, you can take my place as coachman."

"And what about you?"

"I'll walk."

"No, I couldn't permit such a thing. I'd much rather ride on one of these donkeys," cried Pinocchio.

So saying, he approached the first donkey and tried to mount it. But the little animal turned suddenly and gave him such a terrible kick in the stomach that Pinocchio was thrown to the ground and fell with his legs in the air.

At this unexpected sight, the whole company of runaway boys erupted in **raucous**[1] laughter. But the little man didn't laugh. He went up to the **unruly**[2] animal, and, still smiling,

---

[1] **raucous** Sound (laughter, voices, music, etc.) described as *raucous* is rough, harsh, loud. *According to the* Reader's Companion to American History, *Bob Dylan's "first album after his [1966 motorcycle] accident abandoned raucous rock for a quieter, more personal sound."* Behavior described as *raucous* is noisy and disorderly. *As a young man, newspaper tycoon William Randolph Hearst (1863–1951) was expelled from Harvard University for his raucous behavior.*

[2] **unruly** People (or animals) who are *unruly* don't submit to rules, control, or discipline; they're disorderly, unmanageable, uncooperative, disobedient, etc. *According to* Compton's Encyclopedia, *Dennis Rodman's "colorful public stunts and sometimes unruly behavior on the [basketball] court [contributed to] a bad-boy image that eventually [angered] NBA officials."*

bent over him lovingly and pretended to give him a kiss but actually bit off half his right ear!

In the meantime, Pinocchio lifted himself from the ground, and, with one leap, landed on the donkey's back. The leap was so well **executed**[1] that all the boys shouted, "Hurrah for Pinocchio!" and clapped their hands in hearty applause.

Suddenly the little donkey gave a kick with his two hind legs and, at this sudden move, the poor puppet found himself sprawled in the middle of the road. Again the boys howled with laughter. But the little man, instead of laughing, became so loving toward the little animal that, with another kiss, he bit off half of his other ear.

"You can mount now, my boy," he then said to Pinocchio. "Have no fear. That donkey was **agitated**[2] about something, but I've spoken to him and now he seems quiet and reasonable."

Pinocchio mounted and the wagon started on its way. While the donkeys trotted along the road, the puppet heard a very quiet voice whisper to him, "You poor thing! You've

---

[1] **execute (executed)** To *execute* a particular action or activity is to carry it out, perform it, do it, accomplish it (as in *execute a somersault*). *During the Vietnam War, Secretary of State Henry Kissinger helped President Richard Nixon plan and execute a secret bombing of Cambodia.* To *execute* a law or policy is to put it into effect. *In September 1957, speaking of sending troops to enforce racial integration in Little Rock [Arkansas] High School, President Dwight D. Eisenhower said, "I intend to pursue this course until the orders of the federal court can be executed without unlawful interference."* Note: In another sense, to *execute* a person is to put him to death; kill him (especially by carrying out a lawful sentence). *In 1793 French queen Marie Antoinette was executed by guillotine.*

[2] **agitate (agitated)** To *agitate* a person (or animal) is to disturb, upset, or excite him emotionally; to stir up his thoughts, feelings, etc. *When a skunk becomes agitated, it squirts a foul-smelling mist from glands under its tail.* To *agitate* a material substance (water, for example) is to cause it to move with violence or sudden force; to stir it up, shake it up, churn it, etc. *In microwave ovens, high-frequency electromagnetic waves agitate water molecules in food; this results in high temperatures and rapid cooking.*

done as you wished, but you're going to be very sorry before long."

The puppet, greatly frightened, looked around to see where the words had come from, but he saw no one. The donkeys trotted, the wagon rolled smoothly on, the boys slept, and the fat, little driver whistled between his teeth.

After a mile or so, Pinocchio again heard the same faint voice whispering, "Remember, you fool, boys who play and never study regret it sooner or later. Oh, how well I can attest[1] to that! A day will come when you'll cry bitterly, as I'm crying now—but it will be too late!"

At these whispered words, the puppet grew more and more frightened. He jumped to the ground, ran around to the face of the donkey on whose back he'd been riding, and taking the donkey's nose in his hands, looked at him. Imagine his surprise when he saw that the donkey was crying—just like a boy!

"Driver!" cried the puppet. "Did you hear that? This donkey was talking, and now he's crying!"

"That's ludicrous[2]. You must be hallucinating[3]."

"But he really spoke."

---

[1] **attest** To *attest* to something is to confirm, certify, or declare the truth, correctness, or genuineness of it. *Although Barry Manilow's music is dismissed by some critics because of its sentimentality, his fan mail and enormous sales attest to the great pleasure he gives listeners.*

[2] **ludicrous** If something is *ludicrous*, it's laughably absurd or foolish; it's ridiculous. *American humorist and author S. J. Perelman (1904–1979) once wrote: "The effect of the trousers, at least three sizes too large for him, was ludicrous."*

[3] **hallucination (hallucinating)** People who suffer from mental illness or who are under the influence of a drug sometimes believe they see or hear things that don't actually exist. These false impressions are known as *hallucinations*. As a verb, to *hallucinate* is to experience such false impressions. *English novelist John Wain (1925–1994) once wrote: "I'm imagining things, hallucinating a conversation with my sister, who's no longer alive."*

"It's just a **figment**[1] of your imagination, I tell you. Or maybe what you heard was braying. Sometimes that sounds a little like talking."

"But he spoke **fluently**[2], like a person does."

"Perhaps he learned to mumble a few words when he lived for three years with a flock of trained parrots. That might explain it. Now, don't lose time over a crying donkey. Mount quickly and let's go. The night is chilly and the road is long."

Pinocchio obeyed without another word. The wagon started again. They rode all night, and Pinocchio was filled with anticipation. He loved the name of their destination. For him the word "Playland" held **connotations**[3] of ecstasy and delight. Toward dawn they finally reached the much-longed-for country.

---

[1] **figment** A *figment* (as in "figment of the imagination") is something (a story, idea, statement, etc.) merely made up or invented; that is, something that doesn't exist, except in the imagination. *Whereas some heroes of American folklore are mere figments of the imagination (lumberjack Paul Bunyan, for example), others are real flesh-and-blood people (pioneer and nurseryman Johnny Appleseed, for example).*

[2] **fluent** If you're *fluent* (in speech) you're able to express yourself smoothly, easily, readily, effortlessly, etc. *Albert Einstein (1879–1955), perhaps the greatest physicist of all time, was slow in learning to speak; in fact, he was not fully fluent until he was ten.* Note: To be *fluent* in a particular foreign language is to be able to speak it easily and without hesitation. *As a child, journalist William F. Buckley, Jr., had Latin American nurses and French governesses and spoke Spanish and French fluently.*

[3] **connotation (connotations)** Some words suggest certain ideas or concepts in addition to the word's primary meaning. These associated ideas are known as *connotations*. To use the verb, certain words *connote* certain ideas or concepts. For example, the word *home* means "a place where one lives," but it *connotes* warmth, affection, comfort, etc. *American author Vance Packard (1914–1996) once said, "The words 'instant coffee' [seem to be] loaded with unfortunate connotations."*

From the standpoint of government, this great land was completely **unique**[1]. Whereas **conventional**[2] countries had **codified**[3] laws, Playland had no laws or rules at all. The normal state of affairs there was **anarchy**[4] and **chaos**[5].

In physical appearance the population of Playland — which was composed entirely of boys who ranged in age from eight

---

[1] **unique** If you describe something as *unique* (pronounced *you-NEEK*), you mean that there's nothing else like it; it's one of a kind; it's in a class by itself (as in *Bob Dylan's unique singing voice* or *Mel Brooks' unique sense of humor*). *In 1987 journalist James Barron described Liberace's music as a "unique blend of Beethoven and 'Beer Barrel Polka.'"*

[2] **conventional** In one sense, if something is *conventional* it conforms to accepted standards; it's normal, traditional, customary, usual, etc. *A sonnet is a poem, often about love, that follows one of several strict conventional patterns of rhyme.* In another sense, if something is *conventional* it's ordinary rather than unusual or experimental; it's usual, normal, expected, commonplace, everyday, etc. *Frozen TV dinners can be heated in either a microwave or conventional oven.*

[3] **codify (codified)** To *codify* something (a set of laws or rules, for example) is to put it into a complete, systematically arranged collection. *The rules of baseball were codified in 1846 by New York surveyor Alexander Cartwright of the Knickerbocker Baseball Club.*

[4] **anarchy** This word signifies either an absence of any form of government (or political authority) in a society, or the (usually political or social) disorder and (often lawless) confusion that naturally arises from an absence of governmental control. *In 1992, after famine killed more than 300,000 people, (the African nation of) Somalia fell into anarchy and armed thugs prevented world food aid from relieving starvation.* In another sense, the word signifies any state of disorder or confusion. *In 1860 writer and philosopher Ralph Waldo Emerson (1803–1882) said, "There is no chance, and no anarchy, in the universe; every god is sitting in his sphere."*

[5] **chaos** This word (pronounced *KAY-ahss*) signifies either a state of complete disorder, confusion, or turmoil (as in *a classroom in chaos*), or a complete lack of order or organization (as in *a desktop in chaos*). *Writer Katherine Anne Porter (1890–1980) once said, "Human life itself may be almost pure chaos, but the work of the artist is to take these handfuls of confusion and put them together in a frame to give them some kind of shape and meaning."*

to fourteen—was quite **diverse**[1]. Some boys were short, others tall. Some were fat, others thin. Some had fair skin, others had **ruddy**[2] complexions. Some had freckles. Some had buck teeth. In the street there was such merriment and shouting that it was deafening. Everywhere you looked, **throngs**[3] of **frolicsome**[4] boys had **congregated**[1]. Some played marbles or hop-

---

[1] **diverse** If you say that one particular thing is *diverse*, you mean that it consists of differing, sometimes contrasting, elements or parts (as in *Atlanta's diverse economy*). *According to the* Reader's Companion to American History, *folksinger Woody Guthrie (1912–1967) "grew up in Oklahoma in a culturally diverse area, among cowboys, farmers, coal miners, and railroad and oil workers."* If you say that a number of things are *diverse*, you mean that they are varied, unlike (as in *people's diverse interests*). *American photojournalist Margaret Bourke-White (1906–1971) photographed such diverse subjects as the release of World War II concentration camp victims, the rural South during the Great Depression, mining in South Africa, and guerrilla warfare in Korea.*

[2] **ruddy** If you say that a person's face or complexion is *ruddy*, you mean that it has a healthy reddish color. *According to* Compton's Encyclopedia, *Italian explorer Christopher Columbus (1451–1506) "grew up to be a tall, strongly built young man with red hair and a ruddy complexion."* If you say that a thing is *ruddy*, you mean simply that it's red or reddish in color. *According to the* Encarta Encyclopedia, *apricots are "roundish, yellow, and sometimes ruddy on one side, with yellow flesh."*

[3] **throng (throngs)** A *throng* is a large group of people crowded or assembled together. *Civil rights leader Martin Luther King, Jr., delivered his "I Have a Dream" speech to a throng of 250,000 demonstrators during 1963's March on Washington.*

[4] **frolicsome** As a verb, to *frolic* is to play merrily, have fun, make jokes, play pranks, or playfully leap about. The adjective *frolicsome* describes anyone who frolics or tends to frolic; that is, anyone who is merrily playful, full of high-spirited fun, etc. *According to the* American Heritage Dictionary, *Thomas Morton was an "English-born American colonist who was twice [sent back] to England (1628 and 1630) by Puritans who disapproved of his business practices [he sold guns and rum to Native Americans] and frolicsome ways."*

scotch. Others rode on bicycles or painted wagons. Some played hide-and-seek, others tag.

As soon as they'd set foot in that land, Pinocchio, Lampwick, and all the other boys who'd traveled with them began to explore. They wandered everywhere, and they looked into every nook and corner. They became everybody's friend. They couldn't have been happier.

"Oh, what a beautiful life this is!" said Pinocchio when, by chance, he met his friend Lampwick.

"Was I right or wrong?" answered Lampwick. "And to think that you didn't want to come! To think that even yesterday you were ready to return home to see your mother and to start studying again! If today you're free from pencils and books, you owe it all to me. Do you admit it? Only real friends would show such kindness."

"It's true, Lampwick, it's true. If today I'm a really happy boy, it's all because of you. And to think that our teacher, when speaking to me of you, used to say, 'Don't associate with that **crass**[2], loud **boor**[3]! His **unseemly**[1] behavior will only lead you into trouble.'"

---

[1] **congregate (congregated)** When people *congregate*, they gather together into a group or crowd; they assemble. *According to the* Columbia Encyclopedia, *ancient Greek philosopher Socrates "is described as having [ignored] his own affairs, instead spending his time discussing virtue, justice, and [devotion] wherever his fellow citizens congregated."*

[2] **crass** People described as *crass* have no sensitivity, refinement, or delicacy; they're crude, oafish, impolite, vulgar, bad-mannered, etc. *Actor Carroll O'Connor (1924–2001) is best known for his portrayal of Archie Bunker, the crass, bad-tempered, highly prejudiced central character of the 1970s TV sitcom* All in the Family.

[3] **boor** A *boor* (rhymes with *lure*) is a person with rude, clumsy manners (he's coarse, inconsiderate) and little refinement (he's uncultured, ignorant); an oaf, clod, jerk. Note: Don't confuse this word with *bore* (which means "a boring person"). *In the 1984 film* Amadeus, *actor Tom Hulce portrays the title character (brilliantly talented 18th-century composer Wolfgang Amadeus Mozart) as a giggling, pleasure-seeking boor.*

"Poor teacher! Of course he, with his **hypercritical**[2] nature and **genteel**[3] manners, would say something like that," answered the other. "I never could act in **accord**[4] with his ar-

---

[1] **unseemly** If something (one's behavior or appearance, for example) is *unseemly*, it's not in keeping with accepted standards of good taste; it's inappropriate, improper, unbefitting, unbecoming, indecent, etc. *During England's Victorian era (when Victoria was queen, from 1837 to 1901), it was considered unseemly for a woman to display her ankles.* Note: The opposite is *seemly* ("in keeping with accepted standards of good taste").

[2] **hypercritical** The prefix *hyper* means "overly" or "excessively." One who is *hypercritical* is overly or excessively critical; he's faultfinding, nitpicking, fussy, perfectionistic, etc. *French composer Paul Dukas (1865–1935), famous for 1897's* The Sorcerer's Apprentice *(featured in the 1940 animated film* Fantasia*), was hypercritical of his own music and either destroyed or failed to complete the few works he wrote after 1912.*

[3] **genteel** If you say that a person is *genteel* (pronounced *jen-TEEL*), you mean that he acts in a manner suitable to polite society; that is, he's well-bred, refined, courteous, mannerly, elegant, stylish, etc. *In 1958 American hostess and author Amy Vanderbilt (1908–1974) said, "[I am] a journalist in the field of etiquette; I try to find out what the most genteel people regularly do."* Similarly, if you say that a thing (one's childhood, a lifestyle, fiction, a tradition, etc.) is *genteel*, you mean that it belongs to or is suited to polite society. *In 1842 future President Abraham Lincoln (who was born in a log cabin in the backwoods of Kentucky and was almost entirely self-educated) married Mary Todd, a Kentuckian of much more genteel origins (she came from a distinguished family and was educated in a finishing school).*

[4] **accord** When two things are in *accord*, they are in agreement or harmony; they go together without conflict. For example, a student dresses in *accord* with the school's dress code, a swimmer breathes in *accord* with the pace of his strokes, a person's spending increases in *accord* with the growth of his income, etc. *When, in 1925, Tennessee teacher John Scopes presented Darwin's theory of evolution to his high school biology class, he was arrested for violating a state law that prohibited the teaching of any theory not in accord with the biblical story of the Creation.*

chaic[1] **rules.** Do you remember that time he suddenly made a rule that anyone who spoke without raising his hand first would have to sit in the corner and wear a dunce cap? Then he made the rule **retroactive**[2] by a day just so he could punish me for having called out the day before!" Pinocchio smiled knowingly, and then Lampwick continued, "He was awfully old-fashioned, too, wasn't he? The fact that he forced us to learn an **obsolete**[3] language like Latin is proof of that. We didn't even **comprehend**[4] what we were reading! Do you remember how we would memorize a string of meaningless

---

[1] **archaic** If you say that something is *archaic,* you mean either that it belongs to or dates from an earlier period (of culture, art, etc.), or that it's no longer in fashion or use (as a language, word, style, etc.); in either case, it's old, obsolete, antiquated, etc. *According to* Compton's Encyclopedia, *"In the 20th century the Bible has often been updated — mainly to eliminate archaic translations and reflect [modern] usage."*

[2] **retroactive** If something that is enacted (a law or pay raise, for example) is *retroactive,* it's effective as of a prior date. For example, if Joe receives a pay raise on February 1st and the raise is retroactive to January 1st, he is entitled to extra money for January (even though that month has passed). *Enacted by Congress in 1980, the Comprehensive Environmental Response, Compensation, and Liability Act (CERCLA) retroactively required polluters to pay for the cleanup of past hazardous waste disposal sites.*

[3] **obsolete** If something (a word, a type of machinery, etc.) is *obsolete,* it's no longer in use, fashion, or practice (usually because of outmoded design, construction, or style); it's out-of-date, behind the times. *In 1972 Pulitzer Prize–winning architecture critic Ada Louise Huxtable, speaking of railroad terminals in the age of jetliners, said, "Nothing was more up-to-date when it was built, or is more obsolete today, than the railroad station."*

[4] **comprehend** To *comprehend* something is to understand the nature or meaning of it; to grasp it; make sense of it. *In 1985, speaking of the Vietnam Veterans Memorial in Washington, D. C., the* New York Times *said, "Ten years after the war, America may not yet comprehend the loss of those 58,000 lives; but it has at least found a noble way to remember them."*

syllables by **rote**[1], just so we could spit them back **sequentially**[2] when called upon in class?" The puppet nodded, then Lampwick went on, "And he was so petty—always **quibbling**[3] about minor points of grammar. He made me want to scream!" Pinocchio slowly shook his head back and forth as if in disbelief. "You know," continued Lampwick, "it's old fuddy-duddies like him that contribute to the popular **stereotype**[4] of schoolteachers as humorless bores. Do you agree? Anyway, I know that he **despised**[5] me, and that's why he al-

---

[1] **rote** To learn something (a set of grammar rules, a foreign language, a chemical formula, etc.) by *rote* is to memorize it through repetition, without thought of its meaning. *According to the* Cambridge Dictionary of Scientists, *"At school [German physicist Hermann von Helmholtz (1821–1894)] found he did badly at memory work and rote learning, but he enjoyed the logic of geometry and was delighted by physics."*

[2] **sequential (sequentially)** A *sequence* is a following of one thing after another (as numbers, syllables, musical notes, playing cards, etc.) in a particular order. If something is *sequential*, it forms a sequence; that is, it's "in order," consecutive, successive, etc. *In the children's game hopscotch, players toss a small object (a flat stone, for example) into the numbered boxes of a diagram marked (usually with white chalk) on the ground and then hop sequentially through or into the spaces to retrieve the object.*

[3] **quibble (quibbling)** To *quibble* is to raise petty objections, argue over trivial details, etc.; to nit-pick, split hairs. *President Abraham Lincoln once said, "Let us discard all this quibbling about this man and the other man, this race and that race; let us unite as one people throughout this land, until we shall once more stand up declaring that all men are created equal."*

[4] **stereotype** A *stereotype* is a commonly held, preconceived, oversimplified, and often incorrect impression of the characteristics that typify a particular group. For example, according to *stereotype*, psychiatrists wear beards and speak with Austrian accents. *The popular stereotype that all Eskimos live in igloos is inaccurate; in reality, most live in shelters made of stone, wood, or sod.*

[5] **despise (despised)** To *despise* someone (or something) is to regard him with extreme dislike, distaste, hostility, aversion, etc.; to hate him. *In 1962, speaking of the British upper class, journalist Quentin Crewe said, "The children despise their parents until the age of 40, when they suddenly become just like them."*

242

ways **minimized**[1] my accomplishments and tried to **belittle**[2] me in front of the others. But that was okay. Really. I never let his tactics **erode**[3] my **morale**[4]. And today I feel no **antago-**

---

[1] **minimize (minimized)** In one sense, to *minimize* something is to make it seem less significant (or important, valuable, etc.) than it really is; to downplay it (as in *minimize one's accomplishments*). *In his 1946 book* Scientists Against Time, *James Phinney Baxter III wrote: "The was no [tendency to neglect] industrial contractors or minimize the immense contribution they could make."* In another sense, to *minimize* something is to reduce it to the smallest amount or degree (as in *minimize unemployment*). *Oceangoing cruise ships have "stabilizers" that minimize pitching and rolling caused by wave action.*

[2] **belittle** To *belittle* someone (or something) is to speak of him as being unimportant or insignificant; to make him seem little. *Author Mark Twain (1835–1910) once said, "Keep away from people who try to belittle your ambitions; small people always do that, but the really great make you feel that you, too, can become great."*

[3] **erode** When a material object *erodes*, it slowly wears away (as from friction or chemical reaction), as in *ocean waves eroded the rocks.* When something non-physical (peace, happiness, democracy, profit, etc.) *erodes*, it slowly falls apart, becomes less significant, or disappears (as if by wearing away). *President John F. Kennedy once said, "Peace is a daily, a weekly, a monthly process, gradually changing opinions, slowly eroding old barriers, quietly building new structures."*

[4] **morale** A person's (or group's) *morale* (pronounced *muh-RALL*) is the state of his spirits or mood; that is, his mental condition as measured or exhibited by his level of happiness, confidence, enthusiasm, etc. One's morale is generally spoken of as being either high or low (as in *the high morale of the victorious, homebound troops* or *the low morale of the office workers about to be laid off*). *Italian fashion designer Elsa Schiaparelli (1896–1973) once said, "Eating gives a spectacular joy to life and contributes immensely to goodwill and happy companionship; it is of great importance to the morale."*

nism[1] toward him whatsoever. Why? Because I have a **magnanimous**[2] nature and I forgive him."

"What a guy!" said Pinocchio, fondly embracing his friend.

Five months passed and the boys continued playing and enjoying themselves from morning till night. Pinocchio **relished**[3] every bit of it—the toys, the games, the candy, and, perhaps most of all, the cheerful **camaraderie**[4]. But there came a morning when he awoke to find a great surprise waiting for him.

---

[1] **antagonism** This word signifies a strong feeling of hostility, ill will, displeasure, or dislike (as between unfriendly or conflicting people, groups, or countries). *In October 1969 Vice President Spiro Agnew, speaking of the national disharmony between college-aged Vietnam War protesters and older Americans, said, "The lessons of [history are erased in a present-day] antagonism known as the 'generation gap.'"* The adjective is *antagonistic* ("hostile, argumentative"). *When, in 1717, German composer Johann Sebastian Bach (1685–1750) asked to be released from his duties as church organist, he did so in a manner so antagonistic that he was imprisoned for a month!*

[2] **magnanimous** If you're *magnanimous* (pronounced with the accent on the second syllable), you're generous in forgiving an insult or injury; you're not petty or spiteful; you're unselfish, high-minded, etc. The noun is *magnanimity* (pronounced with the accent on the third syllable). *In 1846 novelist and anti-slavery campaigner Harriet Beecher Stowe (1811-1896) said, "What makes saintliness, as distinguished from ordinary goodness, is a certain quality of magnanimity and greatness of soul that brings life within the circle of the heroic."*

[3] **relish (relished)** As a verb, to *relish* something is to enjoy it enthusiastically; to take great pleasure in it. *In his biography (1791) of British author and dictionary compiler Samuel Johnson (1709-1784), Scottish lawyer and writer James Boswell (1740-1795) said: "I never knew any man who relished good eating more than he did; when at a table he was totally absorbed in the business of the moment."*

[4] **camaraderie** The feeling of good-fellowship, goodwill, sociability, or mutual trust that exists between friends or companions is known as *camaraderie*. *According to the* Cambridge Dictionary of American Biography, *film director John Ford (1895-1973) "achieved his greatest [fame] for poetic visions of the American West—its rugged heroes, pioneering families, and sense of male camaraderie."*

Chapter 28 "Donkeys"

On awakening, Pinocchio put his hand to his head and there he found that, during the night, his ears had grown at least ten full inches! He went in search of a mirror, but not finding any, he filled a wash bowl with water and looked at himself in it. His ears had become donkey ears!

He began to cry, to scream. But the more he shrieked, the longer and the more hairy his ears grew.

Hearing those loud cries, a squirrel who lived upstairs came into the room. Seeing Pinocchio so grief-stricken, he asked him, "What's the matter?"

"I'm sick, very, very sick—and from such an awful disease! Do you know how to check for fever?"

"I think so."

"Feel my forehead, then, and tell me if my temperature is **elevated¹**."

The squirrel placed his paw on Pinocchio's forehead and, after a few seconds, looked at him compassionately and said, "My friend, I'm sorry, but I must give you some very bad news."

"What is it?"

"You have donkey fever."

"I never heard of it," said the puppet, who still hadn't quite **assimilated¹** the **ramifications²** of what was happening.

---

¹ **elevate (elevated)** As a verb, to *elevate* something is to raise it to a higher position, level, or rank (from a lower one). *In 1906 President Theodore Roosevelt elevated Spanish-American War hero John Pershing in rank from captain to general.* As an adjective, anything *elevated* is either raised, especially above the ground (as in *elevated railroad*), or increased to a higher than normal amount or degree (as in *elevated temperature*). *Excessive drinking of coffee can cause heart palpitations, insomnia, and elevated blood pressure.*

"Then I'll tell you about it," said the squirrel. "It's an illness that's **prevalent**[3] among lazy boys, especially lazy boys who live in Playland. It **manifests**[4] itself in a very strange way. It

---

[1] **assimilate (assimilated)** To *assimilate* something is to absorb it, take it in. For example, to *assimilate* knowledge is to absorb it into your mind; digest it, grasp it, understand it. To *assimilate* nutrients is to absorb them into your body after digestion. To *assimilate* immigrants is to incorporate or absorb them into society. According to the Columbia Encyclopedia, "*[Charles Darwin's] position as official naturalist aboard the H.M.S.* Beagle *during its world voyage (1831–1836) started [him] on a career of accumulating and assimilating data that resulted in the formulation of his concept of evolution.*"

[2] **ramification (ramifications)** A *ramification* is a (sometimes problematic or complicated) consequence of a particular decision, action, discovery, plan, statement, condition, situation, etc. *In February 1997, after British scientists successfully cloned a sheep, President Bill Clinton asked a bio-ethics advisory committee to look into the ramifications of cloning.*

[3] **prevalent** If you say that something (a belief, a disease, a type of plant, a style, a method of doing something, etc.) is *prevalent*, you mean that it's generally or widely occurring, existing, accepted, or practiced; it's widespread, usual, common, etc. *Magnolia trees are prevalent in Mississippi; in fact, the state nickname is the Magnolia State, the state tree is the magnolia tree, and the state flower is the magnolia blossom.*

[4] **manifest (manifests)** If something *manifests* itself in a particular way, it plainly shows, exhibits, reveals, or gives evidence of itself in that way. *Starvation manifests itself first by weight loss; if unrelieved, it may progress to infections and eventually death.* If one thing *manifests* another, it plainly shows or exhibits it. *About three percent of all children manifest symptoms of attention deficit disorder, with boys outnumbering girls.* Note: As an adjective, the word means "readily seen; obvious, plain, apparent." *While some hereditary defects can be immediately observed, others become manifest later in life.*

changes you into a donkey. Right now you're in **limbo**[1]; you're a **hybrid**[2] creature—part boy and part donkey. But within a few hours the change will be complete and you'll be all donkey, just like the ones that pull the carts."

"Oh, what have I done? What have I done?" screamed Pinocchio, grasping his two long ears in his hands and pulling and tugging at them angrily, as if they belonged to someone else.

"My boy," said the squirrel, to **bolster**[3] the puppet's spirits, "you shouldn't **fret**[4] about it. What's done can't be undone,

---

[1] **limbo** To be in *limbo* (or in a state of *limbo*) is either to be in an intermediate place or state (as between two extremes, outcomes, conditions, etc.), or to be in a state of uncertainly or inactivity, pending some future event. *According to the* World Almanac and Book of Facts, *the question of whether dinosaurs were warm-blooded "has not been resolved; nonetheless, and even with this issue in limbo, we can be confident that dinosaurs were fully efficient creatures."* The word also can signify an imaginary place of nothingness for forgotten, useless, or out-of-date people or things. *In 1954 humorist Fred Allen (1894–1956) said, "When a radio comedian's program is finally finished, it slinks down Memory Lane into the limbo of yesteryear's happy hours."*

[2] **hybrid** In biology, a *hybrid* is a plant or animal that is the offspring of genetically different parents or stock. For example, a mule is a *hybrid* of a donkey and a horse. In general usage, the word signifies anything that is composed of unlike elements or parts; a mixture, a cross. For example, early rock 'n' roll is a *hybrid* of rhythm & blues and country & western. *In 1985, Everette Dennis, Executive Director of Columbia University's Gannet Center for Media Studies, said, "Broadcasters are storytellers, [and] newspapers are fact-gatherers and organizers of information; news magazines are kind of a hybrid of both.*

[3] **bolster** To *bolster* something (a theory, the economy, one's confidence, etc.) is to prop it up, aid it, support it, strengthen it, uphold it, etc. *Twentieth-century British novelist Margaret Drabble once wrote of "inseparable friends who bolstered each other by their mutual devotion."*

[4] **fret** To *fret* about something is to worry about it or be troubled by it; to anguish over it. *When stricken with a rare disease in his mid 40s, golf great Bobby Jones (1902–1971) said, "It's not going to get better; it's going to get worse all the time. But don't fret; remember, we 'play the ball where it lies.'"*

you know." Then he added, "Besides, as far as donkey ears go, they *are* rather nice ones."

Ignoring the squirrel's **diplomatic**[1] remark, the puppet shrieked, "But how could I have caught this awful disease?" Then more quietly he asked, "Do you think it's from eating food **contaminated**[2] with **toxic**[3] substances?"

"No, that's not what causes it."

"Then did I catch some rare, **exotic**[4] infection? Should I be **quarantined**[5]?"

---

[1] **diplomatic** If you're *diplomatic*, you're skilled in handling people, especially in avoiding ill will, hurt feelings, etc.; you're tactful. *In 1960 Australian actor and director Cyril Ritchard (1898–1977), describing matinee audiences, said, "Two thousand dear ladies, all very careful and diplomatic with one another; they're busier watching each other than the show."*

[2] **contaminate (contaminated)** To *contaminate* something is to make it impure or unsafe (as by mixing into it something unclean or harmful), as in *contaminate a reservoir with industrial waste. In July 1963 President John F. Kennedy said, "Continued unrestricted testing [of nuclear weapons] will increasingly contaminate the air that all of us must breathe."*

[3] **toxic** If something (a virus, an insecticide, radiation, snake venom, etc.) is *toxic*, it's capable of causing injury or death (especially by chemical means); it's poisonous. *Laboratory research has shown that cigarette smoke contains about 4,000 chemicals, some of which are highly toxic.*

[4] **exotic** If something (a plant, animal, disease, fashion, language, etc.) is *exotic*, it's interestingly strange or strikingly unusual (often because it comes from or originated in a faraway country). *Since it first opened in 1899, the Bronx Zoo has exhibited many exotic animals, including the platypus, the vampire bat, and the Komodo dragon.*

[5] **quarantine (quarantined)** To *quarantine* someone is to isolate him (keep him away from others), usually to prevent the spread of a contagious disease. *Zoos routinely quarantine newly arrived animals until it can be determined that they don't carry any infectious diseases.* As a noun, the word signifies the condition of such isolation. *Doctors recommend that children with chicken pox be placed in quarantine for seven days after the appearance of the rash.*

"That's not it," answered the squirrel. "And the disease doesn't spread through contact, so you don't have to isolate yourself."

"Then what causes it?"

"You see, all boys who are lazy or who **fritter**[1] away their time playing with toys and playing games sooner or later turn into donkeys."

"Are you sure?" asked the puppet, sobbing bitterly.

"I'm sorry to say that I am. And tears of **remorse**[2] are useless now. You should have thought of all this before."

"But it's not my fault. Believe me, it's Lampwick's fault — Lampwick and his **asinine**[3] ideas!" explained the puppet, in an attempt to **deflect**[4] the blame.

"Who is this Lampwick?"

---

[1] **fritter** To *fritter* away something (time, money, etc.) is to waste it little by little. *British novelist Julian Barnes (born 1946) once wrote of one of his characters: "She had watched her mother's intelligence being frittered away on calculations about the price of tinned food."*

[2] **remorse** A feeling of (often deep or painful) regret (or sorrow, grief, etc.) for a wrongdoing is known as *remorse*. *In June 1995 the Japanese government passed a resolution expressing remorse for the pain Japan caused during World War II.*

[3] **asinine** To describe something (one's behavior, for example) as *asinine* (pronounced *ASS-uh-nine*) is to say that it's silly, foolish, stupid, etc. *According to a February 1990 report from the Associated Press, "a third-grade pupil who took an unopened can of [Billy Beer, a brand of beer named for former President Jimmy Carter's brother] to show-and-tell at school was suspended for three days, an action that the girl's mother said was 'asinine.'"* Note: The word is derived from the Latin word *asin*, which means *donkey*. As such, the word also means "of or like a donkey (in behavior, appearance, etc.); donkey-like," as in *asinine ears*.

[4] **deflect** To *deflect* something (a bullet, public attention, etc.) is to turn it aside or away, or to cause it to be turned aside or away. *The first connection between magnetism and electricity was made in 1819, when Danish physicist Hans Christian Oersted (1777–1851) discovered that a magnetic needle could be deflected by a wire carrying an electric current.*

"A classmate of mine. I wanted to return home. I wanted to be good. I wanted to be a **conscientious**[1] student and to succeed in school, but Lampwick said to me" — and here Pinocchio **modulated**[2] his tone to mockingly **mimic**[3] Lampwick's voice — "'Why do you want to waste your time studying? Why do you want to go to school? Come with me to Playland. There we'll never study again. There we can enjoy ourselves and be happy from morning till night.'"

But the squirrel didn't laugh at the puppet's **parody**[4]. Instead, he asked, "Why did you follow his advice?"

---

[1] **conscientious** If you're *conscientious* (pronounced *con-shee-EN-shus*), you're controlled or guided by your conscience; that is, you're principled (just, honest, upright) or hardworking (careful, thorough, painstaking). *In 1913 British doctor and psychologist Havelock Ellis (1859–1939) said, "It is curious how there seems to be an instinctive disgust in man for his nearest ancestors and relations [apes]; if only [Charles] Darwin could conscientiously have traced man back to the elephant or the lion or the antelope, how much ridicule and prejudice would have been spared to the [theory] of evolution."*

[2] **modulate (modulated)** To *modulate* something is to change it, vary it, adjust it, etc. (by a certain amount or to a certain degree). For example, to *modulate* one's voice is to change its pitch, intensity, or tone. The noun is *modulation*. *In his autobiography, American statesman Benjamin Franklin (1706–1790), speaking of a traveling preacher who arrived in Philadelphia in 1739, said: "Every accent, every emphasis, every modulation of voice, was so perfectly well turned and well placed, that, without being interested in the subject, one could not help being pleased with the [sermon]."*

[3] **mimic** To *mimic* someone is to (sometimes playfully, amusingly, or mockingly) imitate him; that is, to copy his speech, mannerisms, expression, actions, etc. *Parrots can mimic human speech, but they cannot use it to communicate.*

[4] **parody** A *parody* is a humorous or satirical imitation of something (a work of art, an event, a person, etc.). *Many of Mel Brooks' films are parodies; for example,* Young Frankenstein *(1974) is a parody of the horror classic* Frankenstein *(1931), and* Spaceballs *(1987) is a parody of the space epic* Star Wars *(1977).*

"He has a **flair**[1] for the art of persuasion. And I'm not **immune**[2] to temptation. I really did have **misgivings**[3] about the whole affair, but I became so **entranced**[4] by images of endless fun and games that I couldn't think straight! Oh! If I'd only

---

[1] **flair** To have a *flair* for something is to have a natural talent or ability in it (as in *Jackie Kennedy's flair for style, Winston Churchill's flair for colorful speech,* or *Leonard Bernstein's flair for teaching young people*). *In July 1986 British Prime Minister Margaret Thatcher said, "What is success? I think it is a mixture of having a flair for the thing that you are doing; knowing that it is not enough, that you have got to have hard work and a certain sense of purpose."*

[2] **immune** To be *immune* to a particular disease is to have resistance to it; to be unable to catch it. *Children who have had chicken pox are immune to future infection by the virus that causes it.* To be *immune* to a particular influence is to be unaffected by it or unresponsive to it. *According to the* World Almanac and Book of Facts, *"The [1996] senate elections appeared immune to any national trends."* To be *immune* from a particular obligation imposed on others is to be exempt from it. *In 1994 a federal judge ruled that Bill Clinton was immune to lawsuits while President, because they would distract him from his official duties (but the decision was later reversed).*

[3] **misgivings** To have *misgivings* about something (a particular action, plan, policy, decision, etc.) is to have doubts about it; to have a feeling of uncertainty, mistrust, suspicion, skepticism, apprehension, anxiety, or angst about it. *Many of the people who support the practice of using healthy animals in medical testing that will benefit humans do so with deep misgivings.*

[4] **entrance (entranced)** To *entrance* (pronounced with the accent on the second syllable) someone is to fill him with delight, wonder, enchantment, fascination, etc.; to seemingly put him in a trance (as in *entranced by the beautiful music*). *In 1841 German philosopher Ludwig Feuerbach (1804–1872) said that in dreams we "see real things in the entrancing splendor of imagination instead of in the simple daylight of reality."* Note: The word can also refer to literally putting someone into a trance (as in *entranced by a magic spell*).

had a bit of sense, a single **iota**[1] of **foresight**[2], I would never have abandoned the good fairy who loved me so much and who has been so kind to me! And by this time I would no longer be a puppet. I would have become a real boy, like all my friends! Oh, if I see that Lampwick I'm going to tell him exactly what I think of him! We used to be more than **compatible**[3], but now I think he's nothing but a dirty, low-down—" But here, thanks to his sense of good manners, Pinocchio **censored**[4] himself.

---

[1] **iota** An *iota* (pronounced *eye-OH-tuh*) of something is a tiny amount of it; a bit, particle, atom, or speck of it. The word is generally used to refer to non-material things (as in *an iota of common sense* or *an iota of decency*) rather than to physical substances. *In 1979 former Yugoslavian Communist political leader Milovan Djilas said, "One cannot be a Communist and preserve an iota of one's personal integrity."* Note: The word is also the name of the ninth letter of the Greek alphabet (the equivalent of the English "i").

[2] **foresight** *Foresight* is the act or power of looking forward and making thoughtful, careful, or practical decisions about the future. *According to Grolier's Encyclopedia, "The old streets [of Salt Lake City, Utah] were built wide enough to permit a horse and wagon to make a full circle; [today], the generous width of the streets allows for efficient traffic flow, making it appear as though the city planners had great foresight."*

[3] **compatible** When two people are *compatible*, they exist together harmoniously or agreeably; they're friendly; they get along. The opposite is *incompatible*. *An April 1985* New York Times *article said: "What counts in making a happy marriage is not so much how compatible you are, but how you deal with incompatibility."* Note: When two things (computer systems, for example) are *compatible*, they're capable of operating together; they don't cause a conflict. *Blood transfusions can be given only between donors and recipients who have compatible blood types.*

[4] **censor (censored)** To *censor* something (speech, a book, a film, etc.) is to inspect it to see whether it contains anything morally, socially, or politically objectionable (such as violence or a vulgarism) and then to delete or change the offensive material. *Anthropologist Margaret Mead (1901–1978) once said, "Thanks to television, for the first time the young are seeing history made before it is censored by their elders."* Note: As a noun, a *censor* is one who performs such a function.

After abruptly ending his little speech, Pinocchio walked to the door of the room. But when he reached it, remembering his donkey ears, he felt ashamed to show them in public and turned back. To give himself some **semblance**[1] of normality, he took a large bag from a shelf, put it on his head, and pulled it all the way down to his nose.

He went to Lampwick's house and knocked on the door.

"Who is it?" called Lampwick from within.

"Pinocchio!"

"Wait a minute."

After a few minutes the door opened. Another surprise awaited Pinocchio! There in the room stood his friend, with a large bag on his head, pulled all the way down to his nose.

At the sight of that bag, Pinocchio felt slightly happier and thought to himself: "My friend must be suffering from the same thing I am! I'll bet he has donkey ears, too."

But pretending he'd seen nothing unusual, he asked with a **benign**[2] smile, "How are you, my dear Lampwick?"

"Fine."

"Is that really true?"

"Why should I lie to you?"

"Then why are you wearing that bag over your ears?"

---

[1] **semblance** A *semblance* of something is an apparent outward appearance of it (as opposed to a true and accurate reflection of it). *In 1509 Dutch scholar Desiderius Erasmus said, "The nearer people approach old age, the closer they return to a semblance of childhood."* Note: The word can also signify the barest appearance, trace, indication, or amount of something. *Indoor plants provide a semblance of nature to urban apartments.*

[2] **benign** If a person is *benign* (pronounced *bee-NINE*), he's kindly, gentle, gracious, etc. (as in *benign ruler*). If a thing (one's expression, a government, a work of art, etc.) is *benign*, it's either kindly, gentle, etc. (as in *benign smile*), or it's mild, bland, inoffensive, etc. *According to* Grolier's Encyclopedia, *rock music styles of the '70s "range from the benign bubble-gum rock of the Osmond Brothers [to] intentionally [offensive] punk rock."* Note: In medicine the word means "of no danger to health or life; not harmful" (as in *benign tumor*).

"The doctor ordered it because one of my knees hurts," Lampwick explained. "And you—why are you wearing a bag down to your nose?"

"The doctor ordered it because I hurt my foot."

"Oh, poor Pinocchio!"

"Oh, poor Lampwick!"

An embarrassingly long silence followed these words, during which the two friends looked at each other in a knowing way.

Finally, changing the subject, the puppet asked, "Tell me, Lampwick, now that the **novelty**[1] of this place has worn off, do you feel that it was a mistake to come here? I mean, do you ever have **nostalgic**[2] feelings for our old neighborhood or **yearn**[3] for your family?"

---

[1] **novelty** When you speak of "the *novelty*" of something, you're speaking about its quality or state of being new or different. *The Flintstones, the first prime-time animated TV series, debuted in 1960 and quickly became a hit; but the show's ratings declined as its novelty wore off.* If you refer to something as "a *novelty*," you're talking about a particular experience, occurrence, procedure, etc., that is new or different (and whose appeal or success may or may not endure). *The 1950s saw such short-lived film industry novelties as 3-D and "Smell-O-Rama."* Note: The word also signifies any small, cheap, massproduced (often decorative, comic, or sentimental) item whose appeal is usually temporary (as in *miniature Empire State Buildings, hand buzzers, and other novelties*).

[2] **nostalgia (nostalgic)** A feeling of sentimental longing for familiar surroundings or for the pleasant aspects of one's past is known as *nostalgia* (pronounced *nuh-STAL-juh*). If a person is *nostalgic*, he tends to experience such longings. If a thing is *nostalgic*, it tends to remind one of (or sometimes glorify) the past. *In its description of a website celebrating 1980s culture, the Internet Directory asks, "Did you ever get nostalgic for the decade of big shoulders, skinny ties, New Wave music, and power lunches?"*

[3] **yearn** To *yearn* for something (something lost or out of reach, for example) is to have a strong, heartfelt desire for it; to long for it. *In 1978 American humorist and author Mark Twain visited Europe; in his book* A Tramp Abroad *(1880) he lists American dishes he'd yearned for while away, including Sierra Nevada brook trout, Mississippi black bass, and Boston baked beans.*

"No, of course not. Why? Do you?"

"Um...I guess not. But now let me ask you something else. Have you ever suffered from an earache?"

"An earache? Never! And you?"

"Never. Except that this morning my ear has been hurting a little."

"What a strange **coincidence**[1]. Mine has been hurting, too."

"Really? Which ear is it?" asked Pinocchio.

"Both of them. And yours?"

"Both of them, too. I wonder if it could be the same sickness."

"I'm afraid it must be."

"Will you do me a favor, Lampwick?"

"Gladly!"

"Will you let me see your ears?"

"Okay. But before I show you mine, I want to see yours."

"No. Show yours first."

"No, yours first, then mine."

"No, yours."

"No, yours."

For a while longer they continued trading these words back and forth, **vying**[2] against each other for an advantage.

---

[1] **coincidence** A *coincidence* (pronounced with the accent on the second syllable) is an accidental or random occurrence of two (or more) separate events that, by virtue of some striking or notable similarity between them (as of time, place, action, etc.), seems to be not accidental or random. *Allman Brothers Band founder and guitarist Duane Allman died (1971) in a motorcycle accident in Macon, Georgia; by a strange coincidence, the band's bassist, Berry Oakley, also died (1972) in a motorcycle accident, just three blocks from the site of Allman's fatal crash.*

[2] **vie (vying)** When two people (or groups, countries, etc.) *vie* with one another, they strive for victory or superiority with each another; they compete; they're rivals. *According to* Compton's Encyclopedia, *after Christopher Columbus's 1492 voyage "the major European states — England, France, Spain, Portugal, and Holland — vied with one another for nearly four centuries to gain economic advantages in oversees territories."*

Finally, seeing that they were at an **impasse**[1], the puppet said, "Let's stop **bickering**[2]; it's babyish. I have an idea. We're stuck in a **stalemate**[3], right? So let's compromise by taking off our bags at the same time? What do you say?"

"All right," answered Lampwick, who seemed glad that the **deadlock**[4] had finally been broken.

"Ready then!" said Pinocchio. He began to count: "One! Two! Three!"

At the word "Three!" the two boys pulled off the bags and threw them high in the air.

When they saw that they were both suffering from the same **ailment**[5], instead of feeling sad and ashamed, they tried to wiggle their long ears.

---

[1] **impasse** Technically an *impasse* is a road or passage with no exit or outlet. But people usually use this word to refer to a situation or conflict in which no further progress can be made. *In November 1995 an impasse between Congress and President Bill Clinton over the federal budget led to a temporary shutdown of government offices.*

[2] **bicker (bickering)** To *bicker* is to engage in bad-tempered, petty argument; to squabble. *In his inaugural address (January 1989), President George H. Bush said, "The Congress and the [President] are capable of working together to produce a budget. The American people await action. They didn't send us here to bicker."*

[3] **stalemate** In the game of chess, a *stalemate*, which counts as a draw, is a position in which a player cannot make a legal move. But speaking generally, a *stalemate* is any situation in which further action is blocked; a standstill, a standoff, a drawn contest, a tie. *The Korean War (1950–1953) ended in a military stalemate and Korea remained divided into communist North Korea and non-communist South Korea.*

[4] **deadlock** A *deadlock* is a situation or condition (as in a dispute or contest) in which no further progress or activity is possible; a standstill, a tie. *The 1800 presidential election ended in a deadlock, with Thomas Jefferson and Aaron Burr each receiving 73 electoral votes (but the House of Representatives broke the tie, electing Jefferson).*

[5] **ailment** An *ailment* is a (sometimes mild) physical disorder or illness; a sickness, disease. *Acupuncture (a technique of traditional Chinese medicine in which needles are inserted into the skin) has long been used in China for the treatment of such ailments as arthritis, high blood pressure, and ulcers.*

Then they began to laugh at each other. They laughed and laughed until they nearly burst.

But all of a sudden the **hilarity**[1] ended. Lampwick, pale as a ghost, turned to Pinocchio and shouted, "Help, help, Pinocchio!"

"What's the matter?"

"Oh, help me! I can't stand up straight."

"I can't either!" answered Pinocchio, who began to stumble about helplessly.

They had hardly finished speaking when both of them fell on all fours and began running and jumping around the room.

But that was only a **prelude**[2] to the horrors to come. As they ran, their hands and feet turned into hoofs, their faces lengthened, and their backs became covered with long gray hairs. The most horrible moment of all was when the two miserable boys felt their tails appear. Overcome with shame and grief, they began to cry. But instead of moans and wails, they brayed like donkeys: "Haw! Haw! Haw!"

Meanwhile, a loud knock sounded at the door and a voice called, "Open the door! It's the driver of the wagon that brought you here. Open, I say, or it'll be the worse for you!"

---

[1] **hilarity** *Hilarity* is a state of great (sometimes noisy) merriment or amusement. The adjective *hilarious* means "extremely funny." *Actor Don Knotts won five Emmy Awards for his hilarious portrayal of Deputy Barney Fife on the 1960s TV sitcom* The Andy Griffith Show.

[2] **prelude** A *prelude* is a preliminary event (or action, performance, condition, etc.) that precedes and introduces one that is larger and more important; an introduction, an opening. *American historian and writer William Wells Brown (1814–1888) once said, "Our nation is losing its character [and] the loss of a firm national character is the inevitable prelude to her destruction."* Note: In music, a *prelude* is a piece (such as an overture to an opera or the opening section of a suite) that serves as an introduction to a larger composition.

Chapter 29 "The Circus"

When the boys didn't open the door, the little man gave it a violent kick and it flew open. "Fine work, boys!" he said. "You've brayed so well that I recognized your voices immediately, and here I am."

On hearing this, the two donkeys bowed their heads in shame, dropped their ears, and put their tails between their legs.

At first, the little man petted them and smoothed their hairy coats. Then he took out a comb and groomed them. Satisfied with the looks of the two little animals, he bridled them and took them to a marketplace, far away from Playland, in the hope of selling them for a good price.

In fact, he didn't have to wait very long for an offer. Lampwick was bought by a farmer whose donkey had died the day before, and Pinocchio went to a circus owner, who wanted to teach him to perform tricks.

When Pinocchio was led into the circus's stable, his new master, who was tall and had dark hair, filled his feeding bowl with straw. But after tasting one mouthful, Pinocchio spit it out.

Then the man filled another bowl with hay. But Pinocchio didn't like that much better.

"Ah, you don't like hay either?" the man cried angrily. "Wait, I'll teach you not to be so fussy."

He took a whip and gave the donkey a violent blow across the legs.

Pinocchio, **writhing**[1] in pain, brayed, "Haw! Haw! Haw! I can't stand the taste of straw!"

---

[1] **writhe (writhing)** To *writhe* (pronounced with a silent *w*) is to squirm or twist the body (as from pain, violent effort, embarrassment, etc.). *British author William Golding (1911–1993), famous for his 1954 novel* The Lord of the Flies, *once wrote of one of his characters: "He moaned and writhed his body as if the grief were a physical pain."*

"If you find the straw so **revolting**[1]," answered his master, who understood the donkey perfectly, "then eat the hay!"

"Haw! Haw! Haw! Hay gives me a stomachache!"

"Are you telling me that I should feed you meat? Or maybe you have a **yen**[2] for apple pie. Is that it? Maybe you'd also like to tell me how I should prepare your food. Let's see, do you prefer Spanish **cuisine**[3] or French?" Then, angrier than ever, he gave poor Pinocchio another lashing.

After that second beating, the man ordered Pinocchio to keep quiet, and the donkey, lowering his head, **passively**[4] obeyed. The door of the stable was closed and he was left alone. But since it had been many hours since he'd eaten, he started to ache from hunger.

He tasted the hay again. He chewed it well, closed his eyes, and swallowed it. "This hay isn't too bad," he said to himself.

---

[1] **revolting** If something is *revolting*, it causes feelings of disgust or great dislike; it's sickening, awful, offensive, etc. *In 1963, when asked what frightened him, Alfred Hitchcock (the director of the horror classic* Psycho) *said, "I'm frightened of eggs. Have you ever seen anything more revolting than an egg yolk breaking and spilling its yellow liquid?"*

[2] **yen** To have a *yen* for something (a particular food, for example) is to have a craving or desire for it. *In 1994 Pulitzer Prize–winning journalist Anna Quindlen, speaking of doctor-patient relationships, said, "[Patients have] a yen to be treated like a whole person, not just an eye, an ear, a nose, or a throat."*

[3] **cuisine** A manner of cooking (or the art of cookery), especially as characteristic of a particular country or style, is known as *cuisine* (pronounced *kwih-ZEEN*), as in *Mexican cuisine* or *Creole cuisine. American cooking teacher and writer Julia Child stimulated American interest in French cuisine with her popular cooking show* The French Chef *(1962–1976).*

[4] **passive (passively)** People who are *passive* accept or submit to things without objection or resistance; they don't react visibly to situations that might be expected to produce an emotional reaction; they're submissive, unemotional, etc. *In 1986, after Americans were killed by Libyan terrorists in Germany, President Ronald Reagan said, "[Muammar Qaddafi] counted on America to be passive; he counted wrong."*

"But how much happier I'd be if I'd studied! Now, instead of eating hay, I'd be eating a good meal."

Next morning when he awoke, Pinocchio was hungry again. The bowl of straw still sat on the floor beside him, but the thought of it filled him with **revulsion**[1]. He looked for more hay, but it was all gone. He'd eaten it all during the night. He wished that the circus owner would come into the stable to **replenish**[2] his bowl.

"Do you think" shouted his master just then, as he actually did come into the stable, "that I've brought you here only to feed you? Oh, no! You're going to help me make some money, do you hear? Come along, now. I'm going to teach you to play dead, to dance, and to jump through a hoop."

Poor Pinocchio, whether he liked it or not, was forced to learn all these things. After three long months of **rigorous**[3] training — and many, many lashings — he was finally ready for his first performance.

---

[1] **revulsion** A feeling of violent disgust or utter hatred (for someone or something) is known as *revulsion*. *One of Spanish painter Pablo Picasso's most famous paintings,* Guernica *(1937), expresses his revulsion at the German bombing of a northern Spanish town (Guernica) during the Spanish Civil War (1936–1939).*

[2] **replenish** To *replenish* something (a supply, a glass or bowl, etc.) is to make it full or complete again; to refill it. *Vitamin C cannot be stored and must be consumed daily to replenish the body's supply.*

[3] **rigorous** As a noun, *rigor* is the quality of being harsh, severe, rough, etc. (as living conditions, the weather, etc.), or exact, precise, demanding, etc. (as the application or enforcement of a law, mathematics, etc.). Anything described as *rigorous* is characterized by rigor; that is, it's either harsh, rough, tough, etc. (as in *the rigorous conditions of off-road biking*) or strict, exact, precise, etc. (as in *the rigorous logical foundations of geometry*). *President Herbert Hoover was born (1874) into a Quaker family; although his religious training was quite rigorous, he retained few outward signs of his Quaker upbringing aside from his style of dress.*

Large posters in **sensuous**[1] colors were placed all around the town. On them were printed the words "Tonight! First Appearance of the Famous Little Donkey Pinocchio, Star of the Dance!" Below these words was **depicted**[2], in realistic detail, a smiling donkey in a dance costume.

That night the circus tent was full one hour before the show was scheduled to start. The seats around the ring were packed with boys and girls of all ages, impatient to see the famous little dancing donkey.

When the first part of the show was over, the circus owner, doubling as ringmaster, presented himself to the audience and said in a loud, clear voice, "Ladies and gentlemen, boys and girls, I now introduce to you a very special donkey. His **dynamic**[3] dancing—which has been described by some ex-

---

[1] **sensuous** If something (a work of art, for example) is *sensuous*, it appeals to or gratifies the senses (sight, hearing, taste, etc.); that is, it's lush, passionate, exciting, pleasure-giving, etc. (as in *the sensuous richness of Venice's architecture* or *the sensuous imagery of Edgar Allan Poe's poetry*). *In 1985 Czech-born American tennis star Martina Navratilova said, "Being blunt with your feelings is very American; in this big country I can be as brash as New York, as sensuous as San Francisco, as brainy as Boston, [and] as proper as Philadelphia."*

[2] **depict (depicted)** To *depict* something is to represent or reproduce it in a picture or sculpture (by drawing, painting, or sculpting it), or in words (by describing it). *The painting popularly titled* Whistler's Mother *(1872), which depicts American artist James Whistler's (1834–1903) mother in profile, dressed in black, and seated on a straight chair, is actually entitled* Arrangement in Grey and Black Number 1.

[3] **dynamic** If someone or something is dynamic, it's full of energy, spirit, or forcefulness; it's lively, active, intense, in motion, changing, etc. *Singer Tina Turner's dynamic performances helped win her numerous Grammy Awards and an induction into the Rock and Roll Hall of Fame (1991).*

perts as a cross between a slow mambo and a **vivacious**[1] Irish jig, and by others as **reminiscent**[2] of primitive dance in its freedom of expression—has received worldwide critical **acclaim**[3]! His creation of an **idiom**[4] that owes nothing to classi-

---

[1] **vivacious** Anything or anyone described as *vivacious* is lively, high-spirited, perky, active, animated, etc. (as in *a vivacious cheerleader* or *a vivacious hostess*). *In 1992 journalist P. J. O'Rourke, speaking of the popularity of the Kennedy family (John F. Kennedy, Robert F. Kennedy, etc.) with 1960s American voters, said, "We took [them] to our heart [and] it is my opinion that we did it not because we respected them, but because they were pretty; we were smitten by this handsome, vivacious family."*

[2] **reminiscent** If you say that one thing is *reminiscent* (pronounced *rem-ih-NISS-int*) of another, you mean that the one brings to mind memories or thoughts of the other; the one reminds you of the other. *In 1964 President Lyndon Johnson urged a War on Poverty reminiscent of President Franklin D. Roosevelt's New Deal (1930s).* Note: The verb *reminisce* (pronounced *rem-ih-NISS*) means "recall or talk about (often with fondness) past experiences or events" (as in *at the family reunion the three brothers reminisced about their childhood*).

[3] **acclaim** *Acclaim* is an expression of enthusiastic praise, admiration, or approval. *Actor Tom Cruise won critical acclaim (including a Golden Globe Award and an Oscar nomination) for his role in the 1989 film* Born on the Fourth of July.

[4] **idiom** An *idiom* is the distinct style of artistic expression (as in music, art, writing, etc.) of a particular period, country, school, artist, etc. (as in *music videos in the rock idiom*). *According to the* Encarta Encyclopedia, *early 18th-century composer Johann Sebastian Bach understood and used every resource of musical language that was then available, combining such [distinct] idioms as rhythmic French dances, graceful Italian melodies, and intricate German counterpoint all in one composition."* Note: In another sense, an *idiom* is any common phrase or expression whose meaning is not literal but is nevertheless understood, such as "under the weather" or "strike a bargain."

cal traditional and everything to an original, **idiosyncratic**[1] approach to personal style has guaranteed him a significant place in the **annals**[2] of **contemporary**[3] **choreography**[4]! Now

---

[1] **idiosyncrasy (idiosyncratic)** An *idiosyncrasy* (pronounced *id-ee-oh-SIN-kruh-see*) is a characteristic, trait, or mannerism (such as a habit or quirk) peculiar to an individual person. The adjective *idiosyncratic* (pronounced *id-ee-oh-sin-KRAT-ik*) is used to describe anything peculiar or unique to an individual. For example, if you describe someone's style of painting as *idiosyncratic*, you mean that the style belongs to him alone; it's unlike that of any other person, group, school, etc.; it's personal, individualistic, etc. *In 1990 Indian-born British author Salman Rushdie said, "The liveliness of literature lies in its exceptionality, in being the individual, idiosyncratic vision of one human being, in which, to our delight and great surprise, we may find our own vision reflected."*

[2] **annals** If you speak of the *annals* of something, you're talking about the historical records of it, either as actual written or published (often yearly) documents (as in *the annals of the Association of American Geographers*) or in general terms (as in *the annals of the poor*). *According to* Compton's Encyclopedia, *"Perhaps the most stirring accounts of human resourcefulness and courage under fire are to be found in the annals of naval warfare."*

[3] **contemporary** If you say that something is *contemporary*, you mean that it's of the present time; it's current, modern, etc. (as in *the contemporary novel*). *In 1961 violinist Jascha Heifitz (1901–1987) said, "I occasionally play works by contemporary composers for two reasons: first to discourage the composer from writing any more and secondly to remind myself how much I appreciate Beethoven."* If you say that two (or more) people are *contemporary* with each other, you mean that they exist (or existed) at the same time; or, to use the noun, people of the same time period are known as *contemporaries*. *Abraham Lincoln, Edgar Allan Poe, and Charles Darwin were contemporaries; in fact, all were born the same year (1809).*

[4] **choreography** *Choreography* (pronounced *ko-ree-OG-ruh-fee*) is either the art of dancing or the art of arranging (or composing, planning, etc.) dance patterns, steps, movements, etc., for performance. *According to* Grolier's Encyclopedia, *"Jerome Robbins' choreography [for the 1961 film* West Side Story*] is an explosive blend of ballet, acrobatics, and jazz."*

witness for yourselves the **epoch**[1]-making routines of the donkey whose **phenomenal**[2] footwork **eclipses**[3] that of all

---

[1] **epoch** Technically, an *epoch* (pronounced *EP-ik*) is a particular division of geological time. *Peking man (an early species of human beings) is known from fossil remains of the Pleistocene Epoch.* But people generally use this word to signify any period of time marked by distinctive or significant events, features, etc. *World War I's Battle of Jutland, the last great sea battle in which the opponents (Britain and Germany) fought it out (off the coast of Denmark) within sight of each other, marked the end of an epoch in naval warfare.* If you say that something (an event, discovery, invention, etc.) is *epoch-making*, you mean that it's so significant or different that it ushers in (or seems to usher in) a new epoch. *Inventor Thomas Edison (1847–1931) astonished the world with a series of epoch-making inventions (including the electric light, record player, and motion picture).*

[2] **phenomenon (phenomenal)** In science, a *phenomenon* (pronounced *fih-NOM-ih-non*) is an observable event, occurrence, or circumstance, especially one considered extraordinary or remarkable (such as lightning, photosynthesis, magnetism, spontaneous combustion, etc.). But people also use this word to signify anything or anyone considered remarkable or extraordinary (as in *Elvis Presley was a phenomenon*). The adjective *phenomenal* is used to describe anyone or anything considered sensational, spectacular, astonishing, extraordinary, etc. (as in *the phenomenal success of Tiger Woods*). *Pop singer Michael Jackson achieved phenomenal popularity with his album* Thriller *(1982).*

[3] **eclipse (eclipses)** In astronomy, an *eclipse* is a blocking of light between one body and another. And, to use the verb, to *eclipse* something is to cast a shadow upon it (by blocking light directed toward it), as in *the earth eclipses the moon.* But in general usage, if you say that one person or thing *eclipses* another (in a competition or rivalry, for example), you mean that one dims the other by comparison (in performance, reputation, importance, etc.); it surpasses it, outshines it, etc. *According to* Grolier's Encyclopedia, *"Babe Ruth (1895–1948) remains perhaps the most famous baseball player in history despite the fact that most of his batting records have been eclipsed."*

rivals, the donkey who has come to symbolize the very **essence**[1] of modern dance—the one and only Pinocchio!"
This **eloquent**[2] introduction was greeted by **vigorous**[3] applause. And the applause grew to a deafening roar when Pinocchio, the famous donkey, appeared in the circus ring. He was magnificently dressed. He wore a **glossy**[4] new leather bridle with brass buckles. White roses were tied to his ears

---

[1] **essence** The *essence* of something is that part or aspect of it that makes it what it truly is; in other words, it's its most crucial element, most important ingredient, real nature, true substance, central part, etc. *In his inaugural address (March 1925), President Calvin Coolidge said, "The essence of [democracy] is representative government."* Note: The phrase "in essence" means "essentially; fundamentally; basically" (as in *Chinese cooking is, in essence, quick cookery*). Also note: The phrase "of the essence" means "of utmost importance" (as in *in an emergency time is of the essence*).

[2] **eloquent** Verbal expression (speech or writing) described as *eloquent* makes good and appropriate use of language, is appealing to reason or emotion, is fluent, persuasive, forceful, etc. *Cleric and civil rights leader Martin Luther King, Jr., delivered his eloquent "I Have a Dream" speech at the 1963 March on Washington.* A person described as *eloquent* is capable of such verbal expression; he's well-spoken, persuasive. *Perhaps the three most eloquent American Presidents were Abraham Lincoln, Franklin D. Roosevelt, and John F. Kennedy.*

[3] **vigorous** The noun *vigor* means "strength, powerfulness, healthiness, energy, enthusiasm, etc." If a person (a mountain climber, for example) is *vigorous*, he's full of vigor; that is, he's energetic, active, lively, strong, powerful, etc. If a thing is *vigorous*, it involves or requires vigor; that is, it requires strength, activity, enthusiasm, etc. *In 1954 attorney and future Supreme Court justice Thurgood Marshall led a vigorous legal battle against segregation in public schools.*

[4] **glossy** If a material is *glossy*, it has a smooth, shiny surface. For example, high-quality magazines and paperback books have multicolored, *glossy* covers. Note: When the word describes something other than a material, it means deceptively attractive; flashy, showy (as in *glossy production values*). *The narrator of Oliver Goldsmith's novel The Vicar of Wakefield (1766) says, "I chose my wife as she did her wedding gown—not for a fine glossy surface, but [for] such qualities as would wear well."*

and red silk ribbons **adorned**[1] his mane and tail. A pink **tutu**[2] was fastened around his waist. Ballet slippers covered his hoofs. He was a lovely donkey indeed!

The ringmaster, smiling inwardly at the audience's **responsiveness**[3], bowed **flamboyantly**[4] and then turned to Pinocchio and said: "Before starting your performance, salute your audience!"

Pinocchio bent his knees to the ground and remained kneeling until the ringmaster, with the crack of the whip, cried sharply, "Walk!"

Pinocchio lifted himself on his four feet and walked around the ring. A few minutes passed and the ringmaster called, "Trot!" and Pinocchio changed his step.

"Gallop!" and Pinocchio galloped.

---

[1] **adorn (adorned)** To *adorn* something is to beautify or decorate it by adding ornaments, jewels, flowers, pictures, or the like; to dress it up. *Medieval books had wooden covers, sometimes richly adorned with gold and silver work, enamels, and gems.*

[2] **tutu** A *tutu* is a ballerina's skirt; it's usually very short, projects straight out from the hips, and consists of many layers of sheer but stiff material. *When Italian dancer Marie Taglioni (1804–1884) first performed in Paris (1832), she wore a sheer dress with a bell-shaped skirt that inspired the tutu.*

[3] **responsive (responsiveness)** If someone is *responsive*, he reacts readily or favorably to some stimulus or influence (a suggestion, a joke, a new idea, a work of art, etc.); he's receptive, open-minded, agreeable, sympathetic, etc. *During the 1970s, the American Indian Movement (an Indian activist group) staged protests against the U.S. Department of the Interior's Bureau of Indian Affairs and demanded that it become more responsive to the needs of native Americans.*

[4] **flamboyant (flamboyantly)** People described as *flamboyant* tend (often tastelessly) to draw attention to themselves; they're showy, theatrical, unrestrained, exaggerated, etc. *With his piano-pounding and yelping, flamboyant rocker Little Richard (born 1932) helped define early rock-and-roll.* Things described as *flamboyant* are strikingly bold or brilliant; they're colorful, elaborately styled, etc. (as in *flamboyant theatrical makeup*).

"Run!" and Pinocchio ran as fast as he could. As he ran the ringmaster raised his arm and a pistol shot rang in the air. At the shot, the little donkey fell to the ground as if he were really dead. A shower of applause greeted Pinocchio as he rose to his feet. Cries and shouts were heard all around. Pinocchio lifted his head and raised his eyes. There, in front of him, in one of the boxes, sat a beautiful woman. Around her neck she wore a long golden chain at the end of which hung a tiny wooden figure that bore an **uncanny**[1] resemblance to Pinocchio. The letter *P* was **superimposed**[2] on its **torso**[3].

"That's a **replica**[4] of me! That beautiful lady is my fairy!" said Pinocchio to himself, recognizing her. He felt so happy that he tried his best to cry out, "Oh, my fairy! My dear fairy!"

But instead of words, a loud, **discordant**[1] braying was heard in the theater. Then, through some **acoustical**[2] oddity of

---

[1] **uncanny** If you say that something is *uncanny*, you mean that it's peculiarly unsettling, either because it's seemingly inexplicable (as in *Annie Oakley's uncanny accuracy with a rifle*) or because it's strange or unusual (as in *tree stumps with uncanny shapes*). *During his Presidency (1989–1993), George H. Bush was described as an uncanny mixture of John Wayne and Mr. Rogers.*

[2] **superimpose (superimposed)** To *superimpose* something is to place or lay it on or over something else. *To trace a picture, superimpose a transparent sheet and then copy the lines of the original on it.*

[3] **torso** The *torso* is the trunk of the human body; in other words, it's the human body excluding the head, arms, and legs. *Women who dance or exercise often wear a leotard, a snug-fitting, stretchable, one-piece garment that covers the torso.*

[4] **replica** A *replica* of something (a work of art, for example) is an (often small-scale or miniature) reproduction or copy of it. *The Arkansas State Capitol, in Little Rock, is a scaled-down replica of the national Capitol (the dome-shaped building in Washington, D.C., where Congress meets).*

the room, the strange, **dissonant**[3] sound **reverberated**[4] so loudly that all the spectators—men, women, and children, but especially the children—burst out laughing. Pinocchio lowered his head in shame.

"Stop that braying if you know what's good for you!" the ringmaster hissed into the donkey's ear. "What's the matter

---

[1] **discordant** If a sound is *discordant*, it's disagreeable to the ear; it's harsh, jarring, dissonant, etc. *The shower scene in the 1960 horror film* Psycho *is accompanied by a series of high-pitched, discordant violin "screams."* If two (or more) things are *discordant* with each other, they're not in agreement; they're conflicting, differing, inharmonious, at odds, etc. *In his inaugural address (March 1825), President John Quincy Adams said, "Tens years of peace have blended into harmony the most discordant elements of public opinion."*

[2] **acoustics (acoustical)** The branch of physics that deals with sound and sound waves is known as *acoustics*. The adjective *acoustical* (or *acoustic*) is used to describe anything pertaining to sound, the science of sound, or the sense of hearing. *According to the* Columbia Encyclopedia, *"In 1979 a congressional committee [reviewing the November 1963 assassination of President John F. Kennedy] concluded, on the basis of acoustical evidence, that [not one, but] two people had shot at Kennedy—but that interpretation was later criticized as flawed."*

[3] **dissonant** In music, a disagreeable-sounding combination of tones is said to be *dissonant* (and an agreeable-sounding combination is said to be *consonant*). For example, you make a *dissonant* sound when you bang your fist on the piano. *Hungarian composer Béla Bartók (1881–1945) combined Eastern European folk music with dissonant harmony.* But speaking generally, the word describes any harsh or unpleasant sound (whether musical or not). *British poet Samuel Coleridge (1772–1834) once wrote: "No sound is dissonant which tells of life."* Note: The word can also mean "disagreeing, conflicting, incompatible, being at odds, etc." (as in *dissonant colors* or *a lone, dissonant voice*).

[4] **reverberate (reverberated)** When a sound *reverberates*, it echoes or re-echoes (especially repeatedly). *The clatter of breaking dishes reverberated through the house.* The word can also mean "seem to echo or re-echo" or "be much heard" or "have continuing effects." *In 1978 Hungarian-born British novelist Arthur Koestler said, "The most persistent sound which reverberates through man's history is the beating of war drums."*

with you?" Then, in order to teach him that it was **uncouth**[1] to bray loudly in public, the ringmaster smacked him hard on the nose a few times with the handle of his whip. After that a strange smile appeared on the ringmaster's face. But whether it was to win favor with the audience or to unconsciously express a **sadistic**[2] pleasure in watching the donkey suffer was impossible to tell.

To **alleviate**[3] the pain, the poor little donkey stuck out his tongue and licked his nose for a long time. When he finally looked again toward the seats, he saw that the fairy had disappeared!

He felt faint, his eyes filled with tears, and he wept bitterly. But no one could tell, least of all the ringmaster, who, cracking his whip, cried out, "Ladies and gentlemen, boys and girls, because Pinocchio is a classically trained dancer, he of-

---

[1] **uncouth** If a person is *uncouth* he lacks grace or refinement; that is, he's awkward, clumsy, cloddish, etc., or he's uncultured, unsophisticated, unmannerly, etc. *Primitive man covered his mouth when he yawned to prevent his soul from leaving his body; but today we cover our mouths because failure to do so is considered uncouth and rude.*

[2] **sadistic** A *sadist* (pronounced *SAY-dist*) is a person who enjoys being cruel or causing pain. An act or instance of such cruelty is known as *sadism*. The adjective *sadistic* (pronounced *suh-DIS-tik*) is used to describe anyone who acts like a sadist or anything pertaining to sadism (as in *sadistic Nazi prison guards*). *According to the* Dictionary of Cultural Literacy, The Strange Case of Doctor Jekyll and Mr. Hyde *(1886) is "a novel by Robert Louis Stevenson about the good Dr. Jekyll, whose well-intentioned experiments on himself periodically turn him into the cruel and sadistic M. Hyde."*

[3] **alleviate** To *alleviate* (pronounced *uh-LEE-vee-ate*) something (pain, suffering, boredom, overcrowding, poverty, etc.) is to make it less severe or make it easier to endure. *There is no cure for the common cold, and treatment focuses on alleviating symptoms.*

ten **incorporates**[1] steps from the ballet vocabulary into his otherwise **unorthodox**[2] routines. Right now this **monumental**[3] talent, this vision of **virtuosity**[4], will perform — with all

---

[1] **incorporate (incorporates)** When one thing is *incorporated* into another, it is combined into it to form a unified whole; it becomes a part of it; it merges with it. *The Peace Corps (a U.S. government agency that sends American volunteers to developing nations to help improve living standards and provide training) was established in 1961; in 1971 it was incorporated into a larger agency, AC-TION (but ten years later became an independent agency again).*

[2] **unorthodox** If you say that something (an opinion, philosophy, style, manner, method, design, etc.) is *unorthodox*, you mean that it doesn't conform to established or accepted standards, usage, or opinion; it's unconventional, nontraditional, unusual, etc. (as in *folk medicine, faith healing, and other unorthodox forms of therapy*). *In 1963, speaking of creativity, Carnegie Institution president Caryl Haskins said, "It is the gifted, unorthodox individual — in the laboratory, or the study, or the walk by the river at twilight — who has always brought to us all the basic resources by which we live."* Note: The opposite is *orthodox* ("conforming to what is traditional or commonly accepted").

[3] **monumental** If something is *monumental*, either it's of great historical significance (as in *Isaac Newton's monumental contributions to science*) or it's outstandingly great in size, amount, degree, or extent (as in *monumental selfishness* or *a monumental survey*). *Miami experienced one of its most monumental population boosts during the 1960s when about 260,000 Cuban refugees arrived on its shore seeking freedom.*

[4] **virtuosity** A person with masterly skill, ability, or technique in the arts (especially in music) is known as a *virtuoso* (pronounced *vir-chew-OH-soh*). *During his lifetime Johann Sebastian Bach (1685–1750) was better known as an organ virtuoso than as a composer. Virtuosity (pronounced vir-chew-OS-ih-tee)* is the technical skill exhibited by a virtuoso. *According to the* Reader's Companion to American History, *"In August 1935 clarinetist Benny Goodman and his band performed live at the Palomar Ballroom in Los Angeles; the dancers were so moved by the virtuosity of the arrangements and solos that they crowded around the bandstand to listen to a performance (rather than dance to it)."*

the ease and **precision**[1] of a human ballerina—a selection from his vast **repertoire**[2]: an **abridged**[3] **rendition**[4] of the classic ballet *Swan Lake*. He'll begin with a high leap with his front legs extended forward and his hind legs backward. Watch for yourselves how, as he extends his legs in both directions, he at the same time extends the very **parameters**[5] of

---

[1] **precision** The adjective *precise* is used to describe anything (a measurement, an explanation, a description, etc.) that's characterized by attentiveness to detail or accuracy; that is, it describes things that are exact, definite, specific, etc. (as in *an atomic clock is an extremely precise timekeeping device*). The noun *precision* means "the state or quality of being precise; accuracy, exactness, definiteness, distinctness, etc." *Competitive cheerleading squads are judged on such criteria as originality, enthusiasm, acrobatics, and group precision.*

[2] **repertoire** A performer's (singer's, actor's, dancer's, etc.) *repertoire* (pronounced *REP-er-twar*) is the list of works (songs, plays, parts, pieces, etc.) he is prepared to perform (or that he routinely performs). *Country singer Johnny Cash (1932–2003) regularly performed in prisons, and prison songs were an important part of his repertoire.* Note: The word can also signify the entire list of works that exist in a particular artistic field (as in *the Broadway repertoire* or *the cello repertoire*).

[3] **abridge (abridged)** To *abridge* a written text (a novel or play, for example) is to make it shorter (by condensing it or omitting parts of it) while retaining its overall sense. *Modern editions of Johann Wyss's 1813 adventure novel* Swiss Family Robinson *are usually abridged (the narrator's numerous religious comments are omitted).* To *abridge* anything else (a visit, one's freedom, etc.) is to lessen the duration or extent of it. *The First Amendment to the U.S. Constitution states: "Congress shall make no law abridging the freedom of speech."*

[4] **rendition** A *rendition* of something (a dramatic role, a musical composition, etc.) is a performance of it in a particular manner; an interpretation of it. *American singer Kate Smith (1909–1986) was especially known for her moving rendition of Irving Berlin's "God Bless America."*

[5] **parameter (parameters)** The *parameters* (pronounced *puh-RAM-uh-ters*) of something (a field of study, for example) are its boundaries or limits. *According to the* Reader's Companion to American History, *initial performances of (20th-century experimental composer) John Cage's "prepared piano" pieces (which call for metal or wooden objects to be placed on the strings, producing uncharacteristic sounds) were "met with mixed audience reactions; [however], composers were excited by his extension of the traditional parameters of music."*

classical ballet itself! Pinocchio! *Swan Lake!* Leap like a ballerina! Leap!"

The ringmaster sharply **prodded**[1] Pinocchio with the hard handle of his whip, and the donkey jumped a couple of inches off the ground. If he tried to extend his legs while in the air, it wasn't noticeable from the seats.

"And Pinocchio can perform tricks! Pinocchio! Show us how you can jump through the hoop!"

Pinocchio tried twice to jump through a hoop that was held by a female assistant, but each time he came near it, he found it easier to run around it than to jump through it. The third time he started far back to give himself time to gain **momentum**[2]. As he raced toward the hoop, all the boys and girls held their breath expectantly. But the attempt proved **anticlimactic**[3] when at the last second he **veered**[1] to the right and ran around it.

---

[1] **prod (prodded)** Technically, to *prod* a person or animal is to jab or poke it with a pointed object (to cause or force it to move), as in *prod cattle*. But the word is often used to mean "move (a person or group) to action (in a particular situation or circumstance); provoke, urge, motivate, etc." *In 1994 President Bill Clinton prodded Congress to enact an anticrime bill.*

[2] **momentum** *Momentum* is either the motion (or force, speed, etc.) of a moving body (as in *his momentum caused him to fall forward*), or the tendency of an object in motion to stay in motion or gain speed (as in *the truck gained momentum as it rolled downhill*). *Birds fly not only by flapping their wings but by gliding; that is, they hold their wings still and rely on forward momentum to keep themselves in the air.* If you're talking about something non-physical (a course of events, one's career, a story, an idea, etc.), *momentum* is an (often gradual) increase in activity or interest. *The 1963 March on Washington (at which Dr. Martin Luther King, Jr., delivered his famous "I Have a Dream" speech) created the political momentum that resulted in the Civil Rights Act of 1964.*

[3] **anticlimax (anticlimactic)** An *anticlimax* is a weak or disappointing outcome or turn of events where a climax is expected (see *climactic*). *Y2K (the name given at the end of the last century to the possibility that computer operating systems worldwide would malfunction on January 1, 2000, because computers' internal clocks would misread the century change as 1900 instead of 2000) turned out to be so anticlimactic that some people afterwards referred to the non-event as "Yawn2K."*

Immediately after this last **abortive**[2] effort, the ringmaster tightened his grip on the whip and gave Pinocchio a menacing look that seemed to say: "If you **circumvent**[3] the hoop one more time you'll get a lashing you'll never forget!" On his next try, the defeated donkey, with a **dispirited**[4] and re-

---

[1] **veer (veered)** When a moving object (a car, for example) *veers*, it changes direction (especially suddenly); it swerves. *In baseball a "curve ball" is a pitched ball that veers to the left or right.* When something non-physical (a government, a philosophy, a purpose, etc.) *veers*, it changes from one course or position to another. *According to the* Information Please Almanac, *when Fidel Castro took power (1959), "the United States initially welcomed what looked like the prospect for a democratic Cuba, but a rude awakening came within a few months when Castro veered [toward Communism]."*

[2] **abortive** If something (a plan, an attempt, etc.) is *abortive*, it's unsuccessful, failed, ineffectual, useless, etc. (often because progress was halted before it had a chance to succeed). *The Chunnel, a 31-mile-long train tunnel under the English Channel connecting England and France, had two abortive beginnings (1883 and 1974) before its present-day success.*

[3] **circumvent** To *circumvent* (pronounced *sir-kum-VENT*) a physical thing is to go around it (instead of through it); to bypass it. *Canals near Louisville, KY, allow riverboats to circumvent 26-foot waterfalls in the Ohio River.* To *circumvent* a difficulty, a problem, unpleasantness, a law, etc., is to avoid it (often through clever deception); to sidestep it. *Today's ten-pin bowling was devised to circumvent laws against nine-pin bowling (which had been passed because of widespread gambling in the 1800s).*

[4] **dispirited** If someone is *dispirited*, he's in low spirits (as from having lost hope, courage, or enthusiasm); he's sad, depressed, discouraged, disheartened, etc. *During a particularly harsh winter (1777–1778) of the Revolutionary War, General George Washington's soldiers (stationed at Pennsylvania's Valley Forge) became dispirited; in fact, many deserted.*

signed[1] expression on his face, forced himself to leap through it. But as he did so his hind legs got caught. He fell clumsily to the hard floor with a **resounding**[2] thump.

The ringmaster, ignoring the fallen donkey, suddenly announced to the audience, "In his **subsequent**[3] performances, Pinocchio will perform more amazing tricks for your pleasure! So be sure to come back tomorrow night—and bring your friends!"

When he got up, the little donkey was hurt and could hardly limp as far as the stable.

---

[1] **resignation (resigned)** To *resign* yourself to something inevitable or unchangeable is to unresistingly accept it, submit to it, or surrender to it, as in *he resigned himself to the fact that he would eventually die*. The noun *resignation* means "an act of resigning; an unresisting acceptance of, or attitude toward, something inevitable," as in *he accepted the fact that he'd have a long wait in line with resignation*. The adjective *resigned* means "feeling or showing resignation; unresistingly accepting of something inevitable." *Pulitzer Prize–winning author Willa Cather (1873–1947) once said, "I like trees because they seem more resigned to the way they have to live than other things do."*

[2] **resounding** If you describe a sound or noise as *resounding* (pronounced *rih-ZOUND-ing*), you mean that it echoes or rings (especially loudly). *In his "Liberty or Death" speech (1775), American Revolutionary leader Patrick Henry said, "The war [has already] begun! The next [wind] that sweeps from the north will bring to our ears the clash of resounding [gunfire]!"* If you describe anything else as *resounding*, you mean that it seems to echo or ring; that is, it's much mentioned, it causes a stir, it's decisive, it's emphatic, etc. (as in *a resounding success*). *South Africa's first multiracial elections (April 1994) resulted in a resounding victory for the black political leader Nelson Mandela and marked the end of the apartheid era.*

[3] **subsequent** Any event (or circumstance, happening, case, etc.) described as *subsequent* comes after (another) in time, order, or succession; it follows, comes later, etc. (as in *this century and subsequent centuries*). *Actor Tom Hanks won an Academy Awards for his role in* Philadelphia *(1993); his subsequent film,* Forrest Gump *(1994), earned him another.* Note: The word sometimes implies that what follows is a consequence of what went before (as in *the bombing of Hiroshima and Nagasaki and the subsequent surrender of Japan*).

"Pinocchio! We want Pinocchio! We want the little donkey!" cried the children.

But no one saw him again that evening. He spent the night in lonely **seclusion**[1] in the locked stable with nothing to keep him company but his pain.

The next morning the **veterinarian**[2] found a **fissure**[3] in the side of the donkey's hoof.

"What's the **prognosis**[4]?" asked the circus owner.

"It's not good. In fact, this donkey will be crippled for the rest of his life."

"What do I need with a crippled donkey?" said the circus owner to the stable boy. "Take him back to the marketplace

---

[1] **seclusion** This word signifies the state or condition of being alone (apart from others, apart from social contact or activity); solitude, isolation. *England's Queen Victoria spent three years in seclusion after the untimely death (1861) of her husband, Prince Albert.*

[2] **veterinarian** A *veterinarian* is a doctor who treats animals. *British author and veterinarian James Herriot based his best-selling* All Creatures Great and Small *(1972) on his experiences as a rural veterinarian during the years just before and after World War II.*

[3] **fissure** A *fissure* is a (usually long and narrow) opening (in something) made by splitting or a separation of parts; a crack. *Lava (molten rock) erupts not only from volcanoes, but through fissures in the earth's surface.*

[4] **prognosis** In medicine, a *prognosis* is a predicted or expected outcome of a disease, injury, condition, etc. (as in *doctors typically diagnose a disease, suggest a treatment, and offer a prognosis*). *Heat exhaustion can be dangerous, but the prognosis is generally good if treatment is immediate.* Note: The word is often used as a general term for predicting the unfolding or outcome of any course of events (as in *a gloomy prognosis for the company's financial future*).

and sell him. And remember, I've **incurred**[1] a lot of expense feeding and training him, so try to get a good price for him."

The trip to the nearby marketplace took over an hour, for Pinocchio's **affliction**[2] greatly **impeded**[3] his movement. When they arrived, a buyer was soon found. "How much do you want for that crippled donkey?" he asked.

"Five dollars," answered the stable boy.

"I'll give you five cents. Don't think I'm buying him to use for work. I just want his skin. It looks very tough, and I can use it to make a drum for our village band."

After **haggling**[4] over the price for a few seconds, they agreed on ten cents and the donkey changed hands.

His new owner took him to a high, steep cliff overlooking the sea, put a heavy stone around his neck, and tied a rope to

---

[1] **incur (incurred)** To *incur* something (usually something undesirable, such as a loss, an expense, a debt, or another's disfavor) is to become liable or subject to it through your own actions; to bring it on yourself. *British playwright George Bernard Shaw (1856–1950) once sarcastically suggested, "Let [an] Act of Parliament be passed placing all street musicians outside the protection of the law, so that any citizen may [attack] them with stones, sticks, knives, pistols, or bombs without incurring any penalties."*

affliction An *affliction* is anything that causes suffering, harm, misery, distress, etc., especially a physical disorder such as an injury, disease, disability, sickness, or pain. *Helen Keller (1880–1968) was blind and deaf since infancy; despite these afflictions she learned to read and write and was graduated (1904) from Radcliffe College with honors.*

[3] **impede (impeded)** To *impede* something is to slow down or block its movement or progress (by means of obstacles, obstructions, hindrances, etc.). *In the early 1970s President Richard Nixon and his aides tried to impede the investigation of the Watergate case.*

[4] **haggle (haggling)** To *haggle* over something (a price, a deal, etc.) is to argue over it; to bargain, dicker, negotiate, etc. *In April 1958, speaking of unifying the military's ground, sea, and air commands, President Dwight D. Eisenhower said, "It is far more important to be able to hit the target than it is to haggle over who makes a weapon or who pulls a trigger."*

one of his hind legs. Then he pushed him over the **precipice**[1] into the water. Pinocchio sank immediately. His new master sat on the cliff waiting for him to drown, so that he could skin him.

---

[1] **precipice** A *precipice* is high, steep cliff, especially one from which someone might fall. *The northeast side of Ben Nevis, the highest mountain in Great Britain, is a precipice of 1,450 feet.* Note: The word is also used figuratively to refer to any dangerous situation (as in *rescued from the precipice of destruction*).

Chapter 30 "The Shark"

After the little donkey had been underwater for about a half hour, the man on the cliff said to himself: "By this time that donkey must be drowned. I'll pull him up, and then I can begin work on my drum."

He pulled on the rope that he'd tied to Pinocchio's leg. He pulled and pulled and pulled. All at once the **taut**[1] rope **slackened**[2] and he saw gently bobbing on the surface of the water, instead of a dead donkey, a very-much-alive puppet!

Seeing it, the poor man thought he was dreaming and sat there with his mouth wide open and his eyes popping out of his head. Finally gathering his wits, he pulled the rope, with the puppet still tied to it, all the way up.

"What happened to that donkey I threw into the sea?"

"I *am* that donkey," answered the puppet.

---

[1] **taut** If you say that a rope, chord, string, wire, or the like, is *taut*, you mean that it's pulled or drawn tight; it's not loose. *An archer's bow is a flexible piece of wood, fiberglass, or other material, with a tautly bound string or cord running from end to end.* If you say that one's nerves are *taut*, you mean that he's emotionally strained or tense. *British novelist Virginia Woolf (1882–1941) once wrote: "My nerves are as taut as fiddle strings."* If you say that someone's use of something (language or detail, for example) is *taut*, you mean that it's efficient, concise, sparing, etc. (as in *a taut movie script*).

[2] **slacken** When something (a tightly drawn string or an emotionally tense situation, for example) *slackens*, it becomes less tight, tense, or rigid; it loosens, relaxes, etc. *Tuning pegs on a guitar are turned to tighten or slacken the strings so as to adjust their pitch.* When something non-physical (one's interest, one's pace, the economy, etc.) *slackens*, it becomes less active or intense; it slows or dies down. *Whereas the first half of the 16th century saw an intensification of literary activity throughout Europe, the second half was marked by a gradual slackening of activity.* Note: The adjective *slack* means (1) "not tight or tense; loose" (as in *a slack rope*), (2) "economically slow" (as in *a slack summer season*), or (3) "not duly careful or concerned" (as in *a slack worker*).

"You? That's **preposterous**[1]! Are you pulling my leg?"

"Your leg? No, but you pulled me up by my leg."

"No, I was speaking **figuratively**[2]. I meant, are you kidding me?"

"No, I'm serious."

"But how is that possible?"

"Well, do you want to hear my whole story? Untie my leg and I can tell it to you better."

The old fellow, curious to know the puppet's story, immediately untied him.

"You see," said Pinocchio, "I was once a wooden puppet, just as I am today. One day I was about to become a boy—a real boy. But because of my laziness and my hatred of books, and because I listened to bad friends, I ran away from home. One morning, I awoke to find myself changed into a donkey—with long ears, a gray coat, and a tail. I was taken to the marketplace and sold to a circus owner. At the circus, before the entire audience, I suffered the **indignity**[3] not only of being

---

[1] **preposterous** If something is *preposterous*, it's (sometimes laughably) contrary to reason or common sense; it's nonsensical, ridiculous, absurd, etc. *In his* Origin of Species *(1859), British naturalist Charles Darwin (1809–1882) said, "It is preposterous to account for the structure of [a woodpecker or mistletoe] by the effects of [climate alone]."*

[2] **figurative (figuratively)** If an expression is *figurative*, it involves or is based on a *figure of speech;* that is, it uses an expression whose meaning is understood by those familiar with the expression, but whose meaning is not predictable from the actual, literal meanings of the words themselves. For example, if you say that you "put your foot in your mouth," you're using *figurative* language to indicate that you said something embarrassing. *Bill complained, "My wife won't let me out of the doghouse"; then he added, "I speak figuratively, of course."*

[3] **indignity** Humiliating, degrading, or insulting treatment, or the disgrace that comes from such treatment, is know as *indignity. According to Grolier's Encyclopedia, in Alban Berg's opera* Wozzeck *(1925), "the soldier Wozzeck suffers many indignities, including abuse from his captain, being experimented on by a mad doctor, and a beating by a drum major."* Note: In another sense, *indignity* (or *indignation*) is anger aroused by an instance of **unfairness**.

a donkey, but of being made into a **buffoon**[1] — I was forced to wear girlish ribbons, perform dainty ballet steps, and jump through hoops! I was so ashamed. As it turned out, I was a **dismal**[2] failure as a ballerina and I was completely **inept**[3] at jumping through a hoop. Anyway, the **upshot**[4] of the matter was that one night, during a **bungled**[5] performance, I fell while trying to jump through the hoop. My hoof was

---

[1] **buffoon** A *buffoon* is a person who is an object of (often mocking) amusement or laughter; a laughingstock, a fool, the butt of the joke. In a related sense, a *buffoon* is a professional joker; a clown, a jester. *In the mid-19th-century comedy team Abbott and Costello, Bud Abbott played the straight man and Lou Costello the buffoon.*

[2] **dismal** In one sense this word describes anything that causes or expresses gloom, dreariness, depression, etc. *In 1887 journalist Nellie Bly (1867–1922) faked insanity to get inside a mental institution to write an exposé of its dismal conditions.* In another sense the word describes anything characterized by a lack of competence, merit, talent, or skill. *Under the guidance of coach Sid Gillman, football's Houston Oilers rose from a dismal 1-13 record in 1973 to a respectable 7-7 in 1974.*

[3] **inept** If a person is *inept* (at some particular task, assignment, or purpose), he's without competence, ability, or skill (in it); he's blundering, clumsy, awkward, etc. *English critic Alfred Alvarez (born 1929) once told of a "young graduate student, too shy and inept to make conversation."* To describe a thing as *inept* is to say that it displays a lack of judgment (as in *an inept remark*) or a lack of ability (as in *an inept performance*). The noun is *ineptitude*.

[4] **upshot** The *upshot* of something (a disagreement, a course of action, etc.) is its final or eventual outcome, result, or ending. *When a 1928 London exhibition of his paintings was cancelled on grounds of obscenity, British author D. H. Lawrence (1885–1930) explained in a poem: "The upshot was, my paintings must burn [so] that English artists might finally learn."*

[5] **bungle (bungled)** To *bungle* something (a job, task, assignment, etc.) is to perform it unskillfully, inefficiently, or clumsily; to botch it up. *English comic actor Peter Sellers (1925-1980) is probably best known for playing the bungling French detective Inspector Clouseau in* The Pink Panther *(1963) and its sequels.*

maimed[1], and I became crippled. Not knowing what to do with a physically impaired[2] donkey, the circus owner sent me back to the marketplace, and you bought me."

"I know! And I paid ten cents for you. Now, who will give me my money back?"

"But why did you buy me? You bought me to make a drum from my skin! A drum!

"Yes, I did! And now where will I find another skin?"

"Don't worry. There are many other donkeys in the world."

"Is that the end of your story?"

"One more thing," answered the puppet. "After buying me, you brought me here to kill me. But feeling sorry for me, you tied a stone to my neck and threw me to the bottom of the sea. That was very good of you to want me to suffer as little as possible, and I'll always be grateful. And now my fairy will take care of me, even if you—"

"Your fairy? Who is she?"

---

[1] maim (maimed) To *maim* someone is to deprive him of some part of his body (or its use) by causing him severe injury; to cripple, disfigure, disable, or mutilate him. *According to* Grolier's Encyclopedia, *"An estimated 110 million land mines [concealed explosive devises used in war and designed to be detonated by contact] lie buried in some 64 countries; in the 1990s they killed or maimed over 20,000 people each year."* Sometimes the word is used figuratively to mean "make powerless or incomplete (as if by maiming)." *In 1959 journalist John Canaday, speaking of a New York City art museum designed by famed architect Frank Lloyd Wright, said, "The Guggenheim Museum is a war between architecture and painting in which both come out badly maimed."*

[2] impair (impaired) As a verb, to *impair* something is to make it less perfect, less sound, less effective, or less valuable (usually by causing it to suffer injury or loss). *While traveling (1890) on the Congo River in West Africa, Polish-born British novelist Joseph Conrad (1857–1924) contracted malaria, which impaired his health for the rest of his life.* As an adjective, the word *impaired* is used to describe anything that is defective, faulty, imperfect, etc. *In 1818, after twenty years of impaired hearing, German composer Ludwig van Beethoven (1770–1827) became totally deaf.*

"She's my mother. And like all **clairvoyant**[1] fairies—and mothers who love their children—she never loses sight of me. And today this good fairy of mine, this fairy filled with **maternal**[2] love, as soon as she saw me in danger of drowning, sent a thousand **carnivorous**[3] fish to me. They thought I was really a dead donkey and began to eat me. Some ate my ears, others my nose, and others my neck, my mane, my legs, my back, and my tail." When they finished eating my hide and muscle, they came to my bones—or rather, to the wood. After the first few bites, they found that the wood was too hard to eat. They turned and swam away. And that's my whole story."

---

[1] **clairvoyant** The supposed or supernatural ability to see things that are out of sight or to know things that will happen in the future is known as *clairvoyance*. If you're *clairvoyant* you have the power of clairvoyance; that is, you have knowledge of distant objects or future events; you're psychic; you have ESP. *Parapsychology is the study of the ability of the mind to perform such psychic acts as telepathy, telekinesis, and clairvoyance.*

[2] **maternal** In one sense, this word means "pertaining to or characteristic of a mother or motherhood; motherly" (as in *maternal instincts). Bear cubs are born very small and they require maternal care and protection for two or three years.* In another sense it means "related through one's mother"; for example, your *maternal* uncle is your mother's (not your father's) brother. *Former First Lady Eleanor Roosevelt's (1884–1962) parents died by the time she was ten, and she was raised by her maternal grandmother.* Note: The word *paternal* is similarly used to refer to fathers, fatherhood, or a relation through one's father.

[3] **carnivorous** A *carnivore* is an animal that eats meat (or catches other live animals for food); for example, tigers and wolves are *carnivores*. The adjective *carnivorous* ("meat-eating; flesh-eating") is used to describe such animals. *Although the deadly, sharp-toothed, carnivorous species of piranha (a freshwater fish of South America) is by far the best known, most actually feed on plants.* Note: An animal that feeds on plants is said to be *herbivorous* (as in *horses and giraffes are herbivorous*), and an animal whose diet includes both meat and plants is said to be *omnivorous* (as in *raccoons and pigs are omnivorous*).

"Enough of your story!" cried the man angrily. "I wasted ten cents on you, and I want **restitution**[1]!" He thought for a moment and then continued, "I know what I'll do. I'll take you back to the marketplace and sell you as firewood."

"Then sell me. I don't mind," said Pinocchio. But as he spoke, he gave a quick leap and dove into the sea. Swimming away as fast as he could, he cried out, laughing, "Good-bye. If you ever need a skin for your drum, remember me."

He swam on and on. In a little while he had gone so far that he could hardly be seen. All that could be seen of him on the **shimmering**[2] blue surface of the water was a swiftly moving black dot—a tiny black dot that now and then lifted a leg or an arm into the air.

After swimming for a long time, Pinocchio saw a large rock in the middle of the sea. High on the rock stood a little goat who was signaling to the puppet to come to her.

There was something very strange about that little goat. Her coat was not white or black or brown like that of any other goat, but blue—a deep, brilliant blue like that of the hair of the good fairy!

---

[1] **restitution** The act of "making good" or compensating (often by paying money) for (another's) loss, damage, or injury is known as *restitution*. Note: The word is sometimes used informally to signify the repayment (money) itself. *In 1996 a court ruling forced a tobacco company to make restitution (in the amount of $750,000) to a 66-year-old man who developed lung cancer after smoking for 44 years.*

[2] **shimmer (shimmering)** When something (a reflection on water, for example) *shimmers*, it shines with a soft, flickering light; it glimmers. *Impressionistic painting (exemplified by the works of such late-19th to early-20th-century French artists as Claude Monet and Pierre Auguste Renoir) is characterized by indistinct outlines and by a shimmering interplay of light and color.*

Pinocchio's heart beat fast, and then even faster, until he could feel the blood **pulsating**[1] through his wooden veins. He swam as hard as he could toward the rock. He was halfway there when he saw, **hurtling**[2] towards him in the water, a huge shark with an enormous head. It's **mammoth**[3] mouth, wide open, showed three rows of razor-sharp teeth.

Poor Pinocchio! The sight of that **titanic**[4] creature frightened him half to death! He tried to swim away from it, to

---

[1] **pulsate (pulsating)** When something *pulsates* it expands and contracts rhythmically (as does the human heart, for example), or it occurs or proceeds in a rhythmical succession of strokes, movements, sounds, etc. (as do radio waves from space, for example). The noun is *pulsation*. *The "iron lung"(a mechanical device capable of artificial respiration) has an airtight chamber that employs pulsations of high and low pressure to force air in and out of a patient's lungs.* The word is often used figuratively to imply any type of throbbing activity. *In his 1965 book* The City Is the Frontier, *author Charles Abrams says, "A city is the pulsating product of the human hand and mind."*

[2] **hurtle (hurtling)** When something (a train, racecar, bobsled, missile, comet, avalanche, etc.) *hurtles*, it moves or travels with great speed and usually with a rushing sound. *In 1966 Vice President Hubert Humphrey noted, "The earth itself is a kind of manned spaceship hurtling through the infinity of space."*

[3] **mammoth** As a noun, a *mammoth* is large, hairy, extinct, elephant-like mammal (with tusks up to 16 feet long!) of prehistoric times. As an adjective, the word is used to describe anything comparable to a mammoth (that is, anything huge but also heavy, bulky, clumsy, or unwieldy), as in *mammoth oil-tanker*, or anything simply huge (whether bulky or not), as in *mammoth gardens*. *President Lyndon Johnson once complained of "the mammoth task of preparing a 100-billion-dollar budget."*

[4] **titanic** In Greek mythology, the *Titans* were a family of gigantic gods (including Atlas and Prometheus) who ruled the universe. To describe someone or something as *titanic* is to say that it resembles the Titans; that is, it's of enormous size, strength, power, or influence (as in *the titanic struggle known as the Civil War*). *Twentieth-century British philosopher Sir Isaiah Berlin once referred to French Emperor Napoleon I (1769–1821) and German Chancellor Otto von Bismarck (1815–1898) as "great men, titanic figures who achieved superhuman results."*

change his path, to escape, but that gigantic, gaping mouth kept coming nearer and nearer.

"Hurry, Pinocchio, I beg you!" called the little goat on the high rock.

And Pinocchio swam desperately with his arms, his body, his legs, his feet.

"Quick, Pinocchio, the monster's coming closer!"

Pinocchio swam faster and faster, and harder and harder.

"Faster, Pinocchio! The monster will get you! There he is! There he is! Quick, quick, or you're finished!"

Pinocchio swam through the water like a shot—faster and faster. He came very close to the rock. The goat leaned over and held out one of her hoofs to help him up out of the water. Another hoof she waved frantically as a **decoy**[1] to **divert**[2] the attention of the attacker.

But it was too late. Pinocchio found himself between the rows of teeth. The shark took a deep breath and, as he breathed, he sucked the puppet in. Then he swallowed so fast that Pinocchio, falling down into the body of the fish, lay unconscious for a half hour.

---

[1] **decoy** A *decoy* is anything used to lure or deceive others into error, danger, or capture, especially a living or artificial bird or other animal used to lure game into a trap or within shooting range. *Sioux military leader Crazy Horse's (1842–1877) first encounter with U.S. soldiers was on the Oregon Trail at Platte Bridge (July 1865), where he acted as a decoy to draw soldiers out of their defenses.*

[2] **divert** To *divert* something (a stream, traffic, money, etc.) is to turn it aside from a particular direction, course, or purpose. *In Greek mythology Hercules cleaned the Augean stables (King Augeas's stables, which housed a herd of 3,000 oxen and had not been cleaned for 30 years) by diverting the course of two rivers so that they flowed through the stalls.* To divert a person (or his attention) is to distract him; to turn him away from his original interest or focus. *In 1856 presidential candidate Millard Fillmore tried to unite the North and South against foreigners to divert national attention from the controversial slavery issue.*

When he recovered his senses the puppet's mind was **hazy**[1] and he couldn't remember where he was. All around him everything was dark. He listened for a few moments and heard nothing. Once in a while a soft wind blew on his face. At first he couldn't tell where it was coming from, but after a while he remembered what had happened and **deduced**[2] that it was coming from the monster's lungs.

Pinocchio at first tried to be brave, but as soon as he became convinced that he was really and truly in the shark's body, he burst into tears. "Help! Help!" he sobbed. "Oh, poor me! Won't someone help me?"

"Who is there to help you?" said a voice from the darkness.

"Who are you?" asked Pinocchio, frozen with terror.

"I'm a tuna who was swallowed at the same time as you. And what kind of fish are you?"

"I'm not a fish; I'm a puppet. But what are we going to do?"

"Wait here until the shark has digested us, I suppose."

"But I don't want to be digested," shouted Pinocchio, starting to sob. "I want to get out of here. I want to escape."

"Go, then, if you can!"

"How big is this shark?" asked the puppet.

"He's almost a mile long."

While talking in the darkness, Pinocchio thought he saw a faint light in the distance.

---

[1] **hazy** If the atmosphere or air is *hazy*, it's marked by the presence of *haze* (tiny particles of dust, smoke, vapor, etc., that reduce visibility); it's misty, foggy, smoggy, cloudy, etc. *The surface of Titan (Saturn's largest moon) is completely hidden from view by a dense, hazy atmosphere.* If anything else (an idea, a memory, a surface, a line, a detail, etc.) is *hazy*, it's indistinct, unclear, vague, indefinite, etc. *British novelist and essayist Dame Rose Macaulay (1881–1958) once wrote: "I was becoming pretty hazy about right and wrong."*

[2] **deduce (deduced)** To *deduce* something (the answer to some puzzle or problem, for example) is to reach or draw a conclusion about it by reasoning; to figure it out, put two and two together, etc. *By understanding and using the laws of physics, scientists can deduce the internal structure of stars.*

"What's that light?" he said to the tuna.

"It's just an **illusion**[1]. There are no lights in here."

"But I tell you I see it!"

"The fish looked where the puppet was looking and said,

"Now I see it, too. But it must be some kind of **mirage**[2]."

"I don't think so."

"Then it's probably some other poor fish, waiting, as we are, to be digested."

"I want to talk to him. He may be an old fish and may know of some way out."

"I hope so."

"Good-bye, then. When will I see you again?"

"Who knows?" answered the tuna. "It's better to not even think about it."

---

[1] **illusion** An *illusion* is a false mental image or conception of something, such as an object that is seen in a way different from the way it is in reality, an object that is purely imagined, or an erroneous belief. *American novelist John Steinbeck (1902–1968) once said, "The writer must believe that what he is doing is the most important thing in the world – and he must hold to this illusion even when he knows it is not true."*

[2] **mirage** A *mirage* is an optical illusion (caused by a distortion of light) in which an observer sees a realistic but nonexistent object (such as a distant sheet of water over hot pavement). *English detective novelist Ruth Rendell (born 1930) once wrote: "It was [only] a mirage he had seen in that river village, a trick of the heat and light."* Sometimes the word is used figuratively to refer to any delusion, illusion, or fantasy. *In 1961 French anthropologist Michel Leiris (1901–1990) said that a dream is a "mirage surrounded by shadows."*

Chapter 31 "The Reunion"

Pinocchio, slowly feeling his way through the **murky**[1] darkness began to walk toward the faint light that glowed in the distance. The farther he went, the brighter and clearer grew the tiny light. On and on he walked until finally he found, amazingly, a little table set for dinner and lighted by a candle stuck in a glass bottle. Near the table sat a little old man.

At this sight, the poor puppet was filled with such happiness that he nearly fainted. He wanted to laugh, to cry, to say a thousand things; but instead, all he could do was stand still and stutter some meaningless words. At last he managed to utter a cry of joy and, opening his arms wide, he threw them around the old man's neck.

"Oh, Father, dear Father! Have I found you at last? I'll never, never leave you again!"

"Are my eyes deceiving me?" answered the old man, rubbing them with both hands. "Are you really my dear Pinocchio?"

"Yes, yes, yes! It is I! Look at me! And you've forgiven me, 'haven't you? Oh, my dear Father, how good you are! And to think that I...Oh, but if you only knew all that has happened

---

[1] **murky** If a place (a cave or dungeon, for example) is *murky*, it's dim, dark, or gloomy. If the air is *murky*, it's hazy, foggy, misty, or smoky. If water or glass is *murky*, it's darkened, dimmed, or clouded with dirt or other impurities. If something non-physical (one's memory, for example) is *murky*, it's vague, indistinct, or unclear. *According to* Compton's Encyclopedia, *"At the 1920 Olympic Games in Antwerp, Belgium, the pool used for the [springboard diving] competition was part of the city moat; many divers became disoriented when they tried to surface after a dive because the water was dark and murky."*

to me! If you only knew of the **atrocities**[1] I've been subjected to! The day you sold your old coat to buy me my schoolbook, I ran away to a marionette theater, and the owner caught me and wanted to make a fire of me to cook his lamb chop! He was the one who gave me five gold pieces for you, but I met the fox and the cat, who took me to the Red Lobster Inn. There they ate like pigs and I left the inn alone and I met the killers in the woods. I ran and they ran after me. They caught me and hung me from the branch of a giant oak tree. Then the blue-haired fairy sent the coach to rescue me, and the doctors, after looking at me, said, 'If he's not dead, then he's surely alive,' and then I told a lie and my nose began to grow. It grew and grew until I couldn't get it through the door of the room. And then I went with the fox and the cat to the Field of Wonders to bury the gold pieces. The parrot laughed at me and, instead of two thousand gold pieces, I found none. When the judge heard my story, he **summarily**[2] sent me to jail. And when I left the prison I saw a bunch of grapes hanging on a vine. The trap caught me and the farmer put a collar on me and forced me to be his watchdog. But I caught the weasels and he let me go. The snake with the smoking tail started to laugh and burst a blood vessel, so I went back to the fairy's house. She was dead, and the pigeon, seeing me crying, told

---

[1] **atrocities** Shockingly or inhumanly cruel or savage acts (especially unjustifiable acts of violence or torture inflicted by armed enemy forces on prisoners of war) are known as *atrocities* (pronounced *uh-TROSS-uh-teez*). *At the 1946 "Doctors Trial" at Nuremberg (at which Nazi doctors were tried after World War II), prosecutor Telford Taylor's opening statement began: "The defendants in this case are charged with murders, tortures, and other atrocities committed in the name of medical science."*

[2] **summarily** To do something *summarily* is to do it promptly and speedily, without ceremony or formality. *At the end of World War II (1945), Italian dictator Benito Mussolini was captured by his Italian opponents and summarily executed.*

me that you were going to **traverse**[1] the seas so that you could look for me in distant lands. And I said to him, 'Oh, if I only had wings!' And he said to me, 'Do you want to go to your father?' And I said, 'Yes, but how?' And he said, 'Get on my back; I'll take you there.' We flew all night, and the next morning the fishermen were looking toward the sea, crying, 'There's a poor little man drowning,' and I knew it was you, because my heart told me so and I waved to you from the shore—"

"I knew it was you, too," interrupted Geppetto, "and I wanted to go to you. But how could I? The sea was rough and the high waves overturned my boat. Then a terrible shark came up out of the sea, swam quickly toward me, and swallowed me."

"How long have you been here?"

"From that day to this, about two years—two long, weary years that have felt more like two centuries."

"But how have you survived? Where did you find the candle? And the matches to light it with? Where did you get them?"

"In the storm that overturned my boat, a large ship was also overturned. The sailors, who wore lifejackets, were all safe, but they were unable to **salvage**[2] the ship, which **plum-**

---

[1] **traverse** To *traverse* something is to travel across it (as in *Lewis and Clark traversed the western U.S.*), pass through it (as in *the Amazon River traverses Brazil*), or extend over it (as in *the Brooklyn Bridge traverses the East River*). In 1960 *journalist James Morris said, "[The United Nations building] stands ablaze, like a slab of fire; when at last you cross the road to [it], it is like traversing some unmarked but crucial frontier."*

[2] **salvage** To *salvage* something is to save or rescue it from loss or destruction (as from shipwreck, fire, natural disaster, neglect, etc.). *In September 1997 Palestinian leader Yasser Arafat suggested that the U.S. could salvage the faltering Middle Ease peace process by supporting the creation of a Palestinian state.* In a related sense, to *salvage* items that have been discarded or damaged is to retrieve and save them for further use. *The Iraqi city of Al Hillah was built largely of material salvaged from the nearby ruins of Babylon (which had been destroyed by war).*

meted[1] to the bottom of the sea. There, the same terrible shark that swallowed me, swallowed it."

"What! It swallowed a ship?" asked Pinocchio in astonishment.

"In one mouthful. Luckily for me, that ship was loaded with sundries[2]: meat, crackers, bread, raisins, cheese, coffee, sugar, candles, and boxes of matches. With all these supplies, I've been able to live for two years. But the food supply has been gradually dwindling[3], and now it's nearly depleted[4]. And this candle is the last one."

"And then?"

"And then, my child, we'll find ourselves hungry, and in darkness."

"Then, my dear Father," said Pinocchio, "there's no time to lose. We must try to escape immediately."

"Escape? But how?"

---

[1] **plummet (plummeted)** When something (an aircraft, stock prices, the temperature, one's popularity, etc.) *plummets*, it falls or drops rapidly, suddenly, or steeply; it plunges, nose-dives, etc. *About halfway along its 35-mile, northward course from Lake Erie to Lake Ontario, the Niagara Rivers plummets 167 feet (at Niagara Falls).*

[2] **sundries** Small, miscellaneous (often inexpensive) items or articles (especially those that are lumped together as not needing individual mention) are collectively called *sundries*. Skin Diver *magazine once spoke of a certain drugstore that offers "a wide variety of [drugs], magazines, and sundries."*

[3] **dwindle (dwindling)** When something *dwindles*, it becomes gradually smaller or less; it decreases, shrinks, wastes away, etc. *In the decades following World War II, Americans grew increasingly concerned about such environmental problems as pollution, dwindling energy resources, and the dangers of pesticides and radiation.*

[4] **deplete (depleted)** When a supply of something is *depleted*, its quantity or size decreases; it becomes partially or totally used up, emptied out, etc. *In 1974 environmentalists warned that certain industrial chemicals (Freon, for example) could deplete the Earth's ozone layer (a band of ozone in the upper atmosphere that absorbs harmful ultraviolet radiation from the Sun).*

"We can run out of the shark's mouth and dive into the sea."

"That would be a good idea, except for two things — I not a very **proficient**[1] swimmer, and I don't have much **stamina**[2]. I'd never make it to shore."

"That doesn't matter. Swimming is my **forte**[3]! Remember, because I'm made of wood, I can't sink. If you climb on my back, I'll carry you to shore."

"It won't work," answered Geppetto, shaking his head sadly. "Do you think it's possible for a puppet who's only three feet tall to have enough strength to carry me on his back all the way to shore?"

"Can you think of a **viable**[4] alternative?"

"No."

"Then let's try it and see!"

---

[1] **proficient** If you're *proficient* in something (an art, a profession, a branch of learning, etc.) you have an advanced degree of ability or skill in it; you're good at it. *Ancient Greek philosopher Plato believed that one should become proficient in mathematics before beginning a study of philosophy.*

[2] **stamina** Your *stamina* is your ability to endure physical strain or fatigue; your endurance, strength, etc. *Whereas the 100-meter dash is a test of speed, the marathon (a 26-mile cross-country race) is a test of stamina.*

[3] **forte** Your *forte* (pronounced FOR-tay) is the thing you excel at; your strong point. *Baseball great Babe Ruth (1895–1948) excelled at every aspect of the game, but his forte was hitting.*

[4] **viable** If you say that something (a plan, idea, relationship, undertaking, government, etc.) is *viable*, you mean that it's capable of working successfully; it's doable, practicable, possible, etc. *Because of the risk to health from hazardous radiation, many people feel that nuclear energy is not a viable alternative to traditional energy sources.* Note: If you say that a fetus or newborn is *viable*, you mean that it's capable of living outside the womb. Also note: If you say that a commercial product is *viable*, you mean that it's capable of making a profit.

Without another word, Pinocchio took the candle in his hand and, leading the way, said to his father, "Follow me and don't be afraid."

They walked a long distance through the body of the shark. When they reached the throat, Pinocchio turned to his father and whispered, "The shark's sleeping with his mouth open. I can see through it that the sea is very **tranquil**[1]. Follow me closely, Father, and soon we'll be free."

They climbed up the shark's throat into the **posterior**[2] portion of his gigantic mouth. Just then the monster suddenly sneezed, jolting them so violently that they fell back once again to where they'd started.

To make matters worse, the candle went out and the father and son were left in total darkness.

"Now what will we do?" asked Pinocchio.

"Now we're finished."

"Why? Give me your hand, dear Father, and be careful not to slip!"

"Where are we going?"

"We have to try again. Come with me and don't be afraid."

With these words Pinocchio took his father by the hand and they climbed up the monster's throat for a second time. They then crossed the tongue and climbed over the three rows of teeth. But before jumping into the sea, the puppet whispered to his father, "Climb on my back and hold on tightly to my neck. I'll do the rest."

As soon as Geppetto was comfortably seated on his back, Pinocchio jumped into the water and started to swim.

---

[1] **tranquil** If something (a body of water, a town, one's existence, etc.) is *tranquil, it's* calm, peaceful, and quiet. *A hospice (a special hospital for people who are dying) offers relief from pain and a tranquil atmosphere.*

[2] **posterior** This adjective means "situated in or toward the rear or back (of something)." *A firefly has chemicals in the posterior tip of its body that produce a flashing light.*

Chapter 32 "A Real Live Boy"

"Father, we're free!" cried the puppet. "All we have to do now is get to shore, and that's easy."

As he swam he suddenly noticed that Geppetto was trembling with fright.

"Have courage, Father! In a few minutes we'll be safe on land."

"But where's the land?" asked the little old man, growing more and more worried. "I'm looking everywhere, and I see nothing but water."

"I think I see land," said the puppet. For his father's sake, Pinocchio pretended to be peaceful and cheerful—but he was actually far from that. He was beginning to feel discouraged, and his strength was leaving him. Breathing was becoming more and more difficult. He felt that he couldn't go on much longer.

He swam a few more strokes, then turned to Geppetto and cried out weakly, "Help me, Father! I'm dying!"

Father and son were about to drown when they heard a voice call from the sea, "What's the matter?"

"We can't go on!"

"I know that voice. You're Pinocchio."

"Yes. And who are you?"

"I'm the tuna who was inside the shark with you."

"How did you escape?"

"I copied what you did. You showed the way and I followed."

"You've arrived just in time. I beg you! Help us or we're finished!"

"Of course. Climb onto my back, both of you. In a moment you'll be safe on land."

As soon as they reached the shore, Pinocchio jumped to the ground to help his old father. Then he turned to the fish and said, "You've saved my father and me from **catastrophe**[1], and I can't find the words to thank you. May I give you a kiss as an expression of my gratitude?"

The tuna stuck his nose out of the water and Pinocchio knelt on the sand and kissed him affectionately on his cheek. At this sign of love, the poor tuna, who was not used to such things, wept like a baby. Then, ashamed to be seen in such a state, he turned quickly, plunged into the water, and disappeared.

But the ordeal had **debilitated**[2] Geppetto completely, and he could barely stand. Pinocchio offered his arm to him and said, "Lean on my arm, Father, and let's go. We'll walk very, very slowly, and if we feel tired we can stop and rest."

"Where are we going?" asked Geppetto weakly.

"To look for a house or a hut where we can ask for some bread to eat and some straw to sleep on."

They'd walked barely a hundred feet when they saw two beggars **loitering**[3] by the roadside.

---

[1] **catastrophe** A *catastrophe* (pronounced *kuh-TASS-truh-fee*) is any severe misfortune; any (often unexpected) occurrence causing great destruction or distress (often specifically a natural disaster, such as an earthquake, tornado, hurricane, volcanic eruption, or flood). *Bombay, India, has seen a number of catastrophes, including the Great Fire of 1803, the bubonic plague epidemic of 1896, and the harbor explosion of 1944.* Note: Informally, the word can signify any complete or total failure or disappointment (as in *our trip to Mexico was a catastrophe*).

[2] **debilitate (debilitated)** To *debilitate* someone is to cause him to loose energy or strength; to weaken him, enfeeble him, etc. *During his Presidency (1881–1885), Chester A. Arthur was neither happy nor healthy – he mourned the death (1880) of his wife and suffered the debilitating effects of kidney disease.*

[3] **loiter (loitering)** To *loiter* is to stand idly about; to linger aimlessly (in or about a particular place); to hang around (as in *teenagers loitering on street corners*). In some communities loitering is illegal. *When it was pointed out that singer Dinah Shore's 1970s TV talk show was so successful because Dinah herself was so relaxed, comedian Steve Allen (1921–2000) joked, "If she were any more relaxed she would have been arrested for loitering."*

It was the fox and the cat, but they looked so miserable and sickly that they were hardly recognizable. The cat, after maintaining a **façade**[1] of blindness for so many years, had really lost his sight. And the fox, whose muscles had **atrophied**[2], looked old and **emaciated**[3].

"Oh, Pinocchio," he cried in a tearful, high-pitched voice. "Give us something, we beg of you! We're old, tired, and sick."

"Tired and sick!" wailed the cat.

Looking directly into the fox's **gaunt**[4] face, the puppet answered, "I'm wise to your tricks. You fooled me once with

---

[1] **façade** If you're talking about a building, the *façade* (pronounced *fuh-SAHD*) is the (often decorative) front or face of it. *New York City's Grand Hyatt Hotel has a mirrored glass façade.* If you're talking about anything else, a *façade* is a deceptive outward appearance; a false front, pretense, disguise, etc. *American psychologist Elizabeth Kubler-Ross (born 1926) once said, "It is not the end of the physical body that should worry us; rather, our concern must be to release our inner selves from the spiritual death that comes from living behind a façade designed to conform to the external definitions of what and who we are."*

[2] **atrophy (atrophied)** When a part of the body (a muscle or organ, for example) *atrophies*, it wastes away or decreases in size (from disuse, injury, disease, defective nutrition, etc.). *Polio (a highly infectious viral disease preventable through vaccination since 1954) can cause paralysis, muscular atrophy, and deformity.* The word is sometimes used informally to refer to the wasting away of anything. *In 1934 U.S. poet and critic Ezra Pound (1885–1972) said, "If a nation's literature declines, the nation atrophies and decays."*

[3] **emaciated** This word is used to describe people who are extremely or abnormally thin (especially as a result of starvation). *After World War II, photographs of emaciated inmates of German concentration camps stunned the world.*

[4] **gaunt** If a person is *gaunt*, he's thin and bony in appearance (as from exhaustion, hunger, worry, etc.). *In Washington Irving's (1783–1859) story "The Legend of Sleepy Hollow," a gaunt, superstitious, cowardly schoolteacher named Ichabod Crane flees from a legendary headless horseman.*

your **suave**[1] style and smooth talk, but you'll never fool me again. And if now you think that you can **evoke**[2] sympathy with your **pathetic**[3] whining, forget it. You're **incorrigible**[4] thieves and you deserve whatever you get. Good-bye."

Pinocchio and Geppetto calmly went on their way. After a few more steps, they saw, at the end of a long path, a tiny cottage built of straw.

---

[1] **suave** If you say that a person (especially a man) is *suave*, you mean that he's smoothly pleasant, (sometimes superficially or falsely) well mannered, elegant, and sophisticated. He's effortlessly courteous, polished, and relaxed in dealing with others. *Scottish actor Sean Connery (born 1930) first gained fame with his portrayal of fiction's suave British secret agent James Bond (007).*

[2] **evoke** To *evoke* a feeling, memory, image, or the like is to bring it to mind; to call it forth, activate it, etc. *According to* Compton's Encyclopedia, *American artist James McNeill Whistler (1834–1903), famous for his painting popularly titled* Whistler's Mother *(1872), "sought to evoke emotions with patterns of tone and color as a musician would sound with patterns of harmony and melody."* To *evoke* a particular response (laughter, applause, criticism, anger, etc.) is to cause it to happen or occur (sometimes suddenly or unexpectedly); to bring it on, provoke it, etc. *In his inaugural address (March 1909), speaking of proposed changes in banking laws, President William Howard Taft said, "There is no subject of economic discussion so [complex] and so likely to evoke differing views and [opinionated] statements as this one."*

[3] **pathetic** If someone or something is *pathetic*, it arouses feelings of pity, sympathy, or compassion; it's touching, moving, tear-jerking, etc. *In movies, the Frankenstein monster is both terrifying and pathetic.* Informally, the word describes anything that is so poor at living up to expectations that it is seen as miserably inadequate, useless, or feeble (as in *a pathetic excuse*). *Twentieth-century American diplomat George Frost Kennan once spoke of "a rather pathetic affair, attended by only 35 persons."*

[4] **incorrigible** If someone is *incorrigible*, he's incapable of being corrected or reformed; he's hopelessly or incurably bad, unprincipled, immoral, etc. (as in *the incorrigible Mike Tyson*). *In 1981, speaking of lowering the crime rate, Supreme Court chief justice Warren Burger said, "A far greater factor [than ending poverty] is the effect of swift and certain [punishment; however,] there may be some incorrigible human beings who cannot be changed except by God's mercy."*

"That little cottage," said Pinocchio, "has a **rustic**[1] charm and simplicity. I like it. Someone kind must live there. Let's go see."

They went and knocked at the door.

"Who is it?" said a little voice from within.

"A poor father and his poor son, with no food and no home," answered the puppet.

"Turn the key and the door will open," said the same little voice.

Pinocchio turned the key and the door opened. As soon as they went in, they looked all around but saw no one.

"Where are you?" cried Pinocchio, **baffled**[2].

"Here I am, up here!"

Father and son looked up to the ceiling, and there on a beam sat a glowing cricket.

"Oh, my dear cricket," said Pinocchio, bowing politely.

"Oh, now you call me your dear cricket, but do you remember when you threw a hammer at me?"

"You're right. Throw a hammer at me now. I deserve it! But please spare my poor old father."

---

[1] **rustic** If you refer to something as *rustic*, you mean that it pertains to, is found in, or is characteristic of the country (as opposed to the city); it's rural. Rustic people tend to be plain, unsophisticated, unrefined, etc. Rustic objects and structures tend to be plain, simple, or rough in form or style (for example, they might be made of untrimmed lumber). *British novelist Elizabeth Bowen (1899–1973) once wrote: "To look rustic in London, Gera wore a large straw hat."*

[2] **baffle (baffled)** In one sense, to *baffle* someone is to confuse him; to mystify him, perplex him, dumbfound him, etc. *In 1985 Henry G. Miller, President of the New York State Bar Association, said, "The legal system is often a mystery, and we [lawyers] preside over rituals baffling to everyday citizens."* In a related sense, to *baffle* someone is to defeat him in his efforts by confusing him; to stymie him, foil him, etc. *According to* Grolier's Encyclopedia, *"[A maze] was, in ancient times, a structure composed of an intricate series of passageways and chambers, probably at first designed to baffle enemies."*

"I'm going to spare both of you. I only wanted to remind you of what you once did to me. It may teach you that you should always remember the **maxim**[1] that says you should treat everyone with kindness if you wish to be treated with kindness in return. For your own good, you should repeat that over and over until it's **indelibly**[2] imprinted on your mind."

"You're right, little cricket. But I don't need to repeat it over and over, for I've already learned that lesson well. Now, tell me, how did you come to own this pretty little cottage?"

"It was given to me yesterday by a little goat with blue hair."

"Where did the goat go?" asked Pinocchio, suddenly excited.

"I don't know."

"When will she be back?"

"She'll never come back. Yesterday she went away saying, 'Poor Pinocchio, I shall never see him again. The shark must have eaten him by now.'"

---

[1] **maxim** A *maxim* is an expression (sometimes a familiar saying) of a general truth or rule of conduct. *According to the* Columbia Encyclopedia, *ancient Greek philosopher Diogenes "taught that the virtuous [morally excellent] life is the simple life, a maxim he dramatized by living in a tub."*

[2] **indelible (indelibly)** In one sense, if something (ink from a laundry pen, one's fingerprints, etc.) is *indelible*, it can't be erased, removed, washed away, etc.; it's permanent. *British naturalist Charles Darwin (1809–1882) once said, "Man still bears in his bodily frame the indelible stamp of his lowly origin."* In a related sense, if something (a memory, for example) is *indelible*, it makes a permanent impression on the mind; it's unforgettable. *In 1969 Dr. Hans Selye, Director of Montreal's Institute of Experimental Medicine and Surgery, said, "Every stress leaves an indelible [emotional] scar, and the organism pays for it by becoming a little older."*

"Were those her actual words? Tell me what she said **verbatim**[1]."

"That's exactly what she said."

"Then it was she, my dear little fairy!" cried Pinocchio, sobbing bitterly. After he had cried for a long time, he wiped his eyes and then made a bed of straw for Geppetto. Finally, he said to the cricket, "Tell me, where can I find a glass of milk for my poor father?"

"A farmer lives three fields away from here. He has some cows. Go there and he'll give you what you want."

Pinocchio went out into the yard, and, peering into the distance, saw a **pastoral**[2] landscape at the center of which was a little farmhouse.

With great determination, Pinocchio darted across the three fields until, out of breath, he arrived at the farmer's house. He knocked on the door, which was soon opened by the farmer himself.

"Yes?" the farmer asked.

"May I please have some milk for my poor father?"

"How much milk do you want?"

"One cupful."

---

[1] **verbatim** This word means "in exactly the same words; word for word" (as in *repeat verbatim, copy verbatim, dictate verbatim,* etc.). *When a court stenographer is asked to read back a statement made by an attorney or witness, he reads it back verbatim (but without emotion).*

[2] **pastoral** If land is *pastoral,* it's used for pasture (animal grazing) or it's simply rural (it's in the country; it's farm-like). *According to* Grolier's Encyclopedia, *"Cross-country is a fall and winter activity for distance runners, with races of 2–12 miles being run over pastoral terrain."* A landscape, a setting, scenery, etc., described as *pastoral* has the simplicity, peacefulness, or charm associated with rural areas or country life. *The Lake District in northern England is noted for its pastoral beauty.* A work of art (a painting, a musical composition, a literary work, etc.) described as *pastoral* portrays or celebrates the countryside or country life. *English poet Edmund Spenser's (1552–1599) first original work was a series of 12 pastoral poems entitled* The Shepheardes Calendar.

"A cup of milk costs a penny. First give me the penny."

"I don't have one," answered Pinocchio, sad and ashamed.

"That's too bad," answered the farmer, "If you don't have a penny, I can't sell you any milk."

"Never mind, then," said Pinocchio with a **sullen**[1] expression. He turned around and started to go.

"Wait a minute," said the farmer. "Maybe we can work something out. Do you know how to draw water from a well?"

"I can try."

"Then go to that well over there and draw a hundred buckets of water. After you've finished, I'll give you a cup of milk."

"All right."

The farmer took the puppet to the well and showed him how to turn the handle. Pinocchio set to work as best he could, but in a short time he was exhausted and dripping with sweat. He'd never worked so hard in his life.

"Until today," said the farmer, "my donkey has drawn water for me, but now that poor animal is dying."

"May I see him?" said Pinocchio.

"Certainly."

As soon as Pinocchio went into the stable, he saw a little donkey lying on a bed of straw. He was dying from hunger and a life of **drudgery**[2]. After looking at him a long time, the puppet said to himself: "I think I know that donkey! I've seen him before." Bending low over him, he asked, "Who are you?"

---

[1] **sullen** If a person (or his reaction to something) is *sullen*, he shows a gloomy ill humor; he's resentfully silent and unsociable; he's glum, sulky, long-faced, etc. *According to the* Oxford Encyclopedia, *"The reaction of the American military to defeat in Vietnam was sullen disbelief."*

[2] **drudgery** Any heavy, wearisome, tedious, boring, or unpleasant work (scrubbing floors, for example) is known as *drudgery. Cinderella escaped from a life of drudgery and married a prince.*

The dying donkey opened weary eyes and answered, "I'm Lampwick."

Then he closed his eyes and died.

"Oh, my poor Lampwick," said Pinocchio in a faint voice, as he wiped his eyes with his sleeve.

"Why should you feel so sorry about a little donkey that cost you nothing?" asked the farmer. "What about me, who paid good money for him?"

"But, you see, he was my friend."

"Your friend?"

"Yes. He was one of those hearty, **extroverted**[1] types with an **invincible**[2] **optimism**[3] and a **perpetual**[4] smile. You

---

[1] **extrovert (extroverted)** An *extrovert* is a person who is outgoing, friendly, talkative, sociable, unrestrained, etc. Note: The opposite is an *introvert* (a person who is shy, withdrawn, quiet, restrained, etc.). *Robin Williams (born 1951) has delighted audiences with his extroverted, improvisational stand-up comedy and with his excellent performances in a wide range of film roles.*

[2] **invincible** This word describes anything that can't be conquered or defeated (as in *an invincible army*), or anything that can't be subdued or put down (as in *invincible courage*). *In 1978 boxer Leon Spinks surprised everyone by winning the heavyweight crown from the seemingly invincible Muhammad Ali.*

[3] **optimist (optimism)** An *optimist* is a person who expects a favorable outcome (or who expects good things to happen or who stresses the positive). The noun is *optimism;* the adjective is *optimistic. John F. Kennedy's election (1960) as President began a period of great optimism in the United States; in fact, Kennedy himself remarked, "I am astounded at the wave of optimism — there is a tide of feeling that all is well."*

[4] **perpetual** Something referred to as *perpetual* (1) lasts (or is designed to work or remains valid) forever (as in *perpetual treaty*), (2) continues for an indefinitely long time (as in *perpetual holiday*), or (3) continues without interruption (as in *perpetual conflict*). *The Congress of Vienna (a conference of European nations held in 1815, after the defeat of Napoleon) recognized and guaranteed the perpetual neutrality of Switzerland.*

couldn't help but like him. He was **witty**[1] and **personable**[2], too. And on top of all that, he was an outstanding, **versatile**[3] athlete! You see, he was a classmate of mine who—"
"What? A classmate?" shouted the farmer, interrupting Pinocchio's **extemporaneous**[4] little **eulogy**[5]. "You had donkeys in your school?" Then he added sarcastically, "Some lessons you must have had there!"

---

[1] **witty** People described as *witty* are capable of making cleverly amusing remarks. *In his films, Woody Allen often plays a character who is neurotic but witty.* Speech or writing described as *witty* is characterized by or full of clever humor. *Comedian Allan Sherman (1924–1973) gained fame for his witty song parodies, such as 1963's "Hello Muddah, Hello Faddah!"*

[2] **personable** People who are *personable* are pleasing in personality, easy to get along with, pleasant, likeable, agreeable, etc. *TV journalist Barbara Walters (born 1931) is a skillful and personable interviewer of both entertainment celebrities and world leaders.*

[3] **versatile** If a person is *versatile*, he's competent in many or varied skills, tasks, fields of endeavor, etc.; he's multipurpose, many-sided, flexible, all-around, etc. (as in *versatile actor*). *Italian painter, engineer, musician, and scientist Leonardo da Vinci (1452–1519) was the most versatile genius of the Renaissance.* If a thing is *versatile*, it has or is capable of many uses (as in *a versatile plastic*). *Householder magazine once said, "The jigsaw is one of the most versatile power tools."*

[4] **extemporaneous** If something (a speech or musical performance, for example) is *extemporaneous*, it's done (spoken, performed, etc.) on the spur of the moment, without preparation; it's ad-libbed, improvised, off the cuff, unrehearsed, etc. *According to Compton's Encyclopedia, U.S. jazz pianist Jelly Roll Morton's (1890–1941) "dedication to composition and rehearsed performance differentiated him from jazz musicians whose music was solely extemporaneous."*

[5] **eulogy** A *eulogy* (pronounced *YOU-luh-jee*) is a speech praising someone who has recently died. It is usually delivered at a funeral or memorial service. *In his eulogy for Valley of the Dolls author Jacqueline Susann (1921–1974), critic Gene Shalit noted, "Her books were put down by most critics, but readers would not put down her books."*

The puppet, ashamed and hurt by these words, didn't answer. He took his milk and returned to his father.

That day was the **advent**[1] of a new era for Pinocchio. For the next five months, he got up every morning just as dawn was breaking and went to the farm to draw water. And every day he was given a cup of milk for his poor old father.

But that was not all. Using a simple basket he found around the house as a **prototype**[2], he taught himself to weave baskets of his own. In a short time he became quite **adept**[3] at it. Then he learned some advanced basket making techniques. For example, he learned how to create intricate design patterns within the weave and he learned to use a needle and thread to attach colorful glass beads to the outsides of the baskets. He **integrated**[4] each new technique he learned into his overall style. Soon he was producing the most artistic yet

---

[1] **advent** The *advent* of something (especially something important) is the coming into being of it; the arrival of it; the start of it. *In July 1963 President John F. Kennedy said, "Eighteen years ago the advent of nuclear weapons changed the course of the world."*

[2] **prototype** A *prototype* is an original type or form (of something) on which imitations or later versions are based; a pattern, model, etc. *Airplanes used in World War I (1914-1918) were greatly improved versions of the prototype first flown (1903) by the Wright brothers.*

[3] **adept** If you're *adept* at some skill or task, you're very good at it (as from training, experience, or natural ability); you're proficient, capable, competent, expert, etc. *By the time he was a teenager, folksinger Pete Seeger (born 1919) was adept at playing the ukulele, banjo, and guitar.*

[4] **integrate (integrated)** To *integrate* various related things is to bring them together into a whole; to combine or unite them. *Under NAFTA (1992's North American Free Trade Agreement), the United States, Canada, and Mexico became a single, giant, integrated market of almost 400 million people.* To *integrate* a single thing into a larger unit is make it part of it; to add or merge it in. *In 1981 Greece was integrated into the European Economic Community (an economic union, established 1958, to promote trade and cooperation among the countries of western Europe).*

functional[1] baskets anyone had ever seen. A typical basket, for example, might contain diamonds and other geometrical shapes within the weave, and **symmetrical**[2] rows of alternating transparent and **opaque**[3] red beads on either side, toward the top. He sold his masterpieces at the marketplace, and with the money he received, he and his father were able to pay for all their needs.

With some of the money he'd **allocated**[4] for school supplies, he bought himself some used schoolbooks. In the evening he studied by lamplight at the kitchen table.

---

[1] **functional** If you say that something is *functional*, you mean that it's capable of serving the purpose it was designed for, or you're stressing its usefulness as opposed to its structure, form, or beauty. *In 1978 Chinese-American architect I. M. Pei (born 1917), who is known for structures that combine functional concerns with elegance of design, said, "[In architecture] you have to consider your client; only out of that can you produce great architecture."*

[2] **symmetry (symmetrical)** If something has *symmetry*, the corresponding parts of it (its left and right halves, for example) are the same (in size, shape, position, form, arrangement, etc.); they are (or nearly are) mirror images of each other (as in *a broad avenue with symmetrical plantings of trees*). *Human beings, like most animals, have left-right symmetry, but not top-bottom symmetry.* In a related sense, if something has *symmetry*, the parts that make it up are pleasingly balanced; they're well proportioned; they're regular in form or arrangement (as in *the symmetry of a Mozart string quartet*).

[3] **opaque** If an object is *opaque* (pronounced *oh-PAKE*), it doesn't allow any light to pass through (that is, one can't see through it); it's not transparent or translucent; it's solid. *You can make a shadow by placing an opaque object (your hand, for example) between a light source and a surface (a wall, for example).*

[4] **allocate (allocated)** To *allocate* money, time, or the like is to set it apart for a particular purpose; to designate it, earmark it, etc. *In September 1997 the U.S. Senate voted to allocate $34 million for anti-smoking education and enforcement of rules prohibiting minors from buying cigarettes.* To *allocate* a particular product, service, resource, or the like is to distribute it according to a plan; to allot it. *The International Telecommunications Union, a UN agency with headquarters in Switzerland, allocates radio frequencies on a worldwide scale to avoid possible confusion and interference.*

Little by little his efforts were rewarded. He succeeded, not only in his studies, but also in his work. One day he found that he had **accrued**[1] fifty cents. With it he wanted to buy himself some new clothes.

He said to his father, "I'm going to the marketplace to buy myself a coat, a cap, and a pair of shoes. When I come back I'll be so dressed up, you'll think I'm a rich man."

He ran out of the house and up the road to the village. Suddenly he heard his name called, and looking around to see where the voice came from, he noticed a snail crawling out of some bushes.

"Don't you recognize me?" said the snail.

"I'm not sure."

"Do you remember the snail that lived with the blue-haired fairy? Do you remember how I opened the door for you after you kicked your foot through it?"

"Yes, **vividly**[2]. Nothing could ever **efface**[3] my mental picture of that dreadful night," said Pinocchio. "Answer me

---

[1] **accrue (accrued)** To *accrue* something (money, sick leave, etc.) is to accumulate it over time. *During his 23-year major-league career (1954–1976), baseball great Hank Aaron accrued a record-breaking 755 home runs.*

[2] **vivid (vividly)** In one sense, if something (a memory or description, for example) is *vivid*, it's strongly felt or expressed; it forms distinct, lifelike mental images. *The novels of Russian author Leo Tolstoy (1828–1910) paint a vivid picture of his country's life and history.* In another sense, if something (a color, for example) is *vivid*, it's bright, intense, brilliant, etc. *Whereas Dutch painter Vincent van Gogh's (1853–1890) early works portray peasant life in dark colors, many of his later works portray nature in vivid colors.* Note: If you say that a person (or one's personality) is *vivid*, you mean that he's lively, spirited, active, etc.

[3] **efface** To *efface* something is to cause it to disappear, as by erasing it, rubbing it out, wiping it out, etc. *The ancient Egyptians used geometry to determine the boundaries of fields whose dividing lines had been effaced by the annual flooding of the Nile River.* Note: If you say that someone is *self-effacing*, you mean that he tends not to draw attention to himself; he keeps himself in the background, he's modest, humble, low-key, etc.

quickly. Where have you left my fairy? What's she doing? Has she forgiven me? Does she remember me? Does she still love me? Is she very far away from here? May I see her?"

At all these questions, tumbling out one after another, the snail answered calmly, "My dear Pinocchio, the fairy is sick in a hospital."

"In a hospital?"

"I'm afraid so. She's had many problems.

"What kind of problems?"

"Problems with her health—her physical health, I mean. Luckily, so far, her mental **faculties**[1] haven't **deteriorated**[2]. But she's been **beset**[3] by financial problems, too. Her recovery has been **hampered**[4] by a lack of funds. You see, she doesn't even have enough money to buy the medicine that would make her well."

---

[1] **faculties** Your *faculties* (sometimes called *mental faculties*) are the powers of your mind: concentration, memory, reason, judgment, etc. *In 1994 former President Ronald Reagan revealed that he had Alzheimer's disease (a brain disease that gradually destroys the mental faculties) in the hope of increasing public awareness of the illness.*

[2] **deteriorate** When something *deteriorates*, it grows worse (in quality, character, value, etc.); it "goes downhill" (as in *deteriorating neighborhoods*). *After the Civil War (1861–1865), Confederacy President Jefferson Davis, charged with treason, spent two years in prison, where his physical and emotional health deteriorated.*

[3] **beset** To be *beset* by something (troubles, difficulties, etc.) is to be attacked on all sides by it; to be surrounded by it; to be plagued by it, bothered by it, overwhelmed by it, weighed down by it, etc. *When Hannibal (a general from the ancient city of Carthage) and his army crossed the Alps, they were beset by snowstorms, landslides, and the attacks of hostile mountain tribes.*

[4] **hamper (hampered)** To *hamper* something is to hold back, slow down, or interfere with its progress, activity, movement, completion, success, etc. (as in *a runner hampered by knee injuries* or *a space program hampered by a lack of funds*). *In his 1944 play* No Exit, *French philosopher and author Jean Paul Sartre (1905–1980) wrote: "I think of death only with [peace], as an end; I refuse to let [the thought of] death hamper life."*

"Oh, how sorry I am! My poor, dear little fairy! If I had a million dollars I would run to her with it! But I have only fifty cents. Here it is. I was just going to buy some clothes. Here, take it to the hospital, little snail. I **authorize**[1] you to spend it on her medical care in any way you see fit."

"What about your new clothes?"

"What does that matter? I'd like to sell these things I have on to help her more. Until today I've earned only enough money to take care of my poor old father. Now I'll have to **augment**[2] my income so that I can take care of my dear mother, too." Pinocchio thought for a moment and then said, "Will you do me a favor, little snail? From now on, I'd like you to serve as my **liaison**[3] with the hospital. You'll take money to my fairy, and you'll bring news of her condition back to me. Will you do it?"

"Of course."

"Good. Now hurry to my fairy. And remember, I expect you back in two days. By then I should have some more pennies! Oh...one more thing. If fifty cents isn't enough to pay for the medicine, try to borrow the difference from anyone you can. The main thing is that you have to get that medicine one

---

[1] **authorize** To *authorize* a person to do a particular thing is to give him formal or legal power or permission to do it. *In November 1979 the Supreme Court ruled that a warrant to search a particular place does not automatically authorize police to search anyone who happens to be there.* To *authorize* a particular action or activity is to give formal or legal permission for it. *In 1902 Congress authorized the construction of a canal through Panama.*

[2] **augment** To *augment* something is to increase it (in amount, quantity, extent, size, etc.); to make it larger. *During the 1930s Japan augmented its military in an effort to establish greater control over the Asian continent.*

[3] **liaison** A *liaison* (pronounced *LEE-ay-zon*) is someone who provides communication between two persons, groups, organizations, governments, etc.; a go-between, middle man, etc. (as in *a stage manager who served as liaison between the theater group's technical crew and its actors*). *From 1974–1975 future President George H. Bush served as America's liaison with China.*

way or another. Just tell whoever lends you the extra money that I promise to **reimburse**[1] him as soon as I can. Now hurry!"

The little spiral-shelled **courier**[2], **energized**[3] by the urgency of his task, began to run!

When Pinocchio returned home, his father asked him, "Where are your new clothes?"

"I couldn't find any that fit. I'll have to look again some other day."

That night, Pinocchio, instead of working until nine o'clock, worked until midnight, and instead of making four baskets, made eight. If the increased workload **infringed**[4] on his free time, he didn't complain.

---

[1] **reimburse** To *reimburse* someone is either (1) to pay him back money borrowed or (2) to pay him money to cover expenses or losses (as when an insurance company pays one's medical bills or compensates one for something lost or stolen). *If you make purchases from a store with a credit card, you pay the credit card company (on a monthly basis), and the credit card company reimburses the store.*

[2] **courier** A *courier* is a person who carries and delivers messages, news, reports, mail, envelopes, small packages, etc. *In April 1775 American patriot Paul Revere, a courier for the Massachusetts Committee of Correspondence, rode from Charlestown to Lexington (Massachusetts) to warn of approaching British troops.* Note: Overnight shipping companies, such as Federal Express, are also referred to as *couriers*.

[3] **energize (energized)** To *energize* someone or something is to give it energy; to activate it, stimulate it, invigorate it, charge it up, etc. *In 1963 President John F. Kennedy recommended an 11-billion-dollar tax cut to energize the sluggish economy.*

[4] **infringe (infringed)** To *infringe* on something (one's civil rights, a country's air space, a copyright or patent, etc.) is to overstep the boundaries or limits of it; to trespass upon it, intrude on it, violate it, etc. *In 1964 Russian-born French sculptor Jacques Lipchitz (1891–1973) said, "Copy nature and you infringe on the work of [God]; interpret nature and you are an artist."*

After that he neatly put away all his basketry **paraphernalia**[1] and went to bed.

As he slept, he dreamt of his fairy, beautiful, smiling, and happy, who kissed him and said, "My dear Pinocchio! In reward for your **exemplary**[2] conduct and **conspicuous**[3] **valor**[4], I **absolve**[5] you of all your misdeeds. Children who love their

---

[1] **paraphernalia** This word signifies either (1) articles or equipment used in a particular activity (as in *fisherman's paraphernalia*), or (2) miscellaneous objects that go to make up, or are associated with, a particular thing (as in *collectible Barbie paraphernalia*). *British Prime Minister (1957–1963) Harold Macmillan once complained, "Our way was barred by all the usual paraphernalia of [newsmen] and television."*

[2] **exemplary** If something (one's behavior or efficiency, for example) is *exemplary*, it's good enough to serve as an example or model for others; it's excellent, superb, outstanding, etc. *In Greek mythology, Zeus's son Rhadamanthus, in reward for his exemplary sense of justice, was made a judge of the underworld.*

[3] **conspicuous** In one sense, if something is *conspicuous* it's easily seen or noticed. *The Big Dipper is perhaps the most conspicuous constellation in the northern sky.* In another sense, if something is *conspicuous*, it draws attention to itself by being somehow remarkable or unusual. *The Congressional Medal of Honor, the highest U.S. military decoration, is awarded to members of the armed forces for conspicuous bravery in action against an enemy.*

[4] **valor** This word signifies the aspect of a person's character that enables him to face danger (especially in battle) with determination, boldness, and courage (as in *the valor and goodness of King Arthur and his Knights of the Round Table*). *In his inaugural address (March 1889), President Benjamin Harrison, speaking of the Civil War's Union soldiers, said "We owe everything to their valor and sacrifice."*

[5] **absolve** To *absolve* someone of (or from) guilt, blame, or the consequences of a crime or sin is to pronounce him free; to clear, pardon, excuse, or forgive him. *In 1958 U.S. critic and historian Van Wyck Brooks (1886–1963) said, "Nothing is so soothing to our [self-respect] as to find our bad traits in our [parents]; it seems to absolve us."* To *absolve* someone from an obligation, duty, or responsibility is to free or release him from it. *The Declaration of Independence (1776) states: "These United Colonies are free and independent states [and] they are absolved from all allegiance to [England]."*

310

parents and take good care of them when they're old and sick are worthy of praise and love. Continue to be good, and you will be happy."

At that moment Pinocchio awoke, full of amazement. He was astonished to find, on looking himself over, that he was no longer a puppet, but a real live boy! He flexed his arm a few times and watched in wonder as his muscles contracted[1] and relaxed. Then he looked around, and instead of the usual walls of straw, he found himself in a beautifully decorated little room, the prettiest he'd ever seen. In an instant, he jumped down from his bed to look on the chair. There he found a new suit, a new hat, and a new pair of shoes.

As soon as he was dressed, he put his hand in his pocket and pulled out a change purse. On it was written: "The fairy with blue hair returns fifty cents to her dear Pinocchio with many thanks for his kind heart." He opened the purse to find the money, but instead of finding fifty cents, he found fifty gold coins!

Pinocchio ran to the mirror. He hardly recognized himself. The bright face of a tall boy with dark brown hair looked at him with alert blue eyes and happy, smiling lips.

With all these miracles, Pinocchio could scarcely apprehend[2] what was taking place. He rubbed his eyes two or three

---

[1] **contract (contracted)** When a muscle *contracts*, it becomes tense or tight. *Snakes move by alternately contracting and relaxing a set of muscles down each side of the body.* When anything else *contracts*, it becomes smaller (or narrower, more confined, etc.) from the drawing together (or shrinking, concentrating, etc.) of its parts. *Nobel Prize–winning author John Steinbeck (1902–1968) once wrote: "The house creaked loudly as the cooler night air contracted the wood."*

[2] **apprehend** To *apprehend* something is to grasp the meaning of it; to understand it. *Swiss psychiatrist Carl Jung (1875–1961) once said, "We should not pretend to understand the world only by the intellect; we apprehend it just as much by feeling."* Note: To *apprehend* a lawbreaker is to take him into custody; arrest him. *The FBI earned its reputation in the 1920s and 1930s by apprehending bank robbers and gangsters.*

times and pinched himself to make sure that these **cataclys-mic**[1] changes weren't only a dream. But he knew he was awake.

"Where's Father?" he cried suddenly. He ran into the next room, and there stood a **rejuvenated**[2] Geppetto, neat and trim in his new clothes. He was once again a happy wood carver, hard at work on a lovely picture frame.

"Father, Father, what's happened?" cried Pinocchio, as he ran and hugged his father's neck.

"These changes are all your doing, my dear Pinocchio."

"What did I have to do with it?"

"Everything. Your **fidelity**[3] to your parents, your sense of right and wrong, your love of study, your willingness to en-

---

[1] **cataclysm (cataclysmic)** In one sense a *cataclysm* is an event (a war, assassination, economic depression, etc.) that brings about a sweeping or fundamental (usually social or political) change. *The cataclysmic effects of the Great Depression (America's severe economic slowdown of 1929–1941) were felt in Europe and contributed to Adolf Hitler's rise in Germany.* In another sense, a *cataclysm* is a violent geological (earth-related) or meteorological (weather-related) event (such as an earthquake, tornado, or flood) that causes great destruction. *Many scientists believe that the dinosaurs' extinction was caused by a cataclysmic asteroid strike at Mexico's Yucatan Peninsula some 65 million years ago.*

[2] **rejuvenate (rejuvenated)** To *rejuvenate* someone or something is to make it young again (or as if young again); to restore its youthful energy or appearance; to give it renewed energy or strength. *In 1912 German graphic artist and sculptor Käthe Kollwitz (1867–1945) said, "For the last third of life there remains only work; it alone is always stimulating, rejuvenating, exciting, and satisfying."*

[3] **fidelity** This word signifies faithfulness (in fulfilling promises, obligations, duties, etc.) or loyalty to a person or cause. *In 1709 English poet Alexander Pope (1688–1744) complained, "Histories are more full of examples of the fidelity of dogs than of friends."* Note: In another sense, the word signifies the degree to which something is accurately reproduced (as in *high fidelity recording*).

dure hard work—they've all **coalesced**[1] into a brand-new, living, breathing you. And I and our house have changed because it always follows that when bad children become good, they bring happiness to their home and to their whole family."

"And the old wooden Pinocchio, where is he?"

"There he is," answered Geppetto. And he pointed to a puppet leaning against a chair, head turned to one side, arms hanging loosely, and legs twisted under him.

After a long, long look, Pinocchio said to himself with great contentment: "How ridiculous I was as a puppet! And how happy I am to be a real live boy!"

---

[1] **coalesce (coalesced)** When various (usually related) things *coalesce*, they come or grow together to form a whole (a single body, unit, mass, group, etc.); they unite, blend, combine, join, fuse, etc. *Our solar system was born nearly five billion years ago when swirling masses of gas and dust coalesced to form the Sun and the planets.*

Index

aberrant, 57
abode, 141
abolish, 189
abortive, 273
abrasion, 213
abridge, 271
abscond, 114
absolve, 310
abstinence, 55
abstract, 85
abundant, 92
abusive, 4
abut, 137
acceleration, 203
accessible, 162
acclaim, 262
accomplice, 113
accord, 240
accrue, 306
acknowledge, 171
acoustics, 267-268
acquisitive, 182
activist, 127
adage, 227

adamant, 58
adept, 304
adhere, 134
adjacent, 106
adorn, 266
advent, 304
adverse, 84
aesthetic, 23
affiliation, 32
affinity, 223
affirm, 154
affliction, 276
agenda, 20
aggregate, 42
aghast, 13
agile, 192
agitate, 234
ailment, 256
ajar, 5
alienate, 77
allege, 116
alleviate, 269
allocate, 305
allude, 227

allure, 183
amass, 111
ambiguous, 80
amend, 145
amiss, 11-12
amnesia, 90
amnesty, 130
analogy, 42
anarchy, 237
anecdote, 49
annals, 263
annul, 219-220
anonymous, 46
antagonism, 243-244
anticlimax, 272
antithesis, 223
aperture, 9
append, 17
appraise, 26
apprehend, 311
apprehension, 135
apprise, 131
aptitude, 193
arbitrary, 21
archaic, 240-241
aromatic, 207-208
articulate, 96
asinine, 249
aspirations, 16
assailant, 69
assimilate, 245-246
astral, 230
astute, 84
atrocities, 289
atrophy, 296
attest, 235
attribute, 30
atypical, 155
augment, 308
authenticate, 78

authorize, 308
autonomous, 128
auxiliary, 199
avert, 165
avocation, 33
badger, 16
baffle, 298
balk, 168
banter, 187
barrage, 192
bask, 219
beguile, 113-114
beholden, 206
belated, 193
belittle, 243
benchmark, 189
benefactor, 169
benign, 253
berate, 134
beset, 307
bestow, 219
bevy, 208
bicker, 256
bigot, 123
bilk, 47
bizarre, 231
blasé, 85
blatant, 178
bleak, 105
bloated, 206
blunder, 202
bode, 162-163
bolster, 247
bona fide, 132
boor, 239
bountiful, 46
breach, 225
breadth, 70
brevity, 172
brusque, 116

buffoon, 280
bulwark, 122
bungle, 280
bureaucrat, 131
burly, 29
cadaver, 87
caliber, 184
camaraderie, 244
canine, 119
canny, 25
canvass, 77
cardinal, 112
careen, 159
carnivorous, 282
casualties, 164
cataclysm, 312
catalyst, 191
catastrophe, 295
cease, 219-220
celestial, 226
censor, 252
cerebral, 42
champion, 46
chaos, 237
chasm, 156
chaste, 71
checkered, 80
choreography, 263
chronic, 175
circumvent, 273
cite, 80-81
clairvoyant, 282
clamber, 11
clamor, 28
climactic, 218
clique, 183
coagulate, 196
coalesce, 313
coax, 223
codify, 237

cog, 47
coincidence, 255
collaborate, 147
colloquial, 98
colossal, 163
combustible, 69
compatible, 252
compilation, 193
complement, 208-209
component, 83
composure, 178
comprehend, 241
concede, 128-129
concentration, 39
conception, 124
concise, 89
concoct, 66
concurrent, 28
condolence, 153
conducive, 232
confidant, 80
confiscate, 202
conform, 24
congeal, 197
congregate, 238-239
connotation, 236
conscientious, 250
consequential, 5
conspicuous, 310
constrict, 201
construe, 81
contaminate, 248
contemporary, 263
context, 88
contingent, 226
contract, 311
convene, 129
conventional, 237
conversant, 79
conviction, 176

INDEX

convoluted, 115
convulsive, 137
correlate, 91
corroborate, 119
corrugated, 213
corrupt, 54
countermand, 121
counterpart, 62
courier, 309
cower, 29
crafty, 112
crass, 239
crescent, 143
crevice, 134
criteria, 77-78
critique, 188
crux, 222
cryptic, 25
cuisine, 259
culminate, 216
curtail, 63
cynic, 47
dank, 207
dappled, 60
dawdle, 221
deadlock, 256
deadpan, 178
debilitate, 295
deceased, 50
decipher, 22
decline, 56
decompose, 40
decoy, 285
decrepit, 1
deduce, 286
defame, 118
default, 221
defect, 187
defiant, 190
defile, 125

definitive, 79
deflect, 249
deft, 181
defunct, 127
delectable, 208
delete, 98
deliberate, 100
delirium, 201
delude, 110
demeaning, 141
demented, 101
demolish, 189
denote, 82
depict, 261
deplete, 291
deplore, 183
depraved, 148
deranged, 66
desecrate, 147
desist, 181
despair, 2
despicable, 113
despise, 242
detached, 77
deteriorate, 307
detract, 189
detrimental, 40
deviate, 24
devious, 53
dexterous, 191
diagnosis, 78
dichotomy, 172-173
dilapidated, 101-102
dilate, 196
dint, 167
diplomatic, 248
dire, 6
disabuse, 114
disarray, 102
discern, 20

INDEX

disclose, 171
discordant, 267-268
discount, 66
discredit, 124
discrepancy, 99
discriminate, 123
discriminating, 210
disheartened, 167
disheveled, 207
disinterested, 122-123
disjointed, 96
dismal, 280
dismay, 73
dismember, 86
disparity, 43-44
disperse, 4
dispirited, 273
disposition, 31
disputatious, 126
dissect, 86
disseminate, 92
dissonant, 268
dissuade, 63
distend, 56
distorted, 200
distraught, 194
diverge, 162
diverse, 238
divert, 285
divulge, 172
doctrine, 124
document, 130
doldrums, 143
dominate, 163
douse, 12
downcast, 18
dregs, 103
drudgery, 301
dwindle, 291
dynamic, 261

eavesdrop, 25
eclipse, 264
edict, 121
efface, 306
ego, 227
elaborate, 116
elegant, 103
elevate, 245
elicit, 91
eloquent, 265
emaciated, 296
emancipate, 149
embark, 154
embellish, 49
embezzle, 50
embroil, 201
embryonic, 177
empower, 127
emulate, 25
encompass, 39
encumber, 168
endorse, 77
energize, 309
engrossed, 67
enhance, 71-72
enraptured, 21
entice, 169
entrance, 251
enunciate, 73
epoch, 264
equilibrium, 156
equitable, 122
equivalent, 148
erode, 243
erroneous, 75
escapade, 188
essence, 265
esteem, 210
eulogy, 303
euphemism, 153

evasive, 30
evoke, 297
evolve, 174
exasperate, 2
execute, 234
exemplary, 310
exhaustive, 154
exorbitant, 50
exotic, 248
expel, 76
expend, 188
expertise, 79
explicit, 76
extemporaneous, 303
extensive, 91
extradite, 120
extraneous, 43
extremity, 17
extricate, 119
extrovert, 302
exuberant, 28
fabricate, 214
façade, 296
facet, 121
faculties, 307
fallacious, 111
fallible, 131
falter, 3
fanciful, 109
fathom, 44
fertile, 40
festive, 220
fictitious, 66
fidelity, 312
figment, 236
figurative, 279
finicky, 13
finite, 150
fissure, 275
fitful, 59

flagrant, 123
flair, 251
flamboyant, 266
fluctuate, 45
fluctuate
fluent, 236
flux, 44
foil, 51
foresight, 252
forgery, 50-51
formality, 132
forte, 292
fortnight, 133
frailty, 228-229
fraudulent, 49-50
fraught, 63
frenzied, 205
fret, 247
frigid, 12
fritter, 249
frolicsome, 238
frustrate, 53
fugitive, 204
functional, 305
furor, 29
gamut, 50
garbled, 96
garnish, 55
gaunt, 296
generality, 184
generic, 39
genteel, 240
ghastly, 194
gist, 116
glaze, 196
glean, 79
gloat, 129
glossy, 265
glut, 26
gnarled, 74

gory, 201
gradation, 67
graphic, 86
gratify, 219
grave, 86
gravitate, 183
grisly, 87
grotesque, 207
grudgingly, 128
gruesome, 87
gruff, 200
gullible, 47
gusto, 169
habitual, 94
haggle, 276
hallucination, 235
hamper, 307
haphazard, 3
harass, 179
harp, 62
harvest, 111
havoc, 34
hazardous, 63
hazy, 286
heedless, 34
hierarchy, 182
hilarity, 257
hoax, 113
homage, 75
homogeneous, 82
hoodwink, 113
hovel, 103-104
hover, 56
humane, 205
humdrum, 229
hurtle, 284
hybrid, 247
hyperactive, 92
hypercritical, 240
hypothetical, 227-228

idiom, 262
idiosyncrasy, 263
idle, 165
ignoble, 147
illuminate, 9
illusion, 287
immaculate, 76
immensity, 158
immortal, 150
immune, 251
impair, 281
impart, 56
impartial, 124
impasse, 256
impassive, 179
impeach, 126
impede, 276
impetus, 136
impinge, 184
implement, 130
implicit, 221-222
imply, 98
import, 19
impose, 144
imposture, 50-51
impoverished, 166
improvise, 106
inaudible, 203
incapacitated, 166
incarcerate, 128
incentive, 52
incisive, 188
incite, 92
incoherent, 13
incorporate, 270
incorrigible, 297
increment, 174
incriminate, 198
incur, 276
indelible, 299

indeterminate, 46
indict, 198
indignity, 279
indoctrinate, 165
induce, 41
inept, 280
inequity, 34
infamous, 28
infer, 228
infinitesimal, 39-40
inflated, 43
inflection, 90
infringe, 309
infuriate, 7
inhabitant, 106
inhibit, 44
initial, 203
inkling, 164
innuendo, 178-179
inquisition, 125
inscription, 149
insinuate, 110-111
instantaneous, 173
instigate, 197-198
instrumental, 45
integrate, 304
integrity, 121
interim, 140
interminable, 172
intermittent, 5
intervene, 65
intimate, 23-24
intimidate, 190
introspective, 142
intrude, 25
intuition, 52
invalidate, 127
invigorate, 10
invincible, 302
invoke, 151

iota, 252
irksome, 224
jargon, 78
jeer, 179
jeopardy, 51
jocular, 179
jubilant, 28
juncture, 132
jurisdiction, 122
lacerate, 196
latitude, 226
lavish, 103
leeway, 131
lenient, 146
levity, 180
liaison, 308
limber, 3
limbo, 247
litigation, 117
loiter, 295
longevity, 177
lucrative, 51
ludicrous, 235
lunar, 157
lunatic, 101
luscious, 40
luster, 43
magnanimous, 244
magnitude, 186
maim, 281
malaise, 85
malfunction, 171-172
malnourished, 55
mammoth, 284
mangy, 102
maniacal, 114
manifest, 246
manipulate, 150
material, 151
maternal, 282

maul, 197
maxim, 299
mayhem, 178
meager, 36
meddlesome, 38
mediate, 195
medieval, 32
mediocre, 189
meditate, 185
medium, 49-50
memento, 107
mesmerize, 27
methodical, 121
migrate, 157
militant, 126
mimic, 250
minimize, 243
mirage, 287
mirth, 37
misconstrue, 180
misgivings, 251
mishap, 156
misnomer, 36
mobility, 72-73
modulate, 250
mogul, 49
momentous, 220
momentum, 272
monetary, 26
monologue, 90
monotony, 225
monumental, 270
morale, 243
mourn, 94
murky, 288
mutilate, 87
mutinous, 4
naïve, 23-24
namesake, 143
narrative, 96

natal, 171
nautical, 154
negligent, 49
negligible, 52
nepotism, 54
niceties, 100
nimble, 17
noble, 16
nomenclature, 78
nonchalant, 85
norm, 24
nostalgia, 254
notorious, 182
novelty, 254
nuance, 21-22
nurture, 31-32
obese, 231
objective, 120
obligatory, 185
obscure, 159
obsession, 122
obsolete, 241
occult, 151
olfactory, 157
onslaught, 192
opaque, 305
oppressive, 149
optimal, 107
optimist, 302
orifice, 206
pact, 147
painstaking, 92
palatial, 108
pandemonium, 30
panorama, 155
pantomime, 68
parable, 112
paradox, 72
parameter, 271
paraphernalia, 310

paraphrase, 97
parasite, 113
parch, 168
parody, 250
passé, 23
passive, 259
pastoral, 300
pathetic, 297
pauper, 103
peer, 24
peevish, 110
penance, 144
perceptible, 67
perjury, 118
perpetrate, 115
perpetual, 302
persecute, 71
persevere, 167
personable, 303
pertinent, 116
perturb, 61
perverse, 124
pessimist, 225
phenomenon, 264
phobia, 88
phosphorescent, 64
pittance, 36
plumage, 155
plummet, 290-291
podium, 27
populace, 52
porous, 41
posterior, 293
posthumous, 65
potential, 134
potpourri, 209
precarious, 135
precedent, 116-117
precipice, 277
precision, 271

predicament, 141-142
predispose, 57
prelude, 257
premeditated, 199
preponderance, 117
preposterous, 279
prerogative, 118
prestige, 101
pretext, 175
prevalent, 246
probe, 126
procrastinate, 175
prod, 272
proficient, 292
profusion, 60
prognosis, 275
projectile, 193
prominent, 29
proprietary, 5
prototype, 304
provoke, 163
proximity, 136
pulsate, 284
pungent, 156-157
punitive, 53
purge, 58
puritanical, 190
qualm, 214
quandary, 186
quarantine, 248
queasy, 200
quibble, 242
quiescent, 135
quirk, 31
rabid, 9
ramification, 245-246
rampant, 54
ramshackle, 103-104
rationalize, 185
raucous, 233

realm, 151
reap, 99
rebellious, 81
recapitulate, 57
recede, 191
recipient, 218
reciprocate, 206
recoil, 136
reconcile, 197
recount, 115
recourse, 128
recrimination, 126
rectify, 127
recuperate, 89
reek, 83-84
regal, 108
regime, 129
rehabilitate, 58
reimburse, 309
reiterate, 120
rejuvenate, 312
rekindle, 218
relegate, 143-144
relentless, 16
relevant, 78
relinquish, 68
relish, 244
reluctant, 99
reminiscent, 262
remnant, 73
remorse, 249
rendezvous, 59
rendition, 271
renounce, 125
renovate, 104
repellent, 88
repercussion, 6
repertoire, 271
replenish, 260
replica, 267

replicate, 86
reprieve, 146
reprimand, 65
reprisal, 181
repulsive, 83
residue, 43
resignation, 273-274
resounding, 274
responsive, 266
restitution, 283
resuscitate, 199
retaliate, 181
retentive, 182
retract, 190
retroactive, 241
reverberate, 268
reverie, 109
revolting, 259
revulsion, 260
rigorous, 260
roster, 98-99
rote, 242
rowdy, 183
rubble, 102
ruddy, 238
rudimentary, 41
ruffian, 184
rummage, 7
rustic, 298
ruthless, 29
sacrilege, 125
sadistic, 269
saga, 115
salvage, 290
sanction, 54
sanctity, 125
saturate, 194
saunter, 60
savor, 209
scandalous, 118

scanty, 79
scapegoat, 198
scrutinize, 109
seclusion, 275
sedate, 161
seethe, 216
segregate, 58
seize, 140
semblance, 253
senile, 166
sensuous, 261
sequential, 242
servile, 232
shackle, 140
shimmer, 283
shoddy, 104
shrew, 230
sibling, 153
simile, 185
sinister, 30
skimp, 100
slacken, 278
slander, 119
solace, 153
solemn, 77
somber, 70
sophisticated, 91
sordid, 104
sow, 97
sparse, 63
spasmodic, 137
spectrum, 57
speculate, 91
spherical, 13
stagnant, 70
stalemate, 256
stamina, 292
static, 45
stellar, 157-158
stereotype, 242

stern, 17
stigma, 132
stymie, 219
suave, 297
subjective, 79-80
sublime, 210
subsequent, 274
subservient, 33
subside, 137
subsistence, 105
substantiate, 92
subterranean, 45
subtle, 21
succulent, 14
sullen, 301
summarily, 289
sumptuous, 109
sundries, 291
superficial, 79
superimpose, 267
supersede, 23
supple, 60
surrogate, 65
susceptible, 228
suspect, 112
symmetry, 305
tacit, 59
tact, 174
tantalize, 60
taper, 13-14
taut, 278
tepid, 82
terminal, 85
terrestrial, 45
tether, 140
thermal, 41
thespian, 33
throng, 238
titanic, 294
tolerate, 180

INDEX

topical, 27
torrid, 164
torso, 267
toxic, 248
trajectory, 192
tranquil, 293
transform, 173
transgression, 53
transition, 173
transpire, 57
traumatic, 95
traverse, 290
trek, 54
trivial, 88
truant, 141
tutu, 266
ulterior, 112
ultimate, 157
ultimatum, 11
unanimous, 188
unassuming, 96
uncanny, 267
unconscionable, 81
uncouth, 269
unearth, 199
unequivocal, 133
unethical, 53
uniform, 67
unique, 237
unison, 180-181
unorthodox, 270
unruly, 233
unseemly, 239-240
upshot, 280
vagabond, 141
vagrant, 61

valor, 310
variable, 44
veer, 272-273
velocity, 203
vendor, 49
verbalize, 222
verbatim, 300
verify, 66
versatile, 303
veterinarian, 275
vex, 152
viable, 292
vibrant, 22
vie, 255
vigorous, 265
vindicate, 120
virtuosity, 270
visionary, 20
vivacious, 262
vivid, 306
vulnerable, 191
waif, 152
warrant, 94
wary, 52
wean, 55
whet, 212-213
wince, 83
windfall, 39
wither, 137
witty, 303
wreak, 34
wrench, 69
writhe, 258
yearn, 254
yen, 259
zany, 27